SOUTH AMERICAN CINEMA

SOUTH AMERICAN CINEMA
A CRITICAL FILMOGRAPHY
1915–1994

EDITED BY
TIMOTHY BARNARD AND PETER RIST

UNIVERSITY OF TEXAS PRESS, AUSTIN

Printed in the United States of America
First University of Texas Press printing, 1998

Requests for permission to reproduce material from this work should be sent to
Permissions, University of Texas Press, P.O. Box 7819, Austin, TX 78713-7819.

∞ The paper used in this book meets the minimum requirements of ANSI/NISO
Z39.48-1992 (R1997) (Permanence of Paper).

Library of Congress Cataloging-in-Publication Data

South American cinema : a critical filmography, 1915–1994 / edited by
    Timothy Barnard and Peter Rist.
        p.   cm.
    Originally published: New York : Garland Pub., 1996.
    Includes bibliographical references and indexes.
    ISBN 0-292-70871-8 (pbk.)
    1. Motion pictures—South America—Catalogs.   I. Barnard, Tim.
II. Rist, Peter.
PN1993.5.S63S68   1998
016.79143′75′098—dc21   98-39528

English translation of entries by Alfonso Gumucio-Dagron, Isaac León Frías,
Oscar Lucien, Marilú Mallet, Manuel Martínez Carril, Jorge Nieto, Diego Rojas
Romero, and Liliana Sáez copyright © Timothy Barnard.

Les Trois couronnes du matelot by Marilú Mallet translation copyright © Mitch Parry.

Frontispiece: O Cangaceiro, directed by Lima Barreto, Brazil, 1953

In memoriam Paul Lenti

Contents

Preface

This project began a long time ago, in 1980, when João Luiz Vieira—one of my fellow graduate students—and I were studying for the first Ph.D. comprehensive exam in Third World Cinema at New York University. For the benefit of future candidates, we compiled an "essential" filmography, bearing in mind the availability of films through U.S. distributors. We were appalled when the prestigious two-volume *Cinema: A Critical Dictionary*, edited by Richard Roud, appeared that same year, containing only four entries on filmmakers from outside Europe, Japan, and North America: chapters were included on Hong Kong cinema and three directors—Satyajit Ray, Leopoldo Torre Nilsson and Glauber Rocha. It was obvious to us that the continuing dominance of Euro-American cinemas in reference literature was doing a huge injustice to cinemas of the developing world. Indeed, this condition has persisted with the appearance over the last few years of other dictionaries, film guides, and surveys.

I continued to develop the filmography, using it in a "World Cinema" course I was teaching at the University of Western Ontario, to give students a checklist in the event that any "Third World" films showed up locally. I then began to realise that hardly any of the films on the list were available, in any format, in Canada. I consequently conducted an extensive search and printed an availability list in the newsletter I was then editing for the Film Studies Association of Canada in order to help other film educators locate the few titles available for rental in Canada.

Timothy Barnard and I met in 1987 while working on a "Third Cinema Festival" in Ontario and we agreed to produce a critical filmography of approximately 250 "Third World" films. Our book was to function as a corrective to the sort of film dictionaries, like the Roud volumes mentioned above, which usually contain entries on just a few "Third World" "masterworks": typically one or two films by the Indian director Satyajit Ray and perhaps a film by the Senegalese *auteur* Ousmane

Sembène are provided as token representation. The most extensive of these encyclopaedias, the multi-volume *Magill's Survey of Cinema: Foreign Language Films* (1985), contains articles on well over 200 French films, but only 20 from India (including 10 by Ray). Since Western film critics and scholars dominate the field, it is natural that films from North America and Europe should be favoured. As well, the European festival network of Cannes/Berlin/Venice continues to be regarded as *the* showcase for film "art," while everyone looks to Hollywood for entertainment. And yet, Indian film production has led the world (by far) over the last three decades and many other "Third World" film industries have rivalled Hollywood numerically. For example, films made in tiny Hong Kong are invariably more popular than their U.S. counterparts with audiences in many parts of the world. Also, since the advent of Cinema Nôvo in Brazil in the 1960s, many important and provocative "new waves" have sprung up all over the "Third World," from the Senegalese cinema of the 1970s to the remarkably beautiful and challenging 1980s works of the Xi'an provincial studio in the People's Republic of China. Indeed we—Tim and I—are of the opinion that the most significant new film movements are to be found in post-colonial, "Third World" countries.

We initially planned to write some 250 entries on silent, classic sound, and contemporary films from Africa, Asia, and Latin America in a single volume. Each entry would provide a definitive capsule description and analysis of the film and situate it in the social and artistic contexts of its production. We planned to provide extensive technical and production data and use my research to include a guide to print sources in North America. With the advent of video and a continued decline in the availability of films through distributors in Canada and the U.S., we eventually abandoned this idea (acknowledging also that we weren't targeting a specifically North American readership). When our Canadian publisher changed its publishing program after a change in ownership, we rethought the project, realising that we would have far too much material for one book and deciding to deal with each region in turn in greater depth. Susan Ryan in New York City joined us and secured a contract with Garland Publishing for the first volume; other commitments unfortunately prevented her from remaining with the project as a co-editor. But I am hopeful that Susan will be able to co-edit a companion volume on films from Mexico, Central America, and the Caribbean (areas to which she has devoted her research and teaching).

We elected to omit Guyana, Surinam, and French Guiana, even though they are South American countries, because their colonial experience is more recent, and because their historical and cultural development is very closely related to that of the Caribbean region. However, we cover film production in all other South American countries in this volume. My one regret is that I was unable to obtain an internal university grant that would have allowed me to travel to Brazil and view many of the key films that cannot normally be seen. As it stands, I consider myself to be much more an enthusiastic student of South American cinema (and Brazilian cinema in particular) than an "expert." I trust that I will be able to expand my viewing experience in the future, and I welcome any comments that could lead us to produce an additional volume and/or an improved edition of this filmography.

I have a great many people to thank for enabling this project finally to take shape. First, I credit my professor of Brazilian cinema at New York University as being the person who turned my head firmly in the direction of South American cinema. It is no exaggeration to say that Robert Stam taught the best course I ever took: to have the "father" of Cinema Nôvo, Nelson Pereira dos Santos, visit the very first class, followed by the first of many extracurricular gatherings, where students (and Bob) could share their enthusiasm for Brazilian films and culture, was very special and impressive. We saw 35mm prints of Brazilian films never released in New York, and a number of students in that class had essays published in *Brazilian Cinema*, co-edited by Bob, which remains in my view the best book in English on South American cinema. The course was tremendous fun. And it was in this course that I met João Luiz Vieira, whom I think of today as the student who encouraged me the most while I was in graduate school. João is still, for me, the model of collegiality and decency in the rugged world of academia. In a similar vein, another of my professors at NYU, William K. Everson, continues to be a role model for me—in this case as the ideal film historian. While studying under his tutelage and projecting films for his classes, I learned that one has to be sceptical about all accepted, written film history. I discovered that films I'd never even heard of could actually be extremely significant works, especially in terms of a "history of film style." He surely has a more complete understanding of European and American film history than any other person: he has been an avid film-goer all his life; he remembers the films so well and is able to contextualise them in an overall, socio-historical as well as stylistic-historical way. I fantasize that he will read some of this book and be encouraged to seek out a South American film or two—although, given the fact that a Brazilian samba troupe visiting Bob Stam's class, the second time he taught Brazilian cinema, was heard loudly through the thin walls next door while I was projecting a Greta Garbo silent for Bill Everson's Scandinavian film course, I somehow doubt the choice will be Brazilian.

I owe a vote of thanks to all of the contributors, including those few who submitted entries that we were unable to publish. I must also thank my students at Concordia University for suffering through under-prepared classes and having occasionally to read a draft entry for a class. In fact, some of them have been genuinely enthusiastic about the prospect of this book finally appearing in print. Three of our Latin American fine arts students, Ricardo Mendonça from Brazil and Henrique Vera Villanueva and Luis Molina-Pantin from Venezuela have even lent me (perfectly legal) videotape copies of films, and, in Luis' case, copious written material. Henrique has been especially resourceful. Oksana Dykyj and her staff at Visual Media Resources have consistently helped me access available materials and facilities at Concordia University and Anne Harris has done the same at the NYU Cinema Studies Study Center. Charles Silver has also been more than generous to me over the years at New York's Museum of Modern Art Film Study Center. I am fortunate also to have friends who have continued to believe in my ability to get this done, especially Peter and Katie Bordonaro in New York and Paul and Helen Salmon in Guelph, Ontario. On numerous occasions, both families have welcomed my staying with them while I pursued my film viewing—their hospitality knows no bounds. I'm also really grateful that Mitch Parry was able to come aboard the project in its last hour. He has done sterling work editing, writing, and computer "hacking." Finally, my thanks to Shelley Coleman for putting up with all kinds of uncharacteristic—perhaps even unacceptable—behaviour over the last few years, and for her unfailing support and optimism.

P.R.
Montréal, 1995

When the itinerant Dutch filmmaker Joris Ivens, who filmed the Spanish Civil War, the Chinese Revolution, the war in Vietnam, and numerous other social movements and conflicts around the world over a period of nearly 60 years, visited Cuba in 1960 and 1961, his task was two-fold. One project was to train military camera operators. The authorities wanted to be able to document the U.S. invasion they foresaw, correctly, as imminent. Working with wooden models because of a lack of real cameras, asking students to imagine what they filmed rather than showing them rushes, in two months he trained 50 or 60 peasants and workers for the task of military filming.

He also shot two films of his own: *Carnet de viaje* (1960) and *Cuba, pueblo armado* (1961). Here, his young Cuban apprentices had other ambitions. Two aspiring cinematographers, Jorge Herrera and Ramón Suárez, and two assistant directors, Jorge Fraga and José Massip, worked on *Carnet de viaje*. Herrera went on to become one of Cuba's most influential and distinctive directors of photography before his death in 1981. To him we owe the cinematography on *Lucía* (1968), *La primera carga del machete* (1969), and other landmark films. Suárez, before he left the country, worked as director of photography on two of Cuba's most enduring films, Tomás Gutiérrez Alea's *La muerte de un burócrata* (1966) and *Memorias del subdesarrollo* (1968). Fraga, a co-founder of the Cuban film institute ICAIC after the country's revolution in 1959, went on to a career as a director, critic, and teacher. His feature *La odisea del General José* (1968), a film largely unknown outside Cuba, is an exemplary, intimate study of the interplay between nature and human activity.

The director, historian, author, and ICAIC cofounder Massip, with Fraga one of the most promising and today least known of the early ICAIC directors, kept a journal during his work with Ivens. "Th[e] green [of the Cuban countryside] which is so beautiful to the human eye," he wrote, "is not so to the mechanical eye of the photographic lens. With black-and-white film, the different shades of green are lost in a dark and undifferentiated mass. . . . The solution to this problem probably consists in finding an appropriate relationship between the landscape and the sky. Cuba's sky could be the salvation of its countryside. Ivens could not remember a sky to compare with it. Its astonishingly rich plasticity comes not only from the marvellous shade of blue but above all from the extraordinarily varied shapes of its clouds."

There is something just and compelling about Ivens' dual legacy in Cuba. In fact, it is not a duality at all but an expression of the organic unity of art and militancy in Ivens' work and in the early Cuban cinema he helped to inspire. In the following pages, the product of several years' work, the contributors to this volume—some of us, like Ivens, cultural outsiders—have, I believe, strived to attain a similar unity. We have tried to shine light on areas in Latin American film history which until now have unfortunately been viewed as an undifferentiated mass, to recover those different shades of green. We have strived to document and understand melodrama and "guerrilla cinema," *cinéma d'auteur* and a cinema of the people. We have tried to see, and convey, both the wooden cameras deployed in defence of nation and culture and the astonishingly rich plasticity of the Latin American sky and how it may be the salvation of its often-troubled countryside.

The Lumière *cinématographe* arrived in South America in the first months of 1896, and it is perhaps fitting that this book is appearing in the year of that event's centenary. In addition to offering appraisals, and sometimes reappraisals, of the much-studied New Latin American Cinema (c. 1955–1975), we introduce English-language readers to the subject of silent cinema and pre-1955 sound cinema in the region, topics given only a cursory glance in the existing literature. The tragedy, to recall Georges Sadoul's comment about being able to watch the earliest surviving films in an afternoon, is that little remains of Latin America's earliest films. Even sound films have been lost, and films continue to be lost because of poor storage conditions and adverse climates, theft and neglect, and social upheaval and natural catastrophe. While I was in Argentina in 1991–92 carrying out research for this book, the building housing the archives of the Cinemateca Argentina collapsed because of negligence at a construction site next door; screenings were cancelled as a years-long clean-up operation began. The present volume is by necessity, then, an imaginary cinémathèque, as some of its treasures cannot be seen on celluloid.

And yet, as Peter Rist and I propose with this volume, it is through the close study of the films themselves, in tandem with an understanding of their social and political context, the industrial terrain of their production and the individual ambitions of their makers, and their cultural and artistic milieux, that insights into cinema's place in Latin American society lie. Writing such detailed entries has been a great joy and luxury.

A word on the entries themselves and how they are organised and presented. Technical credits are given at the beginning of each entry. At times we were faced with the dilemma of conflicting sources, especially concerning running times, so much so that we often wondered if it was possible for so many different versions of a film actually to exist and leaving us with the task of determining which version is the most prevalent or "correct." Occasionally we privileged some sources over others and hoped for the best, rather than reporting three or four possible running times, for example, in an entry.

On the question of a film's date, two schools of thought exist, that of year of production and that of year of release. The decision of how to date a film is not an easy one, as strong arguments and practical considerations exist for each choice. The year of production is the year of legal copyright and arguably the year of artistic conception, although this is more often than not untrue, considering the gestation period of films today. Choosing to date films this way allows the historian to ignore with a clear conscience all the messy issues around release delays, censorship, etc. On the other hand, this method denies the contradiction of dating a work of art to a time before it was unveiled in public. While this may be justifiable and indeed necessary for any work of art *not* unveiled in public, in all other cases the link between the work of art and its critical and public reception is fundamental. The French film historian Georges Sadoul explained his preference for the latter system in the following way: "The date of a film is in principle that of the first public screening, not of its conception, beginning or end of production, or private screening. In this we have followed the historians of literature who use the date of the first edition, of a book's release to the public, as the identifying one" (*Dictionary of Film Makers*). Curiously, Sadoul's posthumous translator and editor Peter Morris chose not to observe this system in Sadoul's *Dictionary of Films*, arguing that it was less logical and led to "absurdities," for example, when film releases come as much as a decade after production.

In the present volume, the date of a film is its release date. In this way, dates may vary slightly from other literature on South American film. In order to avoid the "absurdities" warned of by Morris, we have given the date of production with the year of domestic release in parentheses in the case of films which experienced lengthy delays before their domestic release, in South America often occasioned by censorship. We do not indicate abnormally long production periods in the technical credits because it is impossible to do so consistently and accurately but have discussed these, when pertinent, in the body of the entry.

With regard to film titles and their English translation, we have in all cases provided the original title as the main reference for each film, and these are indexed at the back of the book, alphabetically and chronologically by country (that is, in the order they appear in the book). An English title of some sort is also provided, unless translation is unnecessary, and indexed. In many cases, the film is universally known by this title in the English-speaking world. In other cases, different commercial release titles exist for different markets, and these have been indicated when known. Occasionally, titles differ within the existing English-language literature or between this literature and what has been given on the film print itself by the film's subtitler. In these cases we have provided all titles that we have encountered and which seem to be still in use, although we have privileged one and put the others in parentheses, with the modest hope that our preference will now become universal. Finally, some films, for example *Barravento*, *Macunaíma*, and *Malayunta*, have, in our view, been unnecessarily burdened with English titles. Many of these, for example *Bad Company* (*Malayunta*), *Jungle Freaks* (*Macunaíma*) and *Tempest* (*Barravento*) are by turns awkward, offensive, or misleading. We have given such titles in parentheses in the heading of the entry and cross-indexed them to the original title in the English-language title index in order to discourage their future use.

Because of the many film and foreign-language terms used in the book, we provide glossaries of film and Brazilian terms. Spanish terms are defined where they appear in the text. The names of institutions have generally been translated into English, except for those common in the English-language literature, such as the Centro Sperimentale in Rome. The original-language name of each institution can be found in the Name and Title Index following the English name assigned to it; the original-language name is also cross-indexed in the same index. The exception to this system, and to our goal of strictly observing institutional names in English and the original language, is that of film festivals. Festivals' actual names can be frustrating to outsiders searching for them in indexes (Montréal's festival is the "Festival des films du monde/World Film Festival") and they have been standardised in this book to the name of the city in which they take place ("Montréal film festival"). Similarly, these festivals' myriad prizes have all been rendered as "Best Film," "Second Prize," etc.

The editors and publisher decided, as this is a reference work which freely borrows—and sometimes presents copious quantities of—factual material from other sources, to limit footnotes to instances where an original idea or original research has been borrowed or directly cited and to which the author is indebted for something more than factual information. To have footnoted more than this would have meant more pages of notes than there are devoted to the films themselves. At the same time, we gladly acknowledge our debt to those South American film historians cited in the Works Consulted who have painstakingly documented the region's film history, occasionally in the face of indifference.

At the end of the book a list of works consulted appears. This list is limited to film books and articles consulted in the course of preparing the present book, and should not be mistaken for a bibliography, which would be a major undertaking in its own right. In the process of synthesizing information obtained from these and other sources (interviews, newspaper clippings, reference works on South American society and culture, etc.), and in our close screenings of the films themselves, we have striven to verify factual information about the films discussed. The present volume, while we hope it will be found to be generally reliable, will not of course be without error, and for this we alone are to blame. We are indebted to our editors at Garland, Marie Ellen Larcada, Phyllis Korper, and Laurel Stegina, for giving us a free hand, for urging us to go the extra mile, and for their patience in waiting for the manuscript and in answering our production queries.

Many people have assisted in the preparation of this book, and for Peter and myself it was a wonderful opportunity to collaborate with colleagues in North and South America, a real group project. We are proud to present the work of some of Latin America's most respected film historians, many for the first time in English. Our contributors were also very helpful in suggesting titles and putting us in touch with other contributors, and for this we are very grateful. Following this preface we list our acknowledgements; we apologise to anyone who has been inadvertently omitted. It should be noted that staff of the institutions listed in the acknowledgements are not listed individually. Behind many such institutions' names then stand many dedicated individuals who went out of their way to assist us. Some of my own most enlightening conversations were with support staff—press officers, projectionists, librarians—who cultivate a thorough knowledge of cinema. We hope they recognise themselves behind the enforced anonymity of the institutional acknowledgement and accept this tribute. In cases where I was able to do research on site at one of the region's film archives, these individuals and the others listed also offered their friendship and became indispensable cultural guides. The founding director of the Cinemateca de Cuba, the late Héctor García Mesa, introduced to me by Paul Lenti during my first visit to Cuba, was an early supporter of the project, as was Robert Daudelin of the Cinémathèque québécoise, then President of the International Federation of Film Archives (FIAF). The indefatigable Manuel Martínez Carril, director of the Cinemateca Uruguaya, spent a week changing reels for me every twenty minutes while trying also to run a cinémathèque. During my sojourn in Cuba in 1989–90, Mercedes Garrido was an unsurpassable guide and loyal friend. This sojourn was made possible by an offer of employment as a translator at the newspaper *Granma*, and I'd like to thank my compatriot Elise Boyer for the offer and for her solidarity while I was in Cuba. My sojourn in the southern cone in 1991–92, made possible by a generous research fellowship from the International Development Research Centre in Ottawa, benefitted similarly from my friendship with Maricel Masat, whose impeccable taste in cinema and *yerba mate* had a great influence.

This book is dedicated to the memory of our contributor Paul Lenti, who died in May 1994 as Peter and I were beginning final preparations for publication. Paul, as a reviewer for *Variety*, had been the first to review my first book, on Argentine film, when I was several years short of 30 and completely new to Latin American film studies. Two years later, when I had saved up enough money to attend my first New Latin American Cinema Festival in Havana, Paul and I met standing next to each other in the aisle of the airplane transporting us to Havana, waiting to go to the washroom. We saw many films together over the years, and through these infrequent encounters and regular correspondence I became acquainted with his brilliance, generosity, and boundless good humour.

Paul, in addition to his thorough knowledge of practically every Latin American cinema, was the recognised authority on Colombian film, and he immediately agreed to contribute to the present volume, as foolhardy as I'm sure he realised the project was. Had he lived to observe Peter and me weather some last-minute crises getting the book to press, I'm sure he would have ended up contributing more than the ten entries included here. Paul's work here is, to my knowledge, his last: he approved some minor editorial revisions in a letter I received the day of his death. After mailing this letter, he received a surprise telephone call from me while I was briefly in New York. We chatted for a half an hour, and I apologised that my schedule kept me from visiting. Paul was at home recovering from minor heart surgery two months' earlier, but already he was taking long walks and travelling to U.S. film festivals. He died four days later, and of course I will always regret not having visited this man I looked up to so much. As a freelance journalist, film festival programmer, and *homme à tout faire*, Paul was for me a model of someone who, despite financial hardship, was blazing his own trail through life. His work editing and translating *Objects of Desire: Conversations with Luis Buñuel* showed what promise his future work held and is the best example of the self-effacing thoroughness and dedication with which he approached every task. Peter and I hope someday to prepare a companion volume on Mexican, Central American, and Caribbean cinema, but I'm not sure how we'll manage without Paul.

T.B.
Toronto, 1995

Acknowledgements

Argentina

Centro Latinoamericano para el Análisis de la Democracia
Embassy of Canada
Fondo Nacional de las Artes
Fundación Cinemateca Argentina
Instituto Nacional de Cinematografía y los Artes Audiovisuales
Sindicato de la Industria Cinematográfica Argentina

Manuel Antín, Oscar Barney Finn, Jorge Miguel Couselo, Leonardo Favio, Rafael Filippelli, Octavio Getino, Daniel López, Jorge López, Claudia Magne, Raúl Manrupe, Maricel Masat, Lautaro Murúa, Alberto Padrilia, Ana Poliak, Alberto Tabbia, Graciela Taquini, Héctor Vena

Brazil

Cinemateca Brasileira
Museu do Arte Moderno (Rio de Janeiro)

Ricardo Mendonça, João Luiz Vieira

Canada

La Cinémathèque québécoise
Concordia University, Cinema Department
Concordia University, Audio Visual Department
Conservatoire d'art cinématographique de Montréal
Festival des films du monde
International Development Research Centre
Mosaic Publishing
Nightwood Editions
Ontario Arts Council

Kathryn Barnard, David Burr, Alberto Ciria, Max Di Bitonto, Erik Dinsmore, Ian Elliot, Maggie Lattuca, John Locke, Kathryn MacKay, Grace Ngan, Barbara Rousse, Jane Sauder, Timothy Savage, Teresa Tarasevic, Carole Thériault, Mark Thompson, Bob Whitney, Cheryl Williams, Ken Yip

Chile

Cinemateca Universitaria
Area de Difusión de la Cinematografía Chilena

Colombia

Fundación Patrimonio Fílmico Colombiano

Cuba

Cinemateca de Cuba
Escuela Internacional de Cine y Televisión

Elise Boyer, Mercedes Garrido, Eduardo Muñoz Bachs, Gaspar Quintana, Armando Suárez

United States

Facets Video
Museum of Modern Art, Film Study Center
New York University, Cinema Studies Department
New Yorker Films

Jerry Carlson, Joel Kanoff, John Montague, Mabel Prelorán, Karen Ranucci

Uruguay

Cinemateca Uruguaya

Venezuela

Cinemateca Nacional

Luis Molina-Pantin, Henrique Vera Villanueva

SOUTH AMERICAN CINEMA

List of Abbreviations

Dir Director
Scr Scriptwriter
Narr Narrator
Intertit Intertitles
Cinematog Cinematographer; Director of Photography
Ed Editor
Anim Animation
Art dir Art director
Mus Music
Choreog Choreographer
Prod Producer/Production company
Act Principal actors
q.v. See

Argentina

Nobleza gaucha

Gaucho Nobility
Argentina, 1915, 60' (at 16 fps), b+w, silent

Dir Eduardo Martínez de la Pera, Ernesto Gunche, and Humberto Cairo *Scr* Cairo *Intertit* José González Castillo, adapted from the poems *Martín Fierro* by José Hernández (1872) and *Santos Vega* by Rafael Obligado (1885) *Cinematog* Martínez de la Pera and Gunche *Act* Orfilia Rico, Celestino Petray, María Padín, Arturo Mario

Following early forays into short actuality films from 1897 and into fiction films from 1908, Argentina produced its first feature film, *Amalia*, in 1914. *Nobleza gaucha*, made the following year, was the country's second feature. Coming at a time when the 1914–18 war had idled European studios and created new opportunities in world markets and before the post-war advance of U.S. cinema smothered Latin American production, *Nobleza gaucha* was a phenomenal success, creating foreign markets overnight for Argentine film and returning 600,000 pesos (despite widespread film piracy) on a 20,000-peso investment. Suddenly the new art had commercial promise, and a brief five-year period of growing production fuelled by foreign sales was inaugurated. Largely in the hands of recent southern European immigrant entrepreneurs, the fledgling industry hoped to take its place alongside the European industries, maintaining high levels of production despite the small domestic market (15 million in 1915; over half of them first-generation immigrants) through extensive foreign sales.

A collaboration between two accomplished still photographers (Eduardo Martínez de la Pera and Ernesto Gunche), *Nobleza gaucha* has been praised by Argentine film historians for its essentially cinematic, not

3

theatrical or literary, treatment. The lead actors were borrowed from the theatre, but Martínez de la Pera and Gunche filmed on location in city and country, providing street-level images of the city through the use of travelling shots from streetcars and trains. The film recounts the kidnapping of a young woman from the rural *estancia* where she works by a lecherous rural landowner, who imprisons her in his Buenos Aires mansion. A gaucho from the *estancia* comes to her rescue, vanquishing the villain and returning with her to the country. In a politically significant coda, the landowner later uses his influence to falsely accuse the gaucho of cattle rustling, but the gaucho defends his honour and the landowner dies in a final chase on horseback. The film's depiction of Argentina's dual reality, countryside and burgeoning city, thus articulates a cultural and political conflict which has deep roots in Argentine society. Seen by the nineteenth-century ruling elite as a battle between "civilisation and barbarism" (Domingo F. Sarmiento), the conflict has been recast by national-popular elements as one between foreign domination and patriotic valour. Reworkings of the mythology can be found in many subsequent Argentine films, including *La guerra gaucha* (1942, q.v.), *Juan Moreira* (1973, q.v.), and *La Patagonia rebelde* (1974, q.v.).

One of the seminal texts of this movement to valorise the gaucho and the national traditions he represents was José Hernández' epic poem *Martín Fierro*. After a disastrous initial release, reportedly due to terrible intertitles, *Nobleza gaucha* was given new intertitles based on *Martín Fierro* and another national literary classic, *Santos Vega*, before achieving the success it did. The man who substituted the prosaic titles with evocative excerpts from these classic poems was José González Castillo, an early collaborator of Argentine filmmakers, a later member of the leftist "Boedo" literary group, and a poet-playwright whose 1914 play about homosexuality, *Los invertidos*, had shocked Buenos Aires. In 1919, González Castillo was to script another important early Argentine film, *Juan sin ropa*, by Camila and Héctor Quiroga. Based on his book, *La lucha por la vida*, it was a fictional reenactment of the repression that year of the country's anarcho-syndicalist movement and also received widespread foreign release. A sound version of *Nobleza gaucha* was released in 1932, prepared by Francisco Mugica, who directed the country's first optical sound feature, *Tango!*, in 1933.

Timothy Barnard

El apóstol

The Apostle
Argentina, 1917, approx. 60',
b+w (with some colour tinting), silent

Scr Alfredo de Laferrere and Federico Valle *Anim* Quirino Cristiani, Diógenes Taborda, and Andrés Ducaud *Prod* Valle

In 1917, Argentina produced what today is credited as the world's first animated feature, *El apóstol*, proof of the effervescence and innovation of its nascent industry, fed by European immigrants and stimulated by the drop in European production during the war. Born in Italy, Federico Valle (1880–1960), *El apóstol*'s producer, was one of those immigrants, arriving in the country in 1911 after working with Georges Méliès, the French film pioneer, and as a newsreel camera operator on three continents from the age of eighteen in 1898. Valle shot the world's first aerial views, with Wilbur Wright piloting, outside Rome. In Argentina, he ran an exhibition company, produced industrial shorts—reportedly of such high artistic value that they had a loyal public following in the cinemas—and, after *El apóstol*, produced dramatic features and operated a decade-long weekly newsreel service. There a generation of film technicians apprenticed—a young Jorge Luis Borges worked there preparing intertitles—and filming in the Argentine interior was opened up. In 1931, he produced the country's first sound feature, *Muñequitas porteñas*, directed by José A. Ferreyra (*Ayúdame a vivir*, 1936, q.v.), using Vitaphone disks. Valle also has the distinction of making the first films with legendary tango singer Carlos Gardel, before his international fame, in 1919.

The experiment of making *El apóstol* in what was still a largely artisanal industry led Valle to bring together disparate talents. Alfredo de Laferrere, the co-scriptwriter, was a popular playwright who became foreign minister in the government of Pedro Eugenio Aramburu (1958). Diógenes Taborda was the country's leading political caricaturist. Quirino Cristiani, also from Italy, was the film's principal animator and today is credited with the film's direction. The result, a satire of president Hipólito Yrigoyen (1916–22 and 1928–30, the country's first president elected by universal male suffrage and the first to be deposed by military coup), came at a time of increasing middle-class involvement in national affairs and on the eve of an explosion of popular culture—radio, magazines, literature—that accompanied this class' gradual ascendance in Argentina's previously oligarchical society.

In *El apóstol*, Yrigoyen is seen dreaming that he journeys to Mount Olympus to seek the assistance of the gods in ridding Buenos Aires of corruption and vice. Full of local flavour, the film was able in this way to make oblique reference to the administration and its ministers and to political issues of the day. A critic described the film as a "Dantean spectacle," with Jupiter's lightning bolts raining down on the city, producing a direct hit on the congress building.

El apóstol, estimated to have been one hour in length, took 12 months to produce and contained 58,000 images; the film once credited with being the world's first animated feature, Winsor McCay's *The Sinking of the Lusitania* (USA, 1918), took 22 months to produce and contained 25,000 images (a third film, made in Italy in 1916, may have been of feature length—at the time that was anything that approached one hour). For its pixillated sequences, *El apóstol* used a seven metre-wide model of Buenos Aires; its cars and pedestrians were manipulated by invisible threads, and eighty ships floated in the harbour. Valle and his team improvised solutions to the problems they faced, such as the running of the camera motor during single-frame shooting. While Cristiani continued making animated films for decades—his 1918 film *Sin dejar rastros* was banned—it was Valle's only incursion into the genre: the following year he produced a puppet feature, *Una noche de gala en el Colón* (also known as *Una Carmen criolla*), which had some animated sequences by Cristiani, and later he turned to dramatic features. Both these early films have been lost, as was Valle's enormous newsreel archive, in a fire in 1926. Impoverished in 1930 when the new military government cancelled a contract to use film in the country's schools, a project Valle had already invested in heavily, he was forced to sell his remaining films to a comb manufacturer for their celluloid content when he was unable to find a buyer willing to preserve them. He was belatedly recognised for his contribution to Argentine culture when Congress voted him a pension in 1959, a year before his death.

Timothy Barnard

El último malón

The Last Indian Uprising
Argentina, 1918, 97' (at 16 fps),
b+w (with some colour tinting), silent

Dir Alcides Greca (1889–1956) *Scr* Greca *Prod* Greca for Greca Film *Act* Flor Silvestre

El último malón is a singular film in Latin American film history. Shot on location in San Javier, near Santa Fe, 300 miles north of Buenos Aires, it reenacts the tragic last uprising of native peoples in Argentine history in 1904. Its director/scriptwriter/producer Alcides Greca, an activist in the Radical Party and a lawyer, was a socialist in his youth as well as a novelist and journalist who later in life was imprisoned for his political beliefs. A committed indigenist, he founded the journal *El mocoví* in San Javier in 1908. Details of the film's production remain a mystery: we don't know how it was financed or produced, who its technical personnel were or, apart from the actress Flor Silvestre, who its principal actors were, nor how Greca achieved such fluency in the medium on his first outing in such a remote area at such an early date.[1] At 97 minutes (silent speed; 65 minutes on today's projectors) it was a half-hour longer than most features of the day. Its production involved the direction of mostly non-professionals, including survivors of the events and 1500 extras for the final battle scene. His goal, to expose the squalid living conditions of Argentina's native peoples, and his strategy of combining documentary and fiction, prefigure by nearly half a century the radical social cinema that emerged in Latin America in the 1960s. His film was in fact rescued from oblivion shortly after his death by Fernando Birri (*Los inundados*, 1961, q.v.), also from Santa Fe, who is considered the modern-day pioneer of that radical cinema. Birri screened a tattered original 35mm print to his students at a new documentary film school in Santa Fe in the late 1950s. (A 16mm copy was made in 1968.) In its social concerns, its regionalism, and its mix of documentary and fiction, *El último malón*'s influence on Birri's work is clearly discernable.

In the last half of the nineteenth century, and especially after 1880, the colonisation of the vast Argentine pampas was undertaken in earnest. The nomadic gauchos and the native peoples were ruthlessly driven from the land ("Fertilise the pampas with the blood of the gauchos" was the exhortation of future president Domingo F. Sarmiento in *Facundo* (1849)).

By the turn of the century, their numbers decimated, the country's native peoples were living out broken lives on reserves or as rural proletariat. It was at one of these reserves near San Javier, Greca's birthplace, that the region's Mocovi Indians carried out the ill-fated rebellion reenacted in the film—"malón" is an Argentine term for an Indian raid or uprising during this period.

After Greca's introduction of the film from his study, the film opens with a documentary prologue on native life in San Javier, showing, for example, the use of both traditional and modern hunting and fishing methods. The film's fiction, which begins with the first of six acts, provides further documentation of this lifestyle, including the depiction of a traditional dance ceremony at an annual celebration. The plot draws its conflict from the grievances and social problems of the day and accurately depicts the composition of native society: a servile old *cacique*, or native leader—by this time the post was at the service of the white authorities—is confronted by his younger illegitimate brother with the demand that he challenge the abuses of the whites. Fearing for his position, the *cacique* refuses, prompting a rebellion which is marred by a lack of discipline and which is finally brutally suppressed after being sensationalised by the press.

Despite its great value as a document of native life, as an early experiment in historical reenactment using participants in the original events, and as an indictment of official policy, *El último malón* was also conceived of as entertainment. Released in major cinemas in Buenos Aires and in cinemas around Santa Fe, its publicity proclaimed its "emotional images of primitive life" and its blend of "art and reality." The film's greatest commercial draw, and its most problematic aspect, was the love triangle inserted into the historical drama. Rosa, the young lover of the old *cacique*, encourages the rebellion and secretly loves the younger brother. Tied up during the rebellion by the *cacique*, she is freed just in time to prevent a total slaughter of the rebels and the death of the younger brother, with whom she flees. An epilogue shows them living happily far away, exchanging a kiss—a custom, an intertitle informs us, they have adopted from white civilisation. Not only does this subplot add more than a touch of melodrama to the film but the depiction of this character and her influence on events are especially problematic, as the contemporary critic Eduardo Romano has argued.[2] Perhaps meant to be mestiza, she appears white, a discrepancy the film makes no attempt to account for. A professional actress, as are, evidently, the two brothers, she dresses and acts like any tragic screen heroine of the day. Her promise of love is also portrayed as a deciding factor in the brother's decision to launch the rebellion, clouding its true political motive. *El último malón* thus stands as a significant, if anomalous and problematic, early experiment in creating a fiction-documentary hybrid in the search for a popular social cinema in Latin America.

Timothy Barnard

1. Jorge Miguel Couselo, "El aporte de Alcides Greca al cine argentino," *Todo es historia*, 49 (1971): 74–9.

2. Eduardo Romano, *Literatura/Cine: Argentinos sobre la(s) frontera(s)*, (Buenos Aires: Catálogos, 1991), 21.

La muchacha del arrabal

The Girl from the Outskirts of Town
Argentina, 1922, approx. 60', b+w, silent

Dir José Agustín Ferreyra (1889–1943) *Scr* Ferreyra *Cinematog* Luis and Vicente Scaglione *Art dir* Andrés Ducaud *Mus* Roberto Firpo; "La muchacha del arrabal," music by Firpo, lyrics by Ferreyra and Leopoldo Torres Ríos *Prod* Tycla Film *Act* Lidia Liss, Jorge Lafuente, Elena Guido, Angel Boyano

"El Negro" Ferreyra (he was mulatto) was the most innovative and prolific of the Argentine silent film directors, producing more than 20 films in the decade ending in 1927. In that year, Argentine film production collapsed entirely from the weight of U.S. competition after five years of decline; only the coming of sound technology in the 30s would revive it. Ferreyra would survive the transition to sound film, one of two directors to do so, but his films wouldn't: of his silent work, only fragments survive. *La muchacha del arrabal* has been completely lost. An autodidact of humble origins who came to film after an early go at painting, a bohemian who frequented the working class cafés of his neighbourhood, Ferreyra brought to film an instinctive talent—often working without scripts and rarely seeing other people's work—for painting bittersweet portraits of the teeming immigrant neighbourhoods of Buenos Aires' south side.

La muchacha del arrabal (an "arrabal" is an outlying working-class district of Buenos Aires where the tango was born at the turn of the century) recounts the somewhat autobiographical tale of a young painter who frequents south side cafés and becomes the lover of a fallen young woman, drawn to the city in search of fame as a tango singer but becoming a prostitute instead. The renowned short story writer and pioneer film critic Horacio Quiroga tempered his praise for the film on its release with the comment that Ferreyra's vision "wasn't much different from that of one of the customers of [the neighbourhood] bars" and that "thinking himself to be creating types, Ferreyra develops instead anonymous individuals, plucked from the crowd." The contemporary Ferreyra scholar Jorge Miguel Couselo counters that this was precisely Ferreyra's merit, "to make dramatic characters from those anonymous souls without heroic qualities."[1] Ferreyra's was a naïve art, but it made a great contribution to the development of silent film language in Argentina, while his melancholic, romantic attachment to the city's south side and its inhabitants would receive many later homages, perhaps most poignantly and unexpectedly in Fernando Solanas' *Sur* (1988).

The tango permeated Buenos Aires working-class culture of the first half of the century, and the history of the tango and that of the cinema are closely intertwined. In a sense, Ferreyra's silent oeuvre is a collection of silent tango films, so closely did they recreate the tango's tenor and milieu on film. Ferreyra, known for exposing early silent film to the influences of the other arts, especially that of art direction, here staged an attempt at synchronisation with the title song, with lyrics by himself and his young acolyte Leopoldo Torres Ríos (*La vuelta al nido*, 1938, q.v.) and live accompaniment by the Roberto Firpo orchestra, one of the leading tango bands of the day. By the end of the decade, the cinemas were full of tango orchestras accompanying silent films; so dependent was the tango on the cinema that when sound film arrived in the 1930s hundreds of musicians were thrown out of work, contributing to the development of an important new dance hall style in the evolution of the music. The film's title song was also recorded a year after the film's release by the country's most famous tango singer, Carlos Gardel.

Timothy Barnard

1. Jorge Miguel Couselo, *El negro Ferreyra, un cine por instinto* (Buenos Aires: Freeland, 1969), 51-2.

Ayúdame a vivir

Help Me To Live
Argentina, 1936, 75', b+w

Dir José Agustín Ferreyra (1889–1943) *Scr* Libertad Lamarque *Cinematog* Gumer Barreiro *Mus* José Vásquez Vigo; "Mi cariño," tango, music by Alfredo Malerba and lyrics by Cátulo Castillo; "Ayúdame a vivir," tango, music by Malerba and lyrics by Atilo Supparo; "Canto a la vida," march, music by Malerba and lyrics by Supparo; "Arrepentida," tango, music by Malerba and lyrics by Rodolfo Sciammarella *Prod* Side *Act* Libertad Lamarque, Floren Delbene, Perla Mary, Delia Durruty

After lying dormant since the late 1920s, Argentine film was given new life in the early 1930s by the introduction of sound technology. U.S. producers were for a time so concerned about the effects of sound on their foreign markets that they made dual- and foreign-language films. Nonetheless, the Argentine industry grew at a dizzy rate throughout the 30s after producing Latin America's first optical sound features, using the Movietone system, in 1933, recapturing lost foreign markets and creating a dynamic domestic film culture. José Agustín Ferreyra, the country's leading silent film maker (*La muchacha del arrabal*, 1922, q.v.) now despondent and penniless in Europe, had been coaxed back to film *Muñequitas porteñas* with Vitaphone disks in 1931, the country's first sound feature. This new debut was auspicious, prompting the critic Roland to write "It again fell to him to be the catalyst of a new stage of Argentine film" while Mario Soffici (*Prisioneros de la tierra*, 1939, q.v.) commented "The voice on the screen was a revelation for Ferreyra, the birth of film with an Argentine accent: this is what he had been waiting for." In the decade after *Muñequitas porteñas*, which is now lost, Ferreyra filmed 15 more features in addition to the score of silent films he had made in the 'teens and 20s. The tango musical, along with comedy the genre which could best satisfy the public's thirst for local flavour in this new entertainment, was the early motor of the industry's revival and a recurring, if problematic, genre in Ferreyra's sound oeuvre.

Ayúdame a vivir was the first Argentine sound film to regain completely Argentina's lost foreign markets—its title is reported to have entered popular slang as a plea for help as far away as Cuba—and its immense success launched the career of Libertad Lamarque. Lamarque became one of Latin America's most popular and enduring screen actresses of the "Golden Age," less known in North America than Brazil's Carmen

Miranda or Mexico's Dolores del Río for having never worked in Hollywood. She did emigrate for a time to Mexico, during Perón's rule in the 1940s and 50s, because a rivalry with Perón's actress wife Evita prevented her from working. She starred in Luis Buñuel's first Mexican film, *Gran casino*, in 1947. Lamarque wrote the script to *Ayúdame*, a script that Ferreyra's protegé Soffici turned down before it was offered to Ferreyra. Unlike Soffici, Ferreyra responded enthusiastically to Lamarque's innovation: an early example of dialogue spontaneously transforming itself into musical numbers, rather than having a narrative break occur between the two. This device has since become common to musicals worldwide and is indeed essential to the genre's sense of spontaneity, to its masking of its narrative devices, and its artifice of unrehearsed musical numbers.

Ayúdame's plot, and especially its treatment, marked a considerable shift for Ferreyra. Here melancholy was replaced by melodrama, the location shooting in the streets and around the port with studio interiors, the immersion in the lower depths and their struggle to survive with a more sanitised image of the middle class, and the leisurely style of the bohemian artisan with the forced pace of a studio director shooting from a daily script. Lamarque plays a young woman who escapes an unhappy family life through marriage; falling ill soon afterwards, she leaves the city to recuperate. On her return she discovers her husband with a lover in their own home. The fleeing lover tumbles down a staircase and Lamarque is falsely imprisoned for pushing her, a charge withdrawn only after the deathbed testament of the lover, whereupon Lamarque is reunited with her husband. Ferreyra's work had succumbed to the melodrama of the era's extremely popular new radio soap operas.

Ferreyra filmed two more vehicles for Lamarque in the next three years, each more successful than the last, managing the occasional personal film in between, like *Muchachos de la ciudad* (1937), filmed concurrently with *Ayúdame*, as his health slowly failed for years before his death in 1943. His sound period is thus viewed ambivalently by Argentine critics. His contemporary Calki, one of his most sympathetic critics, panned *Ayúdame*, declaring that Ferreyra had been "overcome by the wave of commercialism." Jorge Miguel Couselo, writing at a distance of 30 years, found more to praise in the film and sought a more historical interpretation of Ferreyra's chequered sound years, noting that already by the 1930s the cinema was no longer the entertainment of the lower classes and that other directors of the day had adopted a much more deformed style than Ferreyra. Arguing that popular taste had unmistakably altered for the worse in the brief interval between Ferreyra's silent and sound periods,

Couselo suggested that for the first time, Ferreyra, whose talent sprung from a spontaneous intimacy with his surroundings, had found himself out of step.[1] Like other masters elsewhere, however, he proved able when necessary to make a better melodrama than anyone else, even if it was at odds with his own vision.

Timothy Barnard

1. Jorge Miguel Couselo, *El negro Ferreyra, un cine por instinto* (Buenos Aires, Freeland, 1969), 79–81.

La vuelta al nido

Return to the Nest
Argentina, 1938, 77', b+w

Dir Leopoldo Torres Ríos (1899–1960) *Scr* Torres Ríos *Cinematog* Carlos Torres Ríos *Mus* Eugenio de Briganti y Abrain *Art dir* Antonio Scelfo *Prod* Adolfo Z. Wilson for Cinematográfica Terra *Act* José Gola, Amelia Bence, Lita Fernán, Mario González

The early years of the sound period found silent film director Leopoldo Torres Ríos and his cinematographer brother Carlos filming peep shows, but with the growth of the industry in the mid-30s, he was able to return to feature production. He and José A. Ferreyra (*Ayúdame a vivir*, 1936, q.v.) were the only two Argentine silent directors to survive the transition to sound. Despite the unevenness of his subsequent work, often occasioned by commercial imperatives, he was one of the most enduring and influential directors in the country. A constant innovator, he filmed the neo-realist drama *Pelota de trapo* in 1948 and the country's first colour film, *Lo que pasó a Reynoso*, in 1955. He left his mark in a more direct way as well: he was the father of one of Argentina's best-known modern directors, Leopoldo Torre Nilsson (*La casa del ángel*, 1957, q.v.) who apprenticed with him from an early age, and the grandfather of the contemporary director Javier Torre (*Las tumbas*, 1991). While Torres Ríos is remembered more for *Pelota de trapo* and *El crimen de Oribe* (1950), co-directed with Torre Nilsson and marking the latter's debut, he himself remained convinced of the superiority of *La vuelta al nido*, for which he had complete artistic freedom as a reward for previous commercial successes. Upon its completion, however, the film waited months for release and opened for only three days, demonstrating just how tied the Argentine public was to the studio films and formulaic genres which dominated the industry. The film disappeared into oblivion but has been rediscovered as an anomalous art film from the studio era of Argentine cinema.

La vuelta al nido is an intimate portrait of a young couple, their domestic life and the growing staleness of their relationship. Frustrated by her husband's lack of attention, the woman writes him an anonymous note telling him that his wife is cheating on him. A period of doubt and distrust follows which is resolved when she finally reveals the truth and they are reconciled. Torres Ríos was careful to set the film in Argentina's new middle-class milieu: the man is a bookkeeper who spends his days manually tabulating accounts; their home is spacious, modern, and spartan. A few years hence, formal innovations of the sort introduced here by Torres Ríos would become associated in Argentine film with artificial studio worlds or with the upper classes; here Torres Ríos imparted a certain social resonance to the film's narrative ambiguities.

La vuelta al nido was a startling departure from the style of the melodramas, musicals, and comedies that dominated the period. Described by a critic of the day as bearing a "whiff of poetry," it featured a lingering camera and remarkable attention to composition and detail. Preferring the narrative vignette to a more linear unfolding of the drama, the film often opens exterior scenes in the treetops or the sky, slowly tilting down to the action at street level. Extended still-life sequences, like that of the multi-angled views of a statue in a park, break up the story line, and the shot-counter shot technique is eschewed in favour of long takes which capture all the action or pans between two characters in dialogue. There is an extended expressionistic fantasy sequence of the husband murdering his wife with a gun we had earlier seen him buy; for a moment, we are unsure whether he has committed the crime or not. Torres Ríos' use of sound was less innovative, and the film is burdened with an omnipresent, somewhat too melodious soundtrack, although some experimentation is attempted, such as when the man reads the anonymous note at work as the clatter of typewriters gradually becomes deafening. Despite the predictable course of the plot—apart from the fantasy sequence—and the story's happy ending, a certain ambiguity is maintained throughout, a subtle hint of a malaise which will remain after the couple's reconciliation.

Timothy Barnard

Mujeres que trabajan

Working Women
Argentina, 1938, 90', b+w

Dir Manuel Romero (1891-1954) *Scr* Romero *Mus* Alberto Soifer *Art dir* Ricardo Conord
Prod Lumiton *Act* Mecha Ortiz, Niní Marshall, Tito Lusiardo, Pepita Serrador

Manuel Romero was one of the most prolific and successful directors of
the burgeoning Argentine studio system of the late 1930s. By 1937, the
industry's refinement of sound technology was complete, and Argentine
film entered its zenith in domestic and international markets. In that year
the country's largest producer, Argentina Sono Film, made eight films
while Romero himself directed no fewer than five for other producers,
often writing the script as well, as he did for *Mujeres que trabajan*. In the
first decade of his career he filmed more than 30 features. National
production in 1938 stood at 38 features, rising to 56 by 1942, when more
than 30 studios provided regular employment to 4,000 technicians. But
this output was never surpassed, and the studio system itself played a part
in the industry's downfall in the mid-40s as Mexican producers developed
a quicker and cheaper crew system that helped them conquer the Latin
American market.

Romero trained in the U.S.-owned Spanish-language studios of
Joinville, France, in the early 30s, where he scripted one of the films
starring Argentine tango great Carlos Gardel. Gardel was to star in
Romero's first feature, *El caballo del pueblo* (1935), but died in an airplane
crash en route to Argentina to shoot the film. Romero began working in
Argentine film after a stint in popular theatre revues. His love of the
tango led him to direct some of the period's most popular musicals, and
he shared with José A. Ferreyra (*Ayúdame a vivir*, 1936, q.v.) an
instinctive, if less original and bohemian, feel for popular taste. He
worked in—and in Argentina often pioneered—a variety of genres,
including comedy, melodrama, and the *policier*, and his work shows the
considerable influence of American directors like Howard Hawks and
Frank Capra. Today his films are recalled not for any lasting artistic
achievement but because they display his technical command of the
medium and the industry's maturity and, in the better films, because of
a marriage of the commercial with a certain style of social drama. *Mujeres
que trabajan* is the Romero film which went the furthest in this direction

with its sympathetic and, for its time, frank portrayal of the world of single working women. Its theme and all-star female cast reflect a reality of Argentine film in the 30s, when the largest audience for film consisted of women who would often spend the afternoon together at the cinema, seeing a handful of features for one low admission price.

A comedy-drama, *Mujeres* plots the tale of a rich young socialite whose fortune disappears overnight, casting her into the real world as a department store clerk and forcing her to seek accommodation in a boarding house of working women. Here the film's ensemble acting lets loose, featuring the veteran Mecha Ortiz and introducing as the socialite the popular radio actress Niní Marshall, who went on to a career as Argentina's top female film comic. While the film's riches-to-rags story was neither new nor subversive and although the women's world is nothing but wholesome and dignified, behind the gags lay unmistakable social comment. There is periodic discussion of trade unions, and at one point a fellow boarder comments to the fallen heiress that "It's not that I don't like you personally, it's your class I don't like." The film also introduces a single mother who proudly presents her new child to her stunned parents in front of her housemates. There is a distinct impression that we've gone a step beyond Capra and Hawks.

For a time, too, the film seems to portray a world where men are either absent, stupid, or evil and where women manage quite well without them. By the film's end, however, the romantic subplot has taken over completely: Marshall's new working-class friends are boisterously and cheerfully getting her to the church on time for her marriage back into her class. The class tensions the film suggested are miraculously resolved, and the female universe Romero had tentatively sketched is betrayed in favour of one focused on men and how to marry a rich one.

Timothy Barnard

Prisioneros de la tierra

Prisoners of the Earth
Argentina, 1939, 85', b+w

Dir Mario Soffici (1900–1977) *Scr* Ulises Petit de Murat and Darío Quiroga, based on the short stories "Una bofetada" (1916), "El peón" (1918), "El destilador" (1926), and "Los desterrados" (1926) by Horacio Quiroga *Cinematog* Pablo Taberno *Mus* Lucio Demare *Prod* Pampa Film *Act* Angel Magaña, Elisa Galvé, Francisco Petrone, Raúl de Lange

Prisioneros de la tierra was the first and one of the most enduring and darkest expressions of Latin America's most significant film genre, dubbed the "social folkloric" by Argentine film historian Domingo di Núbila. With this film Mario Soffici anticipated the work of others throughout the region and inspired later generations of social filmmakers. In a commentary on *Prisioneros* in which he compares it to John Ford's *The Grapes of Wrath*, released the following year, di Núbila described it as forming part of a vital new "American" cinema, a "classic American cinema, neither North American nor Latin American: American,"[1] thereby expressing the hope of Soffici's generation to build a film industry the equal of its northern rival.

Paradoxically, however, the promise of *Prisioneros* was never fulfilled by the Argentine industry despite the existence of a cultural tradition which could have nourished the genre and an increasingly sophisticated industry which could have refined its achievements. Precisely at the moment of its appearance, in what can only be described as an act of commercial suicide, the Argentine film industry, under the sway of the Argentine bourgeoisie's perennial European cultural obsessions, began a search for a "quality" "European" cinema. Ignoring the realities of its continental working-class markets and the artistic accomplishments of the European social cinema of Jean Renoir and the poetic realists in France and, later, Italian neo-realism, the industry began to produce a slew of studio costume dramas and "white telephone" films whose "European" style had been visibly mutated by the long transatlantic journey.

Prisioneros was filmed on location in Misiones, the adopted home of the Uruguayan short story writer—and early film critic—Horacio Quiroga. It was in this remote and steamy Argentine province that Quiroga, beset with grief and personal demons, wrought his themes of isolation, madness, and death. Soffici's vision of Quiroga's poor *mensús*—indentured labourers harvesting *yerba mate*, a sort of tea, in the infernal heat—was considerably different from that of Hugo del Carril in *Las aguas bajan turbias* (1952, q.v.), a virtual remake despite its different literary source. Soffici's is an uneasy, brooding film, more interested in ambiguity and atmosphere than del Carril's sweeping melodrama. In place of *Las aguas'* schematic plot, stereotyped characters, and obligatory happy ending, *Prisioneros* offers a studied portrait of social rot whose complex, ambiguous characterisations blur the line between good and evil. The company doctor is an immense, aging German whose great humanitarianism, or rather his humanity, has been kicked out of him by alcohol and too many trips upriver. He fails to perform even his minimum task adequately, not of keeping the men healthy but of keeping them alive to work: his drunkenness results in fatal malpractice. He finishes by killing his daughter, who has accompanied him on this voyage to keep him from drink, in a fit of *delirium tremens*. The ruthless *patrón* is a man of culture, somewhat unconvincingly portrayed as being as trapped by destiny as his poor *mensús*, whose frustrated affections for the daughter end in rape. The hero, a rebellious *mensú* whose sufferings attract first the daughter's pity and later her love, exacts his revenge on his exploiter on a forced march through the jungle under the continuous blows of a bull whip, setting him adrift on a raft to die when they reach shore. Jorge Luis Borges, in one of his occasional pieces of film criticism of the day, described this disconcerting sequence as "the most powerful in memory," commenting that usually "brutal people are appointed to perform brutal actions; in *Prisioneros de la tierra* the hero is appointed, and he is almost intolerably efficient." Forced into hiding, the hero's escape with the doctor and his daughter is thwarted by her death. With no reason to live, he emerges to follow her funeral cortège down the dusty road and is immediately shot dead, in Borges' words, by "a single laconic bullet."

Consistently voted the best Argentine film of all time, *Prisioneros* carefully constructs a realistic and oppressive atmosphere. Unlike del Carril, who filmed images of brutal oppression and graphic images of the gruelling harvest under the burning sun, Soffici betrays a greater interest in composition, detail, and pacing and an inclination to shoot at night. The night sequences of the extended prologue on the ship during the trip upriver, when the ship's funnels are framed to loom in the foreground, and the daughter's escape from the *patrón*, described by Borges as a "passionate flight through the tremulous mountain night," are remarkably judicious understatements which reveal Soffici's mastery of the medium.

Soffici was of humble origins and earned his living from a young age at everything from mechanics to performing as an actor in travelling circuses and theatre troupes. He was first shown *Prisioneros'* script by the actor José Gola (*La vuelta al nido*, 1938, q.v.), who saw in the hero the role of a lifetime. Gola died of illness in Misiones early in the shoot and was replaced by the novice Angel Magaña. Soffici's only choice for the female lead, Delia Garcés, was unavailable, leading him to select the non-professional Elisa Galvé through a talent contest, convinced that no other Argentine actress had the proper physique for the role. The script, by Quiroga's son Darío and the scriptwriter Ulises Petit de Murat, was reportedly changed by Soffici to be more linear, adding elements from three additional Quiroga stories to the original source, "Los desterrados." *Prisioneros* was Soffici's fourth feature, and while he remained active into the 1960s, producing other significant films, he was never able to recreate its beauty, authenticity, or force.

Timothy Barnard

1. Domingo di Núbila, *Historia del cine argentino* (Buenos Aires: Cruz de Malta, 1959), I, p. 135.

La guerra gaucha

The Gaucho War
Argentina, 1942, 95', b+w

Dir Lucas Demare (1910–1981) *Scr* Ulises Petit de Murat and Hómero Manzi, based on the collection of short stories of the same title by Leopoldo Lugones (1905) *Cinematog* Bob Roberts *Art dir* Ralph Pappier *Mus* Lucio Demare *Prod* Enrique Faustín for Artistas Argentinos Asociados (AAA) *Act* Enrique Muiño, Francisco Petrone, Angel Magaña, Sebastián Chiola, Amelia Bence

In 1942 four Argentine screen actors (Angel Magaña, Enrique Muiño, Francisco Petrone, and Elías Alippi, whose cancer kept him from the starring role of *La guerra gaucha*), a director (Lucas Demare), and a producer (Enrique Faustín) joined forces to found a "quasi-cooperative" film production company, Artistas Argentinos Asociados (AAA). *La guerra gaucha*, their second film, was by far the most successful and enduring, becoming on its release the most widely seen film in Argentina to that date, surpassing even the seemingly invincible box office records set by *Gone with the Wind* three years earlier. Argentine film was now in its heyday, leading Latin American production in 1942 with 56 features (a figure once matched in 1952 under a system of "quota quickies" but never surpassed in Argentina). But already the industry had begun to stray from the popular formulae responsible for its success, and the salon dramas and lavish costume histories based on foreign classics that reigned in the latter half of the decade had begun to appear. Demare et al., the "angry young men" of the era, sought to stay a nationalist–populist course. They found the perfect vehicle in Leopoldo Lugones' vivid account of the gauchos' war of independence against the Spaniards.

Begun with unrealistically modest start-up capital, AAA soon sought outside funds. These were found in an unlikely place, San Miguel studios, then the country's biggest. San Miguel's owner was then trying to disperse his huge production into more diverse areas through the use of more dynamic and efficient production teams, seeing in them the possibility for both aesthetic innovation and economic salvation. AAA represented an ideal way to try out his theory, and so the young rebels came to be bankrolled by the country's largest studio, offering them access to the finest equipment and the best technicians. Indeed, the Argentine studio system was prolific, employing no fewer than 4,000 technicians full time in 30 studios. More efficient systems in Mexico, in combination with an influx of U.S. investment there and Mexican film production legislation, allowed the Mexican industry to overtake Argentina in Latin American production after this year. The Argentine industry, meanwhile, had become increasingly mismanaged, failing to collect receipts from its extensive foreign sales. From 1942 it was subject to the censorship of a new military government and to a raw stock embargo by the United States that was to last until 1946 and which paralysed production. Ostensibly imposed in retaliation for the country's neutrality during the war, it had as much to do with U.S. investors' decision to enter the Latin American market through Mexico.

Lugones, one of Argentina's pre-eminent writers of the early twentieth century, was a leading member of the *modernista* movement whose early poetry and prose was compared to Walt Whitman and Victor Hugo in its social concerns and formal experimentation. Later he turned to a stilted nationalism and a mystical glorification of nature, and he ended by committing suicide in 1938 after declaring his fascist sympathies. *La guerra gaucha*, described as replete with "battles, duels, cataclysms, blood, sensuality, revenge, triumph, hunger and death," is set at the turn of the nineteenth century in northern Argentina when the gauchos were in revolt against Spanish rule. In the adaptation to screen by the leading scriptwriters Hómero Manzi and Ulises Petit de Murat, the disparate stories and characters of the short stories were woven into a single narrative, creating a tumultuous fresco of the war. Unlike the contemporaneous Hollywood Western, here native people were absent from the action; the gaucho film also inverted the Western's view of colonisation as progress, affording complex ideological readings of the genre.

The film fully embodies the contradictions inherited from Lugones and his work. Writing in the 1960s, the film historian José Agustín Mahieu lamented its "facile patriotism" and persistent "adjectivisation" of the epic form, its "diminished authenticity" and "almost didactic" air.[1] The film is even less in favour today, despite consistently placing high on lists of the best Argentine films ever made. Its national-popular political rhetoric is seen today as excessive, facile and, to some, vaguely reactionary. Nevertheless, the film is a powerful, well-executed epic with a certain stylistic restraint, such as the use of long takes and a limited musical score, which might be said to countervail the excesses of the script.

Shot on location in the hot, dry northern Argentine province of Salta, *La guerra gaucha* relates the battles of gauchos under the commander Güemes during the 1814–18 campaigns. Muiño plays an old priest in town who, while appearing servile to the Spaniards, is actually warning the gauchos of their movements through the ringing of his church bell, a task for which he is eventually savagely punished. Petrone plays the heroic and virile gaucho leader—who nonetheless uses snuff and likes European music—who dies in the penultimate battle. Magaña is his adversary, a Spanish lieutenant who is injured in a duel with Petrone and nursed back to health by the rich landowner Amelia Bence, a fervent nationalist who converts him to the cause. In the final scene he leads the gauchos into battle against his own troops, and the film ends with the appearance of Güemes and more troops on the horizon to save the day.

Timothy Barnard

Awards: Seven awards, including Best Film, Director, Actor (Francisco Petrone), Adapted Screenplay, Argentine Academy of Motion Picture Arts and Sciences, 1942; Best Film, Director, Adapted Screenplay, Association of Argentine Film Journalists, 1942.

1. José Agustín Mahieu, *Breve historia del cine argentino* (Buenos Aires: Editorial Universitaria de Buenos Aires, 1966), 30.

La dama duende

The Phantom Lady
Argentina, 1945, 101', b+w

Dir Luis Saslavsky (b. 1908) *Scr* Rafael Alberti and María Teresa León, based on the play of the same title by Pedro Calderón de la Barca (1629) *Cinematog* José María Beltrán *Art dir* Gori Muñoz *Mus* Julian Bautista *Prod* Miguel Machinandiarena for Estudios San Miguel *Act* Delia Garcés, Enrique Diosdado, Antonia Herrero, Manuel Collado

During the war, Argentina was a haven for European emigrés and others, like Hungarian-born, Hollywood cinematographer John Alton, who later won an Academy Award, were attracted to work in its film industry. Alton, who specialized in film noir, low-key lighting, worked with Luis Saslavsky on *Puerta cerrada* (1938) and was a mentor to a generation of Argentine cinematographers. The French director Pierre Chenal's *Todo un hombre* (1943) and *El muerto faltó a la cita* (1944) made a lasting impression on directors like Saslavsky because of their formal concerns, especially their compositions and use of the camera.

La dama duende, based on a seventeenth-century play by the Spanish "Golden Age" dramatist Pedro Calderón de la Barca, was the period's most extensive and acclaimed collaboration of an emigré community—here, the Spanish Republicans. Of the film's principal talent only Saslavsky and the female lead Delia Garcés were Argentine. The script was written by one of Spain's leading poets of the 1920s and 30s, the communist Rafael Alberti, and his wife María Teresa León. The elaborate decor, the product of seven months' work, was by Gori Muñoz, the leading art director at work in the country. The cinematographer José María Beltrán and the composer Julian Bautista were also Spanish emigrés, as were the principal members of the cast, with the exception of Garcés. As the film historian Domingo di Núbila wrote, there was perhaps more Spanish talent working on this film than was available in Spain at the time. Despite its distant setting and classical theme, it was banned there by Franco.

La dama duende was one of Calderón's *capa y espada*, or cloak-and-dagger comedies, bringing together his many concerns: love, honour, religion, philosophy. In it a widowed young noblewoman becomes determined, despite the taboo prohibiting her remarriage, to seduce an officer temporarily lodged in her castle. Veiled, she presents herself to him at night in his room as a phantom to stir his longing. Complications arise when another couple use the same ruse during this time of carnival to carry out an illicit tryst, and the confusion of identities almost tarnishes the lady's honour and drives the gentleman away. In the end her honour is safe and the two are united. While Saslavsky, Muñoz, and Beltrán were able to find in the text the inspiration to turn in some of their best work, Alberti's contribution is less noticeable. A faithful adaptation of the play, the film bears none of the twentieth-century sensibility of Alberti, whose poetry had been influenced in its imagery, rhythm, and radical juxtapositions by the silent cinema of Buster Keaton, Charlie Chaplin, and Sergei Eisenstein.

As important in the work of Calderón as the classical themes of love and honour was his baroque stylisation, and here lay the principal attraction of the work to the aesthete Saslavsky. Calderón's mirrors, secret passageways, and elaborate interiors were ideally suited to the development of Saslavsky's aesthetic of interior space, of which he is the recognised Argentine master. The sumptuous mise-en-scène reflected the first time in Argentina that an art director had also designed all the costumes and furniture, while Beltrán's camera was judiciously formal; di Núbila commented that Saslavsky would rather lose conviction than a good shot. The exteriors provide a subplot of local revelry and the opportunity for some music and dance. The social polarisation and antagonism of the two milieux are reflected in the treatment, and although the exteriors were shot on location, the costumes and decor give them a fairy-tale quality.

Saslavsky began filmmaking in 1931, before Argentine film had been brought back to life by the coming of sound technology, when he made the independent experimental feature *Sombras*, shot in 16mm and now lost. In the 30s he worked occasionally in melodrama, but he was clearly unsuited to working in popular genres in the studio system. His *La fuga* (1937), also lost, has legendary status as one of the best films of the era. While *La dama duende* is his surviving masterpiece, he was able to continue filming until 1979, the year he made the baroque *El Fausto criollo*. His total output in Argentina reached nearly 30 features, more than half of them made before 1950; soon after making *La dama duende* he left the country, spending 14 years in France, where he was able to make a few films, including one starring Yves Montand. He is recognised as the leading exponent of an art cinema in Argentina, a socially, industrially, and even artistically problematic tendency there. Lesser directors, confusing decor with art, produced a deluge of "white telephone" films and sterile adaptations of foreign literary classics in the years following *La dama duende*, contributing to the commercial ruin of the industry. Saslavsky was one of the few to produce an art cinema of merit, and his affinity with Calderón's hermeticism is clear. It has been said of Calderón that what prevented him from achieving the truly great artistry of authors like Shakespeare and Cervantes was his idealism, his lack of interest in popular characters or events. The contrast between the film's unconvincingly-shot exteriors of popular revelry and Saslavksy's interiors, where Calderón's themes are played out and his form is at its most compelling, confirms the similarity between the two artists. Uncannily, we can read in Goethe's appraisal of Calderón a comment on Saslavsky's own remote and uncompromising style: "He is rather theatrical throughout, even stagey . . . [he] stands on the threshold of over-refinement. Shakespeare on the contrary gives us the rich red grape from the vine. According to our taste we can enjoy the single berries, press them out and sip the juice or fermented wine. With Calderón, on the other hand, nothing is left to the choice or taste of the spectator: we receive from him the spirits already drawn off and distilled, seasoned with many spices, or flavoured with sweets; we must accept the beverage as it is, as a delicious and palatable stimulant, or else refuse it."

Timothy Barnard

Awards: Best Film, Argentine Academy of Motion Picture Arts and Sciences, 1945; Five awards, including Best Film and Best Director, Association of Argentine Film Journalists, 1945.

Las aguas bajan turbias

Troubled Waters [Muddy Water] [Dark River]
Argentina, 1952, 85', b+w

Dir Hugo del Carril (pseudonym of Piero Bruno Ugo Fontana) (1912–1989) *Scr* Eduardo Borrás, based on the novel *El río oscuro* by Alfredo Varela (1943) *Cinematog* José María Beltrán *Art dir* Gori Muñoz *Mus* Tito Ribero *Prod* del Carril for Lina C. de Machinandiarena *Act* Hugo del Carril, Adriana Benetti, Raúl del Valle, Gloria Fernández, Pedro Laxalt

Las aguas bajan turbias takes up the theme of Mario Soffici's *Prisioneros de la tierra* (1939, q.v.), the exploitation of *yerba mate* harvesters in the tropical north around the turn of the century. Hugo del Carril, in addition to directing, played the lead role and accompanied himself on guitar singing a few regional songs. This was his second Argentine film as director, after making two others abroad before *Las aguas bajan turbias*, and he would film a dozen more by 1975. In the 1930s and 40s he had been a matinée idol, the star of many of the most important tango films. Del Carril was also a devoted Peronist, and *Las aguas* is unmistakably stamped with the populist rhetoric of the era. And yet the film was based on a novel by a communist author, Alfredo Varela, who was languishing in Perón's prisons at the time; del Carril had to seek special permission to adapt the book, which was granted on condition that neither it nor Varela be named in the screen credits.

The film opens like a Peronist newsreel of the day, with a command-ing voice-over narrative telling us that the exploitation we are about to witness is a thing of the past and that the remote Upper Paraná region, where the film was shot on location, is now an area of "civilisation and progress." Del Carril plays a man who, with his brother and other poor *yerba mate* harvesters, or *mensús*, are tricked into indentured labour in the Upper Paraná, a river whose waters transport the bodies of rebellious workers back south. Del Carril substantially modified the tone and message of Varela's novel, giving the heroine a sexual innocence and her relationship with del Carril's character a chaste sentimentality at odds with the carnal and brutal relationship depicted in *El río oscuro*. Rather than have the two flee to safety together, as del Carril has them do, Varela had the man abandon the woman and flee alone. Significantly, the communist Varela depicted the rebellion set in motion by del Carril's character as being only a transition from feudal to capitalist exploitation.

Del Carril assembled some of the best talent in the country, and *Las aguas* marked the return to Argentina of cinematographer José María Beltrán (*La dama duende*, 1945, q.v.), recently awarded the Best Cinematography prize at the Cannes film festival for *La balandra Isabel llegó esta tarde* (Venezuela, 1949, q.v.). The cinematography is stark and powerful—numerous critics have commented that the film is narrated by its images—and quite unlike the nuanced images found in *Prisioneros de la tierra*. The latter is a film of shadows that rarely depicts the open exploitation of the *mensús; Las aguas* is a film of cruel suffering filmed under the blazing heat of the tropical sun. The acting and musical score are melodramatic, creating a film which is part social protest and part humid romance.

In its social conviction, the quality of its production and especially in the feeling of authenticity the location shooting conveys, *Las aguas* stood in marked contrast to most of the films of the decade of Juan Domingo Perón's rule (1946–55). Few other films produced in this period are worthy of mention, with the exception of the work of Lucas Demare (*La guerra gaucha*, 1942, q.v.), Leopoldo Torres Ríos (*La vuelta al nido*, 1938, q.v.), and Carlos Hugo Christensen (*La balandra Isabel llegó esta tarde*). The decade's production was polarised into "white telephone" melodramas on the one hand and lifeless action films on the other, with a serving of comedies and musicals. The best talent in the country sat idle, produced far below standard work, or went into exile; censorship was suffocating. Through import quotas, artificially low admission prices, and production subsidies which favoured "quota quickies," levels of production were achieved which have not been matched since, and yet the quality of the films produced was consistently the worst in Argentine film history. The dream of a popular social cinema, put within reach by films like *Prisioneros de la tierra*, was paradoxically dashed during this period of political populism. The damage done to Argentine film by this period and especially by the military coup which brought it to an end in 1955 would only be repaired in the late 1950s with the emergence of the young *nuevo cine* generation. By then the project of creating a popular social cinema had given way to an "auteur" cinema by an urban intelligentsia.

Timothy Barnard

Awards: Best Film, Director, Supporting Actor (Pedro Laxalt), Argentine Academy of Motion Picture Arts and Sciences, 1952; Four awards, including Best Film and Director, Association of Argentine Film Journalists, 1952; Honourable Mention, Venice, 1952.

La casa del ángel

The House of the Angel [U.K.]
[End of Innocence - U.S.]
Argentina, 1957, 78', b+w

Dir Leopoldo Torre Nilsson (1924–1978) *Scr* Beatriz Guido, Torre Nilsson, and Martín Rodríguez Mentasti, based on the novel of the same title by Guido (1954) *Cinematog* Aníbal González Paz *Art dir* Emilio Rodríguez Mentasti *Mus* Juan Carlos Paz *Prod* Martín Rodríguez Mentasti for Argentina Sono Film *Act* Elsa Daniel, Lautaro Murúa, Berta Ortegosa, Bárbara Mujica

The "discovery" of *La casa del ángel* at the Cannes film festival by some of France's leading film critics, who later put the film on their annual ten-best lists, marked Argentina's return to the world film stage and Leopoldo Torre Nilsson's international debut. Torre Nilsson was the first and for a long time the only Latin American filmmaker to be admitted into Europe's pantheon of art film directors and to be distributed widely in the United States. *La casa del ángel* also heralded the imminent renewal of Argentine cinema by an even younger group which, by 1961, the year Torre Nilsson was awarded the International Critics' Prize in Cannes for his masterpiece *La mano en la trampa*, was premiering its debut films in Europe, where they enjoyed a brief vogue. Although he was not yet 40 when he made *La mano en la trampa* and nearly 20 films would follow in the next 15 years, this was to be the pinnacle of his career. Despite a few commercial successes, he would never regain the expressive powers he demonstrated during this brief period, resulting in a career marked more by disappointment than by achievement, despite his legendary status.

Torre Nilsson had grown up in a privileged film milieu, apprenticing with his father Leopoldo Torres Ríos (*La vuelta al nido*, 1938, q.v.) while barely a teenager in the late 1930s. His first solo film, *Días de odio*, made in 1953, came after co-directing two films with Torres Ríos. *La casa del ángel* began a ten-film cycle over seven years in collaboration with his novelist wife Beatriz Guido: she scripted or co-scripted nine of these films, mostly adapting her own novels. Her influence on Torre Nilsson, especially in his most accomplished and thematically and stylistically similar *La casa del ángel*, *Fin de fiesta* (1960), and *La mano en la trampa*, is unmistakable. Not only are these Torre Nilsson's most thematically compelling works, they are also sublime expressions of a unique form created to express Guido's themes. This was to be Argentina's most fruitful and sustained collaboration between filmmaker and author.

Guido's favoured theme of the period was the repressive world of the country's disappearing oligarchy. To Guido, this world, with its cruel sexuality and asphyxiating social conventions, always appeared perverse and macabre. In *La mano en la trampa*, set in the 1950s, this world was dealt a death blow when Elsa Daniel discovers her mother and aunt to have kept a mentally handicapped sister captive in the attic for decades. Daniel, with Lautaro Murúa one of Torre Nilsson's acting stable during this period, plays in *La casa del ángel* the youngest daughter in a family ruled over by a cold, distant patriarch and a mother so obsessed with carnal sin she forces her daughters to bathe in their bedclothes. Daniel's awakening sexuality, which includes a crush on Murúa, a friend of her father's, is fed by a nanny who paints vivid pictures of the devil lurking in men's bodies while spiriting Daniel away in secret to lust over Rudolph Valentino at the cinema.

Murúa plays an idealistic young opposition politician—the setting is the 1920s, Argentina's first and last full decade of democracy—engaged in a campaign against corruption and press censorship. Caught short by revelations of his late father's corruption and censorship when in power, he sinks into despair and apathy. To protect his family's honour, however, he half-heartedly proceeds to duel the opponent who revealed his father's crimes. The night of the duel, to be hosted by Daniel's father, Murúa visits Daniel in her room and rapes her. As Daniel lays in bed afterward, her voice-off telling us she wishes Murúa dead, shots are heard: he has won the duel. The film then finishes on the scene it opened on in flash-forward: Daniel is seen cleaning up after a dinner of her now-aged father and Murúa. Her emotionless voice-over tells us of her mother's death and her sisters' marriages and the lonely life she leads caring for her father, a frequent host of Murúa: "I wander the city in the saddest neighbourhoods, but he is always there, and I'm not sure if he is dead or alive, if we are both ghosts."

What held Torre Nilsson in the international eye for nearly a decade was a superbly crafted, singular aesthetic that consummately expressed Guido's claustrophobic world of denial and guilt. In *La casa del ángel*, Torre Nilsson's most audacious expression of this aesthetic, the black-and-white cinematography made use of extreme shadows, high contrast, and spot lighting that often revealed only part of an actor's face. The mise-en-scène, frequently described as baroque, matched Guido's gothic sensibilities. While Torre Nilsson had in fact little in common with the "new waves" emerging or about to emerge in Europe at the time, he shared with these directors a willingness to engage in radical formal experiments. His camera work, said by Richard Roud to be "Wellesian," revelled in extreme and disorienting angles and movements. More than his superb craftsmanship, Torre Nilsson created a form which, like Robert Bresson in France and Michelangelo Antonioni in Italy, embodied his thematic concerns. Torre Nilsson himself, however, after viewing Bresson's *Le Procès de Jeanne d'Arc* at Cannes in 1962, pointed out the differences in their styles: "There are those who believe that you must strip away so many things in order to be left with pure synthesis, without realising that genius is born of abundance, the abundance of a Tolstoy, a Dostoevsky, a Joyce." These were the early literary heros of a filmmaker who was also a—little accomplished—author, poet, and playwright. If Torre Nilsson rejected high modernist minimalism, if he insisted on creating a dense atmosphere through a baroque mise-en-scène and exaggerated camera and lighting effects, accentuated in *La casa del ángel* by Juan Carlos Paz's dissonant, atonal musical score, his great achievement, like Orson Welles, was to have done this with such rigour and simplicity, avoiding any impression of clutter or superfluity.

After 1963 and the end of his collaborations with Guido, Torre Nilsson undertook some critically and commercially disastrous English-language co-productions. As the decade progressed and the generation he opened doors for had them closed by censorship and a hostile market-place, he survived by making more and more commercial films, including a blockbuster *Martín Fierro* (1968), which won him little praise from the critics. In the early 1970s he undertook adaptations of two Argentine novels which fit his criterion of "abundance": Roberto Arlt's *Los siete locos* (1973), and Manuel Puig's *Boquitas pintadas* (1974), as well as Adolfo Bioy Casares' *La guerra del cerdo* (1975). They revealed a middle-aged Torre Nilsson to be an excellent craftsman who had lost all his idiosyncratic genius. He died at the age of 54, two years after the new military dictatorship had banned his last film, *Piedra libre* (1976), an ignominious end to the career of the country's most celebrated and talented stylist. His son, Javier Torre (*Las tumbas*, 1991), is continuing the family vocation but has not yet revealed any special talent.

Timothy Barnard

Awards: Five awards, including First Prize and Best Director, National Film Institute (INC), 1957; Special Mention to Elsa Daniel, Cannes, 1957.

El jefe

The Leader [The Boss]
Argentina, 1958, 90', b+w

Dir Fernando Ayala (b. 1920) *Scr* David Viñas and Ayala, based on the short story of the same title by Viñas *Cinematog* Ricardo Younis *Art dir* Mario Vanarelli *Mus* Lalo Shifrin *Prod* Ayala and Héctor Olivera for Aries Cinematográfica Argentina *Act* Alberto de Mendoza, Orestes Caviglia, Leonardo Favio, Duilio Marzio

One of the characteristic and most dynamic features of the new currents in Argentine film in the late 1950s and early 60s was the collaboration between parallel new generations of filmmakers and authors emerging after the downfall of Juan Perón in 1955. For 15 years prior to the collaboration between Beatriz Guido and Leopoldo Torre Nilsson (*La casa del ángel*, 1957, q.v.), "quality" Argentine cinema had been overwhelmingly reliant on foreign authors, resulting in studio versions of European classics such as Luis Saslavsky's *La dama duende* (1945, q.v.). With *El jefe* and *La casa del ángel*, made a year earlier, Argentine cinema inaugurated a new relationship between national authors and directors, which was to multiply in the coming years. Some directors, like Manuel Antín (*La cifra impar*, 1961) and René Mujica (*El hombre de la esquina rosada*, 1962) sought to adapt the country's most prestigious—and difficult to film—authors, Julio Cortázar and Jorge Luis Borges. Others sought to depict contemporary social issues in an innovative style in the mainstream of the industry or its margins with the aid of younger writers. In the case of Fernando Ayala and the young leftist writer David Viñas, the conditions which led to such a collaboration soon changed, with Viñas moving towards increasingly critical commentaries on Argentine society while Ayala soon became established as a journeyman director of commercial fare.

El jefe recounts the relations among a group of young delinquents in the new middle class suburbs of Buenos Aires. Their increasingly sophisticated activities end in tragedy, the death of a young woman picked up by the group's *jefe*, or leader. His bravado then crumbles and his spell over his followers is broken; they go their separate ways, some following a new gang leader and others renouncing their delinquency. The film's resemblance to Nicholas Ray's *Rebel Without a Cause* (1955) is unmistakable, especially in the development of Leonardo Favio's supporting role as a junior member of the gang, too intelligent to be attracted by the thrills of intimidation but driven into the gang's arms—and into adulation for its dynamic leader—by an adolescent rebellion against the conservatism and impotence of his father, a representative of the country's declining oligarchy. But the film went beyond exposing the delinquency of contemporary Argentine youth and insinuating that its characters were typical—and logical—products of modern society. The image of the *jefe* was widely recognised as an allegory for the influence Perón held over Argentine society through the mixture of intimidation and rewards that bound his followers to him.

El jefe is a carefully crafted film that, while not aspiring to the singular vision of Torre Nilsson or the radical experiments of the generation to follow, reveals considerable flair. Aspects of the mise-en-scène, such as the lighting effects, stand out, and the production standards are on a par with European cinema of the time. The film's evidently sizeable budget is an indication of the new hopes of the film milieu following the introduction in 1957 of new film legislation and the creation of a national film institute—charged with granting subsidies and cash awards—after the industry was dismantled by the new military government of 1955. Despite this new hope, three major studios closed their doors in 1957, crippled by the events of the preceding years. *El jefe* was the first feature produced by Aries, a company whose beginnings were in advertising and which is co-owned by Ayala and Héctor Olivera (*La Patagonia rebelde*, 1973, q.v.), who continue to produce each others' films nearly 40 years after its founding in 1956. For 35 years the company alternated between these two directors' more or less serious work and commercial comedies and adventure films, of which it was the country's largest producer. In 1991, Aries gave up its production activities, apart from the occasional film by Olivera and Ayala, in favour of distribution. *El jefe* was the first of several Aries films (*La Patagonia rebelde, Tiempo de revancha*, 1981, q.v.) that situated social commentary in a well-crafted commercial drama, seemingly always at a time of social change and at a moment propitious for box office success.

Timothy Barnard

Awards: Six awards, including Best Film, Director, Actor (Alberto de Mendoza), Association of Argentine Film Journalists, 1958; Second Prize, Best Director, Best Actor (de Mendoza), National Film Institute (INC), 1958; Best Spanish-language Film, Mar del Plata, 1959.

Shunko

Argentina, 1960, 76', b+w

Dir Lautaro Murúa (b. 1927) *Scr* Augusto Roa Bastos, based on the memoir of the same title
by Jorge W. Abalos *Cinematog* Vicente Cosentino *Art dir* Saulo Benavente *Mus* Waldo de los
Ríos *Prod* Leo Kanaf for Producciones San Justo *Act* Lautaro Murúa, Gabriela Shoo, Raúl
del Valle, Marta Roldán, Angel Greco, Graciela Rueda

Shunko, Chilean-born stage and screen actor Lautaro Murúa's first film as
director, was one of the first independent productions of the early 1960s
to be associated with the emerging *nuevo cine* movement. Unlike many
films of the loosely defined group, who preferred urban themes, *Shunko*
was shot on location in the remote province of Santiago del Estero.
Shunko—the nickname of the film's child star—was based on the memoirs
of primary school teacher Jorge W. Abalos, published in an obscure
provincial edition and discovered and adapted by the Paraguayan author
Augusto Roa Bastos. Murúa relates that Roa Bastos' script had to be
modified on location, "writing as we filmed," because of shooting
problems. Despite its box office success and critical acclaim, *Shunko*, like
Murúa's *Alias Gardelito*, made the following year, was shut out of the
national film awards, with their important cash value, by the newly-
created National Film Institute (INC), prompting public controversy and
accusations of political manipulation by the films' producer.

In the film Murúa plays a schoolteacher who arrives in a remote
region to teach the children of poor shepherds and farmers at the local
schoolhouse—a few benches under a tree. The film was shot in the same
region as Abalos himself taught, and the young actors were local children,
many of whom had never seen a film. The schoolteacher becomes
embroiled in tugs-of-war with the parents, who would rather have their
children at home working than at school. Murúa enters into a brief affair
with a single mother, a poor woman leading a harsh rural existence,
before they cut it off because of gossip. Like other parts of the film's
narrative this subplot seems a bit clichéd in its treatment, but it does allow
for the development of a female character and allows the director to work
out his concerns of cultural (mis)understanding. In the end, Murúa wins
the mountain people's trust by saving a young girl after a serious accident.
The community pitches in to build a new schoolhouse and Murúa departs,
confident that the value of education has been accepted by the community
and that he has been enriched by the wisdom of the local culture.

In both its narrative and formal treatment, *Shunko* reveals the influence of Murúa's mentor Leopoldo Torres Ríos (*La vuelta al nido*, 1938, q.v.). A simplicity and tenderness bordering on sentimentality are complemented by a meticulous attention to detail. On the one hand is a frank realism, highlighted by Murúa's determination to film in direct sound despite the obstacles and his daring use of the native language Quechua, subtitled in Spanish. The film historian José Agustín Mahieu hailed this aspect of the film as a landmark study of rural/urban and native/white cultural conflict which captured the dilemma of a now-static traditional culture destroyed by European values without hope of accommodation between them.[1] On the other hand was a poetic lyricism, springing from Murúa's belief that "We must sacrifice realism to authenticity," a dictum which allowed him to engage in formal experiments that undermined the film's realism, such as the interlude of local people pounding corn in a long-shot silhouette to a soundtrack of wooden percussion instruments.

Murúa had begun working as an actor in Argentina in the mid-1950s. His most notable work was with Torres Ríos and his son Leopoldo Torre Nilsson (*La casa del ángel*, 1957, q.v.), and *Shunko* is dedicated to the former, who died the year it was released. Murúa had starred in Torres Ríos' last film the year before, when he had been able to direct a few scenes. This, and not early experiments with short films like the majority of his generation, was Murúa's initiation into directing. In the next 15 years, before his exile to Europe in the mid-70s, Murúa was able to direct only three more films (*La Raulito*, 1975, q.v.), earning his living as a film and stage actor. *Alias Gardelito*, seen as one of the major films of the period, was an urban film that depicted a marginal class of petty criminals. A more elliptical, unsentimental style captured the alienation of the characters and the hostility of the city. Here again Roa Bastos, then establishing himself in Argentina as a novelist (*Hijo de hombre*, 1960) and screenwriter, wrote the script. In 1989, Roa Bastos was awarded Spain's prestigious Cervantes literary prize. Murúa has been unsuccessful in his attempts to bring Roa Bastos' monumental *Yo, el Supremo* (1974), his masterwork, to the screen.

Timothy Barnard

Awards: Best Film, Best Director, Association of Argentine Film Journalists, 1960; Best Spanish-language Film, Special Mention, Mar del Plata, 1961.

1. José Agustín Mahieu, *Breve historia del cine argentino* (Buenos Aires: Editorial Universitaria de Buenos Aires, 1966), 68.

Prisioneros de una noche

Prisoners of One Night
Argentina, 1960 (released 1962), 87', b+w

Dir David José Kohon (b. 1929) *Scr* Carlos Latorre *Cinematog* Alberto Etchebehere *Mus Re Concierto* by Antonio Vivaldi; various tangos, foxtrots, charlestons, and Argentine jazz *Prod* Leopoldo Torre Nilsson and Néstor Gaffet for Angel Producciones *Act* María Vaner, Alfredo Alcón, Osvaldo Terranova, Juan J. Edelman

In the late 1950s, a disparate group of aspiring young filmmakers, armed with new state production subsidies, set in motion an explosion of short fiction and documentary film production, mostly in 35mm, that was to be the seed of the Argentine *nuevo cine* movement. Between 1958 and 1963 some 200 shorts were made by the movement's rising talents. "Movement" is a misnomer, as much for the lack of cohesion and common formal and thematic interests among the filmmakers as for its extremely short life. Many directors made only one or two features before withdrawing or being incorporated into the commercial mainstream; by the time the younger director Leonardo Favio appeared on the scene in 1965 (*Crónica de un niño solo*, q.v.), the dream of sustaining an independent movement had been shattered.

While the filmmakers gained some exposure and acclaim for their work at European festivals, foreign sales were harder to obtain. Today their work is virtually unknown in Europe and North America, even by specialist Latin American film critics, in direct contrast with the art-house successes of Brazilian Cinema Nôvo and of Cuban cinema in the late 1960s and early 70s. The conventional view from afar is that the reason for this, and indeed for the films' failure in their own market, is because this was an "intellectualised cinema designed for a small elite, [bringing] to the screen, with the technical fluidity of the European cinema, the world view and individualistic experiences of the Buenos Aires middle class."[1] Much is wrong with this assessment. While it may stand as a fairly accurate summary of the work of directors like Rodolfo Kuhn (*Los jóvenes viejos*, 1961) or Manuel Antín (*La cifra impar*, 1961), it fails to acknowledge the social concerns of the movement's leading directors, Lautaro Murúa (*Shunko*, 1960, q.v.) and David José Kohon. Murúa's early films in particular enjoyed considerable box office success, posing the question of just why the movement was unable to take root in Argentina: censorship and the open hostility of government and film institute officials must be seen as a large part of the answer; the unwillingness of the mainstream of the industry (and its trade union) to tolerate an auteurist rump must also be considered. We must also wonder whether, in addition to factors such as the movement's early appearance and short life, its invisibility in the northern metropolis is not due to the latter's willingness to accept the exoticism of the young Brazilians and the revolutionary rhetoric of the Cubans—the two poles of our conception of the South, tropicalism and revolution—but not the more European-derived formal experiments and literary adaptations of the Argentines.

David Kohon made his first short in 1950, but it was his second, *Buenos Aires*, filmed in 1958 but never seen publicly because of censorship, that gave him the opportunity to make his first feature, *Prisioneros de una noche*. Like *Buenos Aires*, *Prisioneros* presented a poetic yet gritty view of the city, one of the hallmarks of this *nuevo cine* generation's films. Produced by Argentina's leading filmmaker, Leopoldo Torre Nilsson (*La casa del ángel*, 1957, q.v.), who brought with him to the project the cinematographer Alberto Etchebehere (who the following year would film Torre Nilsson's masterpiece, *La mano en la trampa*), *Prisioneros* was shot almost entirely at night in the streets of Buenos Aires. It is a hallucinatory vision of the city and the mundane yet tragic lives it hides. Its portrait of a transient, doomed love is one of the best expressions of the movement's often-cited melancholy and romantic fatalism. Foreign critics, calling the film "kaleidoscopic," noted a resemblance to the "poetic realism" of French director Marcel Carné's films made with poet Jacques Prévert (e.g. *Quai des brumes*, 1938; *Le Jour se lève*, 1939), and indeed *Prisioneros* was scripted by a poet, Carlos Latorre. *Quai*'s "fog of despair" (Simone de Beauvoir) had earned it accusations by Vichy of demoralising France and thus contributing to its defeat in the war. To this atmosphere Kohon added some of the *nuevo cine*'s most radical formal experiments, giving it an affinity also with the French *nouvelle vague*, especially to films like Jean-Luc Godard's *A bout de souffle* (1960), which Kohon was surely unfamiliar with at the time *Prisioneros* was shot.

Prisioneros recounts a one-night affair between two of the city's anonymous souls. Alfredo Alcón plays a man who works in the vegetable market at night and as a phoney bidder at auctions on weekends, living in a refurbished train car in the city's train yards. María Vaner, whose mysterious sadness we gradually learn is caused by her unwilling prostitution to make ends meet, is a ballroom dance instructor who lives in a rooming house. One of her co-lodgers, a man who performs with a boa constrictor in the market, is a regular client. The night of the lovers' encounter they wander the city, slowly falling in love in its alternately delirious and desolate locales: an amusement park, the deserted docks, cafés, train stations, markets. Stalked by her co-lodger, who has paid for her company that night, they are attacked and Vaner is abducted. Alcón searches the city for her all night, finally finding her at dawn in the flower market, one of her professed haunts. Amidst the intoxicating bustle of the market—the city is always swirling about them, forcefully occupying the frame—they affirm their love and agree to meet the next day. Vaner then returns to her rooming house and confesses her co-lodger's murder to the waiting police.

Adding to the hallucinatory effect of travelling through the sprawling city in one night, Kohon undertook a series of stylistic experiments. The disorienting montage sequences and sudden camera movements are among the less successful of these. His musical experiments were more rewarding. At several points Vivaldi's *Re Concierto* appears on the soundtrack, recorded at 45 rpm and played back at 33 rpm. He also created sound collages of tangos, jazz, and ballroom dance music to accompany the couple as they walk the city's streets, past its cafés and record stores. "When you walk along the streets of Buenos Aires, this sort of mixing happens," he explained, adding "If the images themselves were already somewhat hallucinatory, these sound mixes accentuated this impression." Even the acting style he imposed on his cast and his manner of filming them was unconventional. Only one close-up appears in the film, when Vaner confesses her crime. Throughout the film she delivers her lines in a flat, emotionless monotone, as Kohon insisted real people really speak, and as we might expect a woman in her position to speak. These experiments, especially his handling of the actors, drew the criticism even of the film's production company, and the film was shelved for two years until after the release of his somewhat less experimental *Tres veces Ana* (1961, q.v.), a portent of Kohon's troubled career.

Timothy Barnard

Awards: International Critics' Prize (FIPRESCI), Cineforum Prize and Best Young Director, Santa Margherita (Italy), 1961.

1. Ana López, "Argentina, 1955–1976: The Film Industry and Its Margins," *The Garden of Forking Paths: Argentine Cinema*, eds. John King and Nissa Torrents (London: British Film Institute, 1987), 57. López does acknowledge Murúa as a "[possible] exception" to this formulation.

Tres veces Ana

Three Times Ana
Argentina, 1961, 115', b+w

Dir David José Kohon (b. 1929) *Scr* Kohon *Cinematog* Ricardo Aronovich *Mus* Excerpts from popular music *Prod* Marcelo Simonetti for Silvestras *Act* María Vaner, Luis Medina Castro, Walter Vidatre, Alberto Argibay, Lautaro Murúa

With *Tres veces Ana* David Kohon (*Prisioneros de una noche*, 1960, q.v.) further developed his project of an intellectual cinema portraying the residents of Buenos Aires, their melancholy, and the chance encounters and fleeting loves the city offers them. A three-part anthology, *Ana* again features María Vaner, the lead actress of *Prisioneros*, here playing not one but three sad and inscrutable women: Kohon's films are striking portraits of young women which go against all cinematic convention. Plain, sad, drab (in all but the second episode), they are also more conscious of how events are unfolding and, despite the pervasive fatalism of Kohon's films, more in control than the men, who are hopelessly dependent on them.

In *Ana*'s first vignette, "La tierra" ("Land"), Vaner plays a shop clerk who lives with her mother in the suburbs. An affair with a young man who takes the same train into town ends in pregnancy; he persuades her to have an abortion and they drift apart. A chance encounter on the street draws them back together, but almost ruefully, as if resigned to a life together that won't be as happy as before. In the second episode, "El aire" ("Air"), Ana is a promiscuous, empty-headed beach bunny. The action takes place one night in a crowded beach house outside Buenos Aires where a group of friends and circumstantial acquaintances meet to drink, talk, and dance. Kohon's themes of the distances which separate us and the hollow, mechanical nature of our relations are expressed here through a furtive encounter between Ana and a newcomer to the group, a student. Here too we see another recurring theme in Kohon's work, one not often associated with the *nuevo cine* filmmakers, the role of class in our social relations and personal destiny, brought to light by Kohon's pairing of lovers from different classes, particularly in his later films. In *Ana*'s third sequence, "Las nubes" ("Clouds"), Ana literally assumes a phantom form. Walter Vidarte plays a day-dreaming young clerk who notices Ana intently gazing down at him in the street from a third-story window. He becomes obsessed with her, returning often to the corner to gaze back at her, a silent, expressionless vigil for them both. She appears in his dreams and fantasies more remote and ephemeral than ever, dressed in black. Finally, walking under her balcony, an opportune wind blows her flowerpot at his feet and he seizes the opportunity to return the pieces to her, only to discover the apartment inhabited by a middle-aged seamstress who keeps a mannequin in the window.

Just as Ana's remoteness and the film's fatalism and melancholy increase from one vignette to the next, so too is there a progression in Kohon's style as he searches for the means to give form to the episodes' moods and titles. In this he is well served by the work of Ricardo Aronovich, one of Latin America's finest contemporary cinematographers, who in 1964 shot the Brazilian Cinema Nôvo classic *Os Fuzis* (q.v.) and who at the end of his career shot Costa-Gavras' *Missing* in 1982. "La tierra," the most "terrestrial" tale and the one with the most conventional narrative, is shot in the city's streets, cafés, train stations, and lovers' hotels. It is the most directly shot, a street-level portrait of daily routine. Kohon's approach in "El aire" is more abstract, with little in the way of narrative development and camera and editing techniques that accentuate this: there is an abundance of tightly-framed shots in the cabin, disjointedly edited, forming an abstraction seemingly suspended in space. In "Las nubes," not only is Vidarte a dreamy clerk whose co-workers ridicule him for having his "head in the clouds" and Ana an apparition he can't touch or feel; the entire episode seems to take place off the ground. Vidarte works in an upper-story office, providing background vistas of the sky above the city. The camera tends to low angle shots and tilts up the sides of buildings and into the sky. At one point, when Vidarte is fantasising Ana's presence in his room and they are pretending to be at an amusement park while sitting on chairs, the camera cuts loose, lunging drunkenly around the room. Here too the social commentary becomes more explicit, especially in the comments of one of Vidarte's workmates, played by Lautaro Murúa: "A bunch of zombies," he laments, looking out onto the city, "a city of ghosts."

While *Tres veces Ana* established Kohon as the most formally gifted of the *nuevo cine* generation, he was no luckier than the rest in being able to maintain a career. Many of the young filmmakers, not finding a market for their work and faced with less and less state support and increasing censorship as the decade progressed, contributed only one or two films before moving on, or relied on advertising work between occasional features, something Kohon refused to do. His next film, *Así o de otra manera* (1964), was never released. Only three more films would follow in more than 15 years. His most conventional, *¿Qué es el otoño?* (1976), was banned by the military government that took power that year because of its references to the country's "disappearances." In it, a middle-aged architect, recognised as the most brilliant of his generation in his youth, commits suicide when unable to find work. Speaking about film in the early 1960s in 1982, shortly after his last film was released, Kohon said, in a manner as incisive and poetic as his films, "With more than ninety per cent of the country's film releases made up of foreign films and exhibition in the hands of private firms, all that one can accomplish are these interludes, these brief springtimes, like in the early 1960s and from 1973 to 1975. Their fleeting perfume hits us suddenly from time to time, with the sweetness and rage of infertile beauty. We're still here and yet we feel ourselves to be phantoms."

Timothy Barnard

Awards: Three awards, Association of Argentine Film Journalists, 1961; Third Prize, National Film Institute (INC), 1961; Special Jury Prize, La Palma (Spain), 1962.

Los inundados

Flooded Out
Argentina, 1961, 87', b+w

Dir Fernando Birri (b. 1925) *Scr* Birri and Jorge A. Ferrando, based on the short story of the same title by Mateo Booz (pseudonym of Miguel Angel Correra) *Cinematog* Adelqui Camusso *Art dir* Saulo Benavente *Mus* Ariel Ramírez *Prod* Universidad Nacional del Litoral and Productora América Nuestra (PAN) *Act* Pirucho Gómez, Iola Palomba, María Vera, Roberto Pérez

Returning to Argentina in 1956 from studies with the Italian neo-realists at the renowned Centro Sperimentale in Rome (alongside the Cubans Julio García Espinosa and Tomás Gutiérrez Alea and would-be filmmaker Gabriel García Márquez), Fernando Birri inaugurated a documentary film school within the university of his native Santa Fe, the first of its kind in Latin America. Initially, Birri and his students produced a series of photomontage documentary shorts. The most important of these, *Tire dié*, a study of child beggars in Santa Fe made in 1958, was re-shot as a 16mm short film, finished in 1960. *Tire dié* was later proclaimed one of the first Latin American social documentaries. In 1959 Birri shot two other shorts, *La primera fundación de Buenos Aires* and *Buenos días, Buenos Aires;* the latter was included in the anthology film *Che, Buenos Aires* (1966). By 1961 Birri was able to shoot the shoestring feature *Los inundados*. A picaresque saga of a Santa Fe family uprooted by a seasonal flood, the film shows the clear influence of Birri's Italian mentors. *Los inundados* was based on a short story by Santa Fe author Mateo Booz, of the same literary generation as Alcides Greca, whose film *El último malón* (1918, q.v.) was a model of social enquiry and documentary narrative for Birri, who rescued the film from oblivion on his return to Santa Fe. *Los inundados* stars a local vaudeville actor (Pirucho Gómez) and a host of local actors and non-professionals, all dubbed by themselves in order to preserve the local accent, despite the primitive recording facilities available in Santa Fe.

Los inundados opens with Gómez speaking to the camera of the events to follow: he and the numerous members of his family, flooded out of their home, will be shunted by the authorities across the countryside in a boxcar until they are finally returned home, whence Gómez, again addressing the camera, will wonder aloud when the next flood will be. The tone of the film is thus set: this will be not so much an exposé of social conditions or the manipulations of officialdom as an often-comic jaunt through the social landscape. Despite Birri's being considered the "godfather" of the region's social protest cinema, there is little of the latter movement's explicit political denunciations in *Los inundados* or in his three solo short films of the period. Gómez' character has a loveable aversion to work and lets his oversized wife run the family while he plays cards or *bocci*. The picaresque approach creates thematic ambiguities, however, such as when his daughter is date-raped by her boyfriend, an event recounted like all the others as part of life's ups and downs. Politicians are depicted as inherently duplicitous and cynical, yet somehow bumbling and benign, in their attempts to buy votes with promises of assistance while nonetheless trying to keep the uprooted families out of their jurisdiction. Nevertheless, the film caused a considerable stir when released in Argentina, and the film institute initially turned down requests from foreign festivals to screen it, overlooked it in the awarding of its annual cash prizes for merit, and resisted giving it an "A" classification so that it could benefit from the exhibition quota system in place at the time.

The technical challenges of filming a regional feature on a small budget were great, and formally *Los inundados* at times seems limp and artless compared to other works of the period. Cinematographer Adelqui

Camusso, who studied in Rome with Birri, shot the film in functional, static medium shots, held together by a recurring *chamamé*, a jig-like accordion air popular in northern Argentina. When the film workers' union insisted on a full complement of technicians for the shoot, such as make-up artists Birri had no need of, he got them to agree to an apprenticeship system which saw two of his students assigned to help every union member, giving rise to an incredible 150 people on the shoot.

After filming another documentary short in Santa Fe (*Pampa gringa*, 1963), Birri left the country definitively in 1963, a year after the military deposed the centrist Arturo Frondizi government, eventually settling in Italy. There he made a series of experimental and documentary films under the aegis of his Laboratory of Film Poetics but largely disappeared from view. During this period he filmed political documentaries (*Remitente: Nicaragua (Carta al mundo)*, 1984 and *Mi hijo el Che*, 1985); portraits of other artists (*Castagnino, diario romano*, 1966 and *Rafael Alberti, un retrato del poeta, por Fernando Birri*, 1983); and an experimental film (*Org*, 1968), signed under the pseudonym FERMAGHORG. His theoretical perspective, outlined in intermittent manifestos, conference proceedings, poems, and other writings, evolved from the search for a "nationalist, realist, critical and popular cinema" of his beginnings in Argentina, when "film which is complicit in . . . underdevelopment [*subdesarrollo*] is sub-cinema [*subcine*]" to a desire for a "cosmic, raving and lumpen cinema," or "cosmunism," whose "sensual hedonistic erotic communism" accommodated "madness and rigour [going] hand-in-hand." In 1986 he was named director of the new International Film and Television School in Cuba, which brought together students from Asia, Africa, and Latin America; he remained there until 1992. In Cuba, he was able to make his second feature fiction film in 1988, *Un señor muy viejo con unas alas enormes*, freely adapted from a short story by García Márquez, the school's founder. Subsequent attempts to mount feature productions, in Argentina and Spain, have been unsuccessful. The film school he founded in Santa Fe lived on into the 1970s, graduating such contemporary Argentine filmmakers as Gerardo Vallejo (*El camino hacia la muerte del viejo Reales*, 1971) and Nicolás Sarquis (*La muerte de Sebastián Arache y su pobre entierro*, 1972), both directors with strong regional and social concerns.

Timothy Barnard

Awards: Special Jury Prize, Karlovy Vary, 1962; Best First Film (shared), Venice, 1962.

Crónica de un niño solo

Chronicle of a Boy Alone
Argentina, 1965, 70', b+w

Dir Leonardo Favio (b. 1938) *Scr* Jorge Zuhair Jury and Favio *Cinematog* Ignacio Souto *Mus* Arcángelo Corelli and Alessandro Marcello *Prod* Luis de Stéfano and Walter Achúgar *Act* Diego Puente, Tino Pascali, Oscar Espínola, María Vaner

A late addition to the heterogenous body of work known as the *nuevo cine*, *Crónica de un niño solo* was young film actor Leonardo Favio's first feature film. While Favio himself was able to shoot five more features in the next decade, *Crónica* was in many ways the culmination of the *nuevo cine*, as many of its members were unable to film regularly beyond the early 1960s, and censorship worsened after a military coup took place in 1966. An impressionistic tale of a young boy (non-professional Diego Puente's first screen role) who moves from an institution for indigent children to jail to a shantytown and back to jail again, *Crónica* creates a juvenile universe only occasionally disturbed by adults. It is also partly autobiographical: Favio himself spent part of his childhood in such an institution, placed there by a mother unable to care for him, and later emerged as one of Argentina's leading young actors in the 1950s. *Crónica* is dedicated to director Leopoldo Torre Nilsson (*La casa del ángel*, 1957, q.v.), in whose films Favio came to fame as an actor.

Crónica elicited considerable critical acclaim and favourable comparisons with the austere French director Robert Bresson. The French critic Marcel Martin termed *Crónica* a film halfway between Jean Vigo's *Zéro de conduite* (1932) and François Truffaut's *Les 400 coups* (1959), classic films about rebellious children in an oppressive social environment. In this unusually assured and mature first film Favio, at the age of 27, depicted the lot of indigent children in an manner both poetic and precise. On the film's release a medical doctor working with juvenile delinquents was prompted to write to Favio, praising his ability to render "every scene" of the film "clinically perfect."

Like Bresson and other European contemporaries, Favio prefers the long take to cutting and reframing to follow the (minimal) dialogue and on-screen action rather than adopting a shot-counter shot structure. Ignacio Souto's beautiful black-and-white cinematography—Favio's 1960s films are among the last great Argentine black-and-white films, as the country's art film directors switched to colour in the late 1960s—is distinguished by seemingly simple yet intricate tracking shots and a propensity to wander off and leave the action off-screen. In the long and languorous river scene, the camera tilts into the trees, and the young boy's escape from prison, an extended sequence showing him pull the bolt with his belt buckle, affords the camera the opportunity to probe the interior of his cell. Favio borrows a technique from his European mentors when he films the boy running from prison: a five second tracking shot is repeated four times to represent his flight. The use of music for effect is limited to four brief occasions in the film, and Favio's peculiar 90° overhead ceiling shot appears here for the first time.

Twice in the film Favio lingers in the boys' universe—during one of the film's opening sequences, as they whisper amongst themselves in bed at night in the institution, and late in the film, when Puente and a friend are swimming in a river upstream from a rival group of boys. The former sequence establishes Favio's uncommon approach, his refusal to depict dramatic events through the standard cinematic techniques: when the boy strikes an official, the scene is shot from behind as a medium travelling shot, and Favio cuts on the action with no reaction shot. During the river scene, the boys are shot completely naked with no attempt to shoot them from behind or from the waist up. Separated from Puente, the other boy is chased through the woods by their rivals, but rather than using the scene to develop an emotional response on the part of the spectator, the sequence is filmed silent, the camera luxuriating in the forest setting.

Favio, who was born in the provincial city Mendoza, captured the dreariness of provincial life in the even more elliptical, austere, and disaffected films which followed, *Este es el romance del Anicieto y la Francisca, de como quedó trunco, comenzó la tristeza . . . y unas pocas cosas más* (1966) and *El dependiente* (1967), both low-budget films co-scripted with his author brother Jorge Zuhair Jury. This triptych established him as one of the greatest poets and stylists of Argentine film, one with a particularly realist and sombre social vision. None of these films was a commercial success, and in the 1970s Favio changed course with a series of flamboyant, whimsical colour films (*Juan Moreira*, 1973, q.v.), although his idiosyncratic formalism remained.

Timothy Barnard

Awards: Special Jury Mention, Mar del Plata, 1965; Special Mention, International Critics Jury, Mar del Plata, 1965; Special Mention, Acapulco, 1965.

La hora de los hornos

The Hour of the Furnaces
Argentina, 1968, 260', b+w

Part One: "Neocolonialismo y violencia"
            (Neo-colonialism and Violence), 95'
Part Two: "Acto para la liberación"
            (An Act for Liberation), 120'
Part Three: "Violencia y liberación"
            (Violence and Liberation), 45'

Dir Grupo Cine Liberación (Fernando E. Solanas (b. 1936) and Octavio Getino (b. 1935)) *Scr*
Solanas and Getino *Cinematog* Juan Carlos Desanzo (director of photography) and Solanas
(operator) *Sound* Getino *Prod* Solanas

By virtue of its collective production, clandestine distribution, formal
heterogeneity and experimentation and direct engagement with the
Argentine military dictatorship of the day and with neo-colonialism the
world over, *La hora de los hornos* articulated the most radical formal and
political aspirations of the New Latin American Cinema, then entering its
zenith. This self-defined "guerrilla cinema," its makers declared in a
manifesto a year after its completion, constituted a major break with the
models of Hollywood and of European auteur cinema: *La hora de los
hornos* heralded a "third cinema" wherein the camera is used as a "rifle,"
the film an "unfinished, unordered, violent work," and the "proletarian-
ised" filmmaker works with "a camera in one hand and a rock in the
other." At a time when national liberation movements and student
protests were proliferating, this agit-prop film essay's appeals to the
revolutionary rhetoric of Ernesto "Che" Guevara and Frantz Fanon fired
the imaginations of filmmakers and activists in Argentina and around the
world and was hailed abroad as the paradigmatic "Latin American protest
documentary."

In reality, the "Grupo Cine Liberación" was composed of two people,
Fernando Solanas, its principal figure, and the Spanish-born writer Octavio
Getino, winner of the Cuban Casa de las Américas literary award in 1963
for his book of short stories *Chulleca*. Travelling a reported 18,000
kilometres around the country, they filmed in semi-clandestinity with a

young assistant, Gerardo Vallejo (*El camino hacia la muerte del viejo Reales*, 1971), and a novice director of photography, Juan Carlos Desanzo, who would become a leading Argentine cinematographer (*Juan Moreira*, 1973, q.v.), with Solanas operating the 16mm camera and Getino on sound. Today Solanas is generally credited with having directed the film and Getino with co-authoring it.

Solanas had made a couple of short films in the early 1960s as part of a wave of aspiring young filmmakers before being incorporated into the lucrative world of advertising, where he established himself as one of the leading figures of the industry, allowing him to self-finance *La hora de los hornos*. Earlier, he had studied music. An opportunity to work on a feature film seemed to present itself in 1965, when a group of Argentine short film makers and journalists developed a project with the Italian filmmaker Valentino Orsini. A watered-down script was presented to the Argentine film institute for funding but was rejected. One month later the democratic government of Arturo Illia (1963–66) was overthrown in a manner very similar to the fictional script of the aborted film project, and one of the most repressive and turbulent periods in Argentine history was inaugurated under General Juan Carlos Onganía (1966–70).

La hora de los hornos is divided into three parts of unequal length totalling over four hours. The first, "Neocolonialismo y violencia" ("Neo-colonialism and Violence"), is the most experimental and politically broad, a rhetorical "film-act" that foretold and urged on a tri-continental revolution. In the second and third parts, "Acto para la liberación" ("An Act for Liberation") and "Violencia y liberación" ("Violence and Liberation"), the filmmakers' radical Peronism, a bane of the film's admirers in the West, and especially in the rest of Latin America, came to the fore. As the country mobilised against the military, Juan Perón continued to exert considerable influence and fascination from exile, so much so that he returned to lead the country in 1973, nearly 30 years after his first election in 1946 and after the country's military and political elite had spent nearly two decades trying to eradicate his memory. Part Two chronicles these first presidencies, which had become popularly mythologised as a "golden age" in Argentina, and the underground Peronist movement of the 1950s and 60s. Part Three is a series of interviews with mostly-Peronist activists about the prospects for a revolutionary Latin America.

Today, Part One, site of most of the filmmakers' formal experimenta-tion and less dated in its political perspective, is the only one widely available for screening. Divided into 13 subsections ("History," "Dependency," "Political Violence," "Ideological Warfare," etc.), it considers political repression and the need for and prospects of revolutionary liberation in the developing world in general and Argentina in particular, with analyses ranging from colonialism to the role of the mass media. After the credits, the film is dedicated to the Argentine revolutionary Ernesto "Che" Guevara, who died leading a guerrilla movement in Bolivia in 1967. It then opens with syncopated Afro-Cuban music accompanying intermittent images, intercut with black leader, of popular revolt and repression, along with images of a torch being carried through a dark street. There follows a series of quotes to the same music—of Fanon, Aimé Césaire, Fidel Castro, Scalabrini Ortiz, Juan and Evita Perón—and intertitles of slogans and enigmatic single words ("ideology"; "impunity"). The effect is intoxicating and mesmerising. For the next hour and a half, the film offers its call to arms through a unique summation of cinema's vanguard techniques. There are masterful quotes of the European avant-garde, from the 1920s to the 1960s, among them collage, Dziga Vertov's pioneering candid street scenes (*Chelovek S Kinoapparotom*, 1929), Jean-Luc Godard's pithy intertitles, and Luis Buñuel's sardonic view of the bourgeoisie. Accompanying the filmmakers' commentary (and not the other way around) are snippets of mass media effluvia, mock travelogues, archival and found footage, footage from other films (including Fernando Birri's *Tire dié* (1960), about child beggars in Argentina), kitsch effects (lightning bolts raining down on Argentina's entombed oligarchy), and images of city life and rural poverty. One of the most inventive and compelling of the film's techniques is its juxtaposition of these images with music and sound effects: opera music over images of the rural poor; violent and initially unidentifiable sounds of a punch clock over images of workers leaving work (intertitle: "Daily, systematic, minute violence").

La hora de los hornos is more than a modernist film essay, however: by adopting as a principal slogan Fanon's statement that "All spectators are cowards or traitors" (painted on a banner over the screen at the first public Latin American screening at the Viña del Mar film festival in Chile in 1969), Solanas and Getino set for themselves no less a goal than to abolish the passive spectatorship of the "first" and "second" cinemas of classical Hollywood and contemporary Paris and replace it with revolutionary action incited by the film. The distinguishing features of this new cinema, "third cinema," were not only textual—the unrelenting series of questions, challenges, and appeals to the viewer to join the struggle—but also built into the film's structure and its means of distribution and exhibition. Because of censorship and political repression, normal commercial distribution was out of the question. Instead, a circuit of clandestine screenings for small groups was organised, primarily through the Peronist trade unions. There, the film's projection was actually interrupted during Part Two so that the audience could conduct impromptu debates amongst themselves in response to the issues raised by the film. No documentary record of these undoubtedly marathon screenings seems to exist. Several were interrupted by police raids, however, and arrests were made. While a standard 260 minute version was shown abroad, Getino reports that within Argentina changes were made to the film by "exhibitors" according to the type of audience. There is nothing to indicate, however, that the standard version was actually ever modified as a result of audience discussions, despite the film's appeals for input and the group's claim that it was an "unfinished" work. At the same time, many Argentines were able to see the film commercially in neighbouring Uruguay, where it was advertised as a film censored in Argentina. Finally, after the return of Perón in 1973, the film was released commercially in Buenos Aires, although initially no exhibitor could be found. On this occasion Solanas and Getino added an opening title explaining when the film was made and proclaiming the victory of the "Justicialist[Peronist] Revolution." The end of Part One was also changed: in place of the famous five-minute silent freeze-frame close-up of the dead "Che" Guevara's face, a brief "update" on political events since 1968 appeared.

The project of a "guerrilla cinema" that *La hora de los hornos* proposed was developed theoretically in an essay published by Solanas and Getino in 1969,[1] the year after the film's completion. Widely translated and reprinted and appearing contemporaneously with similar theoretical work elsewhere in Latin America (notably Cuban filmmaker Julio García Espinosa's "Por un cine imperfecto" ("For an Imperfect Cinema") published in 1970), "Hacia un tercer cine" ("Towards a Third Cinema") proclaimed that history had provided a moment in Argentina when "political and artistic vanguards" were to meet. In the most lucid commentary on the film available, U.S. scholar Robert Stam praised it as "one of the high points" of the convergence of these two vanguards in film history.[2] Discounting the film's Peronist politics, Stam tempered his praise with the observation that the film's much-vaunted "openness" was to be found in its structure of allowing debate but not in its discourse, which was "stridently unequivocal." Indeed, there is little ambiguity or subtlety in the filmmakers' political analysis. The leftist Argentine critic Raúl Beycero, writing in 1982, criticised the film's "acritical" Peronism.

Citing the contradiction between Peronism (an essentially corporatist ideology) and the Marxist rhetoric of *La hora de los hornos* (a contradiction that became painfully obvious to all "Left Peronists" after Perón's return in 1973), he noted that "to incite armed struggle as a (truly incomprehensible) corollary of an analysis of Peronism appears to be a mixture of opportunism and a lack of a certain fundamental political soundness." On the film's form, Beycero notes its rapid montage, images intercut with intertitles and discontinuous soundtrack, and the way these same techniques are "habitually" used in advertising, where they are "strongly compulsive, seeking an irrational adhesion, a momentary enthusiasm." Calling the use of the same techniques in *La hora de los hornos* politically "incoherent," he describes the result as a "feature-length advertisement for the Peronist revolution."[3]

The film's Peronism can perhaps be overlooked with hindsight, as Stam suggests we do, and explained in part by the fact that resistance to the military was organised primarily through the Peronist labour movement. But few commentators other than Beycero and the French critics Louis Marcorelles[4] and Pascal Bonitzer,[5] the latter writing in *Cahiers du Cinéma*, have expressed much disquiet over the more vexing issue of the film's formal strategies. Unlike Bolivia's Jorge Sanjinés (*¡Fuera de aquí!*, Ecuador, 1975, q.v.), for example, the other New Latin American Cinema director perhaps most concerned with creating new formal structures and new relationships with the film audience, Solanas reveals an astonishing disregard for the politics of mise-en-scène and the filmmaker's relationship to the film's *subjects*. While *La hora de los hornos'* shooting conditions and the prevailing sense of political urgency may have mitigated against the development of new strategies for the mise-en-scène (Solanas' later films are saturated with attention to mise-en-scène), troubling practices remain. The scenes of rural poverty, for example, display a startling objectification of the subjects, deploying the zoom (ubiquitous in world cinema in the late 1960s) almost rapaciously, filming them as passive victims. We even see people on city streets being filmed against their will. They are ciphers in the film's argument, footage to juxtapose with opera music later in the editing room, where the film's brilliance is constructed—in its montage, its extraneous material, its use of intertitles. But where the European avant-garde generally used these same techniques to construct ambiguity and polysemy (with the exception of Sergei Eisenstein's montage), to create complex, "open" works, *La hora de los hornos* appears relentlessly single-minded and, paradoxically, hermetic. It is agit-prop cinema made by an intellectual, not intellectual cinema.

In the late 1960s and early 70s, as the country saw widespread popular protest against the military government, the now-enlarged group undertook a number of other activities, including a trade union newsreel (*Cine informe*) and numerous short films. In 1971 Solanas, Getino, and Vallejo interviewed Perón in Madrid. Two films resulted: *Actualización política y doctrinaria para la toma del poder* and *La revolución justicialista* (both 1972). They were distributed through the same Peronist circuits as *La hora de los hornos*, and Getino reports that the demand for the latter exceeded that for their first film, requiring over 50 16mm copies to be made. With the abdication of the military in 1972, the election of a stand-in for Perón (Héctor Cámpora) that same year, and finally Perón's sweeping election victory of 1973 (before dying in mid-1974, leaving power to his vice president and second wife Isabel), the country's political climate, and Cine Liberación's strategy, changed. Solanas began a feature fiction film, *Los hijos de Fierro*, transforming the epic gaucho poem *Martín Fierro* into a parable of Perón's exile and return. Exiled himself with a new military coup in 1976, he finished the film in France in 1977 and it was not seen in Argentina until 1983, after the restoration of democracy. Getino shot the fiction film *El familiar* in 1972, which, judging it to have been overtaken by events, he withheld until 1975.

In 1973–74, as an indication of the group's change of strategy, Getino headed the film classification board, releasing all foreign and Argentine films banned under the military and trying to develop progressive classification procedures. Significantly, the group opposed other attempts to make a "guerrilla cinema" during this period, objecting strongly to the film *Los traidores* (1974), directed by Raymundo Gleyzer and the far-left Grupo Cine de la Base and about the betrayal of Peronism by its own right wing. Gleyzer would be abducted after the 1976 coup and never heard from again, the most well-known victim from the film milieu of the repression of that period.

After spending his exile in Peru and Mexico, Getino returned to Argentina in the mid-1980s, writing several detailed studies of the Argentine film industry and serving briefly as head of the film institute in 1989–90, when the film industry was paralysed by the country's economic crisis. With *Tangos, el exilio de Gardel* (1985, q.v.), filmed in Paris and Buenos Aires, Solanas returned to the stage, ironically, as one of Latin America's leading auteurs. *Tangos*, an art-house hit in Europe, was followed by *Sur* in 1988. In 1989 the new president, Carlos Menem, the first Peronist to hold the job since Perón and his widow, publicly offered him the job of running the film institute. Solanas declined in order to continue filming and soon afterwards had a falling out with Menem over cultural policy, leading to his eventual renunciation of Peronism. His increasingly shrill accusations that Menem's neo-liberal policies were a betrayal of Peronism prompted Menem to file suit for defamation. In May 1991, the day after a flamboyant court appearance, Solanas was shot in the legs several times in broad daylight, delaying completion of his most recent film, *El viaje* (1992).

Timothy Barnard

1. Octavio Getino and Fernando Solanas, "Hacia un tercer cine," *Hojas de cine* (Mexico City: Fundación Mexicana de Cineastas, 1988), 29–62; "Towards a Third Cinema," *Cineaste*, Vol. 4, No. 3, (1970/71): 1–10.
2. Robert Stam, "*The Hour of the Furnaces* and the Two Avant Gardes," *The Social Documentary in Latin America*, ed. Julianne Burton (Pittsburgh: University of Pittsburgh Press, 1990), 250–66.
3. Raúl Beycero, "El cine y la política en la Argentina de hoy," *Ensayos sobre cine argentino* (Santa Fe: Universidad Nacional del Litoral, 1986), 24–5.
4. Louis Marcorelles, *Living Cinema: New Directions in Contemporary Film-making* (New York: Praeger, 1973), 110–12. Marcorelles comments that the film's style "can prove anything or nothing."
5. Pascal Bonitzer, "Cinéma politique," *Cahiers du Cinéma*, 222 (1970): 37. Bonitzer comments that the film "Uses the 'documentary effect' to convert itself into spectacle . . . directing itself to the spectator's feelings. . . . A documentary which becomes the purest and most perfect fiction."

Hermógenes Cayo [*Imaginero*]

[The Image Maker]
Argentina, 1969, 56', b+w

Dir Jorge Prelorán (b. 1933) *Scr* Prelorán *Cinematog* Prelorán *Ed* Prelorán *Sound* Prelorán *Mus* Leda Valladares, Rodrigo Montero, and Anastasio Quiroga *Prod* Prelorán

Jorge Prelorán is Latin America's best-known and most prolific ethnographic filmmaker. He has over 60 films to his credit, including one feature fiction film, *Mi tía Nora* (Ecuador-U.S., 1982), and his work has been nominated for an Academy Award. Prelorán studied architecture in Argentina and the United States and cinema at UCLA. He made his first film at the age of 18, but his film career really began with his return to

Argentina in 1962, armed with the first of several grants from U.S. foundations. By the time he returned to the U.S. in 1975, to teach at UCLA, he had shot on average more than three films per year in remote corners of Argentina. He worked virtually alone, with no crew (one early assistant, Raymundo Gleyzer, who in his own films would develop a much more radical view of the country than Prelorán, "disappeared" in 1976 after the military coup of that year). Armed with a hand-held 16mm camera, Prelorán shot silent and edited his films himself afterwards—often many times over: different versions of his films abound, as he returns to them over the years and re-edits them, an inexplicable vanity.

Many of Prelorán's early short films were commissioned by the National Art Fund to document traditional indigenous arts and handicrafts. Generally they follow a standard documentary format, with voice-over narration, although Prelorán's later interest in imparting to his films a personal vision is evident in certain stylistic devices, such as brief montage sequences and experiments with the camera, rapid zooms and pans. In *Hermógenes Cayo*, his best-known and most acclaimed work and the first of several lengthier "personal" films, these elements are more prominent and find more mature expression.

In its focus on one man, *Hermógenes Cayo* also introduced what would be a distinguishing feature of the later feature documentaries, or "ethnobiographies." Hermógenes is an old man who lives a rudimentary, solitary life in the barren province of Santiago del Estero, working as an *imaginero*, or carver of religious icons from local cactus wood. The film also crystallised what would become a common feature of Prelorán's mature work, the independence of sound and image. Despite the fact that synchronised sound in 16mm, without the need for a sound technician, was now widely available, Prelorán preferred to record a separate soundtrack and shoot silent. With *Hermógenes Cayo*, the soundtrack was recorded in a single interview after Prelorán had visited his subject several times in order to get to know him—another hallmark of Prelorán's modus. The film script was then written around the interview, although the image and sound tracks do not always correspond. Prelorán's questions have been excised, leaving us with a monologue by Hermógenes, ruminating on his work and life. He died soon after the principal shooting was complete and Prelorán returned before the film was finished to shoot footage of his grave, which closes the film. Prelorán always worked on a small budget on a 2:1 shooting ratio, leaving very little room for footage to go unused.

Prelorán's oeuvre constitutes an indisputably valuable record of native life and arts through the 1960s and 70s. His belief in extricating himself from the viewer's gaze, which became more pronounced in the later films and was compensated by an aesthetic of creating a discontiguous commentary on the images by the subject himself, allows us to contemplate these cultures with a minimum of overt interference on the part of the filmmaker. No one else in South America at the time "gave voice" so literally and with such dedication to indigenous culture, and while Hermógenes' monologue can tire at times, it is a unique cinematic experiment. That some of the scenes were obviously staged—that is, that Prelorán introduced mise-en-scène to his work—is discreetly acknowledged and ultimately of little importance. What is unfortunate is Prelorán's insistence on handling all aspects of the films' production himself, when he clearly lacks the technical skill and artistic talent to execute some of the little flourishes he attempts, which come across as amateurish. This approach is explained as the product of budgetary restraints and a desire to come into intimate, one-on-one contact with his subject, but it seems that an equally important consideration was Prelorán's determination to sign feature films with one name, a conceit which would be unthinkable in any other area but the ethnographic.

Prelorán's work studiously avoids political issues and commentary, and while this is understandable in the commissioned shorts on indigenous culture, this absence is more noticeable in the independently produced features. In these "ethno-biographies," even the individual's own social environment is only sketchily provided. His one fiction film, the independently produced *Mi tía Nora*, which addressed intergenerational conflict in an upper class Ecuadorean family, curiously did not feature a single native person with a speaking part, although the theme of the indigenous culture's achievements and its distance from white society in Ecuador was taken up. In Argentina, after the fall in 1983 of the military dictatorship whose imminence sent Prelorán back to the United States permanently in 1975, a few other directors took up feature ethnographic filmmaking. The most notable of these was Raúl Tosso's *Gerónima* (1986), like *Hermógenes Cayo*, a biographical study, in this case of a Mapuche woman in Patagonia. But here modern society and its devastating impact on Gerónima are integrated into the film, and a disjointed voice-over monologue by the subject, more experimentally counterpointed with the images, evokes a world of alienation and repression.

Timothy Barnard

Juan Moreira

Argentina, 1973, 105', colour

Dir Leonardo Favio (b. 1938) *Scr* Jorge Zuhair Jury and Favio, based on the novel of the same title by Eduardo Gutiérrez (1879) *Cinematog* Juan Carlos Desanzo *Mus* Pocho Leyes and Luis María Lumaldo *Prod* Juan Sires for Producciones Cinematográficas Centauro *Act* Rodolfo Bebán, Elcira Olivera Garcés, Edgardo Suárez, Jorge Villalba

After filming three sparse, low-budget—and commercially disastrous—black-and-white films in the 1960s, beginning with *Crónica de un
niño solo* (1965, q.v.), Leonardo Favio changed course with *Juan Moreira*,
a big-budget colour film. While his trademark pans and tracking shots
remain, and in fact become more elaborate, *Juan Moreira* introduced new
techniques to Favio's singular style. Among this cacophony of effects are
zooms, often at lightning speed; delirious hand-held camera sequences;
rapid editing, often on contrasting images; and extreme close-ups, either
held longer than one expects or seen only fleetingly. The mise-en-scène
alternates between the vast emptiness of the pampas and occasionally
overwrought interiors, while the soundtrack, liberally employed, ranges
from a mystical chorus to piercing sound effects. Throughout the film,
vibrant, mostly red hues predominate, especially in the sensuous panoramas of the pampas. Gone are the acclaimed rigour and spare beauty of
the earlier films and their reticent, elliptical narrative, replaced by a
tumultuous helter skelter of styles and techniques which nonetheless, in
Favio's hands, imparts a certain grandeur and epic quality to the film. For
the first time, too, in Favio's work we sense the presence of the fantastic,
which would reappear in Favio's next two films. While the overall effect
of the film is stunning, confirming in our minds that we are in the
presence of a gifted stylist, there is also the unmistakable impression that
this talent is undisciplined and easily distracted by trifles and trompe l'oeil.
This tendency was to become accentuated in Favio's next two films before
the military coup of 1976 sent him, a vocal Peronist, into exile. His
filmmaking career, only recently resumed (*Gatica, el mono*, 1992), can thus
be divided into two—now three—periods, the first a triptych of uncompromising and ascetic black-and-white films in the 1960s, and the second a
period of flamboyant colour films in the 1970s.

Eduardo Gutiérrez' serial novel of the late nineteenth century,
considered one of the seminal works of national mythology in Argentine
letters—that of the gaucho as a noble rebel—was the first written account

of the popular myth of the gaucho Juan Moreira, the subject of many other stage and screen adaptations. Like *La guerra gaucha* (1942, q.v.), which depicted the gaucho as the true national hero in his resistance against Spanish domination early in the nineteenth century, Gutiérrez' *Juan Moreira* mythologised and made martyrs of the gauchos of the latter part of the century, when the Buenos Aires oligarchy was massacring the native peoples and conscripting or driving off the roaming gauchos in their drive to "civilise" the hinterland of the pampas. Moreira, after killing a landowner who cheated him and had him jailed, is forced into a solitary existence on the pampas, for a time living in squalor with some surviving native people, before being courted, manipulated, and finally assassinated by warring political factions from the city.

Juan Moreira was filmed between the abdication of the military government in 1972 and the triumphant return to power of Juan Domingo Perón in 1973 after nearly 20 years of exile in Spain, when the national mythology around Juan Moreira had considerable resonance and sentimental appeal. Like *La Patagonia rebelde* (1974, q.v.) and especially Fernando Solanas' *Los hijos de Fierro* (1972–77), *Juan Moreira* incorporated elements of popular national mythology at a time when appeals to this mythology were pervasive. Favio, himself a mythologised figure in Argentine popular culture because of his background as a poor provincial waif who had become a film star by the age of 20, a pop singer and a Peronist of the slightly mystical variety that reveres Perón's first wife, Evita, was ideally suited to this task of national mythological reconstruction. When pandemonium broke out amongst the crowd of one million gathered to greet Perón on his return to the country, forcing the landing of his plane elsewhere, it was Favio who was placed before the multitude to appeal for calm. *Juan Moreira* was released a few weeks later, the day of Perón's assumption of power, going on to become the country's biggest box office hit in history, as *La guerra gaucha* had been before it, with nearly two million admissions. This feat was surpassed by Favio's *Nazareno Cruz y el Lobo* in 1975, which obtained 3½ million admissions. By the time of Favio's comeback in 1992 with *Gatica*, film attendance in Argentina had dropped precipitously to an average of 50,000 admissions for national films; nonetheless *Gatica*, a simultaneously frank and sentimental view of Perón's Argentina in the 1950s, obtained a half-million admissions that year, confirming Favio's status as both the country's most popular director and one of its most idiosyncratic stylists.

Timothy Barnard

La Patagonia rebelde

Rebellion in Patagonia
Argentina, 1974, 110', colour

Dir Héctor Olivera (b. 1931) *Scr* Osvaldo Bayer, Fernando Ayala, and Olivera, based on the history *Los vengadores de la Patagonia trágica* by Bayer (1972-74) *Cinematog* Víctor Hugo Caula *Mus* Oscar Cordozo Ocampo *Prod* Ayala for Aries Cinematográfica Argentina *Act* Héctor Alterio, Luis Brandoni, Federico Luppi, Pepe Soriano

One of the most successful and controversial films in Argentina and one of the best known abroad, *La Patagonia rebelde* reenacts an episode of labour strife and eventual slaughter in the remote south of the country in 1920-21, a time of considerable labour activism. Until investigated by Osvaldo Bayer as part of a three-volume history of Patagonian labour and social unrest, the incidents depicted in the film were virtually forgotten, and Héctor Olivera's adaptation found extraordinary resonance in the Argentina of Juan Perón's third presidency of 1973-74—audiences are reported to have cheered many scenes and to have jeered military figures in the film. The subject matter, a denunciation of the way military, political, and national and foreign economic interests had thwarted the legitimate aspirations of exploited workers, coincided with a national discussion of these issues as the country emerged from years of a military dictatorship that had finally allowed Perón's return from exile when the country faced possible civil war. The film is also an example of how mainstream elements in Argentine society such as Olivera, known previously as a director of entertainment films, and Aries, the country's largest and most commercial film production company, had been politicised and vitalised by the years of military rule and the prospects for a democratic centre-left government under Perón (which proved to be illusory).

Combining a modern and topical theme, labour activism, with a setting reminiscent of earlier gaucho epics and a treatment closer to "spaghetti" Westerns of the period, *La Patagonia rebelde* proved to be a potent updating of a genre. The film quickly moves the viewer through a carefully crafted, taut plot, performed by some of Argentina's top actors of the day: A general strike in favour of the *peones* working on rural estates in the south results in the country's first-ever rural collective agreement, signed by the landowners under pressure from a sympathetic military commander sent by the progressive president Hipólito Yrigoyen (1916–22 and 1928–30) to investigate. Later, when the agreement is breached and the general strike is resumed (and tainted by the activities of a self-proclaimed and lumpen "Red Council"—the film is as much about the treachery of the Left as of the Right), the commander returns convinced the workers have betrayed his trust. Under orders from Yrigoyen, himself under considerable foreign pressure, to end the strike "at any cost," the commander has the workers ruthlessly slaughtered. The entire story is told in flashback, as the film opens a few years later in Buenos Aires when the military commander is assassinated by the sole survivor of the massacre.

La Patagonia rebelde appeared precisely at a time when Perón's government veered to the right and para-military death squads began to appear and the left-wing guerrilla activities of the years of the dictatorship intensified. The film's release was at first delayed by the military representative on the film institute's classification board. Perón died, throwing the country into even more turmoil, less than a month after it was finally released. A bitter debate developed over the film, as it was denounced by military and right-wing figures and, according to the director, a screening in the interior of the country was interrupted by left-wing guerrillas, who lectured the audience on the film offering proof of the military's capacity for mass slaughter. Eventually it was voluntarily withdrawn from circulation in the midst of its release on these grounds, when its certain prohibition was imminent, although critics suggest that the film had recouped its investment and Aries was acting with an eye to the future. Indeed, Olivera was able to stay and work in Argentina throughout the years of military dictatorship, when many others in the film industry were forced into exile or silenced and some of Patagonia's actors, including Federico Luppi (Tiempo de revancha, 1981, q.v.), were blacklisted.

Timothy Barnard

Awards: Second Prize, Berlin, 1974.

La Raulito

Tomboy Paula
Argentina, 1975, 90', colour

Dir Lautaro Murúa (b. 1927) *Scr* José María Paolantonio *Cinematog* Miguel Rodríguez *Art dir* German Gelpi *Mus* Roberto Lar *Prod* Elida Stantic for Helicón Producciones *Act* Marilina Ross, Duilio Marzio, María Vaner, Luis Politti

La Raulito—the title is an untranslatable nickname, indicating that "little Raúl" is actually a girl—is a study of a double marginalisation, of a poor woman. The film is based on the life of María Esther Duffau, who had spent many years dressing as a man while living on the margins of society, at times as a vagrant. In 1948 she had a small role in the Argentine neo-realist classic *Pelota de trapo* by Leopoldo Torres Ríos (*La vuelta al nido*, 1938, q.v.) as a tomboy who played soccer—a strictly male sport—with the neighbourhood boys. No more than 12 years old, she was working delivering groceries, which is how she met the film's producer Armando Bo. She later became a friend of the famous boxer Gatica and eked out an existence through menial labour and petty crime and passed in and out of jail and psychiatric institutions. She was known to Buenos Aires intellectual circles in the 1960s and when *La Raulito*'s scriptwriter José María Paolantonio (*El juguete rabioso*, 1984) located her in the early 1970s in order to film her life—director Lautaro Murúa (*Shunko*, 1960, q.v.) was brought in later—she refused his offer of payment, saying that he couldn't provide her with what she most wanted in life, a family. She was by now in her mid-30s. As depicted in the film, her mother had died when she was very young, and she had fled from her drunken father, who molested her.

 La Raulito was the first of Murúa's films to fulfil his contention that in a country like Argentina film should assume an almost journalistic role. Filmed as a street chronicle, quickly and on a low budget, *La Raulito* follows actress Marilina Ross in a loosely connected series of incidents based on Duffau's life. At times it seems like a documentary, as when Ross delivers a monologue on her life in an interview with a prison official: the camera is held on her, with no cut-aways or reaction shots, even to her provocative comments directed at the official, as if it were the filmmakers interviewing her. Indeed Ross is the film's principal focus and attraction, holding the screen virtually alone throughout the film in a reserved, convincing performance. Because of its budget and shooting conditions, the film is less rigorously structured than Murúa's renowned work in the 1960s, with rougher edges created by the hand-held camera and the somewhat slapdash editing and musical effects.

For La Raulito, her sex is more of a nuisance than anything else, another obstacle to survival once it is discovered. Her sexuality remains enigmatic and confused. In the film's most extended subplot, she befriends an older newsstand dealer and convinces him to take her on as a helper, even though he doesn't need one. By now aware of her sex and the fact that she is homeless, he takes her in, and a seemingly happy domestic interlude unfolds as they shop and eat out together and sleep in the same bed. But she slips out quietly after he tries, not very forcefully, to seduce her when comforting her. He once asks her why she wants to be a man and she replies, ambiguously, "I want to be a woman." She later tells a sympathetic psychiatrist at a mental institution for women that confinement is easier for men than for women, that she can't even play soccer, her passion. To his reply that they are going to build a soccer field, she says in disgust "So I can play with *them*?," pointing to her catatonic fellow-inmates, suggesting that even when marginalised or institutionalised men are able to retain a piece of themselves and their bond with each other that women don't.

Released just nine months before the military coup that intensified the repression already under way under Perón's widow Isabel's rule, *La Raulito* was one of the last films of the period to address social issues. Surprisingly, it was allowed to be exhibited, even though film censorship was severe: 160 films, both Argentine and foreign, were banned in the 18 months before the coup. Murúa, however, like many other film workers and cultural figures, was forced into exile shortly after the film was released when a bomb exploded in front of his home while he was out. He relocated to Spain, where *La Raulito* had been a great success, working as an actor in film and theatre. He was able to make only one film in exile, a sequel to *La Raulito* called *La Raulito en libertad* (1977). Back in Argentina after the return of democracy, he was able to film *Cuarteles de invierno*, in 1984 and has since worked as a theatre director and acted in theatre and film; he has been unable to direct again.

Timothy Barnard

Awards: Best Director and Best Actress (Marilina Ross), Panama, 1975; Best Actress (Ross), Cartagena (Colombia), 1979.

Tiempo de revancha

Time of Revenge
Argentina, 1981, 112', colour

Dir Adolfo Aristarain (b. 1943) *Scr* Aristarain *Cinematog* Horacio Maira *Mus* Emilio Kauderer *Prod* Héctor Olivera and Luis Osvaldo Repetto for Aries Cinematográfica Argentina *Act* Federico Luppi, Ulises Dumont, Haydée Padilla, Julio de Grazia

Coming one year before the military defeat in the South Atlantic that brought about the Argentine dictatorship's downfall, *Tiempo de revancha* was the film that broke its censorship and blacklists and regained Argentine film's presence in important foreign markets and festivals. Federico Luppi, one of the country's leading actors, returning to the screen after passing five years on the blacklist, gives a powerful performance as a specialist mining dynamiter with a militant labour history who feigns injury in order to collect compensation. The character's return to his profession as a dynamiter after being blacklisted for his union activism—the very mention of which was taboo in the early years of the dictatorship—paralleled Luppi's own return to the screen and was emblematic of the changes under way in Argentine society. Suspected by his employer, Luppi is subjected first to a battery of tests and then to intimidation and ruses to get him to talk: for Luppi has feigned muteness, a potently symbolic injury in a society reduced to collective silence. Finally, motivated now more by a visceral sense of justice, a blind thirst for revenge against the institutions of power than by his fraud, Luppi cuts off his tongue to ensure his victory.

Practically everything about the film, from its title to Luppi's profession as a dynamiter to the web of power that suggests foreign interests and shady elements, points to a symbolic reading. Yet as an allegory it was somewhat inverted: the struggle in the final years of the dictatorship was to speak the truth, not to remain silent. While this amorphous political subtext may have been necessary to elude the censors and may in fact be seen as contributing to the film's force, to its pervasive climate of repression and complicity, it was also determined by the film's essential nature as a commercial suspense film. Unlike, most notably, neighbouring Chile's experience under dictatorship in the 1970s, in Argentina a skeleton film industry survived, allowing veteran directors to turn out safe films and, perhaps more importantly, providing apprenticeship opportunities for young directors like Adolfo Aristarain. Aristarain was an ambitious young director with a confessed "mania" for Hollywood who subsequently made an unsuccessful pilgrimage there. Long inactive on his return to Argentina, he resurfaced in 1992 with the sentimental drama *Un lugar en el mundo*, in which Luppi plays an activist who has taken refuge from life in Patagonia. The film enjoyed considerable box office success and was the second of Aristarain's films in little over a decade to be hailed as leading a recovery from two different crises in the industry.

With *Tiempo de revancha*, Aries owners Héctor Olivera (*La Patagonia rebelde*, 1974, q.v.) and Fernando Ayala (*El jefe*, 1958, q.v.) again demonstrated their uncanny ability to anticipate social and political trends in a commercial film. Here they uncharacteristically took on a young talent: Aries' success was based on using a small stable of journeyman directors to make lowbrow commercial films, with an occasional topical middlebrow film directed by one of its co-owners. With *Tiempo de revancha*, the formula was little changed: take a topical theme, develop it to the limits imposed by the censorship or prevailing mood of the day, and deliver it in an entertainment film with higher than normal production values, made possible by Aries' position as the country's leading and wealthiest producer. The endeavour would be more successful if it appeared, as did *Tiempo de revancha* and the films by Olivera and Ayala cited above, at a time when Argentines were returning to the cinemas en masse after a period of cultural desolation. To some, the formula has produced some of the most compelling films in the Argentine industry's recent history and stands as a model for producing a social cinema with broad appeal in a small national industry. Olivera would repeat the success several times in the following decade (*No habrá más penas ni olvido*, 1984, a black comedy about Peronist infighting in the 1970s; *La noche de los lapices*, 1986, based on a true story of schoolchildren abducted during the dictatorship; and *El caso María Soledad*, 1993, based on scandals involving a provincial government), but with each film the strategy appeared more shallow, cynical, and opportunistic.

Timothy Barnard

Awards: Seven awards, including Best Film, Director, Actor (Federico Luppi), Association of Argentine Film Journalists, 1981; Best Film, Cartagena, 1982; Best Film (shared), Montréal, 1982; Best Film, Biarritz, 1982; Best Film, Havana, 1982; Best Actor (Luppi), Chicago, 1982.

Camila

Argentina-Spain, 1984, 97', colour

Dir María Luisa Bemberg (1922–95) *Scr* Bemberg, Beda Docampo Feijoo, and Juan Batiste Stagnaro *Cinematog* Fernando Arribus *Ed* Luis César D'Angiolillo *Art dir* Miguel Rodriguez and Esmerelda Almonacid *Prod* Lita Stantic for Gea Producciones (Argentina) and Impala (Spain) *Act* Susú Pecoraro, Imanol Arias, Héctor Alterio, Elena Tasisto

In the aftermath of a film industry devastated under the repressive rule of the military dictatorship, María Luisa Bemberg emerged and quickly established herself as a chronicler of the conditions for women in Argentina, both past and present. Drawing from both Argentine history and fictional creations, Bemberg has examined the largely unexplored and marginalised social and cultural position of women.

Bemberg began her filmmaking career relatively late, in her late forties, after working in the theatre and as a scriptwriter. During the 1970s two of her scripts were made into films by other directors: *Crónica de una señora*, by Raúl de la Torre (1970) and *Triángulo de cuatro*, by Fernando Ayala (1975). Bemberg shot two of her own scripts as short films, *El mundo de la mujer* in 1972 and *Juguetes* in 1978. In 1981 she made her first feature film, *Momentos*, the story of an upper-class woman who attempts to give meaning to her life amidst feelings of frustration at her repression and of social shame because of her husband's affair. Though not drawn from events in her own life, Bemberg does consider the film to have an autobiographical quality. Following *Momentos*, Bemberg returned to an earlier script, *Señora de nadie* (1982), to portray the life of a woman who leaves her home and family to seek sexual and emotional fulfillment. After her affair ends, leaving her alone again, the woman finds friendship with a gay man. Given the scandalous subject and what Bemberg terms the "very mild feminism" of the film, it is not surprising that it encountered problems. The military government felt that the presentation of a homosexual was unpalatable, and Bemberg included the character over their objections. The furore over the film ultimately dimmed when it was premiered on the eve of war with Britain in the South Atlantic. Despite these problems and the lack of local press, the film did well at the box office. *Señora de nadie* has the distinction of having presented the first gay character in Argentine cinema.

Following *Señora de nadie*, Bemberg opted for another controversial project, the presentation of the life story of Camila O'Gorman, the daughter of an upper-class family who scandalised nineteenth century Argentine society during the dictatorship of Juan Manuel de Rosas (1829–52) by running away with her priest Ladislao Gutiérrez. The two lived in secrecy in a provincial village until they were discovered and arrested. Then, without trial and despite the fact that Camila was pregnant, both were executed by firing squad, in 1847. So notorious was this affair that the only previous successful attempt to dramatise it was in 1912, when the country's filmmakers were making dramatic short films out of national history. The film was immediately and forever banned. Subsequent attempts to bring the story to screen were unsuccessful.

In order to "hit the audience in the heart and in the pit of their stomach" simultaneously, Bemberg shot the film in a highly romantic style with lush colours. There are stark contrasts drawn between the opulence of the O'Gorman lifestyle and the simplicity of the provincial town to which the lovers flee, the former a façade of civilisation atop a foundation of repression and terror, the latter an idyllic existence almost free from the social repressions of the government. The richness of Bemberg's contrasts is furthered by the inclusion of geo-political machinations, both historical and current. It is ironic that it was during the Rosas era that Argentina lost the Malvinas/Falkland Islands to the British, in 1833. A more chilling irony lay in the Rosas government's use of a form of populist nationalism, backed up by terror. Throughout *Camila* Bemberg makes such parallels manifest, concluding with a tilt shot up from the bodies of Camila and Ladislao to the Argentine flag.

National politics notwithstanding, the central concern of the film is the struggle of Camila, the struggle of a woman to gain an identity and break free from the constraints of family, Church, and State. Susú Pecoraro's performance of Camila is exemplary. Her transition from naïveté to maturity coincides with her rebellion against all social norms. She abandons her privileged lifestyle for a meaningful life teaching at a local school. Her tragedy lies only in realising too late that her social position will not protect her from the brutal backlash against such rebellion.

Camila was a breakthrough film for Bemberg, garnering a great deal of international attention, including an Academy Award nomination for Best Foreign Film. Following *Camila*, Bemberg continued to dramatise the position of women in Argentine and Latin American society in a series of increasingly prestigious and costly international co-productions. Her next film, *Miss Mary* (1986), starring Julie Christie as a British nanny working in rural Argentina in the 1930s, was reportedly the first Latin American film to break the $1 million barrier in production costs. Later films refined a strategy of polished productions using one major European star: *Yo, la peor de todas* (1990), with Dominique Sanda, was based on the life of Juana Inés de la Cruz, a seventeenth century Mexican nun who established herself as an excellent poet before the Inquisition forced her to renounce her writings. Most recently, Marcello Mastroianni starred in *De eso no se habla* (1993), another period piece set in rural Argentina and Bemberg's last film before her death in 1995.

David Douglas

Awards: Best Actress (Susú Pecoraro), Karlovy Vary, 1984; Best Actress (Pecoraro, shared), Havana, 1984.

La historia oficial

The Official Story
Argentina, 1985, 112', colour

Dir Luis Puenzo (b. 1946) *Scr* Aída Bortnik and Puenzo *Cinematog* Félix Monti *Art dir* Abel Facello *Mus* Atilio Stampone *Prod* Cinemania S.A., Historias Cinematográficas S.A. and Progress Communications *Act* Norma Aleandro, Héctor Alterio, Chunchuna Villafañe, María Luisa Robledo

After the fall of the 1976–83 military dictatorship, Argentine film underwent a remarkable renaissance, attracting considerable foreign attention at the same time as domestic production and attendance increased substantially. *La historia oficial* was the first and one of the surprisingly few films of the period to deal directly with the recent past, taking up the controversial issue of the young children of the country's "disappeared," who were born in captivity before their mothers' execution, adopted by collaborators of the regime, and eventually sought out by the families of the disappeared.

La historia oficial is set in 1983, just before the dictatorship toppled and as its web of coercion and collaborators is unravelling. Norma Aleandro plays a middle-aged history teacher, married to businessman Héctor Alterio, who has risen from his working-class roots to a comfortable position thanks to business dealings of the sort encouraged by the regime's disastrous *plata dulce* ("easy money") economic policies, designed to

appease and enrich its upper-middle class backers. Slowly, Aleandro begins
to realise the extent of the repression her country has just lived through
(it is thanks to the Argentine dictatorship that the word "disappeared"
entered the popular lexicon, as up to 30,000 people from all walks of life
were abducted, tortured, and executed by paramilitary death squads). She
also begins to suspect the true nature of some of her husband's business
dealings and is confronted with the possibility that their adopted daughter
may be the child of a victim of the repression. Her voyage of discovery
becomes a journey through the Argentine political landscape of the time:
she meets an old friend who has just returned from years of exile; observes
the Mothers of the Plaza de Mayo demonstrating silently in front of the
presidential palace for the return of their disappeared children, as they
have done every Thursday since 1977—the only organised, public dissent
in the country for most of the dictatorship; meets a woman who may be
the grandmother of her adopted daughter; and finally confronts her
husband concerning the mysterious circumstances surrounding the
adoption and the true identity of their daughter.

La historia oficial's release had a tremendous cathartic effect on a
middle-class audience faced with the question of how to deal with the
atrocities that had been carried out in its midst, atrocities on such a scale
and undertaken with so much active collaboration or passive complicity
of "ordinary citizens" that many commentators have compared the period
to pre-war Nazi Germany. The film also earned the praise of foreign
critics who saw in this "women's film" a frank examination of the past.
The film's title, of course, encourages this interpretation, promising as it
does to debunk the dictatorship's propaganda. And yet *La historia oficial*
can be seen to articulate another myth, cherished by the middle and upper
classes, that they did not realise the extent of and certainly weren't in any
way implicated in the repression (a claim bitterly mimicked by the title
of Raúl Beycero's 1988 film *Nadie nada nunca*—"Nobody Never Nothing"). Similarly, the film manages to convince us, through its melodramatic treatment of Aleandro's dilemma and our identification with her, that
her plight is more traumatic than those of the characters who have a
marginal existence in the film, like her daughter's natural grandmother. In
this way the film accomplishes the bizarre feat of shifting the burden of
suffering under the dictatorship from those who lost family members
through torture and execution to those who adopted their children. Later,
Argentine society would see many of the latter obtain custody of the
children in court by arguing that they could provide them with a better
home.

In 1986 *La historia oficial* became the first Latin American film to win the coveted "Oscar" for Best Foreign Film. Overnight, Argentine films became the hottest ticket at international film festivals, a phenomenon actively promoted by the democratic government of Raúl Alfonsín (1983–89), as much for the international prestige and legitimacy it conferred on the country's democratisation process as for any direct benefit to the national film industry. Just as instantly Luis Puenzo, who heretofore had directed only two feature films in the early 1970s and was known in Argentina only as the most successful director of advertising, was elevated into the pantheon of world film directors. Able to command large budgets, considerable artistic freedom, and the attention of leading actors through the performance of Aleandro, who shared a Best Actress award at the Cannes film festival, Puenzo has since filmed two mega-projects which were poorly received by both critics and the public and which revealed him to be a director of mediocre talent. The first, *The Old Gringo* (1989), featured Gregory Peck and Jane Fonda and was based on the novel by Mexican author Carlos Fuentes. The second was a Franco-Argentine production of Albert Camus' *La peste* (1992), filmed in Buenos Aires and starring William Hurt, which was never released in North America.

Timothy Barnard

Awards: Best Actress (Norma Aleandro, shared), Best Film, Ecumenical Jury, Cannes, 1985; Best Actress (Aleandro), Special Mention, Cartagena (Colombia), 1985; Best Film, Best Supporting Actress (Chunchuna Villafañe), Chicago, 1985; Second Prize, Best Screenplay, Havana, 1985; Best Film, Quito, 1985; Best Foreign Language Film, Academy of Motion Picture Arts and Sciences ("Oscar"), 1986.

Tangos, el exilio de Gardel

Tangos: The Exile of Gardel
France-Argentina, 1985, 119', colour

Dir Fernando E. Solanas (b. 1936) *Scr* Solanas *Cinematog* Félix Monti *Mus* Astor Piazzolla; songs and lyrics by José Luis Castiñeira de Dios and Solanas *Choreog* Susana Tambutti, Margarita Balli, Robert Thomas, and Adolfo Andrade *Prod* Solanas and Envar El Kadri for Tercine (France) and Cinesur (Argentina) *Act* Miguel Angel Solá, Marie Laforêt, Philippe Léotard, Marina Vlady, Georges Wilson, Lautaro Murúa

Exiled to Paris in 1976 after the military coup and an attempt on his life, Fernando "Pino" Solanas (*La hora de los hornos*, 1968, q.v.) made several unsuccessful attempts there to mount a feature production. Before beginning to shoot *Tangos, el exilio de Gardel* in 1985 (the idea had been born in 1980 and filming was initially scheduled to start, under the title *Los tangos de Homero*, in 1982), Solanas had made only one film abroad, the commissioned television documentary *Le Regard des autres* (1979), a frank portrait of the physically disabled. *Tangos* was in fact salvaged by production grants made available under the generous cultural policies of the democratic government of Raúl Alfonsín (1983–89), making it the first Franco-Argentine co-production. Featuring a number of well-known second-string French and exiled Argentine actors, *Tangos* was to become, more so than the more conventional *La historia oficial* (1985, q.v.), the film to announce Argentina's cultural renaissance to the world, becoming a major art-house attraction in Europe and a box office hit in Argentina when it was released there in 1986. A standard two-hour version of the film now exists, with 125 or 130 minute versions in circulation on its release; an even longer version had premiered at the Venice film festival in 1985 but was hastily cut in response to critical consensus that it was too long.

   Tangos, described by one French critic as a "dazzlingly manifold" work, "profuse, baroque, even burlesque," seemed to mark a radical departure for Solanas after his agit-prop underground documentary *La hora de los hornos*. Indeed some on the Left in Latin America rejected the film as a betrayal of the radical "third cinema" aesthetic Solanas had postulated, seeing in it a mistakenly nostalgic revival of a discredited popular form, the tango musical, and Argentine intellectuals' infatuation with European culture and their eagerness to be accepted into it. While there is no doubt that a great distance had now been travelled since the earlier film (an evolution mirrored, curiously enough, by Brazilian director Ruy Guerra's contemporaneous film *Opera do Malandro* (1986)), perceptive critics noted how *Tangos* did in fact share many of *La hora*'s stylistic traits, above all a "musical" structure that here was foregrounded by recitative prologues to each act, composed by Solanas (who had a musical education) and Argentine film composer José Luis Castiñeira de Dios. So, too, could each film be said to share a multiplicity of techniques and strategies to express its concerns, the one documentary/political and the other narrative/cultural, one of whose many points of convergence was a search for a popular form, as different as this was conceived.

Tangos' multi-layered narrative is structured into a prologue and four acts, announced by young street performers in Paris singing the songs penned by Solanas and Castiñeira de Dios. Each act is, in turn, divided into episodic vignettes, whose fluid transitions are indicated by subtitles ("Letters from Exile," "Absences," etc.). Throughout the film a variety of oddball and vaguely nostalgic technical effects are used, such as lightning crossing the screen and irises (these were also seen in *La hora de los hornos*), and the film abounds in visual gags—at one point Solanas, playing a bit part, literally comes apart, shedding limbs before exploding and being put back together. The result is not so much Brechtian, as the structure and sung introductions might suggest, as it is vaudevillian. European critics, who saw in *Tangos* an inspired marriage of First and Third World aesthetics, credited Solanas with rejuvenating modernism with the materials of a non-European culture. In *Tangos* Solanas was not only paying homage to a lost Argentine tango culture, as some would suggest; in the face of the impasse of "third cinema," he was returning, he relates, to early twentieth-century creole theatre, which was often episodic in structure, and to the vaudeville with which it often played in itinerant circuses in Argentina at the turn of the century, to create a cinema at once populist and intellectual, folk and modernist, the quintessential aesthetic of the Third World artist in the metropolis.

Tangos' principal narrative thread concerns the attempts of a group of exiled Argentines to mount a *tanguedia*—part tragedy, part comedy, and part tango musical, a neologism coined by Solanas that clearly represents his own film. *Tangos* shares the *tanguedia*'s concerns: its authorship is obscure, it has no definite ending (which would betray the spirit of the exiles' odyssey), and it seeks to communicate Argentine culture to Europeans in a language they understand. As a work-in-progress, and true to the norms of the musical genre, we see only "impromptu" rehearsals of the *tanguedia*, showcasing the talents of contemporary choreographers and of legendary "new tango" composer and bandoneonist Astor Piazzolla, who revolutionised the music in the 1960s and achieved a following in Europe. *Tangos* also features a cameo performance by the Osvaldo Pugliese orchestra, playing the octogenarian Pugliese's own style of syncopated big-band tango music. *Tangos'* recorded soundtrack was itself a big hit in Argentina, introducing a new generation to Piazzolla's unique abilities as a composer and virtuoso bandoneonist.

In addition to the mounting of the *tanguedia* and the explorations of its protagonists' troubled lives and relationships offstage, two fantastic subplots are added to the mix to fill out Solanas' ruminations on identity and exile, culture and politics. Lautaro Murúa plays an Argentine writer in France researching the European years of the Argentine General José de San Martín, one of the great liberators of Spanish America, who chose to live the last thirty years of his life in France out of bitter disillusionment with the fruits of his campaigns. Elsewhere, sporadic reference is made to Carlos Gardel, the legendary tango singer who swept Europe in the 1920s and died in a plane crash over Colombia in 1935 when making a triumphant return to Argentina to star in Manuel Romero's *El caballo del pueblo* as Argentina's sound film industry began to take off. Gardel, who was born in France, raised in Uruguay and who found fame as an Argentine tango singer in Europe, has always embodied Argentina's problematic cultural relationship with the metropolis and its own crisis of cultural identity; his "exile," of course, is strictly an invention of Solanas', a metaphor for the experience of Argentine intellectuals and artists, like himself, who have felt estranged from their own land and drawn to Europe. In one of the film's concluding scenes, Murúa receives a visit from San Martín and then, joined by Gardel, the three of them listen to Gardel on a phonograph singing "Volver"—"To Return"—a scene that trades on more national myths, obsessions, and nostalgia than one would think possible in a single film frame. Solanas would return to this cinema of symbolism and metaphor, and to the tango, in *Sur* (1988).

Timothy Barnard

Awards: Special Jury Prize, Francesco Pasinetti Prize for Best Foreign Film, UNICEF Prize, Venice, 1985; Second Prize, Association Française de Cinéma d'Art et Essai Prize, Biarritz, 1985; Scriptwriters' Association Prize, Huelva, 1985; Arte y Ensayo Prize, Troia, 1985; Best Film (shared), Best Musical Score, Havana, 1985; Five awards, including Best Film and Best Director, Association of Argentine Film Journalists, 1986; Best Cinematography, Best Art Direction, Cartagena (Colombia), 1986.

La película del Rey

A King and His Movie
Argentina, 1985, 107', colour

Dir Carlos Sorín (b. 1944) *Scr* Jorge Goldenberg and Sorín *Cinematog* Esteban Courtalón *Art dir* Margarita Jusid *Mus* Carlos Franzetti *Prod* Axel Harding for Carlos Sorín Cine S.A. *Act* Ulises Dumont, Julio Chávez, Villanueva Cosse, Roxana Berco, Miguel Dedovich

La película del Rey was Carlos Sorín's first film, but like many others who came to prominence during the "boom" years of the mid-1980s, he had been working in film professionally since the late 1960s. Like many of his generation, who came of age at an unfavourable moment in Argentine film, when the careers of many talented *nuevo cine* directors were floundering and censorship was severe, Sorín apprenticed in and earned his living from advertising. He first worked in advertising as an assistant to Alberto Fischerman (*The Players vs. Los Angeles Caídos*, 1969; *Los días de junio*, 1985), one of the leading members of this *cine publicitario* generation, which also included Juan José Jusid (*Tute Cabrero*, 1967; *Made in Argentina*, 1986) and Raúl de la Torre (*Crónica de una señora*, 1970; *Pobre mariposa*, 1985). With few exceptions, this group's tenuous careers were interrupted by the 1976–83 military dictatorship, and much of their work in the 1980s, in contrast with their early experimentalism and interest in avant-garde literature and theatre, was quite conventional, rendering study of their films problematic.

Sorín began working as a cinematographer for even more experimental and marginal filmmakers, shooting Edgardo Cozarinsky's legendary . . . (*Puntos suspensivos*) in 1970 before Cozarinsky relocated to Europe, and Miguel Bejo's *La familia unida esperando la llegada de Hallewyn* in 1971. Neither film screened publicly in Argentina, although Bejo's film won a prize at the important Third World film festival at Mannheim. Sorín also shot two films which were never completed, including Juan Fresán's and Jorge Goldenberg's *La nueva Francia* in 1972. This was the extent of his professional experience before the 1976 coup, when he returned exclusively to advertising.

La película del Rey is a film-within-a-film, a rumination on cultural creation through a comic look at an obsessed filmmaker. The film opens on the pre-production bustle of a film crew about to depart for Patagonia to shoot a film called *La nueva Francia*. In between the myriad and intoxicating pre-production activities the young director David (Julio Chávez) explains the film's subject, which is, of course, the same as the incomplete 1972 film of the same title, in a television interview: In 1860 a Frenchman named Orélie Antoine de Tounens declared himself King of a quixotic "Kingdom" in southern Argentina, a remote area populated largely by indigenous peoples, at the time not under the formal jurisdiction of Argentina or Chile. His aim was to improve the welfare of the Araucanian people and to introduce them to monarchical democracy, setting up a government in which they would participate. Their own culture had predicted the arrival of a white man to free them from the tyranny of Spanish rule, and he was welcomed into their midst. For 17 years, without money, under attack from the Chileans, unassisted by the French he hoped to establish ties to, and apparently without personal ambition, Orélie Antoine the First persisted before acknowledging defeat and returning to France to die. In response to a comment that this was a European-imposed enlightenment, David replies "And what in our country isn't European? Go to Patagonia today to see the results of the alternative."

Mirroring Tounens' adventures, things go wrong for David from the start: a financial backer withdraws, and the film union won't allow its actors to work for less than scale. This first of many defections leads David to make the first of many compromises to his epic film: local non-professionals will take their place, and it will be filmed silent and dubbed later. His rag-tag actors, however, including an immense prostitute and a Buenos Aires street vendor David "discovered" for the role of the King (Miguel Dedovich), can't ride horses, remember their lines, or stay out of trouble. As the money runs out the ever-dwindling entourage moves from a hotel to an orphanage to tents pitched on the windswept plains. David's loyal producer, played by veteran character actor Ulises Dumont, frantically tries to raise more money, but their madcap misadventures come to an end when the King himself, unpaid in weeks, abandons them. David is left to film wire mannequins and torches stuck into the ground, like Tounens, determined to continue, when the army runs him out of town.

Slyly, Sorín surreptitiously ends this comedy of manners with the experimental footage of Patagonia that he and others had long dreamt of; these final images are, in fact, copied from the unseen footage of *La nueva Francia*. The novelist and critic Tomás Eloy Martínez, who had participated in this film, wrote at the time of *La película del Rey*'s release "I had always hoped that *La nueva Francia* would have the same immortality as

Eisenstein's *Que viva Mexico!:* a fountain that other films could drink from indefinitely." After a wait of over a decade, Sorín drank deeply in these last few minutes of the film, giving us troubled, haunting images of Patagonia's barren spaces (often filmed at dusk), unlit interiors, creating a paradoxical sense of confinement, and the King's final monologues before a court of mannequins. If Sorín constructed the film's narrative to attract audiences and money-lenders in order to film, however fleetingly, his vision of Patagonia, he has done so with good humour. But he may also be suggesting that, in the end, it is not such experimental visions which are untenable as much as the epic designs of the mainstream. His own film, however, does not systematically attempt the earlier film's formal experiments or political analysis, and contemplation of Tounens' project is drowned in farce. The attempt to clothe his experiments in a commercial narrative was only partially successful from another point of view: until it was noticed at festivals abroad, *La película del Rey* languished at the box office in Argentina.

On the basis of this film, Sorín was offered a co-production opportunity with a British producer; the result was *Eversmile New Jersey* (1989), starring British actor Daniel Day-Lewis, known for choosing his roles very carefully, as a proselytising dentist travelling through Patagonia on motorcycle. The film was not a success at the box office, however, and the ensuing crisis in the Argentine film industry prevented Sorín from filming again until 1993, when he completed *Fast Forward.*

Timothy Barnard

Awards: Five awards, including Best First Film, Association of Argentine Film Journalists, 1986; Best First Film, Venice, 1986; Best Film, Biarritz, 1986; Best First Film, Valladolid, 1986.

Hombre mirando al sudeste

Man Facing Southeast
Argentina, 1986, 105', colour

Dir Eliseo Subiela (b. 1944) *Scr* Subiela *Cinematog* Ricardo de Angelis Jr. *Art dir* Abel Facello *Mus* Pedro Aznar *Prod* Luján Pflaum for Cinequanon *Act* Lorenzo Quinteros, Hugo Soto, Inés Vernengo, Cristina Scaramuzza

Hombre mirando al sudeste is a beautifully stylized film with intelligent dialogue and complex characters. Evoking the mood of crisis, its bleak imagery and haunting soundtrack are skillfully paced to bring the audience gradually into the space of the director's metaphysical concerns. *Hombre mirando al sudeste* marked a return to an auteur cinema in Argentina, and Subiela's style is both personal and political, without yet being either ponderous or self-indulgent, as many would complain his later films were (*Ultimas imágenes del naufragio*, 1989; *El lado oscuro del corazón*, 1992).

Because of its ostensible concern with an extraterrestrial's visit to our planet, *Hombre mirando al sudeste* has often been identified with science fiction. In part, this is due to a marketing strategy which helped it become one of the most exported Argentine films of the mid-1980s boom. Still, to view the film as science fiction is to miss the point. It is not interested in the genre's usual accoutrements but rather poetically explores the spiritual crisis seen to affect Argentina in the 1980s. Its "literary" narrative style and construction lends it comparison to an Argentine tradition of the fantastic as seen in the work of Jorge Luis Borges, Adolfo Bioy Casares, Felisberto Fernández, and Julio Cortázar.

One day Rantes, played by Hugo Soto, appears unannounced at the Borda mental hospital on the outskirts of Buenos Aires. Claiming to be on a mission from another planet, Rantes looks and speaks like a human being. He is cogent and alert; his steady voice and poise in refuting the examining psychiatrist's sceptical questions seem to belie any pathology. The psychiatrist initially believes Rantes is seeking refuge in the asylum from some criminal misdeed, but no official record is found of his existence. The doctor's increasingly obsessive curiosity about Rantes leads him into an ambiguous friendship with him. Here another possible interpretation of Rantes' existence occurs to the audience, that of his being Christ, as Rantes speaks of the ethical stupidity of humanity as it moves inexorably to its own destruction.

Despite his grandiose concerns for the deterioration of the planet and the oppression of the weak, Subiela forgoes an epic or documentary style, focusing his attention on the psychiatrist's forlorn state and Rantes' new life at the asylum. Already at the beginning of the film the doctor is in the midst of a profound crisis of confidence in his profession and his own self-worth. As he becomes increasingly vulnerable to Rantes' prophet-like charisma, so is the audience led into a deeper appreciation of the alien's despair. These two theatre-trained actors bring an intensity to their dialogue and to their moments of solitude, which seem to represent a social malaise.

What gives the film the full power of a mystery and the narrative beauty of a fable is the absence of a definitive explanation of Rantes' identity. His otherworldliness is made clear by his telekinitic powers, and yet the film's strength lies in the suggestion that Rantes could yet be a mortal, a man who is as imaginative and sincere in his delusions as he is in his moral precepts. That he might be both an alien and a human allows Subiela to make righteousness and truth seem absurdly out of place, yet lyrically necessary, in our world.

Some critics maintain that the film's ethical critique is dulled by Rantes' ambiguity and the lack of a clearly delineated social context for his message of doom. Yet it is also possible to read the film as an exploration of the meaning of absence. In the context of a country still grieving over the revelations of its recent past, still trying to comprehend "disappearance" as a political modus, *Hombre mirando al sudeste* uses the sign of the alien to reflect upon the presence of displaced phantoms still wandering among us. If Rantes does not have a specific past, it is because he represents what is still missing from our hollow present. His mission, he confesses, is to redeem humanity by trying to salvage its atrophied ethical dimension.

Federico Hidalgo

Awards: CIGA Prize for Best First Film (shared), OCIC Award, San Sebastián, 1986; Special Mention by the OCIC, UNEAC Caracol Award (shared), La Giraldilla de La Habana municipal award, Havana, 1986; Nine awards, including Best Film, Director, Actor (Lorenzo Quinteros), Association of Argentine Film Journalists, 1987.

Malayunta

[Bad Company]
Argentina, 1986, 92', colour

Dir José Santiso (b. 1945) *Scr* Jacobo Langsner and Santiso, based on the play *Pater Noster* (1977) by Langsner *Cinematog* Eduardo Legaría *Mus* Litto Nebbia *Prod* Santiso Cine *Act* Federico Luppi, Miguel Angel Solá, Bárbara Mujica

In 1981, the year the film *Tiempo de revancha* (q.v.) broke the military dictatorship's blacklists and censorship in the film industry, a group of theatre people formed Teatro Abierto ("Open Theatre"), a theatre co-op dedicated to the same ends. Apart from the weekly demonstrations of the Mothers of the Plaza de Mayo, demanding information concerning their "disappeared" children, there existed no other organised resistance to the dictatorship at that time. Teatro Abierto's first theatre was burned down, but it continued functioning until 1986; its activities are documented in the film *País cerrado, teatro abierto* (Arturo Balassa, 1981, not screened publicly until 1990). One of Teatro Abierto's productions was Jacobo Langsner's *Pater Noster*, a thinly veiled allegory of life under a dictatorship which had initially been met with open support by large numbers of Argentines and whose atrocities were carried out with the complicity, or outright collaboration, of many. (The country's leading writer, Jorge Luis Borges, praised the Junta members as being "gentlemen" after meeting with them.) It was precisely this complicity that *Pater Noster*, premiered in Uruguay in 1977 and mounted in Argentina by Teatro Abierto in 1981, confronted. Adapted to the screen by José Santiso as *Malayunta* (after a famous tango, "Mala Junta," meaning mismatch) after the return of democracy, it proved to be the most profound, disturbing, uncompromising, and novel of all the films of the new democratic period to examine the years of terror.

Santiso, a theatre director, Teatro Abierto member, and director of photography or camera operator on a number of films in the 1960s and 70s, is a professed admirer of the cinema of Orson Welles, Alfred Hitchcock, and Fritz Lang. In this first film he created a dark vision worthy of these masters of moral disquiet. Shot almost entirely in a run-down apartment, *Malayunta* introduces us to a middle-aged working class couple down on their luck who rent a room from a bohemian artist. The artist ridicules their humble decency, forbids them to cook in the flat—he lives on bread and milk—and keeps them awake with his all-night debauchery. The audience initially sides with the couple, poor sods with only a couple of suitcases to their name humiliated by a smart-ass artist who pays the rent on the apartment with what they pay him for a room. Our empathy increases when Federico Luppi is attacked one day in a park by a seeming lunatic demanding to know what Luppi has "done with" his brother.

The film changes course abruptly—like Hitchcock, Santiso can create a mesmerising world of brusque shifts on a single set—when the couple takes over the apartment and ties the artist up in his room. Insisting that they "love him like a son" and that he is "ill" and "needs their help"—much of the audience is still with the couple and treating the film as an ironic comedy of manners—they attempt to force him to abandon his "unhealthy lifestyle." When Luppi binds him to a chair with barbed wire while Bárbara Mujica cooks him red meat, we realise the manipulation we have fallen prey to. The horror then relentlessly continues to its inexorable finish—the artist's dismemberment—which is compounded by our realisation that for the couple, this is routine business. The analogy is laid bare: a generation of Argentines, concerned to save the country from the atheistic communism said to be threatening the country in the 1970s, collaborated in the systematic slaughter of some 30,000 students, trade unionists, schoolteachers, and others accused of being "terrorists." The audible discomfort of audiences watching the film is not, then, just a reaction to the drama being played out on screen. *Malayunta*'s implacable challenge to its audience is to confront Argentina's recent history in a way that allows for none of the catharsis of a film like *La historia oficial* (1985, q.v.). Santiso, like his mentors, has expertly crafted a disquiet which goes far beyond the drama on screen, radically politicising it for an era in which the most "normal" people can be torturers and still walk the streets.

Timothy Barnard

Awards: Second Prize, Taormina, 1986; Jury Prize for First Film, Chicago, 1986; Special Mention, First Film, Troia (Portugal), 1986.

Tango, bayle nuestro

Tango, Our Dance
Argentina, 1988, 75', colour

Dir Jorge Zanada (b. 1950) *Scr* Zanada *Cinematog* Gabriel Perosino, Marcelo Camorino, Juan
Carlos Lenardi, Carlos Torlaschi, Yito Blanc, Andrés Silvart, and Jaun Carlos Ferro *Mus*
Daniel Binelli *Choreog* Marcial Bo, María Luz Audisio, and Zanada *Prod* Zanada for Cóndor
Films

In the Argentine film production boom during the first years of democracy following the period of military rule from 1976–83, a number of
feature-length documentaries were made, ranging from archival historical
reconstructions to quirky personal films like *Tango, bayle nuestro*. Written,
produced, and directed in 16mm by a young filmmaker who admits in
voice-over at the beginning of the film's prologue that "I hated the tango.
I found it old and out-of-date, it filled me with a profound shame, the
shame of what is ours . . . ," *Tango bayle nuestro* is a rediscovery and
valorisation of Argentine popular culture. In a film-essay style worthy of
comparison to the films of French director Chris Marker, the film is a
meditation on the subtle links between culture and politics, between daily
life and great events. Its heretical attempt to reconcile two seemingly
antagonistic cultures, that of the tango and the radical youth culture of the
director, is announced by the opening dedication, "To Hugo del Carril
and Cine Liberación": while both tango singer and filmmaker Hugo del
Carril (*Las aguas bajan turbias*, 1952, q.v.) and the radical underground
film collective Cine Liberación (*La hora de los hornos*, 1968, q.v.)
represented (very different varieties of) militant Peronism, the juxtaposition is somewhat analogous to a dedication to Frank Sinatra and John
Lennon.

Many consider that the tango first appeared as a dance in the late 1800s
(Jorge Zanada believes it was first danced—without women—by soldiers
fighting in the war against Paraguay) and that the musical form appeared
only later, as accompaniment. Like jazz in North America, the tango in
its heyday in the mid-twentieth century was essentially dance music,
despite the vanguard elements of both we remember today, and there were
hundreds of neighbourhood dance halls in Buenos Aires at the time.
Tango dancing—after a visit to the cinema—was the principal working-
class Saturday night activity, and the film explores the dance's complexity

and variety of styles, revealing a popular culture of great depth and intricacy. A few of these clubs still exist, with a declining and aging clientele, and Zanada takes his camera onto the dance floor and into the homes and workplaces of the dancers to talk to them about the tango. Most consider the dance style known abroad, the stiffly elegant dance made famous in Europe and in numerous non-Argentine films, to be a "complete fraud," a sterile standardisation. Their dance has a greater variety of styles and is practised with a gentler rolling of the hips, producing a less tense eroticism than the international style. Zanada also interviews foreigners who have come to Buenos Aires to learn this "real" dance, including U.S. film actor Robert Duvall, and young Argentine dancers who want to save the form through innovation while respecting its traditions.

Intercut in a disconnected collage with the images of the dancing and the interviews with dancers and scholars are sequences of a more "vanguard" choreography, still lifes of Argentina's industrial ruins, archival footage of the 1955 and 1976 military coups, and brief dramatic vignettes, including a couple fleeing the street violence of the former coup. In the safety of a cemetery they unearth a coffin filled with an elegant dance dress and newspaper clippings about the tango; the viewer is left to make his or her own interpretation of the sequence. The soundtrack includes the middle-of-the-road tangos danced to in the clubs, a "new tango" score by bandoneonist and composer Daniel Binelli (which includes percussion, unheard of in the traditional tango), and snippets of U.S. pop music on radio stations. The voice-over narration weaves in and out of these disparate sounds and images, at times poetic and melancholy like a tango lyric, at times ruminating on the larger cultural significance of the dance, how for example machismo is embodied in its steps and the ways a people move and dance might be seen as part of larger social structures.

Timothy Barnard

Boda secreta

Secret Wedding
Argentina-Netherlands-Canada, 1989, 95', colour

Dir Alejandro Agresti (b. 1961) *Scr* Agresti *Cinematog* Ricardo Rodríguez *Ed* René Wiegmans *Art dir* Rodolfo Pagliere and Juan Carlos Alvarez *Mus* Paul Michael Van Brugge *Prod* Juan Collini for Cogurccio (Argentina), Kees Kasander and Denis Wigman for Allarts (Netherlands), and André Bennett and Brigette Young for Cinéphile (Canada) *Act* Tito Haas, Mirta Busnelli, Sergio Poves Campos, Nathan Pinzón, Floria Bloise, Elio Marchi, Carlos Roffe

Alejandro Agresti was the youngest active Argentine feature film director when he made *Boda secreta*, his third feature film. With a formidable command of cinematic technique, he was regarded as an extremely promising director, capable of expediting international co-productions. But after *Boda secreta* he chose to remain in The Netherlands, the key partner on this film and his second feature, *El amor es una mujer gorda* (1987).

Born in Buenos Aires, Agresti began making films at sixteen and later worked in the Argentine film industry as a camera operator. In 1986 he directed his first feature, *El hombre que ganó la razón*, and secured finishing funds for this film in The Netherlands. Kees Kasander launched *El hombre* at the Rotterdam film festival in 1987, and with his partner at Allarts Enterprises, Denis Wigman, co-produced Agresti's next film, *El amor*, with the Argentine film institute. With its extreme angles and complex tracking camera moves—especially in the flamboyant opening shot, reminiscent of Orson Welles—Néstor Sanz's black-and-white cinematography is extremely striking. But after an amusing reflexive opening, where José, a journalist, sabotages the shooting of a film which he believes distorts the reality of Argentina, *El amor* becomes mired in José's self-pity as he unsuccessfully searches for his "disappeared" lover.

At the beginning of *Boda secreta*, a naked man (Tito Haas) is seen clambering up and out of the Buenos Aires subway and running through the streets. He is picked up by police who determine that he must be Fermin García, a unionised bus driver, who was arrested for political activities in 1976 and "disappeared." Suffering from amnesia, "García" is released and he travels on a bus to Mendieta, a small provincial town. When his former lover, Tota (Mirta Busnelli), fails to recognize him, he adopts the alias of Alberto González. He befriends the town bum, Pipi (Sergio Poves Campus), whom he learns had been tortured. After being employed by Doña Patricia (Floria Bloise) to play the piano in her restaurant, he gradually learns that nothing has really changed. The town's dignitaries have continued in their fascist ways, especially the priest (Nathan Pinzón) who imagines that García/González is a KGB agent. Fermín and Tota plan a secret wedding. The priest is mysteriously drowned and Pipi is blamed. González gets him off and takes the blame—we believe that he did kill the priest—and as he is driven away on another bus, this time in captivity, he reveals his true identity. But Tota calls out "I'll wait for you Alberto" as she runs after the bus. . . .

Agresti's cinematic style, evident in *El amor*, dominates *Boda secreta*. Early in the film the subjective camera tracks past a line of derelicts in a corridor. In the same shot the camera scans a woman being interrogated by the police, moves into another room, and proceeds to crane up and tilt down to frame Fermín in an almost vertical angle. Such trajectories leading to entrapment, more Langian even than in Fritz Lang's own films, abound in *Boda secreta*. The high angle is often accentuated by juxtaposing it with a very low-angled shot. In addition, the strange camera positions force the spectator to "see things" differently, somewhat akin to the *ostraneniye* workings of Cubism and Futurism of the 1920s, and provide a surrealist or "magical realist" sense to the piece. Once in Mendieta, Ricardo Rodríguez' camera often observes the near-empty streets and buildings staticly and from a distance, or from a laterally tracking position, reminiscent of Jim Jarmusch's ironic and satirical view of small-town America. Indeed one could accuse Agresti's flamboyant visual style of being both highly derivative of other contemporaneous filmmakers such as Raúl Ruiz (*Les Trois couronnes du matelot*, 1982, q.v.) and the Coen brothers (*Blood Simple*, 1984), and far too obvious. On the other hand, the prominent elements of visual style in *Boda secreta* are appropriate in the contexts of paranoia, memory loss, and political oppression, which are working against the protagonists' sanity and combine with the film's action in suggesting that the events of the past dominate the present.

Agresti continued to make films in The Netherlands for Allarts—directing part of the anthology film *City Life* (1990), followed by solo efforts, *Luba* (1990) and *Modern Crimes* (1992)—but only with the Spanish-language *El acto in cuestria* (1993), which was shown at the Cannes film festival, did he regain the support of the critical establishment.

Peter Rist

Awards: International Critics' Prize (FIPRESCI), Best Actor (Tito Haas), Best Actress (Mirta Busnelli), Rio de Janeiro, 1989; Best Film, Dutch Film Days, 1989.

Después de la tormenta

After the Storm
Argentina-Spain, 1991, 105', colour

Dir Tristán Bauer (b. 1959) *Scr* Rubén Alvarez, Graciela Maglie and Bauer *Cinematog* Ricardo de Angelis Jr. *Mus* Rodolfo Mederos *Prod* Edgardo Pallero for Killarney (Argentina) and Televisión Española (TVE) and Sociedad Estatal Quinto Centenario (Spain) *Act* Lorenzo Quinteros, Patricio Contreras, Ana María Picchio, Eva Fernández

Tristán Bauer, a painter, began work in film as a cinematographer on independent productions and as a member of an activist documentary collective, "Cine y Testimonio." All of these experiences are evident in *Después de la tormenta*, an unusually accomplished first feature which demonstrates a rare concern for formal issues in a social film, at the same time as it does not hesitate to adopt a commercial narrative. Using both leading professional actors such as Lorenzo Quinteros (*Hombre mirando al sudeste*, 1986, q.v.) and non-professionals, all rehearsed in video, *Después de la tormenta* recounts a modern-day odyssey from the working class to the depths of degradation and poverty in a shantytown. A working class family is forced out of their home when the local factory closes; the mother takes work as a maid, the young son begins a life of petty crime which will land him in jail, and the father suffers the humiliation and impotence of being unable to find work of any kind. Leaving his wife, the man undertakes a solitary journey back to his poor rural roots in search of dignity, but there, old wounds with his aged father and his brother are reopened and his illusions of rural dignity are shattered by their servility to the local *patrón*. He returns to his wife and finds a menial job. While this marital reconciliation suggests a guarded optimism for their ability to make the best of their shattered lives, their son's criminalisation is depicted as irreversible and the film unflinchingly insists on the social and economic collapse all around them.

Cinematographer Ricardo de Angelis (*Hombre mirando al sudeste*, 1986, q.v.) shot *Después de la tormenta* in long languorous pans and tracking shots which present terribly, paradoxically beautiful images of Argentina's industrial ruins and shantytowns. The lighting—in factories and shacks, on grey days in the shantytown or in the pre-dawn light in the country—is realistically dim yet nuanced, and Bauer reveals a fascination with industrial forms. In this and other ways—the use of direct sound, for example—we have a sense of the film as a document. This is accentuated by an acting style which shuns melodrama and excess and presents us instead with a sparse realism, a quiet despair. There is limited recourse to music for effect, and again, rather than succumbing to the temptation of using music for simple emotional underscoring, Bauer commissioned "new tango" composer and bandoneonist Rodolfo Mederos to create a deft score of chamber music and folkloric and melancholic tango themes.

Involving several years' preparation, *Después de la tormenta* came to fruition just as Argentina's industries—including its film industry—were collapsing in the country's worst economic crisis since the return of democracy nearly a decade earlier. Its study of the social problem of thousands of newly-unemployed middle-aged industrial workers couldn't have been more timely. A subsequent privatisation of state assets of massive proportions has since fuelled a recovery of foreign investment and profit rates while creating social disparities on a scale long unseen in Argentina. The film industry managed its own miraculous recovery in 1992–93, somehow escaping the wave of neo-liberal economic policies affecting all activities dependent on state support. Legislation introduced during this period placed a tax on home video rentals to finance domestic film production and in 1994 co-productions with domestic television were encouraged and the name of the national film institute, INC, changed to the National Institute for Film and Audiovisual Art (INCAA). With this increased support the industry, which some believed to be, like the Brazilian film industry, fatally crippled during this period, regained production levels on a par with historical levels. In 1994 Bauer filmed a successful documentary on the life of Argentine author Julio Cortázar (*Cortázar*) and announced plans to film a biography of Ernesto "Che" Guevara in 1995.

Timothy Barnard

Awards: Best First Film (shared), San Sebastián, 1990; First Prize, Huelva, 1990; Best Photography and the OCIC and Vigía Awards, Havana, 1990; Best First Film, Chicago, 1990.

Bolivia

La profecía del lago

The Prophecy of the Lake
Bolivia, 1925, approx. 80', b+w, silent

Dir José María Velasco Maidana (1901-1989) *Prod* Velasco Films *Act* Donato Olmos Peñaranda, Emmo Reyes, N. Sotomayor, N. Laguna

La profecía del lago was the second feature film produced in Bolivia, following by eight days the completion of *Corazón Aymara*, directed by the Italian immigrant Pedro Sambarino. It was also the first Bolivian film to fall victim to the censor; today the film's fate remains a mystery and for decades it has been considered lost. In 1988 a few rolls of film were found among the belongings of José María Velasco Maidana's first wife, and they are believed to be part of *La profecía del lago*, although they have not yet been restored.

The film's theme was subversive for its time and even today would prove controversial for many. In the film a woman from Bolivia's high society, the wife of a government official, has an affair with an indigenous man. The story was reportedly inspired by a real-life incident. Having been lost practically since its completion, that is the only detail of the film's plot that is known to us. Everything else that is known about the film comes to us from brief and vague notices in the press of the day and from interviews the author of this review was able to carry out with the actor Donato Olmos Peñaranda and the sculptress Marina Nuñez del Prado, who worked on the film.

The newspaper *La Verdad* announced the film's opening in the Teatro Paris in La Paz in July 1925 but gives no further information on the film. In September of that year *El Diario* reported that "the municipality has

83

ordered the film to be incinerated." Legend has it that in order to circumvent this order to destroy the film, Velasco Maidana hid the film in a wall of his house. His last wife, the U.S. painter Dorothy Hood, relates that he told her that in order to prevent the film's destruction he appeared before the authorities and said "You can burn me alongside my work." Velasco Maidana himself could recall none of this when this author visited him at his home in Houston, Texas, in 1978.

The film's theme was especially subversive in the context of Bolivian society of the day. The early 1920s in Bolivia were especially unstable politically and socially, as the transition from a feudal society to a modern economy based on mining threatened the power of the ruling classes. The native peoples, who were being converted from peasants to miners after the discovery of huge reserves of tin in the north of the country, worked from sun to sun in the mines, rebelling on several occasions. In 1921 President Bautista Saavedra (1921–25) declared: "We are going to eliminate the Aymara and Quechua because they constitute an obstacle to our progress."

The censor's concerns were not misplaced, as the film was a slap in the face to a society which viewed itself as pure white and avoided all contact with the native population. It would not be an exaggeration to say that Velasco Maidana's film was a revolutionary act in this context, exposing the racism of the ruling classes and portraying indigenous people as human beings with full rights of citizenship. These rights would only be gained in fact with the National Revolution of 1952, a quarter of a century after the film was produced.

Despite the little we know about it and its apparent loss, *La profecía del lago* is an extremely important precursor to modern Bolivian cinema. Film production since this date in Bolivia would bear the social perspective of the filmmakers. Since this early period right up until the present day, Bolivian cinema has been, despite a chronic shortage of resources, a fiercely independent cinema engaged with the country's social problems.

Alfonso Gumucio-Dagron

Warawara

Bolivia, 1930, approx. 90',
b + w with some colour tinting, silent

Dir José María Velasco Maidana (1901–1989) *Scr* Antonio Díaz Villamil, based on his novel *La voz de la quena Cinematog* Mario Camacho *Mus* César Garcés B. *Prod* Velasco Maidana for Urania Film *Act* Juanita Tallansier, José María Velasco Maidana, Emmo Reyes, Guillermo Viscarra Fabre, Arturo Borda, Marina Nuñez del Prado, Dámaso Eduardo Delgado, Raúl Montalvo, Mario Camacho, Donato Olmos Peñaranda, Yolanda Bedregal, Juan Capriles

By 1930 Bolivia had produced four silent feature films, all of them since 1925. Despite this late start and sparse output, this was more than production levels have ever been since. All early production was by independent artisans, as there was no industrial infrastructure, laboratories, or skilled technicians. Each film was the product of the efforts of the director and a few friends who lent their money, hoping neither for fame—cinema then was not considered a serious art form—or fortune.

Nonetheless, pioneer filmmaker José María Velasco Maidana (*La profecía del lago*, 1925, q.v.) embarked on the country's first "super-production," initially entitled *El ocaso de la tierra del sol* but eventually exhibited as *Warawara*, which means "star" in the native language of Aymara and is the name of the female lead in the film. The result was a monumental work, a sort of *Intolerance*, only one set in one of the poorest countries in Latin America. The film's production took nearly two years, and Velasco Maidana's and author Antonio Díaz Villamil's prestige was such that they were able to obtain the collaboration of Bolivian personalities already famous for their work: the poets Yolanda Bedregal, Guillermo Viscarra Fabre, and Juan Capriles, the painter Arturo Borda, and the sculptress Marina Nuñez del Prado. The press of the time gave the film ample coverage which, together with surviving photographs and other documentation, provides us with a fair idea of the film's themes, the film itself being lost.

Warawara's principal theme is the conquest of America. The Inca capital Cuzco, in present-day Peru, has been taken by the Spanish, who are advancing on the Kollasuyo across the Andes. On the altiplano, peaceful Aymara communities are seen, ignorant of the peril which threatens them. After bloody battles with the advancing Spanish, the Aymara take refuge in the mountains. These historical events, which took several years to unfold, are narrated in the film through the lives of its two principal characters, the Aymara princess Warawara and the young Spanish captain Tristán. They fall in love, but Aymara resistance to the Spanish separates them.

While this love story is the film's connecting thread, the essential aspect of the film is Velasco Maidana's plea on behalf of the indigenous Aymara communities, arguing for the recognition of a new national identity based on this mixing of Spanish and native blood. In this way Velasco Maidana returned to the theme which prompted the banning of *La profecía del lago*, the relationship between white and native society. This insistence on Bolivian identity as being the product of an encounter between these two cultures was still a taboo theme at the time.

With *Warawara* special sets were designed for a film's production for the first time in Bolivia. Artists and architects themselves built a recreation of the Aymara palace. Velasco Maidana's home in La Paz was filled with women sewing costumes for the actors. In a makeshift laboratory, Raúl Montalvo and José Jiménez (the latter co-director of *Hacia la gloria*, 1932, q.v.) developed the film by hand while Velasco Maidana played violin in the next room to entertain the crew. The only modern equipment used in the production was the Ernemans camera Velasco Maidana had brought from Buenos Aires. Editing was done by the naked eye with a small moviola and a pair of scissors. According to Montalvo, the finished film was seven reels long, at 300 metres per reel. By the time it premiered in January 1930 at the Teatro Princesa in La Paz, accompanied by live music composed by César Garcés B., it was already famous. Critics applauded the film, saying that it marked "the birth of a new art and a new national industry." Nevertheless, the film's exhibition was cut short with the arrival of imported sound films in July of that year, and its distribution in the interior of the country did not have the same impact as it did in La Paz. One of the two prints of the film was shipped to Germany—its European release was also hampered by the advent of sound film—from whence it never returned; the other disappeared, as did, eventually, Velasco Maidana.

Velasco Maidana was a singular personality in Bolivian culture, a filmmaker, visual artist, and music composer and director. His paintings and engravings are exhibited in museums but are not the principal aspect of his work. His films have disappeared after opening a path for others. His music, however, remains. Velasco Maidana founded the National Conservatory of Music and remained active as a composer and conductor all his life. His frustrating experiences in film drove him from Bolivia; after shooting a few short documentaries there in the early 1930s, he spent a few years in Argentina and returned to Bolivia in 1936 to mount the successful ballet "Amerindia," which toured successfully in Germany. In 1943 he began an extensive tour of Latin America as an orchestra director, performing in the region's principal recital halls. The tour ended in Mexico City, where he remained until relocating to Houston, where he died without ever returning to Bolivia. Interviewed there by the present author in 1978, he had completely forgotten any details about his film career.

Alfonso Gumucio-Dagron

Hacia la gloria

Towards Glory
Bolivia, 1932, b+w with some colour tinting, silent

Dir Mario Camacho and José Jiménez *Scr* Moisés Alcazar *Cinematog* Camacho *Art dir* Arturo Borda *Prod* José Durán for Cinematografía Bolivia *Act* Donato Olmos Peñaranda, Arturo Borda, Matilde Garvía, Manuel B. Sagárnaga, Angélica Azcul, Valentina Arze

By the end of the 1920s Bolivian cinema consisted of a handful of documentary shorts and just four feature films, none of which has survived and none of which seemed to create an opportunity for further attempts to create a market for national films. In addition to the two features by director José María Velasco Maidana (*La profecía del lago*, 1925, q.v.; *Warawara*, 1930, q.v.) and the drama *Corazón Aymara*, filmed by the Italian Pedro Sambarino in 1925, there was the experiment of the archaeologist and amateur photographer Arturo Posnansky and Bolivian film pioneer Luis Castillo, *La gloria de la raza*, filmed in 1926. This was a blend of fiction and documentary on the Uru civilisation, which was then disappearing. It was thus a considerable challenge for the three young enthusiasts behind *Hacia la gloria*, the co-directors Mario Camacho and José Jiménez and producer José Durán, to undertake the film's production. All three had been heavily involved in the production of Velasco Maidana's last film, *Warawara*, and had seen first hand the frustration its fate caused him. The three undertook the project despite all this, and the result was a film which, like others before it and despite limited resources, took up a theme which discomfited the national bourgeoisie, demonstrating a sense of rebellion and criticising social hypocrisy. The filming, between October 1930 and mid-1931, was undertaken in a cooperative spirit among the four principal personalities behind the film—Camacho, Jiménez, Durán, and art director and actor Arturo Borda. The film was originally to have been scripted by Castillo, who was said to have carried the script in his head; after he withdrew and sold a version of the script to the project, the film faced legal action by a former collaborator of Castillo's who claimed it was in fact a script of his that Castillo had undertaken to film in 1927 but never had.

The story was a melodrama: The child of a La Paz bourgeois and his young mistress is abandoned on the banks of the Choqueyapu River a few days after birth. A poor woman finds him and raises him. Eventually he becomes an airplane pilot and is injured in combat when sent to war. In the field hospital where he is treated he encounters a nun who comes to recognise him as her own son; through her he learns that the girlfriend he is to marry is actually his sister. This complicated web of relationships is narrated by letters written by the characters which appear on the screen. Finally, the troubled young man is seen leaving on a train, with no destination in mind.

In addition to being an emotional drama, the film's backdrop was a war, and here *Hacia la gloria* had the fortune—or misfortune—to prefigure the actual declaration of the Chaco War, which Bolivia and Paraguay waged from 1932–1935 for control over territory in the desolate Chaco jungle. The war cost both sides an estimated 50,000 lives, and the territory Bolivia lost as a result doubled the size of Paraguay. While it may seem that the film's setting was an advantage, in fact the war didn't have much impact on its distribution. At the time, *Hacia la gloria* was waging its own war, against sound film, which had arrived in Bolivia in 1930 via imported films dubbed in Spanish; the Bolivian public had very quickly become accustomed to the "talkies."

While *Hacia la gloria*'s directors had considerable technical experience in the country's artisanal silent film industry, developing their own 35mm footage in a small makeshift laboratory and doing their own hand tinting of various scenes, they did not have the means or expertise to make a sound film. Nevertheless, they advertised the film on its release in 1932 as the country's "first sound film," with "clear sound" and "music perfectly adapted." Their ingenious strategy was to place the actor Emmo Reyes behind the screen of every exhibition; with the aid of phonograph records and a variety of homemade sound effects, he was able to provide sound effects and music for some of the film's scenes. Reports indicate that he was so successful that audiences applauded battle scenes with airplanes firing at each other.

However, local critics didn't much like the film, and the public's reception was also lukewarm. The situation in the country at the time was critical, as war was officially declared soon after the film's release, although confrontations had been taking place for a year previous, and the army was drafting young men to fight. Jiménez was so young that he wasn't drafted, allowing him to travel the country's interior, showing the film in towns and mining communities, where it was seen as having bellicose aims. Jiménez wrote that the film was also seen as one of Bolivia's first "social outcries," as a "cry of rebellion."

With the coming of the Chaco War the first period of Bolivian film came to an end. During the war two films were made, *La campaña del Chaco* by Camacho (1933) and *La guerra del Chaco* by Luis Bazoberry (1936). These films today have great value as historical documents but at the time they were failures. It would be another fifteen years before Bolivian film would be revived by a group of short film makers in the late 1940s.

Hacia la gloria is estimated to have been approximately 50 minutes in length, but only fragments remain in the archives of the Cinemateca Boliviana.

Alfonso Gumucio-Dagron

La vertiente

The Watershed
Bolivia, 1959, 65', b+w

Dir Jorge Ruiz (b. 1924) *Scr* Oscar Soria *Cinematog* Nicolás Smolij *Prod* Enrique Albarracín for Instituto Cinematográfico Boliviano (ICB) *Act* Rosario del Río

"Jorge Ruiz is one of the six most important documentary filmmakers in the world," the Scottish filmmaker and founder of Canada's National Film Board (NFB) John Grierson declared during a visit to Bolivia in 1958, the year before *La vertiente*'s release. His comment was prompted by the projection of the short film *Vuelve Sebastiana* (1953), a semi-documentary account of the indigenous Chipayas communities on the altiplano. The film, through the story of a young indigenous girl, depicts the customs and difficult living conditions of one of the oldest cultures in the Andes. Even at this early date Jorge Ruiz was experimenting in his films with non-professional actors, real people from the community, as Jorge Sanjinés would do many years later (*Yawar Mallku*, 1969, q.v.). There is no doubt that Ruiz was advanced for his time. While he was interested in ethnographic film, he transcended the merely descriptive through the use of fictional narratives, generally written by Oscar Soria or Luis Ramiro Beltrán.

Ruiz was Bolivia's first professional filmmaker. Everything that had gone before was the work of isolated artisans. Ruiz dedicated himself to cinema and contributed to the industry's professionalisation in the early 1950s, having begun making short films in 1942. By the late 1950s and early 1960s, he was the only active filmmaker in Bolivia. He was instrumental in the training of the first generation of professional technicians. This was made possible by the National Revolution of 1952, the second popular revolution in Latin America, after that of Mexico. The new Nationalist Revolutionary Movement (MNR) government supported film by creating the Bolivian Film Institute (ICB).

La vertiente was the first feature film that Ruiz undertook for the ICB. While Bolivian cinema has usually focused on the highlands of the altiplano, *La vertiente* reveals Ruiz's interest in the country's tropical region, a neglected theme despite the fact that this region accounts for most of the country's territory. There are two principal axes to the story: the first, somewhat banal, is a love story between a schoolteacher and a handsome alligator hunter. The second documents the collective efforts of the people of the community of Rurenabaque to install facilities for fresh water. The former story line seems inspired by Mexican melodramas of the day, while the latter has great impact, accountable perhaps by the fact that the film simply recorded a real event: the film was made to coincide with the community's efforts but also to stimulate them. Ruiz had suggested the idea to President Hernán Siles Zuaco (1956–60), who endorsed it as supporting the principles of "self-help" and "local efforts" that the revolution was espousing. The result is a mix of genres, part Mexican-style romance and part social documentary, focusing on the community's efforts. And although this latter component of the film is crucial, Ruiz was able to edit the film with great dexterity in order to intermingle the genres, to the point that the barriers between them seem to dissolve and it is difficult to distinguish between them, so that it entertains its audience while expounding on the country's development needs.

Mayakovsky would have applauded the way in which the film creates poetry out of such a theme, the way in which the ideology of development in the first years of the revolution becomes in a sense the film's protagonist. In one scene, after the pipes have been fitted to carry the water, someone yells "Let it flow!" and immediately the townspeople expectantly and suspensefully place their ears near the pipe to hear the distant water begin to flow. This poetry of work and progress is one of the film's great qualities.

While not simply a government propaganda film, *La vertiente* is a political film, reflecting the aspirations of a new society trying to break with its feudal past. The film concludes with a speech that articulates the MNR government's philosophy. Ruiz relates that when the film was nearly complete the U.S. embassy offered money to finish it on condition that he film scenes showing the pipes as being stamped "Donated by USAID," which was not even the case. Ruiz rejected the offer, although later in his career he would resort to making many documentary films commissioned by the agency. His early films of the 1950s remain his best, as they were made independently. In the 1960s and 70s he made dozens of commissioned industrial films in Bolivia and throughout Latin America as well as a couple of commercial features in Bolivia in the late 1960s, never again producing personal work that demonstrated the extent of his talent.

The fate of the ICB is a sad chapter in Bolivia's film history. Closed in 1964 after a military coup, when Ruiz left the country, it was, surprisingly, reopened by the same military government the following year under the leadership of Jorge Sanjinés (*Yawar Mallku*, 1969, q.v.). It was closed again, however, in 1967, in the face of Sanjinés' own increasingly radical films (*Ukamau*, 1966) and their success abroad. The fifteen years' production at the ICB have since been lost, however. Negatives stored at an Argentine film lab were destroyed because the Bolivian government left a small account unpaid. Copies were stored at Bolivian Television under very poor conditions and quickly deteriorated beyond use. Finally, some films from the ICB period were maliciously destroyed because of their themes of the 1952 revolution, agrarian reform, etc., so that today nothing of the agency's work, apart from *La vertiente*, remains.

Alfonso Gumucio-Dagron

Yawar Mallku

[Blood of the Condor]
Bolivia, 1969, 72', b+w

Dir Jorge Sanjinés (b. 1936) *Scr* Oscar Soria *Cinematog* Antonio Eguino *Mus* Alberto Villalpando *Prod* Ricardo Rada for Ukamau *Act* Vicente Verenos, Benedicta Mendoza Huanca, Marcelino Yanahuaya, Danielle Caillet

No other Bolivian film is as well known throughout the world as *Yawar Mallku*, which confirmed Jorge Sanjinés as a major figure of the New Latin American Cinema, a movement that aligned itself with popular democratic struggles throughout the continent. *Yawar Mallku* was no exception, and its political engagement was consistent with the evolution of Sanjinés' work and his increasing politicisation. After studying photography in Bolivia and philosophy in Chile, Sanjinés began making short films with Oscar Soria in the early 1960s, with whom he also established a film school and a ciné club. Sanjinés also spent time with the photography department of USAID in Bolivia and was director of the Bolivian Film Institute from 1965–67, accepting the challenge of directing the agency under the military. In two years there he managed to produce some documentaries with social concerns alongside the mandatory pro-government newsreels. His first short film as a solo director, *Revolución* (1964), won the Joris Ivens Prize at the Leipzig film festival, and his first feature, *Ukamau*, made in 1966, announced his arrival as a major force in Latin American cinema. Despite his forced departure from Bolivia after *El coraje del pueblo* (1971, q.v.), scattering later production throughout the region (*¡Fuera de aquí!*, Ecuador, 1975, q.v.) until finally able to film again in Bolivia in the 1980s (*La nación clandestina*, 1989, q.v.), Sanjinés is one of the principal figures of Latin American film of the period. In these early, pre-exile films, he and the Grupo Ukamau collective formed around him in 1968 (Antonio Eguino, who would later film *Chuquiago* (1977, q.v.), Soria, former scriptwriter for Jorge Ruiz (*La vertiente*, 1959, q.v.), and Ricardo Rada developed, through their method of filming with non-professional actors based on real events, a unique and compelling aesthetic and political engagement.

Yawar Mallku was the group's first independent production, and it came at a critical time in Bolivian society. Ernesto "Che" Guevara, the Argentine revolutionary who had helped lead the Cuban revolution, had been killed leading an insurrectionary movement in Bolivia in 1967. The country was in political turmoil as popular sectors sought to overthrow a military government backed by the U.S.; by 1969 military dictatorships supported by the U.S. were predominant throughout the region. The Bolivian military and the U.S. intelligence services openly manipulated Bolivian politics and society, which were radically polarised.

The film was originally planned to tell the story of a rural schoolteacher, but a newspaper article about the forced sterilisation of rural indigenous women (on top of everything else an absurd concept in an underpopulated country like Bolivia) by the U.S. Peace Corps led the filmmakers to adopt this theme as the central focus of the film. Here a foreign "Progress Corps" is discovered sterilising women without their knowledge; the indigenous community rebels and attacks the foreigners, but the Bolivian army intervenes and the community's "Mallku"—which means both condor and leader in Aymara—is wounded. He is taken to La Paz in search of medical care, but there the peasants find only indifference and racism. Their urban plight, seeking help in various places and from various sources, would be reworked in Eguino's later film *Chuquiago*.

Yawar Mallku is a parable of imperialism: the foreign control of fertility was a real event, but here it is taken as a starting point for a larger historical analysis. Medical mutilation is seen as a symbol of U.S. intervention in Bolivia and Latin America, and when the "Mallku" discovers this, what is really being depicted is a class awareness of this intervention. The sterilisation also serves as a powerful metaphor for the silencing of the region's culture.

Yawar Mallku's black-and-white photography is one of the most beautiful expressions of New Latin American Cinema, despite the film's budget of only $40,000. Here Sanjinés consolidated his ability to film with non-professional actors, indigenous Aymara whose only film acting experience was in his earlier films. His collaboration with the community of Kaata, depicted in the film, had no precedent in Latin American cinema. In order to film in the community, Sanjinés had to abide by its decisions, which, as the film illustrates, were taken in group assemblies, with final approval going to community elders.

The film's release in La Paz in July 1969 caused a veritable political upheaval. When the first spectators arrived at the cinema the doors were locked, and a notice indicated that the city had banned the film's exhibition, acting on "higher orders." It is believed that these orders came directly from the U.S. embassy. The spectators organised a march through the streets of La Paz, an unprecedented protest because of a film, which was repressed by police using tear gas and water cannons. In the following days, however, protests continued in the press, leading to the film's release and to its even greater impact in Bolivia and abroad; the film is credited with initiating debate on the role in Bolivia of the Peace Corps, which was expelled from the country in 1971.

Alfonso Gumucio-Dagron

El coraje del pueblo

Courage of the People
Italy-Bolivia, 1971 (released 1979), 94', colour

Dir Jorge Sanjinés (b. 1936) *Scr* Oscar Soria *Cinematog* Antonio Eguino *Mus* Nilo Soruco *Prod* Walter Achúgar and Edgardo Pallero for Radiotelevisione Italiana (RAI) (Italy) and Ukamau (Bolivia) *Act* Domitila de Chungara, Eusebio Gironda, Federico Vallejo, Felicidad Coca García

In 1973 the French film critic Guy Hennebelle included *El coraje del pueblo* on his list of the twenty best films of all time. While most European critics probably wouldn't share his views, there is no doubt that director Jorge Sanjinés' third feature is one of the best films to emerge from Bolivia. Both in its theme and its style, it is one of the most representative works of the New Latin American Cinema which developed in the 1960s and 70s.

The initial title of the film was *La noche de San Juan*, as it depicts events that took place at the Siglo XX mining camp on the eve of Saint John's Day (24 June) in 1967. On that day, the Bolivian army attacked the camp at dawn and massacred the union leaders and miners working there. This was not the first time that Bolivian military authorities had tried to crush the country's vigorous miners' unions by force; similar massacres had taken place in Catavi in 1919, 1942, and 1949; at Uncía in 1923; and at Siglo XX in 1965. Tin and blood: it was a high price to pay for miners whose work drove Bolivia's economy from the colonial era to the 1970s, when gas (and cocaine) replaced it as the country's principal export.

The film's story can be summarised quickly: Mining families are shown celebrating Saint John's Eve, the coldest day of the year, by fires in front of each home. The army attacks suddenly, slaughtering the defenceless workers. From this event, which opens the film, Sanjinés constructs in extended flashback an image of daily life in the mining camp, showing the problems of obtaining supplies, health, and work. The settlement is shown as a model of solidarity, ideological conviction, and political resolve that the military could not tolerate: this small group of workers was a "bad example" that had to be eliminated.

Once again Sanjinés (*Yawar Mallku*, 1969, q.v.) demonstrated his preoccupation with using film to give voice to a collective memory and sense of community within Bolivia's indigenous population. The film's style is more poetic than documentary, and the initial massacre scene, understood as representing the state's widespread violence against the poor, gives way to a sober and intense analysis of the political relationship among miners, peasants, students, and guerrillas, the latter active in the country a few years earlier under the leadership of Ernesto "Che" Guevara. The film is in a sense a keen history lesson, exploring the role of women in trade union struggles as well as the importance of unions and of popular means of communication, such as mining community radio stations. Despite the involvement of the Italian television network RAI, which that year financed a quartet of films on "Latin America Seen by its Filmmakers," Sanjinés again filmed with little money, achieving an extraordinary beauty in 16mm. The most remarkable aspect of the film is that Sanjinés used survivors of the massacre to interpret their own roles in the film: in this way they may be said to be not only non-professional actors but historical actors, allowing Sanjinés to eliminate all distinction between fiction and reality, creating a cinema which mixes the force of testimony with the plasticity of spectacle.

Sanjinés had been able to make *El coraje del pueblo* under conditions of unusual freedom in Bolivia. A populist military leader, General Juan José Torres, was president in 1970–71, and under his rule there was freedom of expression and association. Parliament had been dissolved and in its place, in the same building, a People's Assembly functioned under the famous miners' leader Juan Lechín. There industrial workers, miners, peasants, journalists, students, and others met. But all this ended abruptly with a coup d'état in 1971 by Colonel (later General) Hugo Bánzer (1971–78), which brought severe repression in its wake. The filming of *El coraje del pueblo* was completed days before the coup, and Sanjinés edited it in Italy, where it was screened in a shortened version on television, going into theatrical release in 1973 in Europe and, to a lesser extent, in Latin America. Sanjinés later filmed in Perú, Ecuador (*¡Fuera de aquí!*,

1975, q.v.), and twice in Bolivia in the 1980s (*La nación clandestina*, 1989 q.v.). *El coraje del pueblo* could not be screened publicly in Bolivia until 1979, although following a clandestine screening in 1975, cinematographer Antonio Eguino (*Chuquiago*, 1977, q.v.) was detained. He was released after 15 days following pressure within Bolivia and from abroad.

Alfonso Gumucio-Dagron

Awards: Annual OCIC (International Catholic Cinema Office) Award, 1972.

Chuquiago

Bolivia, 1977, 87', colour

Dir Antonio Eguino *Scr* Oscar Soria and Luis Espinal *Cinematog* Eguino *Mus* Alberto Villalpando *Prod* Carlos Sforzini for Ukamau *Act* David Santalla, Néstor Yulra, Edmundo Villarreoi, Taliana Aponte

The city of La Paz, the highest capital in the world, has a strange topography. It is situated at the foot of a great cleft in the Andean altiplano at a height of nearly 4,000 metres above sea level, criss-crossed by rivers carrying water from the Andes to the country's tropical regions in the south and east before finally joining the magnificent torrent of the Amazon. La Paz's topography is marked not only by these geographical elements but also by its social structure. In the lower parts of the city live the city's bourgeois, taking advantage of a more agreeable climate and more open space. On the more crowded slopes leading up into the heights of the altiplano live the city's poor, many of them rural immigrants who have arrived in La Paz over the past 30 years.

The city's social topography is the subject of Antonio Eguino's feature *Chuquiago*, his second after *Pueblo chico* (1974). "Chuquiago" is the city's Aymara name, a reference to the fact that its rivers contained gold. The Spaniards gave it a religious name, after Nuestra Señora de La Paz. The film is made up of four stories, which together make a whole: it was filmed in sections, in 16mm, for budgetary reasons. At $80,000, a paltry sum by international film production standards, it was the most expensive Bolivian fiction film made to that date.

The four stories make up a perfect description of La Paz' social classes. Each story has one principal protagonist. In "Isico," an indigenous boy from the altiplano makes his first visit to the city, without being able to speak Spanish. Quickly faced with a marginal existence, he works loading goods in the city's markets, and it seems clear that his future holds nothing better. In the second story, "Johnny," the adolescent son of a worker tries to deny his class and ingratiate himself with the local middle class, who, of course, reject him. Johnny learns English and dreams of going to the United States; his very name is an indication of his infatuation with leaving his class. His desperation to obtain money leads him into a life of crime. "Carlos" relates the last days, told in flashback from the vantage point of his funeral, of a middle class bureaucrat, a typical public servant, who dies on his way home from a brothel after a drunken "bachelor's Friday night out." In the last story, "Patricia," a young bourgeois woman abandons her revolutionary dalliances of her university days to marry in her class and return to a life of comfort. As the film ends and we see her driving off on her honeymoon, Isico appears, struggling up the hill under the weight of a heavy load.

Each story is told in a different style. "Isico" has a sobriety appropriate to the altiplano, underlining the tragic quality of the boy's life. "Johnny" reveals the border between white and indigenous culture in the city: the character crosses back and forth from one to the other before finally becoming marginalised in both. Life—and death—in "Carlos," on the other hand, is recounted in the style of an Italian comedy, emphasizing the comic talents of the actor, David Santalla, the best known person in the film, and we are led to judge him kindly. "Patricia" touches on political issues directly, but at the same time it is the weakest of the stories because it doesn't achieve a critical analysis of Bolivia's bourgeoisie.

Each story closes without leaving any opportunity for hope: each character appears condemned to the fate of his or her class, unable to develop beyond its prescribed limits. *Chuquiago* is undoubtedly a pessimistic film, reflecting the country's circumstances in the late 1970s, soon before the fall of the dictatorship of General Hugo Bánzer (1971–1978). It is also a bitter testament to the fact that despite the popular social revolution of 1952—the second, after Mexico, in Latin America—there had been no substantial social integration. Social injustice still reigns as well as a racism camouflaged by social conventions determined by class.

Chuquiago was the first real popular success in Bolivian film. The public appreciated its honesty and its realism as well as its polished production values. It didn't achieve the international fame of the films made by the Grupo Ukamau under Jorge Sanjinés (*Yawar Mallku*, 1969, q.v. and *El coraje del pueblo*, 1971, q.v.), by now in exile, but in Bolivia it broke box office records for a national film with 400,000 admissions, beating the U.S. release *Jaws* that same year. This is more impressive when one considers that the country's population is only six million people, many of them living in rural regions, and that the country has extremely low rates of film attendance, averaging only one film per person per year. Unfortunately, because of the country's ridiculously low film admission prices, Ukamau barely recovered its investment. Co-scriptwriter Luis Espinal, a filmmaker and film critic who had denounced Eguino's detention in 1975 after a clandestine screening of *El coraje del pueblo* and who later denounced attempts to prevent that film's first public screening in 1979, was abducted, tortured, and murdered in 1980. Eguino was able to make one more film, the epic *Amargo mar*, in 1984.

Alfonso Gumucio-Dagron

La nación clandestina

The Clandestine Nation
United Kingdom-Spain-Germany-Japan, 1989, 125', colour

Dir Jorge Sanjinés (b. 1936) *Scr* Sanjinés *Cinematog* César Pérez *Mus* Cergio Prudencio *Prod* Beatriz Palacios for Channel Four (U.K.), Televisión Española (TVE) (Spain), A2F (Germany), and Japan TV (Japan) *Act* Reynaldo Yujra, Delfina Mamani, Orlando Huanca, Roque Salgado

With *La nación clandestina*, Jorge Sanjinés, Bolivia's most important filmmaker (*Yawar Mallku*, 1969, q.v.; *El coraje del pueblo*, 1971, q.v.; *¡Fuera de aquí!*, Ecuador, 1975, q.v.), returned to the most fundamental motivations for his film career. In Sanjinés' words, *La nación clandestina* represents his "search for the national identity of Aymara culture, whose people make up forty per cent of the population of La Paz and who resist domination by, and the power and morality of, the ruling classes."

Indigenous peasants from Bolivia's altiplano emigrate to the city for the same reasons as others around the world do, the dream of a better life and the mirage of consumer society. In Bolivia and elsewhere, many end up in miserable shantytowns around large cities, but in Bolivia the problem is accentuated by the refusal of white society to grant them the rights of citizenship, as we saw in the treatment of the "Mallku" in Sanjinés' earlier film *Yawar Mallku*.

While the theme is a common one, Sanjinés' treatment of it in *La nación clandestina* is unique, with a less explicit political emphasis and a more profound cultural awareness and stylistic experimentation. Through its depiction of its principal character and the existential anguish which consumes him in the city, the film suggests that the cultural syncretism of Bolivia is not yet complete, at least from the native point of view. To support this view that the Aymara are not yet integrated into national life, Sanjinés concentrates on the drama of this cultural uprooting and the denial of native identity in the city.

The film depicts the pilgrimage on foot of Sebastián Mamani, an Aymara living in La Paz, to his native village, from which he had been expelled. There, he knows, death awaits him. Most of the film is taken up with his solitary journey across the altiplano, carrying an elaborate mask for his final, ritual act. This act, a ritual dance he performs until his death, is the film's most powerful sequence, portrayed with a force and the weight of tragedy hitherto unseen in Sanjinés' work. The dance's leitmotif is woven into the film's dramatic structure as a vicious circle from which the protagonist cannot escape. He appears fated from the beginning to end his life through this supreme effort of dancing to redeem himself in death, dancing not only with his body but with all his shattered spirituality.

La nación clandestina employs an aesthetic of long takes and camera movements which preserve the continuity of the action and give the film a documentary flavour. This style—reminiscent of the films of the Hungarian director Miklós Jancsó—is not new in Sanjinés' oeuvre: beginning with *El enemigo principal* (Peru, 1973) and continuing in *¡Fuera de aquí!*, Sanjinés has tended to create sequences whose duration corresponds to real time. The long take, as Sanjinés has written, is a fundamental part of his aesthetic, permitting him to surround reality without interrupting it. It also facilitates his use of non-professional actors, who lack the training to re-do scenes. For Sanjinés, unlike Jancsó, the long take is much more than a formal device, it is the embodiment of a consideration of the ethical dilemmas of filmmaking and the depiction of social reality and the marginal lives of his characters.

La nación clandestina—a title Sanjinés first used in 1970 for a project that was never completed—is a parable of alienation and repression.

Sanjinés insists that within Bolivia two races have been superimposed on the same land without coming to co-exist: a European nation, descended from immigrants, and an indigenous nation, exiled in its own country. Others argue that Bolivia, since the revolution of 1952, has experienced a process of racial, social, and cultural mixing and integration which has affected all strata of society, a belief supported by the election of an indigenous vice-president, Víctor Hugo Cárdenas, in 1993, an unprecedented event in Latin America. Sanjinés, however, reaffirmed with this film his belief in the purity of the Aymara, kept at the margins of modern Bolivian society.

Alfonso Gumucio-Dagron

Awards: Best Film, San Sebastián, 1990; Jury Prize, Glauber Rocha Prize (awarded by the foreign press), Havana, 1990.

Brazil

Exemplo Regenerador

Moralizing Example
Brazil, 1919, 7', b+w, silent

Dir José Medina *Scr* Medina *Cinematog* Gilberto Rossi *Prod* Rossi for Rossi Filme *Act* Lucia Laes, Waldemar Moreno, José Guedes de Castro, Carlos Ferreira

Although the cinema was introduced early to Brazil and quickly captured the interest of several recently-arrived European immigrants, who produced the first short actuality films, the Brazilian market developed slowly until the standardisation of electrical service in Rio de Janeiro and São Paulo around 1907. As early as 1906, however, films based on famous crimes (known as *posados* or posed films) proved to be extremely popular. Between 1908 and 1912—the *Bela Epoca* or "Golden Age" of Brazilian cinema—production soared. Brazilian entrepreneurs produced adaptations (most notably, *Os Guaranis* (Antônio Leal, 1908), based on the José de Alencar novel), reenactments of contemporary crimes, "sung" films in which singers and musicians accompanied each show behind the screen, comedies about *carioca* life, satires, and melodramas. Audiences flocked to the cinemas and production grew to more than 100 short films per year.

However, soon after the 1911 establishment of a powerful cinematographic trust aligned with foreign distributors which purchased theatres and distributed foreign films, production declined drastically. Unable to place their films in theatres, production companies closed and by 1912 Brazilian cinema was in crisis, surviving until the late 1920s in the form of regional cycles led by devoted artisanal cinephiles and which, given Brazil's vast territory, were relatively insular. Some of the cycles produced extraordinary films and filmmakers: Silvino Santos in Amazonia, who produced an extraordinary record of the region in the 1920s and also a wonderful "outsider's" view of Rio de Janeiro in 1932 (*Terra Encantada*); Edson Chagas and Gentil Roiz in Recife (Pernambuco), whose *A Filha do Advogado* (1927) was successfully distributed in Rio and São Paulo despite all odds; Humberto Mauro (*Ganga Bruta*, 1933, q.v.) in Cataguases (Minas Gerais), whose *Brasa Dormida* (1928) and *Sangue Mineiro* (1929) remain among the most important and innovative Brazilian silent films.

In São Paulo, filmmaking was the domain of newly-arrived European immigrants. Gilberto Rossi, for example, arrived in São Paulo from Italy in 1911, expecting to tap into an unexploited cinema market. Instead, he found a market dominated by foreign films, and sought recourse in industrial and commissioned films, which sustained Rossi's and other struggling filmmakers' fictional efforts for almost two decades. During World War I, they produced literary adaptations and films exalting patriotic themes and Brazilian history. Films reenacting contemporary crimes continued to be popular. In 1919, Rossi entered into a partnership with Arturo Carrari (for documentary) and the Spanish writer José Medina (for fiction). Rossi and Medina produced a series of significant films: *Como Deus Castiga* and *Exemplo Regenerador* (both 1919), *Perversidade* (1921), *Carlitinho* (1921), *A Culpa dos Outros* (1922), and *Do Rio a S. Paulo Para Casar* (1922).

Exemplo Regenerador is the only one of their films to survive. It hardly seems representative of the kinds of films being produced then by Rossi, Medina, and others: it addresses neither patriotic or historical themes, nor a contemporary crime. But it is remarkable insofar as it clearly evidences a desire to experiment with narrative and cinematographic form. Apparently, Medina was intent in proving to Rossi the advantages of U.S.-style continuity editing and produced an agile and narratively efficient short film in the process.

The narrative is simple, elegantly structured, and centred on a well-to-do couple threatened by the husband's amorous adventures. The film begins on the day of their first wedding anniversary. The husband has forgotten the anniversary and announces to the wife that he cannot stay with her because of an important meeting. When he leaves, their servant (a white or mulatto actor—J. Guedes de Castro—in blackface) suggests to the wife that she has yet to conquer her husband's heart and proposes a plan of action. Meanwhile, we see the husband in his chauffeur-driven car going off and arriving at his assignation. A title announces "An hour later." At home, the servant is pouring champagne into two glasses. At his lover's house, the husband receives a letter which says that, at that very moment, his wife is imitating his behaviour: "an eye for an eye." He rushes to his car and drives off, worried and muttering to himself. When he arrives home he finds his wife laid out on a chaise lounge, a burning cigar on an ashtray, two glasses with champagne, and a man resting with his head on a table (all shown in point-of-view close-ups or medium shots). When he pulls out his gun and yells, "What does this mean?" (intertitle), the man raises his head and we realise he is the servant. In close-up, the servant exclaims dramatically: "This is what may happen to you if your 'meetings' continue." After a fade out and in, we once again see the couple in a long shot, this time all amorous and affectionate. The servant comes into the background of the shot, smiles, and leaves.

Although in the context of international silent cinema circa 1919 (three years after D.W. Griffith's *Intolerance*), this seven-minute narrative hardly seems significant, for Brazil in this period of crisis, *Exemplo Regenerador* is evidence of an innovative spirit and cinematographic fluidity, markedly influenced by Griffith's moralizing melodramas, that was rarely exploited in other contemporary films. Its judicious use of close-ups for dramatic impact, well-realised outdoor shots (when the husband is in his car), careful lighting for sets, and filmic narrative structure indicate that Medina and Rossi were clearly interested in pushing the medium beyond the limits of their own and others' stilted theatrical narratives. Given Brazil's subsequent history, it is also, of course, interesting that the film's real "hero" is the savvy servant, who—blackface or not—is represented as possessing a wisdom that the upper class protagonists cannot even aspire to.

The temptation to read into this narrative a racial/class critique of modernity is supported by Medina's *Fragmentos de Vida* (1929), a film about São Paulo in the city symphony genre (the same year as Adalberto Kemeny's *São Paulo, Sinfonia da Metrópole*). Although both films exhibited a similar fascination with the new cosmopolitan modernity of the city and its streets, Medina's city symphony largely bypasses the dynamism of the new urban centre and merely suggests its effects by focusing on two vagabond characters who are unable to "make it" in the new urban centre.

Medina did not film again until 1942, when he produced, wrote, and directed the short *O Canto da Raça*, based on a poem by Cassiano Ricardo. All we know about this film is that it was seized and burnt by Getúlio Vargas' censors for *bairrismo* (local chauvinism or an excessive allegiance to one's own region to the detriment of the national ensemble). Although Medina lived until 1980, *O Canto da Raça* was his last film.

Ana López

Limite

[The Boundary]
Brazil, 1930, 120' (at 18fps), b+w, silent

Dir Mario Peixoto (b. 1910) *Scr* Peixoto *Cinematog* Edgar Brasil and Rui Costa *Ed* Peixoto
Act Olga Breno, Taciana Rei, Raul Schnoor, Brutus Pedeira, Carmen Santos, Mario Peixoto,
Iolanda Bernardes, Edgar Brasil

Over a long period of time, *Limite* garnered a legendary reputation as the great unseen Brazilian film. Mario Peixoto was only eighteen when he directed it, and soon after its release he pulled it out of circulation and took it with him to a remote Brazilian island (according to Georges Sadoul, who was himself unable to screen it).[1] But it was restored between 1958 and 1971, and its reputation has been enhanced by being seen to such an extent that in a recent poll of Brazilian film critics, *Limite* topped the list of the "30 most significant films in the history of Brazilian Cinema."

Limite's central focus is a scene of three people—two women and a man—on a row boat, adrift at sea. They all look dishevelled and exhausted, and the film recounts their stories, by turns, in flashback. The first, lighter-haired woman (Olga Breno) escaped from prison with the help of a guard, but her new life as a seamstress is visually revealed to be similarly entrapping, and she takes flight again. The second woman (Taciana Rei), who initially was shown to be lying in the bottom of the boat (perhaps dead), is revived, and her story is shown to be no more exalting: she is unhappily married to a drunken pianist. The life of the man (Raul Schnoor) is even worse. He is widowed and having an affair with a woman who, her husband (Peixoto) informs him, has leprosy. At the end of the film the man, desperate for water, dives into the ocean, apparently to retrieve a barrel, and possibly commits suicide. After a raging storm, only the first woman appears to survive, albeit in handcuffs: imprisoned once again.

From this plot description, one can understand that the film's title was intended to express the "limits" to which human beings can be stretched in life. But the greatness of the film lies in its style, which also pushed the boundaries of narrative filmmaking. Despite his young age, Peixoto had already travelled to Europe and been influenced by the avant-garde filmmaking of the 1920s. *Limite* has been compared to this body of work, and its relation to the French Impressionist tradition of Jean Epstein,

Germaine Dulac, and Dimitri Kirsanov's *Ménilmontant* (1926) is clear. As in their films, camera movement, camera angle, lighting, and various editing devices are used by Peixoto along with the representation of nature to express character psychology and emotion. But in *Limite*, the repeated use of extreme camera angle and position, the insistence on eliding key information and framing characters closely and claustrally, and the forceful representation of natural elements as highly sensuous and tangible, pushes cinema passionately further to the edge.

The opening of the film introduces the viewer to all these devices of *limite*. The film's first shot is a low-angle view of some crows perched on a rocky hillside. This image dissolves to a strange shot of a pair of hands, handcuffed across a woman's neck, against a stark black background, causing both face and hands to appear to be disembodied. Another dissolve isolates the cuffed hands in close-up, and a further dissolve replaces the clenched fists with Breno's eyes in extreme close-up. Yet another dissolve slowly reveals sunlight shimmering on the surface of a wall of water, which in turn dissolves back to the eyes looking directly into the camera lens. This shot series can only barely suggest a narrative line, but already, a strong sense of desperate, passionate struggle against entrapment and a link between this human struggle and the forces of nature are presented. Once the three characters in the boat are revealed, they are viewed from every conceivable direction, but the variety of scope is deliberately limited through a consistent use of high angle and a resistance to providing any kind of wider perspective on the row boat's location. Like a detective film, key narrative information is withheld from the audience in *Limite*, but unlike films in the classical genre, Peixoto never widens the scope, and one experiences frustration throughout the film. The unravelling of the first woman's story is typical. One has to infer that she escapes from prison by piecing together the limited amount of information given: a swish-pan from a woman behind bars leads to the ground, a glimpse of a door closing, a pair of legs, a struggle between a man and a woman. This single long take is followed by a series of tracking shots, occasionally viewing her but also expressing her dynamic perspective of escape. Her subsequent train journey is expressed through a single image of train wheels in motion, but the euphoric sense is immediately contradicted when the train wheels dissolve into the hand wheel of a sewing machine, and a series of close shots of the woman from a number of tight positions intercut with details of a tape measure, a spool of thread, the sewing machine, and, especially, a pair of scissors, leads the viewer to infer that she is again living in a kind of prison.

In its oscillation between tightly framed images of potential exhilaration (full of dynamic movement) and static, frustrating entrapment, *Limite* presents an incredibly passionate and suspenseful vision of alienated youth in a tropical paradise. Unfortunately, Peixoto was never able to complete another film. He began two in 1931, collaborated on a screenplay in 1950, and worked on another project for Embrafilme in 1983. But his one finished film, *Limite*, is a truly unique work which now needs to be seen widely outside of Brazil in order to gain its rightful place as one of the world's genuinely great experimental narrative films.

Peter Rist

1. Georges Sadoul, *Dictionary of Films* (Berkeley: University of California Press, 1972), 194. In an entry on Peixoto in *Dictionary of Film Makers*, Sadoul wrote that the director hadn't "allowed anyone to see it since 1940" (p. 197).

Ganga Bruta

[Brutal Gang]
Brazil, 1933, 88', b+w

Dir Humberto Mauro (1897–1983) *Scr* Mauro, based on an idea by Octavio Gabbus Mendes *Cinematog* Aphrodísio P. de Castro and Paulo Morano *Mus* Hekel Tavares; Joracy Camargo; Radamés Gnatalli; Heitor Villa-Lobos; and Mauro *Prod* Adhemar Gonzaga for Cinédia *Act* Durval Bellini, Déa Selva, Lu Marival, Décio Murillo, Andréa Duarte

Ganga Bruta was described as being a "landmark in the history of Brazilian cinema" by the French film historian Georges Sadoul.[1] It had a profound influence on many of the future Cinema Nôvo directors of the 1960s when they saw it during a retrospective in 1961. One of the leading figures of that movement, Glauber Rocha (*Barravento*, 1962, q.v.) declared it to be "one of the twenty best films of all time" in 1963.

Ganga Bruta was Humberto Mauro's sixth feature film as a director and his second after moving from Cataguases to work at Cinédia studios in Rio de Janeiro. It was also his first sound film and took about eighteen months to complete while Adhemar Gonzaga's company struggled financially. The delay ensured that the film's public acceptance would be poor since the sound on disc contained little dialogue, and audiences were already accustomed to the technical perfection of Hollywood "talkies." In fact, *Ganga Bruta*'s reception was disastrous and almost ruined Mauro's future as a director. He only managed to complete six more features including his last, *O Canto de Saudade*, in 1952, but he had a long career as a maker of short films (228) and medium-length films (8), predominantly documentaries. Most of these were made at the National Institute of Educational Cinema (INCE), where he became technical director in 1936. In effect he functioned as a kind of film laureate of Brazilian culture, and in 1952, when *Ganga Bruta* was rediscovered during a major retrospective of Brazilian cinema in São Paulo, Mauro began to receive the acclaim his work warranted. He directed his last short, *Carro de Bois*, in 1975 and died in his home town of Volta Grande in Minas Gerais at the age of 86.

Ganga Bruta begins with the wedding of an engineer, Dr. Marcos Rezende (Durval Bellini), who kills his bride (Lu Marival) that night when he learns of her affair with another man. After acquittal from his crime of passion, he leaves town to manage a construction plant, which he revitalises. He stays in the house of the owners, Décio (Décio Murillo) and his infirm mother (Andréa Duarte), and falls in love with the much younger Sônia (Déa Selva), Décio's fiancée. Amidst a lush tropical setting, by a waterfall, Rezende saves Sônia from drowning but later is unable to rescue Décio from the same fate after they fight over Sônia. In a bizarre conclusion, Sônia and Marcos are married, following the double funeral of Décio and his mother.

It is clear from a brief description of the plot that *Ganga Bruta*'s melodramatic events went beyond the limits of Hollywood decorum even in the contemporaneous pre-code era. But the film's style was even more remarkable. While the first Senhora Marcos is being killed, the camera lingers on the ugly visage of the doctor's manservant. From here on, close-ups, particularly of hands and feet, are seen regularly. Apart from suggesting allusions to Luis Buñuel's films of the period, such closeness reflects an attempt to draw the audience closer to the emotions and physical sensations of the characters. It also provides a symbolic texture and marks the film as a highly subjective one. Although Marcos does not appear to be a particularly sympathetic character, the audience is often drawn in to identify with his gaze, especially when he witnesses the lovers Décio and Sônia passionately embrace (and where a flashback reminds him of a woman's betrayal). Everything works to heighten the passion: the intensity of the camera's gaze, the tropical decor, the hazy atmosphere, and the soft focus of the lens, enhanced by the shadows of leaves. But the most remarkable and original aspect of Mauro's lyrical style is that it is very much a mixed one. The scenes in which Marcos goes to get drunk in a bar are truly naturalistic, wherein the illusion of reality is completed by the use of non-professional actors. And most of the exteriors appear to have been shot on location. As such, *Ganga Bruta* is a true precursor to Italian neo-realism and Brazil's own Cinema Nôvo. Indeed, Rocha recognised and lauded the film's mixed style when he wrote that the first five minutes were "Expressionist," followed by "realist documentary in the second sequence," developing into a "Western" with a fight in the bar, all expressed with "a force like that of classic Russian cinema."[2] One of the other remarkable features of the film, the sound track, was lost for a long time. The original Vitaphone discs of Brazilian music no longer exist, but much of the sound was found while restoring the film in the early 1970s, recreating the full lyrical effect of Mauro's audio-visual mélange.

Peter Rist

1. Georges Sadoul, *Dictionary of Films* (Berkeley: University of California, 1972), 123.
2. Glauber Rocha, "Humberto Mauro and the Historical Position of Brazilian Cinema," *Framework* 11 (1979): 7–8 (originally published in 1963).

It's All True

U.S.-Brazil-Mexico, 1941–42, unfinished, b+w and colour

Dir Orson Welles (1915-1985) with Norman Foster ("My Friend Bonito") *Scr* Welles, with Foster and John Fante ("My Friend Bonito," based on the short story, "Bonito, the Bull," by Robert Flaherty), and Robert Meltzer ("Carnaval," a.k.a. "The Story of Samba") *Cinematog* Floyd Crosby, with Alex Phillips ("My Friend Bonito"), Harry J. Wild ("Carnaval"), and George Fanto ("Jangadeiros," a.k.a. "Four Men on a Raft") *Art dir* Herivelto Martins *Mus* Martins, Ataulpho Alves, Mário Lago, David Násser, Grande Otelo, Vicente Paiva, Pixinguinha, Rubens Soares, and others *Choreog* Martins *Prod* Welles and Richard Wilson for RKO Radio and the Office of the Coordinator of Inter-American Affairs (OCIAA) (U.S.) *Act* Jesús Vásquez Plata, Domingo Soler, Jesús "Chucho" Solórzano, Silvério Pérez, Fermín "Armillita" Espinosa in "My Friend Bonito"; Grande Otelo and Pery Ribeiro in "Carnaval"; Manuel "Jacaré" Olimpio Meira, Jerônimo André de Souza, Raimundo "Tatá" Correira Lima, João "Jacaré" Olimpio Meira, Francisca Moreira da Silva, José Sobrinho in "Jangadeiros"

As a rare attempt to create an inter-American dialogue on film, *It's All True* has been perhaps the most mystifying and maligned of Orson Welles' film projects, and its lack of completion in 1942 has tended to obscure rather than foreground its broader historical and cultural implications. The idea for the project took root in a series of conversations between Welles and Duke Ellington in June 1941. Welles wished to tell the "story of jazz" on film, and he promptly engaged Ellington as a co-scriptwriter, composer, and arranger of the musical soundtrack. This was the fifth project Welles initiated while under contract at RKO Radio Studio, and it would have been his third feature film to be released, following *Citizen Kane* (1941) and *The Magnificent Ambersons* (1942).

As the project evolved, a screenplay based on Louis Armstrong's life was written by Elliott Paul, with Armstrong himself cast in the lead role, and this was joined to plans for three other episodes. In addition to the tenuous boundary between "real" and "staged" events, which Welles planned to work into the characterisation, mise-en-scène, and plot of each segment, there was a thematic emphasis on the achievement of dignity by the working person, along with the celebration of cultural and ethnic diversity in North America. Of the four stories, only "My Friend Bonito" went into production, with Norman Foster as director on location in central Mexico. Adapted by Foster and John Fante from Robert Flaherty's story (which, in turn, was based on an actual incident in Mexico City in 1908), the episode was to explore the close friendship which develops between a rural mestizo boy and a fierce young bull being groomed for the ring. Bonito's bravery at the "moment of truth," coupled with his sudden display of obedience and affection toward the boy, would help him win his pardon from the audience in Mexico's Plaza "El Toreo."

Shooting for this segment was temporarily suspended in mid-December 1941, when Foster was called back to Hollywood by Welles to direct *Journey into Fear*, also at RKO. In the meantime, the geographic emphasis, sponsorship, and strategies around *It's All True* had shifted drastically upon Welles' appointment as "Good Will" Ambassador to Latin America in late November 1941, by Nelson Rockefeller, then Head of the Office of the Coordinator of Inter-American Affairs (OCIAA). As Brazilian journalist Edmar Morel quipped, "we [Brazil] sent Carmen Miranda up there, and they sent us Orson Welles; there was an exchange." "Bonito" would be linked to two Brazilian segments to be shot during Welles' tour through South America in 1942, while Welles kept open the possibility of attaching a fourth episode, vacillating between the Inca Atahuallpa's insurrection against Francisco Pizarro's conquest of Peru, and the jazz episode.

The first of the Brazilian segments, a documentary of the Rio de Janeiro carnival, went into production in early February 1942. Finding the festivities in full swing upon his arrival, Welles mobilized a twenty-six member U.S. crew to shoot continuously in both black and white and Technicolor (its first known use in South America), lighting the night scenes with anti-aircraft searchlights borrowed from the Brazilian armed forces. Dissatisfied with the necessarily impressionistic results in terms of narrative content—the Technicolor rushes were dazzlingly impeccable—Welles decided to approach the subject in a manner analogous to the story of jazz. He would stage the "history of *samba*" for the camera, following its social and musical trajectory from the hillside slums to the posh casinos of beachside Rio. The shooting of these fictional scenes—done entirely in three-strip Technicolor and choreographed by composer and musician Herivelto Martins—began at the local Cinédia studio and at various locations around Rio in late March of 1942.

The second Brazilian segment was devoted to a reenactment on location of the voyage of the four poor northeastern fishermen, or *jangadeiros*, over 1,500 miles on a raft from Forteleza to Rio to petition Brazilian President Getúlio Vargas for improved working conditions and inclusion in his social security legislation. Following a series of disagreements and miscommunications between Welles and RKO executives, the U.S. production company sought to shut down *It's All True* in late spring. However, in the wake of the charismatic and articulate *jangadeiro* leader Manuel "Jacaré" Olimpio Meira's tragic disappearance into the Atlantic Ocean in the course of shooting the reenactment of the *jangadeiros'* triumphant arrival in Rio, Welles was able to negotiate a small amount of black-and-white stock, the use of a silent Mitchell camera, and a skeleton crew through an RKO foreign manager, so that he could render homage to "Jacaré" by shooting the remaining scenes of "Jangadeiros."

Contrary to rumour, Welles did not immediately abandon the project when he discovered upon his return to Los Angeles that RKO had no intention of allowing him to complete *It's All True*. However, he was unsuccessful in securing the rights to the footage prior to his departure for Europe in 1947. The footage then "disappeared" until 1980, when large amounts of negative were discovered at Paramount Pictures. Roughly 30,000 feet of *It's All True* (mostly pertaining to the "Jangadeiros" segment) were preserved on acetate "safety" stock by the American Film Institute at the UCLA Film and Television Archive facility. Then, in 1986, Richard Wilson, a long-time associate of Welles and associate producer of the Brazilian episodes, initiated the difficult task of organising the footage and preparing a short documentary on the film's making in Brazil. Extensive research was conducted by Wilson and the author of this article over the next five years in Brazil, Mexico, and the United States, and the project was completed by Bill Krohn and Myron Meisel in 1993 with production funding and supervision from Les Films Balenciaga (France). At present, around 125,000 feet (or almost twenty-four hours) of *It's All True* nitrate footage remain unused in the UCLA vault, about 51,000 feet of which have been deemed "worth preserving." But, to date, no one has been able to locate the 50,000 feet of sound negative containing unique recordings of over thirty *samba* and *frevo* songs Welles had intended to use in connection with "Carnaval."

As it was designed and shot by Welles, *It's All True* would have been a thematically and stylistically heterogeneous text, a trait which appears to have been more strategic than aleatory, in view of the film's discourse on "reality" vs. "representation," and in conjunction with its goal of strengthening cultural reciprocity and understanding across the Americas. In "Bonito," the even, grey tones of Floyd Crosby's frontal compositions, emphasizing action in the middle distance, contrast considerably with the stark, expressionistic play of light and shadow and terse compositions filmed in shorter takes by George Fanto in "Jangadeiros." As well, many of the shots in "Jangadeiros" resemble Sergei Eisenstein's dynamic compositions, in that human action and the placement of objects are organised along a diagonal axis. By filming what was already an especially colourful event in Technicolor, Welles achieved in "Carnaval" an unusually high degree of saturation and spectral range in each shot, thereby underscoring the tonal opposition between the austere, sparse compositions of "Jangadeiros" and the jubilant and lush pre-Lenten celebration. In contrast to many "Good Neighbor" films of the period, which used Latin American locations as "scenic backdrops" or created friendly yet often conflationary and garish "national" stereotypes—often at the expense of historical and cultural specificity—Welles insisted on casting non-professionals, such as Jesús Vásquez ("My Friend Bonito") and Francisca Moreira da Silva (the bride in "Jangadeiros"), and black actors, such as Grande Otelo ("Carnaval") in roles normally reserved for Hollywood stars. He made extensive use of locations and research to penetrate beyond the touristic façade of nationally showcased culture and bring the uninitiated spectator in contact with vernacular forms of music, handicrafts, and religion. Welles also formed genuinely collaborative relationships with Latin American scholars, writers, and musical talent. Perhaps most importantly, in attempting to establish an analogy between the struggle for social dignity and forms of cultural expression in North and Latin America, Welles violated the traditionally tacit, yet now explicit, boundary between the cinematic representation of social reality within the United States as opposed to abroad.

Whatever the ultimate cause for *It's All True*'s demise in the early-1940s, the same methods and characteristics which provoked its censorship and industrial neglect point us in the direction of stylistic and thematic resemblances to subsequent film practice in Europe (namely Italian neo-realism) and to socially committed filmmaking in Latin America with films such as *La escalinata* (César Enríquez, Venezuela, 1949), *Rio Quarenta Graus* (Nelson Pereira dos Santos, 1955, q.v.), and *Barravento* (Glauber Rocha, 1962, q.v.). Undeniably, the film left the indelible sense of a "rare and lost opportunity" for the communities involved in its making, while its unique characteristics and circumstances have prompted its inclusion by Latin American film historians and critics as part of a cinematic legacy that continues to reverberate in present-day practice.

Catherine Benamou

Carnaval Atlântida

Brazil, 1952, 105', b+w

Dir José Carlos Burle (1910–1983) *Scr* Burle, Berliet Junior, and Vitor Lima *Cinematog* Amleto Daissé *Ed* Waldemar Noya and Burle *Art dir* Martim Gonçalves *Mus* Lírio Panicali *Prod* Atlântida *Act* Oscarito, Grande Otelo, Cyll Farney, José Lewgoy, Eliana Macedo, Colé Santana, María Antonieta Pons

Although the *chanchada* was despised by critics and intellectuals through the 1960s (Glauber Rocha even argued that it was a "conformist cancer of underdevelopment" and Cinema Nôvo's "worst enemy"), the genre's unique combination of irreverent parody and carnivalesque songs and dance began to be reassessed in 1973, thanks to the pioneering acuity of critic Paulo Emilio Salles Gomes, who argued that, above all, the *chanchada* was Brazilian and had allowed for the development of a specifically Brazilian cinematic subjectivity. Heir to the long-standing parodic tradition of Brazilian cinema since the silent period and to the *carnaval* films produced to take advantage of the new sound technology in the early 1930s, the *chanchada* was perfected as a form by the *carioca* Atlântida studios (established in 1943 by Moacyr Fenelon) in the late 1940s and 50s. Reasonably well capitalised and counting on the creative talents of seasoned directors, energetic apprentices—like Carlos Manga, who choreographed the musical numbers of *Carnaval Atlântida* and would later direct many of the best *chanchadas* of the decade—and the most popular comedians of the period (especially the "couple" of Oscarito and Grande Otelo), Atlântida had another unique commercial advantage: an association with the exhibition chain controlled by Luiz Severiano Ribeiro which guaranteed its access to screens. Unlike Vera Cruz in São Paulo, its goals were inspired by Hollywood but defined by the marketplace: the production of popular films for popular audiences.

No film among the Atlântida *chanchadas* exemplifies this paradigm as clearly and self-consciously as *Carnaval Atlântida*. A film producer called Cecilio B. De Milho (a not too subtle allusion to Cecil B. DeMille) is attempting to film the life of Helen of Troy in the style of a Hollywood "super" production and enlists the help of an old classics teacher, Professor Xenofontes (Oscarito). Others around him, especially two typical *carioca malandros* (scoundrels) (Grande Otelo and Colé Santana) and Lolita, the producer's own sexy niece (María Antonieta Pons; a.k.a. "The Cuban Hurricane"), argue that the adaptation should be less serious, more popular, and perhaps even completely "unfaithful" to the original. When even the Professor is convinced—especially by the seductive latin rhythms of Lolita—the producer gives up the serious project until some future date (when "conditions" improve) and surrenders to the pleasures of a carnivalesque song and dance extravaganza.

As Brazilian film scholar João Luiz Vieira has argued, *Carnaval Atlântida* is a "practical manifesto of a more realistic policy for Brazilian cinema" that clearly establishes a dichotomy between "elite" (history, "seriousness") and the popular culture of the *povo*.[1] As Lolita says to her uncle, "The people want to sing, to dance, and to have fun." No scene illustrates this more clearly than the one, early in the film, in which De Milho shows his sets for his epic version of Helen of Troy: they are ponderous, artificial, theatrical, and precariously built, and the toga-clad actresses are simply ridiculous. Meanwhile, Grande Otelo and Colé imagine what they would do with the sets, and the film presents their subjective vision: using the same sets, the same actresses, the epic becomes a *carnaval*. The singer Blecaute, dressed in a toga, enters and begins to sing the 1953 carnival hit song "Dona Cegonha" while Grande Otelo dances and stumbles around his too-large toga and animates the previously frozen actresses into song and dance. Here, and elsewhere in the *chanchada* genre, parody emerges as the only possibility within underdevelopment for a cinema that attempts to imitate Hollywood standards and ends up laughing at itself in happy complicity with its audiences.

Ana López

1. João Luiz Vieira, "A Chanchada e o Cinema Carioca (1930-1955)," *História do Cinema Brasileiro*, ed. Fernão Ramos (São Paulo: Art Editora, 1987), 165.

O Cangaceiro

The Bandit
Brazil, 1953, 105', b+w

Dir Lima Barreto (1906–1982) *Scr* Barreto and Raquel de Queiroz *Cinematog* Chick Fowle *Ed* Oswald Hafenrichter *Art dir* Carybé and Pierino Massenzi *Mus* Gabriel Migliori *Prod* Cid Leite da Silva for Companhia Cinematográfica-Vera Cruz *Act* Alberto Ruschel, Milton Ribeiro, Marisa Prado, Vanja Orico

O Cangaceiro was by far the most successful of the eighteen features produced at the Vera Cruz studio in São Paulo, breaking Brazilian box office records and being distributed in 22 other countries. But its critical and commercial success came too late to save the most ambitious attempt at creating an indigenous Brazilian film industry of international quality.

Post-World War II São Paulo saw an explosion in cultural activity, including the founding of the Museum of Modern Art, which showcased cinema (like its New York inspirational model). Also, whereas only a handful of films had been made in São Paulo during the previous two decades, close to thirty film production companies were founded between 1949 and 1953. Among the first of these was the most prestigious, Vera Cruz, which hired the only Brazilian filmmaker with an international reputation, Alberto Cavalcanti, as its managing director. They had a mandate to make Brazilian pictures of quality, unlike the previously popular *carioca chanchadas* made in Rio, which were despised in polite circles. While Vera Cruz attempted various genres, including musicals and comedies, far too much money was lavished on each production, and a certain pretentious Europeanness is thought to have hindered their films' success in the home market. This is not surprising, since many technicians came from outside of Brazil, including, in the case of O *Cangaceiro*, the Anglo-Argentine cinematographer Chick Fowle and the Austrian editor Oswald Hafenrichter. Ironically, with this film Vera Cruz discovered a successful formula with one of its last productions. In its combination of Hollywood Western and native Brazilian folklore of the *sertão* (backlands), O *Cangaceiro* gave birth to the "Northeastern" or *cangaço* genre. But Vera Cruz was forced to relinquish O *Cangaceiro*'s lucrative distribution rights to Columbia before the State Bank of São Paulo closed it down in 1954.

Using rural São Paulo locations to represent the *sertão*, O *Cangaceiro* is set in the near past, the late 1930s, and loosely based on the real lives of outlaw bandits such as Virgulino Ferreira—"Lampião." A band of *cangaceiros* led by the ruthless Captain Galdino (Milton Ribeiro) is terrorising the northeast. In a village they capture the local schoolmistress, Olivia (Marisa Prado), but a lieutenant, Teodoro (Alberto Ruschel), the most sympathetic of the bandits, falls in love with her. Galdino tries to convince Teodoro to leave Olivia behind and rejoin the gang on a mission of plunder, but the couple flees into the *sertão*. Teodoro is shown to be relatively sensitive, peace-loving, courageous, and honest, much like the cowboy heros of "classical" Westerns. Also, O *Cangaceiro* is conventional in its melodrama and romance, but it deviates from the Hollywood norm by having its hero tragically killed in the end. As the camera tracks out with the walking Teodoro, he is shot three times from behind by an offscreen Galdino.

O *Cangaceiro* is also significantly different from the Hollywood model (as well as Argentine gaucho epics and Mexican *comedias rancheras*) in its resistance to making the bandit characters likeable and in its matter-of-fact attitude to banditry. There are also some scenes of extreme brutality in O *Cangaceiro*: at one point a mulatto woman is branded in the mouth. In all these ways, O *Cangaceiro* prefigures revisionist Westerns of the 1960s and 70s, particularly Italian "spaghetti" Westerns, and looks forward to the Brazilian Cinema Nôvo theme of the *cangaço*. Additionally, though many of the film's characters are phenotypically white—especially the very light-skinned Olivia, who also dresses in white—an attempt was made in O *Cangaceiro* to reflect the racial admixture of the legendary *mestiço sertanejos* and *vaqueiros* of Euclides da Cunha's great work of non-fiction literature, *Os Sertões* (1902). And, as a final example of O *Cangaceiro*'s interesting collusion of traditional entertainment conventions and newly introduced folkloric elements, one could cite the fairly authentic Brazilian music track, which spawned a minor hit in the United States. On July 16,

1955, "The Bandit (O'Cangaceiro)," sung by Eddie Barclay, reached #18 on the *Billboard* singles chart.

Peter Rist

Awards: Best Director and Best Actor (Milton Ribeiro), Association of Brazilian Film Journalists, 1953; Best Adventure Film, Special Mention for Musical Score, Cannes, 1954.

O Canto do Mar

Song of the Sea
Brazil, 1953, 100', b+w

Dir Alberto Cavalcanti (1897–1982) *Scr* Cavalcanti, José Mauro de Vasconcelos, and Hermilo Borba Filho, based on Cavalcanti's film *En rade* (France, 1927) *Cinematog* Cyril Arapoff *Ed* José Cañizares *Mus* Guerra Peixe *Prod* Cavalcanti for Kino Filmes *Act* Aurora Duarte, Cacilda Lanuza, Margarida Cardoso, Alfredo de Oliveira.

Born in Rio de Janeiro, Alberto Cavalcanti studied law and architecture in Switzerland. He moved to Paris, where he was involved in the artistic avant-garde and worked as an art director for Marcel L'Herbier in the early 1920s. In 1926 he directed his first films, including a city symphony documentary, *Rien que les heures*, which remains among his best-known work. In 1934 he accepted John Grierson's invitation to join the G.P.O. Film Unit in the United Kingdom where he made a number of documentaries including *Coal Face* (1935). In 1942 he moved to Ealing Studios where he directed a series of remarkable fiction features under Michael Balcon, including *Went the Day Well?* (1942) and *Nicholas Nickleby* (1947). By the time he returned to Brazil in 1949 to become head of production at the new Vera Cruz studio in São Paulo, he had directed more than 45 films in his illustrious career. But the overly ambitious attempt to create a Hollywood-style studio in Brazil failed and Cavalcanti was fired.

Although disappointed with his Vera Cruz experience, Alberto Cavalcanti remained in Brazil after leaving Vera Cruz, agreed to head a new production company in São Paulo—Kino Filmes—and concentrated on new filmmaking projects and chairing the National Cinema Commission (CNC), which was developing a master plan for a National Film Institute (which were heatedly debated in a series of round-table seminars on national cinema issues in 1951–53; hopes for a film institute were frustrated until 1966).

The production company Kino Filmes was similar to Vera Cruz in spirit—studio-based production—and was designed to take advantage of the cinematic boom that even in late 1952 still enthused *paulistanos*. Purchasing its equipment and facilities from Maristela, another São Paulo production company nurtured in the shadows of Vera Cruz and led astray by the lure of studio-based filmmaking, Kino used Cavalcanti's prestige to sell stock to the public and produced only two of his films, *O Canto do Mar* and *Mulher de Verdade* (1954), before folding in 1954.

Although the production of *O Canto do Mar* was exceptionally difficult for Cavalcanti—producing and directing, dealing with inexperienced actors, and managing difficult location shooting in Pernambuco—1953 was a productive year: he was awarded the "State Governor's Award" for his contribution to Brazilian cinema, published his book *Filme e Realidade*, prepared the script for *Mulher de Verdade*, and weathered a critical polemic over *O Canto do Mar*.

An adaptation of *En rade* (1927)—Cavalcanti's biggest European success—*O Canto do Mar* recounts the tragic lives of those who flee from the drought of the northeastern *sertão* to the coast as a first step to migration to the south. The film begins with a prologue that introduces the region and its problems via a poetic voice-over narration and a montage of graphically-matched images. The refrain "There is no rain" accompanies images of the parched earth, the departure of anonymous *sertanejos* on foot and crowded trucks, their arrival at the seashore, and their impassioned first encounter with the sea. This almost documentary introduction (highly reminiscent of a Griersonian aesthetic and Cavalcanti's own earlier work in the U.K.) is followed by a social-realist narrative focused on one family's troubles: Zé Luis, the mentally disturbed and alcoholic father; María, the mother who has been hardened and prematurely aged by years of poverty and harsh labour washing clothes for others; a teenage daughter who yearns for the luxury and fast living of the city; Raimundo, an adolescent son who has to shoulder too much responsibility for the family and his father and yearns to go south with his flirtatious and unfaithful girlfriend Aurora; and Silvino, a toddler who will die prematurely for lack of medical attention, nutrition, and perhaps even love.

The family unhinges as a result of a series of calamities—the death of Silvino, Aurora's betrayal of Raimundo, Maria's inability to deal with her daughter's desires, Zé Luis' increasing drunkenness—which propel the film from melodrama into the realm of a tragedy presented in episodic, rather than strictly linear, form. Furthermore, this tragedy unfolds in a world which the film carefully and respectfully captures—alongside the narrative—in almost-documentary breathtaking sequences of *frevo* dancing, a *macumba terreiro*, typical *bumba-meu-boi* celebrations, dignified funeral rituals, the back-breaking labour of washerwomen and sailors, and the developing urban centre of Recife.

Thus, although in many ways a "typical" 1950s film not unlike the best Vera Cruz productions, *O Canto do Mar* already stylistically, even if not in terms of its production methods, points the way to the independent neo-realist-inspired films of social analysis and criticism that are normally cited as precursors of Cinema Nôvo, such as Alex Viany's *Agulha no Palheiro* (also 1953) and Nelson Pereira dos Santos' *Rio Quarenta Graus* (1955, q.v.). *O Canto do Mar* had an ambivalent reception: box-office receipts were low and, although consecrated intellectuals like Jorge Amado and Vinicius de Moraes praised the film, film critics panned it as "mystificatory" and "depressing." As Cavalcanti himself said years later, "In Brazil I tried to create a conscience of the nationality of films; films would have not only local colour but a real national, social colour."

Ana López

Awards: Best Film, Association of Brazilian Film Journalists, 1953; Best Director, Karlovy Vary, 1954.

Nem Sansão Nem Dalila

Neither Samson Nor Delilah
Brazil, 1954, 90', b+w

Dir Carlos Manga (b. 1928) *Scr* Victor Lima *Cinematog* Amleto Daissé *Ed* Waldemar Noya and Manga *Art dir* Both Velez *Mus* Lírio Panicali, Luiz Bonfá *Prod* J.B. Tanko for Atlântida *Act* Oscarito, Fada Santoro, Cyll Farney, Eliana Macedo, Carlos Cotrim, Wilson Grey, Wilson Vianna, Ricardo Luna, Werner Hammer

While the Vera Cruz studios in São Paulo suffered, in Rio de Janeiro the *chanchada* thrived. And in the able hands of Carlos Manga—an ex-law student fascinated by MGM musicals, who had apprenticed at the

Atlântida studios in every possible job category and begun his directing career in 1953 with the *chanchada A Dupla do Barulho*, starring Oscarito and Grande Otelo—it became even a pointed political instrument. As film scholar Jean-Claude Bernadet has argued,[1] *Nem Sansão Nem Dalila* is one of the best political films of Brazilian cinema because it clearly lays out how those in power ally themselves with populism to remain in power even after a populist coup, as well as the reactions that follow the recognition that such an alliance is impossible and does not lead to power for either side (perhaps politically—yet certainly not stylistically—comparable to Glauber Rocha's *Terra em Transe*, 1967, q.v.).

The film is an obvious parody of Cecil B. DeMille's Biblical super-epic *Samson and Delilah* (1949), which had been released in Brazil a few years earlier. Manga's version retains some elements of the original—especially the "spectacle" scenes—but creates an allegorical parody around a central carnivalesque inversion: what would happen if Samson's hair were a hairpiece? As the double negation of the film's title already indicates, the film is an elaborate proof of what Paulo Emilio Salles Gomes described as the Brazilian cinema's "creative inability to copy."

While a pompous professor called Incognitus (Werner Hammer) presents his newly invented time-machine to the media, in the Dalila beauty salon, Hélio (Cyll Farney) questions the invention and Dalila (Eliana Macedo) sighs that she would like to return to paradise, while the other salon personnel bustle around them: the manager Artur (Carlos Cotrim), the manicurist Miriam (Fada Santoro), and the barber Horácio (Oscarito), who is having a bad day, is late for work, and is severely reprimanded. Horácio's first customer, the truculent Chico Sansão, orders him to trim his beard and not to touch his hair: when Horácio carelessly strokes it, Sansão's wig comes off in his hands. Fleeing from Sansão's fury, Horácio jumps into a jeep driven by Hélio which ends up crashing into Professor Incognitus' house. Without any marks of temporal or spatial discontinuity, we are transported to the Gaza of the Philistines, centuries before Christ.

In this Gaza—not surprisingly figured in Brazilian terms—Horácio is able to obtain Sansão's wig (he exchanges a lighter for it), enters Gaza as Sansão, and becomes governor. When he assumes power, he also assumes the posture and rhetoric of the populist leader Getúlio Vargas and caricatures them. As Sergio Augusto remarks in his analysis of the film, this was the only political posture that working class Horácio/Sansão could possibly be familiar with: Vargas had taken over the country in 1930 after a revolution and ruled as a dictator from 1937, when a coup established the "Estado Nôvo" or New State, until the army ousted him in 1945. Elected president in 1950, Vargas ruled until his mysterious suicide in 1954. Horácio/Sansão's legislative measures in *Nem Sansão Nem Dalila*'s Gaza—equal rights, representative government, a Ministry of Inventions, a national labour day ("to compensate for all those other days in which nobody works"), etc.—invert Vargas' populism and his speeches and political slogans clearly mirror his rhetoric: "Workers of Gaza! Our national politics is in a shameful state! Corruption is everywhere! Everyone refuses responsibility!"

Caught in a complex web of political action, intrigue, and counter-intrigue, Horácio/Sansão loses his wig to Artur (as chief of the military forces), who takes over and announces his marriage to Dalila. Before the ceremony is completed, Miriam steals the wig from Artur but drops it into the fire. In the confusion that ensues, Horácio attempts to escape in the jeep, crashes once again, and wakes up in the present, in a hospital room where he has been recuperating from the first accident. It was all a nightmare.

Almost completely eschewing music and dance (a palace "dancer" is featured in two scenes, but there are no musical numbers as such), Manga produced both a satire of the subaltern position of the Brazilian cinema (the wig is, after all, a perfect metaphor of fakery) as well as a perfect parodic allegory of populism and demagoguery without any explicit links to present-day figures or events (firmly ensconced, as Sergio Augusto argues, in the satiric tradition of Mark Twain's *A Connecticut Yankee in King Arthur's Court*).

The *chanchada* continued to be popular throughout the 1950s, degenerated in the 60s, gave rise to the erotic *pornochanchada* in the 70s, and finally found a new home in television, where the Globo *telenovelas* have reinvented and reinvigorated the parodic political irreverence of the genre for the small screen in series such as *Que rei sou eu?* (1990) which, like *Nem Sansão Nem Dalila*, portray the present through an off-centred replay of the past.

Ana López

1. Jean-Claude Bernadet, *Trajetória Crítica* (São Paulo: Polis, 1978), 210-11.

Rio Quarenta Graus

Rio 40 Degrees
Brazil, 1955, 100', b+w

Dir Nelson Pereira dos Santos (b. 1928) *Scr* dos Santos, from a synopsis by Arnaldo Farias *Cinematog* Hélio Silva *Art dir* Julio Romito and Adrian Samailoff *Mus* Radamés Gnatalli *Choreog* Portela and Unidos de Cabaçu *samba* schools *Prod* dos Santos, Ciro Freire Curi, Mario Barros, Luiz Jardim, Luis-Henri Guitton, and Pedro Kosinski *Act* Jece Valadão, Glauce Rocha, Roberto Batalin, Claudio Moreno, Antônio Novais, Ana Beatriz, Modesto de Souza, Jackson de Souza, Zé Kéti, Sadi Cabral

Ironically, with *Rio Quarenta Graus*, the demise of the ambitious Vera Cruz studio project in 1954 ushered in the kind of independent, low-budget feature film production that would characterise the most significant movement in Brazil's cinema history: Cinema Nôvo, the "new wave" of the 1960s. Nelson Pereira dos Santos, who has been called the "father" and "pope" of Cinema Nôvo, as well as its "conscience," was born in São Paulo in 1928 and studied law before working in cinema as an assistant director in 1951. At Brazilian conferences in 1951–53 he led other young aspiring filmmakers by introducing a number of propositions advocating a truly national cinema, and with this, his first film, he was able to put these ideas into practice.

In 1953, dos Santos worked as assistant director to Alex Viany on *Agulha no Palheiro*, which is notable for being the first Brazilian feature to adapt the principles of Italian neo-realism, such as shooting on location, using non-professional actors, and dealing with contemporary, popular subject matter in a very simple, direct, non-dramatic manner. Dos Santos always championed neo-realism and considered the use of its principles—which radically oppose the Hollywood-style model imitated by earlier attempts at a Brazilian industry—to be a "political" act. And, though *Rio 40 Graus*'s opening is accompanied by a popular *samba* ("Voz do Morro") from the most recent carnival, the tight *chanchada* narrative form is rejected for an episodic structure in which central characters are replaced by the city of Rio de Janeiro and its people. In addition to being neo-realist in its production methods, *Rio 40 Graus* was prototypically Cinema Nôvo in being collectively funded by its cast and crew. Also symptomatic of *Rio 40 Graus*' radicalism is the fact that after production was finished in 1955, its nation-wide release was delayed until March 1956 after it was removed from Rio screens by the local censor.

Rio 40 Graus begins with panoramic, aerial views of the picturesque city. But the direction of movement is towards the poor *favelas* (slums) and a cut to a closer view reveals a group of poor Afro-Brazilians. Instantaneously, in this transition we are reminded of the world of Luis Buñuel's 1950 Mexican film *Los olvidados* (another of dos Santos' sources, no doubt) and Brazil's socio-political reality, which had previously been almost entirely absent from Brazilian screens. The film then focuses on five young boys, working as peanut vendors who trade their wares in different parts of Rio—Copacabana beach, Sugar Loaf mountain, Corcovado mountain (and the statue of Christ the Redeemer), Maracana soccer stadium, and the zoo at the Quinta da Boa Vista. Such a scenario allows for various "stories" to be cross-cut, and interestingly, as the boys interact with others, more narrative threads are introduced. Thus a veritable mosaic of Rio life is mapped out, covering all social strata. For example, close by Copacabana a pregnant young woman tries to persuade the father-to-be, a sailor, to marry her. On the beach itself, a politician, accompanied by his wife and daughter, plots to marry off his daughter to a deputy minister for personal gain. Meanwhile, one of the peanut vendors tries to get money from a beach bum who had tricked him earlier.

One of the boys is eventually killed and another is attacked by a gangster (Jece Valadão) who is trying to control the peanut racket. Less seriously, a third loses his pet lizard in the zoo. He breaks into this unfamiliar territory and, in a subjective sequence of shots, is shown to be transported into a magical domain. But his euphoria is shortlived and he is arrested by a cop as a snake devours his pet. Such negative encounters with police characterise the boys' lives in *Rio 40 Graus* and function as a motif representing the oppression of the underclass by figures of authority. The situation also represents a Brazilian reality, where *pivetes* (children) are forced by economic circumstances to be marginalised and to work at an early age in occupations which have very close links with crime.

The film also explores the pitfalls of the two cultural activities that are most relevant to the lives of the poor majority of Brazilians: *carnaval* and *futebol* (soccer). The selling of peanuts in Maracana stadium leads to focus on a young new player who is initially booed by the fans. An understanding of the fragility of fame and the fickleness of the public is achieved when a goal is scored and the jeers turn to cheers. The film ends at night in the *favelas*, where it began, with preparations for *carnaval*. One of the participants is a girl who had been glimpsed earlier. She is being crowned the local district "Carnival Queen" after being pushed by her hard-working, obese mother, while her father, an aging trombone player, drowns his sorrows in drink. But this critical scene is cross-cut with a celebratory one: a *samba* festival.

Rio 40 Graus is truly a landmark film. In its neo-realist production methods and its complex, episodic, anti-rhetorical narrative exposition, it is a prototype for Cinema Nôvo. Among so many characters some are inevitably stereotyped, and at times the film lapses into melodrama. But in its focus on poor Afro-Brazilians and their interaction with the other levels of society, *Rio 40 Graus* lay the groundwork for a film movement which would tell the truth about the miserable plight of Brazil's marginals, while championing the richness of their culture. Indeed, *Rio 40 Graus* manages to be simultaneously popular and political.

Peter Rist

Orfeu Negro

Black Orpheus
France-Italy-Brazil, 1958, 103', colour

Dir Marcel Camus (1912–1982) *Scr* Jacques Viot and Camus, based on the play *Orfeu de Conceicao* by Vinícius de Moraes *Cinematog* Jean Bourgoin *Mus* Antonio Carlos Jobim and Luís Bonfá, including "O Nosso Amor" and "A Felicidade" (Jobim) and "Manha de Carnaval" (Bonfa) *Prod* Sacha Gordine for Dispat Film (France), Gemma Cinematográfica (Italy), and Tupan Filmes (Brazil) *Act* Breno Mello, Marpessa Dawn, Lourdes de Oliveira, Lea Garcia, Adhemar da Silva, Alexandro Constantino, Waldetar de Souza, Jorge dos Santos, Aurino Cassanio

Orfeu Negro is not, strictly speaking, a Brazilian film. The director Marcel Camus and most of the crew were French (or Italian), and the principal partners in the co-production deal were French and Italian. But the Portuguese-speaking cast was predominantly Brazilian (except for Camus' wife, the American dancer Marpessa Dawn), and the music by Carlos Jobim and Luís Bonfá, which gives the film much of its character, is authentically Brazilian. *Orfeu Negro* has almost certainly been seen by more non-Brazilians than any other film shot in that country and is likely to have provided a first introduction to Brazilian culture for more Europeans and North Americans than any other art work. An indication of this is the fact that the film has been in continuous release in North America since 1958, is widely available on video cassette, and is regularly shown on television. Such a situation is unfortunate, because it means that for many people, Brazil is represented by the picturesque mountaintop playground for the poor and simple but mostly happy people of African descent shown in Camus' film.

Orfeu Negro places the Greek legend of Orpheus and Eurydice in a modern Rio de Janeiro setting. It relies even more on its European source than on the Brazilian play, *Orfeu de Conceicao*, on which it is only loosely based. Forty-eight hours of carnival are encompassed by the film. On the first day, Eurydice (Dawn) travels across town to visit her cousin. She is frightened by carnival revellers but falls asleep on a streetcar and is awakened by its driver, Orpheus (Breno Mello). He teases her and is, in turn, pestered by his gregarious fiancée, Mira (Lourdes de Oliveira), clad in hot pink, while the kindly older driver, Hermes (Alexandro Constantino) shows Eurydice the way to her cousin Serafina's mountain-top home. Serafina (Lea Garcia) and Orpheus are neighbours, so that when he goes home and escapes Mira, he finds Eurydice and jokingly professes his thousand-year love. Orpheus plans to masquerade as the sun, Serafina as "Queen of the Night," and Mira as "Queen of the Day" in the next day's parade. That night, Orpheus and Eurydice become lovers, and after a sunrise accompanied by its musical motif, "Manha da Carnaval," Serafina gives up her veiled costume to Eurydice so that the young couple can celebrate together. During the carnival pageant Mira discovers the ploy, and she attempts to fight Eurydice, who escapes, only to encounter the masquerading figure of death, who has been haunting her ever since she arrived in Rio. Hermes saves Eurydice and sends her to apparent safety at the streetcar terminal. It is now night. Orpheus attempts to rescue his beloved from the clutches of death, but when he throws the switch to illuminate the garage he accidentally electrocutes her. In a desperate attempt to bring Eurydice back to life, Orpheus attends a *macumba* ceremony. As in the myth, he is warned by a medium that if he turns around to face the source of Eurydice's voice he will lose her forever. He does so and sees only an aged black *macumba* priestess. Continuing his quest, Orpheus visits the morgue, and carries Eurydice's dead body back to the top of the mountain, only to meet his own accidental death when Mira throws a stone in anger. Carrying on (black) Orpheus' musical spirit, three young children—two boys and a girl—greet the new day, believing the strains of "Manha de Carnaval" played by Benedito on Orpheus' guitar to actually cause the sun to rise.

Orfeu Negro was shot on location in the streets of Rio de Janeiro and on Sugar Loaf mountain during the carnivals of 1957 and 1958. The film has been mistakenly labelled a "documentary" of Brazilian carnival, but the integration of the main narrative with real-life activities is exemplary, and from the moment when young Afro-Brazilian men in bright blue, yellow, and red shirts burst through the title card, dancing the *samba*, Jean Bourgoin's colour cinematography is strikingly dramatic. The blue, yellow, and violet costumes of the central masquerade band match its apparent cosmos theme as well as the residential setting at the "top of the world." However, while the panoramic vistas of Rio's sunsets and sunrises are rendered mesmerisingly beautiful, the abject poverty of Rio's hillside-dwelling *favelados* is totally bypassed by Camus in favour of showing an unbelievably idyllic and simple lifestyle. Orpheus lives side-by-side with domestic and farm animals and is a friend to everyone, especially young women and small boys. Irony is intended through the (uncredited) art direction, where vertical bars substitute for walls, giving the impression of a cage. But this image of entrapment is belied by Orpheus' free-spirited nature, and only in retrospect, after his death, does it seem at all ominous.

The central conceit of *Orfeu Negro*, the overarching structure of Greek tragedy, is one of the reasons for its worldwide success. One could criticise such imposition of an outside culture as being emblematic of the film's non-Brazilian, European nature, and this would be justified. More important is that the central characters' demise is attributed to their mythic fates, obscuring the miserable socio-political reality of Brazil's *favelados*, the wretched conditions under which a majority of Brazil's black population lives—for example, the neighbourhood's smiling white grocer willingly grants food on credit to Serafina and Eurydice. Politically, then, *Orfeu Negro* fails to look forward to the emergence of Cinema Nôvo. But on the level of art and culture it succeeds in a number of ways. The beauty of the landscape, the exuberant, predominantly black, non-professional cast, and the music by Luís Bonfá and Antonio Carlos Jobim are truly memorable. Moreover, the delicate guitar-accompanied vocals of "A Felicidade" and "Manha de Carnaval," and the percussion and group vocals of Rio's *samba* schools ushered in the first wave of interest in Brazilian jazz and popular music, leading to the "Bossa Nova" craze.

Peter Rist

Awards: Best Film, Cannes, 1958; prize at Venice, 1958; Best Foreign Language Film, Academy of Motion Picture Arts and Sciences ("Oscar"), 1960.

Barravento

[The Turning Wind] [Tempest]
Brazil, 1962, 80', b+w

Dir Glauber Rocha (1928–1981), begun by Luis Paulino dos Santos *Scr* Rocha, Luis Paulino
dos Santos, and José Telles de Magalhães *Cinematog* Tony Rabatony *Ed* Nelson Pereira dos
Santos *Mus* Washington Bruno and Batatinha *Prod* Rex Schindler, Braga Neto, and David
Singer for Iglu Filmes *Act* Antônio Sampaio, Luiza Maranhão, Lucy Carvalho, Aldo Teixeira,
Lidio Cirillo dos Santos

Barravento is usually regarded as being the first important work of
Cinema Nôvo. It was also the first feature film directed by Glauber
Rocha, with Nelson Pereira dos Santos the most significant figure in
Brazilian film history. Rocha was born in Bahia in 1938. As a student in
Salvador and Rio de Janeiro he was an activist and turned to journalism,
cinema, and the theatre in order to express himself. Like dos Santos, he
was involved in promoting a truly indigenous national cinema and wrote
many key articles while he was becoming involved in filmmaking. He
directed his first film, *O Pátio*, an experimental short, in 1959 and before
taking over the direction of *Barravento* in 1960 he made another short, *A
Cruz na Paca*. All of Rocha's first three films were shot in Bahia, and he
maintained a life-long interest in its (mainly African-based) culture.

Barravento is a story of a Bahian fishing community, set in the small
fishing village Buraquino. Firmino (Antônio Sampaio) has returned to
Buraquino after becoming politicised in the big city. He tries to convince
the fishermen that they are foolish to give up 90% of their profit to the
proprietor of the net and cuts the net so that they will return to the
self-sufficiency of *jangada* (small wooden craft) fishing. Firmino also
persuades a prostitute, Cota (Luiza Maranhão), to seduce Aruã (Aldo
Teixeira), who is believed to be protected by Iemanjá, the Goddess of the
Sea, and as such he must remain a virgin. But Naína (Lucy Carvalho) is
in love with Aruã and is initiated into *candomblé* by a priestess who
believes that Naína is already under Iemanjá's spell. Firmino is the catalyst
for a number of drownings (including that of Cota, his lover), and
following the tempest (*barravento*) and his physical struggle with Aruã, he
leaves the village again. At the end of the film, Aruã also leaves after
promising Naína that he will return for her in a year's time.

The meaning of *Barravento* is highly ambiguous. It is structured
dialectically in both its style and narrative. The central characters seem to

be living contradictions. For example, while Firmino acts like a Gramscian man of the people, in being educated "outside" and by trying to demystify the local religious and working practices, his actions cause a great deal of destruction and suffering. Also, while Aruã's god-like status is undermined by Cota's seduction of him, his sexual awakening seems to cause the *barravento*. Furthermore, while the drownings would normally be attributed to nature, the presence of the sea goddess Iemanjá—through Naína and Aruã's characters—cannot be discounted. Stylistically, the realism achieved through the use of on-location shooting and non-professional actors is counterpointed by the excesses of Eisensteinian montage and delirious camera movement. A heightened lyricism is achieved; in one scene, the realism of sunlit waves is modified impression-istically through the cinematography and modified again through the musical accompaniment of *macumba* drumming. A contrast is also apparent in the oscillation between a predominantly observational, long-shot shooting style and the inclusion of close-up inserts. This is especially evident in the somewhat ethnographic scenes of *candomblé* and *capoeira* (fight/dancing) where the music is rarely synchronised with the image. At times the structure seems more dichotomous than dialectical.

While it has been forcefully argued that *Barravento* achieves a dialectical synthesis between religious alienation and progress, and between past and present fishing methods, projecting to the future use of *jangadas*,[1] one could also interpret the film as being somewhat schizophrenic or incoherent. Rocha himself disowns this "unfinished" early work which was started and finished by the two unrelated dos Santoses, Luis Paulino and Nelson Pereira, and claims, not surprisingly, that it is not really "his" film. But with its shifting, elusive text, which only partially explains the "exotic" nature of its subject and in its refusal either to endorse or criticise traditional Afro-Brazilian culture, *Barravento* looks today to be a remarkably sophisticated precursor to poststructuralist, postmodernist deconstructions of Western ethnographic practice such as can be found in the films of Trinh T. Minh-ha and Kidlat Tahimik.

Peter Rist

Awards: Best First Film, Karlovy Vary, 1962.

1. See for example Randal Johnson, *Cinema Novo X 5* (Austin: University of Texas Press, 1987), 121-27; Ismail Xavier, "*A Narrativa Contraditória*" (Ph.D. diss., University of São Paulo, 1979), quoted in Johnson, 121-27; William van Wert, "Ideology in the Third World Cinema," *Quarterly Review of Film Studies*, 4, No. 2: 216-22.

Os Cafajestes

The Hustlers
Brazil, 1962, 100', b+w

Dir Ruy Guerra (b. 1931) *Scr* Guerra and Miguel Torres *Cinematog* Tony Rabatoni *Ed* Nello Melli and Zélia Costa *Mus* Luís Bonfá *Prod* Gerson Tavares, José Sanz, and Jece Valadão for Magnus Filmes *Act* Jece Valadão, Norma Bengell, Daniel Filho, Luci Carvalho, Glauce Rocha

According to Glauber Rocha, *Os Cafajestes* inaugurated Brazilian Cinema Nôvo in Rio de Janeiro, but the film was an anomaly in the "new cinema" apogee of 1960–62: it generated a nationwide public scandal and censorship (and subsequent box-office success) and hardly fit within the parameters of the new Cinema Nôvo movement. Unlike *O Pagador de Promessas* and *Barravento* (both 1962, q.v.), it eschewed a northeastern *sertão* theme for Rio de Janeiro's chic Zona Sul, and unlike other urban Cinema Nôvo films of the period, it chose not to contrast the decadence of the bourgeoisie with a sentimentalised view of popular classes (for example, *Cinco Vezes Favela* (1962), a compilation film sponsored by the leftist Centre for Popular Culture and the National Students' Union and even Nelson Pereira dos Santos' earlier *Rio Quarenta Graus* (1955, q.v.)).

Os Cafajestes is, to some degree, traceable to Ruy Guerra's biography and his status as a "foreigner." Born in Mozambique in 1931, when it was still a Portuguese colony, Guerra moved to Europe in 1950 and studied at IDHEC in Paris from 1952–54. When he arrived in Brazil in 1958, he forged an uneasy alliance with the filmmakers of what became known as Cinema Nôvo (Rocha was resentful of his "foreignness" and even accused him of plagiarism in the unfinished short *Cavalo de Oxumaré*, 1960–61). Guerra also brought artistic allegiances which were markedly different from the resolutely neo-realist pedigree of Cinema Nôvo.

The first scene of *Os Cafajestes* sets up the paradigm which will structure the entire film: the camera tracks through a tunnel, in and out of focus, and emerges in Copacabana, documenting the streets to the accompaniment of a solo saxophone, until it focuses upon two of the fictional characters, Jandir (Jece Valadão) and a prostitute (Glauce Rocha). Thus, although not inspired by neo-realism, the film is nevertheless structured by the elegant juxtaposition of documentary material that "could have been" part of a neo-realist-influenced film about Rio de Janeiro and the nearby beaches and a complexly narrated fictional "story."

Os Cafajestes tells the story of Vavá (Daniel Filho), a young playboy whose banker father has fallen on hard times, his relationship with the amoral hustler Jandir, who is accustomed to the malaise of the urban underworld, and their attempts to blackmail two women—Leda (Norma Bengell), who is also the ex-mistress of Vavá's father, and Wilma (Lucy Carvalho)—by "selling" their nude photographs to their relatives.

Throughout the film, the camera (and sound track) functions with great independence. It is subservient neither to the characters nor to the diegesis. At one point Jandir, Vavá, and Leda discuss their scheme to blackmail Wilma, but the camera, instead of focusing on them, shows Wilma climbing rocks nearby. But beyond its independence, the camera—and by extension, the cinema—are literally and metaphorically equated with psychosexual violence. The camera is an instrument that reveals and lays bare, not only the social underworld, but the psychic deformations it produces. It is with a camera, after all, that Jandir and Vavá blackmail, seduce, and humiliate the women. The photographs (which we never see) bare their bodies and translate their nudity into nakedness. The film camera establishes a direct link between their photographic violence and its own work whose own visual violence is most clearly seen in the pivotal sequence shot where Jandir convinces Leda to swim naked and then drives off with Vavá and her clothes while she helplessly chases the car. When they turn back towards her, they drive in circles and photograph her. The frenzied 360° tracks of the hand-held camera record Leda's nakedness and humiliation. Captured by it in ever closer and more frenzied circles and mercilessly dominated by its gaze, she collapses on the sand. Here, as elsewhere in the film, the camera is aggressive and penetrating, a phallic instrument equated with violence, manipulation, subjugation, and exploitation. While criticising the moral sordidness of its characters, the film also speaks of its own amorality and a freeze frame, trapping Leda, Jandir, and Vavá, ends the sequence.

It was this sequence—Brazilian cinema's first frontal nudity—and the film's general angst—its amoral bourgeois universe is not juxtaposed to any other moralizing system—that shocked censors and incited audiences: ten days after its release, the film was criticised by the church, the army, and the government and banned by censors in Rio de Janeiro with great press coverage. When it was subsequently approved for restricted audiences (twenty-one-years old and above), it was a resounding commercial success (beating all box-office records in São Paulo).

Ana López

O Pagador de Promessas

The Given Word
Brazil, 1962, 97', b+w

Dir Anselmo Duarte (b. 1920) *Scr* Duarte and Dias Gomes, based on the play of the same
title by Gomes (1960) *Cinematog* Chick Fowle *Art dir* Jose Teixeira de Araujo *Mus* Gabriel
Migliori *Prod* Oswaldo Massaini for Cinedistri Productions *Act* Leonardo Vilar, Glória
Menezes, Dionízio Azevedo, Geraldo del Rey, Othon Bastos, Norma Bengell, Antônio
"Pitanga" Sampaio, Roberto Ferreira

In winning the prize for Best Film at the 1962 Cannes film festival, over
Robert Bresson's *Le Procès de Jeanne d'Arc*, Michelangelo Antonioni's
L'Eclisse, Tony Richardson's *The Loneliness of the Long Distance Runner*,
and even Luis Buñuel's *El ángel exterminador*, *O Pagador de Promessas*
brought considerable prestige to Brazilian film. However, it is mistakenly
believed to be a key film in the Cinema Nôvo movement, having more
in common with the Brazilian traditions of melodrama and *chanchada*
than the new films by Glauber Rocha, Ruy Guerra, and Nelson Pereira
dos Santos that were simultaneously impressing Parisian critics. The
theatrical origins of *O Pagador* are also apparent, but through a change of
setting to Bahia and the inclusion of the Afro-Brazilian rites of *candomblé*
and *capoeira*, as well as the use of Cinema Nôvo actors such as Antônio
Sampaio, the film does fit the "new wave" mould somewhat.

A naive *sertanejo*, Zé (Leonardo Vilar), believing that his donkey has
been miraculously cured, drags a cross from his inland home village to the
church of Santa Barbara in the Bahian port city and capital, Salvador.
Most of the film's action (and all of the play's) takes place on the church
steps where Zé is stopped by Father Olavo (Dionízio Azevedo). But while
the Catholic church denounces Zé as a heathen, his cause is championed
by the leftist press and by the ordinary people of Salvador. The film
begins at a *terreiro* shrine where the *candomblé* god Yansan is worshipped,
and the congregation that gathers on the steps becomes a syncretic one.
(Both Yansan and Santa Barbara offer protection from storms and
lightning.) Among the people who gather there is the bowler-hatted
mulatto *cordel* poet, Dede (Roberto Ferreira), who tries to sell his
Esmeralda poem and who functions as a kind of folkloric political
commentator when he recognises that what the priest is protecting is his
"business." A simple prostitute, Marli (played by a *chanchada* star, Norma
Bengell), becomes one of Zé's followers, while her pimp, Bonitão (Geraldo

del Rey) attempts to seduce Zé's wife, Rosa (Glória Menezes). When she resists, Bonitão denounces Zé to the police as a Communist. When the police try to arrest Zé, a riot ensues and he is killed. Only then is he allowed into the church, as his followers carry his dead body to the altar.

The cinematographer on *O Pagador*, Chick Fowle, had worked for the Vera Cruz studio in the 1950s, and the director Anselmo Duarte had been a leading man in many of these São Paulo-made melodramas as well as Rio's *chanchada* comedies in the 1940s. Thus, not surprisingly, *O Pagador* is quite conventional, in the Hollywood mould, in its compositional and editing styles and its treatment of character. However, it presents a scathing critique of the institution of the Catholic Church in Brazil and suggests that a network of corruption oppresses the racially mixed poor people of Bahia. It also intermittently celebrates the rituals of *candomblé*, and especially the musical fight/dancing of *capoeira*. In addition, *O Pagador de Promessas* provided an excellent forum for the different acting traditions of Brazilian film and theatre to come together: Vilar had played Zé on stage, Bengell was able to cross-over from *chanchada* to Cinema Nôvo, Sampiao had recently starred in Glauber Rocha's *Barravento* (1962, q.v.), while del Rey went on to play the central character in Rocha's next film and Othon Bastos later became the lead of Leon Hirszman's *São Bernardo* (q.v.) in 1972.

Peter Rist

Awards: Best Film, Cannes, 1962; prizes at San Francisco; Cartagena; Acapulco; Edinburgh.

Ganga Zumba

Brazil, 1963, 108', b+w

Dir Carlos Diegues (b. 1940) *Scr* Leopoldo Serran, Rubem Rocha Filho, and Diegues, based
on the novel *Ganga Zumba, Zumbi dos Palmares* by João Felicio dos Santos *Cinematog*
Fernando Duarte *Ed* Ismar Porto *Mus* Moacir Santos; the *Afoxé* group Filhos de Gandhi; and
traditional Brazilian folklore *Prod* Jarbas Barbosa, Carlos Diegues, and Roberto Quartim *Act*
Antônio "Pitanga" Sampaio, Luiza Maranhão, Elizer Gomes, Lea Garcia, Jorge Coutinho,
Teresa Rachel, Cartola

Ganga Zumba was twenty-three year old Carlos Diegues' first feature film
and the first significant work of Cinema Nôvo to treat Afro-Brazilian
history from an insider's perspective. Though not himself black, Diegues,
like Glauber Rocha, was born in the Brazilian northeast—in Maceió,
capital of Alagoas—and shared an interest in Brazil's African heritage.
Indeed, Diegues' first professional film, the short *Escola de Samba, Alegria
de Viver* (1962), focused on black culture. This film has since come to be
regarded as patronising in its critical view of *carnaval* as a kind of opiate
of the people, and *Ganga Zumba* works somewhat to correct *Escola de
Samba*'s outsider's viewpoint.

 Ganga Zumba begins ambiguously. Over a series of etchings and/or
paintings—the film is in black and white—a voice tells of the development
of *quilombos*, villages for escaped slaves. The voice-over continues: "The
most famous was Palmares that stood free for nearly a century. In 1640
it was governed by a Bantu king called Zambi who had turned the place
into a haven of peace and liberty." The action of the film begins at night
and with the camera moving past close-ups of hands and faces, shifting out
of focus, and with editing alternating close views and long shots and
cutting from house to field, only gradually can the audience clearly discern
the narrative. A sad group of white-clad slaves chanting and speaking in
an untranslated African language are gathered around one of their own,
beaten and manacled, while the long-haired mulatto overseer looks on
from the doorway of the plantation house. Before the credits appear, the
group disperses and another slave woman walks from the house to kneel
beside the tree to which the man—presumably her husband—is shackled.
Thus the first scene of the film dialectically contrasts the opening photo-
montage.

 The main action of the film begins in a sugarcane field. In broad
daylight, a slave attempts to escape. Rapid cutting and camera movement

enhance the dynamism of this event. But he is caught and when he is whipped, we retrospectively interpret a similar cause of the slave's demise in the pre-credit prologue. In one of many sequences where slaves gather together to tell stories and enact African rituals, a young black man, Antão (Antônio Sampaio), learns from his elder Arorobo that he is King Zambi's grandson. Palmares is never seen in *Ganga Zumba*, but in being discussed often as the slaves' haven, it gathers a mythical status. When a man arrives clandestinely at night from Palmares, an escape party forms rapidly. Antão prepares himself for his role of Ganga Zumba by killing the wicked foreman with the aid of his lover, Cipriana. He cuts out the overseer's heart and carries it to Arorobo in his hat. In turn, Arorobo gives Antão an amulet, the bracelet of Oxumare, the god who protects Palmares. Cipriana travels with Antão, Arorobo, and the rest of the group, but leaves to go her own individual route, taking up with another ex-slave who is working as a fisherman. Following a number of setbacks, Arorobo is killed, but Antão decapitates an informer in their midst, and the remaining runaways are saved by warriors from Palmares. At the end of the film, in extreme long-shot, Antão, framed by an idyllic tropical setting of rocks, waterfall, and rainforest, is proclaimed Ganga Zumba and travels up a slope into the far background with his young bride and entourage, presumably to the promised land of Palmares.

Like Glauber Rocha's *Barravento* (1962, q.v.), the style of *Ganga Zumba* includes a mixture of long takes and Eisensteinian montage as well as long shots alternating with close-ups. But, unlike the earlier film, Diegues' stylistic choices seem to be much more deliberate. Often the slaves are filmed at night, and when a rockface is not used as backdrop, a bright figure-filled foreground is complemented by a darkened background. Such a unity of style seems to connote a collective Africanness, and it is in these scenes—of storytelling, singing, and *capoeira*—that the continuity of African culture in the Brazilian setting is conveyed. Indeed it could be argued that *Ganga Zumba* is not only the best realised affirmation of Afro-Brazilian culture in Cinema Nôvo's first wave but also the director Diegues' most successful representation of his own stated "goal" of the movement, published in issue number two of *Movimento* in May 1962: ". . . to study in depth the social relations of each city and region as a way of critically exposing, as if in miniature, the socio-cultural structure of the country as a whole."

Peter Rist

Vidas Secas

Barren Lives
Brazil, 1963, 115', b+w

Dir Nelson Pereira dos Santos (b. 1928) *Scr* dos Santos, based on the novel of the same title by Graciliano Ramos (1938) *Cinematog* Luiz Carlos Barreto and José Rosa *Ed* Rafael Justo Valverde and Nello Melli *Art dir* João Duarte *Mus* Leonardo Alencar *Prod* Luiz Carlos Barreto, Herbert Richers, and Danilo Trelles *Act* Atila Iório, Maria Ribeiro, Gilvan Lima, Genivaldo Lima, Jofre Soares, Orlando Macedo

Vidas Secas is one of the true masterpieces of Cinema Nôvo and Brazilian cinema as a whole. In world cinema it stands as a great example of literary adaptation and as an ideal work of neo-realism, more exemplary than most of its Italian forebears, while its filmic treatment of peasant life has never been surpassed.

Nelson Pereira dos Santos followed *Rio Quarenta Graus* (1955, q.v.) with another important precursor to Cinema Nôvo, *Rio Zona Norte*, featuring *chanchada* star Grande Otelo, in 1957. But this second part of an intended three-part trilogy on Rio life and popular culture was too costly, and the director was unable to start another feature for four years. This was going to be the adaptation of Graciliano Ramos' novel, *Vidas Secas*—literally translated as "Dry Lives"—but it rained on the *sertão* in 1961, so that cast and crew improvised a completely different project, *Mandacaru Vermelho*—variously called a "Bossa Nova Western" and "Romeo and Juliet of the *sertão*." It wasn't until after he directed the important and controversial but neglected adaptation of the (self-proclaimed) reactionary writer Nelson Rodrigues' *Boca de Ouro* in 1962 that dos Santos was able to return to the northeast to make his film of *Vidas Secas*.

Graciliano Ramos' classic novel in the Brazilian naturalist tradition was written in 1938. It has an anthology structure, wherein a series of short stories are loosely connected by having each focus on a different member of a peasant family—including the dog, Baleia—battling drought, hunger, and other impoverishments such as the lack of education. In the film, dos Santos collected the separate stories into a linear narrative but obeyed most of the other structuring principles of the literary source, including a shifting double perspective about which Antônio Cândido writes: "Without recourse to introspection, inner life is described through the situation of a character within a context of actions and events."[1] While the novel is written in the third person throughout, Ramos describes what the characters seem to be thinking and feeling. In the film, occasional point-of-view shots translate this relative subjectivity. Burning white shots of the sun transfer the sensation of dry heat to the film audience, while birds in the sky are rendered in low-angle shots, apparently representing the family members' desires for food, freedom, and escape. The camera is placed at the level of the children to view through their eyes, and, most strikingly of all, the dog Baleia's perceptual subjectivity is represented as she is dying, shot by her master to put her out of her misery.

Vidas Secas, the film, begins in 1940 and ends in 1942 with Fabiano (Atila Iório), his wife Vitoria (Maria Ribeiro), and their two sons (Gilvan and Genivaldo Lima) on the road, looking for a place to live away from drought and hunger. During the first journey, they are forced to kill their parrot for sustenance, and after a few days they discover an abandoned ranch. Their arrival is accompanied by winter rains, and they elect to stay. However, the absentee landlord, played by Jofre Soares, soon returns. He attempts to evict the family, but when Fabiano convinces him of his ability as a *vaqueiro* (cowherd), they are allowed to remain. Their daily life on the ranch is interspersed by two trips to the nearest town. On the first, Fabiano is cheated out of his full wages by the landlord and is also denied access to the marketplace: he is not allowed to sell pork. On the second occasion the whole family travels to town for a festive holiday. Separated from his wife and children (who are attending church), Fabiano is again cheated, this time at cards. He fights back but is thrown in jail, and Vitoria and the two boys wait outside overnight for his release. When summer and the inevitable drought recur, the family has no option but to leave their ranch haven and the dead Baleia behind. They slowly trek past the now-familiar *caatinga* (scrub vegetation) of the barren desert-like *sertão*.

Dos Santos and cinematographer Luiz Carlos Barreto were able to devise a "dry, harsh" style for *Vidas Secas* which not only complemented the subject matter and the novel's style but also set the pattern for films using the *Nordeste* as theme. White dominates the image. Blank white frames are interspersed with shots of birds in the sky. After Fabiano's night in jail, an extremely bright light shines through the bars of his cell. This is immediately followed by a shot of the sun rising over a rooftop, with the blinding light facing the camera, bleaching out the image. Such an elemental approach is matched on the soundtrack. There is very little dialogue and music is only heard twice in the film—on both occasions it is diegetic: the landowner's daughter's violin lesson and a *bumba-meu-boi* ceremony in town. The other examples of sound (such as birds singing) are discreet, and as an audience we find ourselves in the position of being attentive to minimal yet intensely descriptive sound and image tracks. Editing provides us with sequences within which an impression of the rigours of daily life is balanced by a naturalist perspective on the "connect-edness" of humans and the rest of the natural world. Dialogue would be superfluous. A typical sequence of shots is as follows. Fabiano has just been shooting at the birds: Long take, straight at the sun, over distant hills—cut—Fabiano in medium shot whispering in the background —cut—repeat of the first shot of the sun—cut—the dog, Baleia, sleeping—cut—Vitoria at the doorway of the house, praying—cut—younger boy—cut—Baleia, again—cut—deep focus shot, with mother and child in doorway, and father below the house—cut—Fabiano kneels down—cut—track out from sun—cut—track left in bushes—cut—birds on trees against sun—cut—cattle—cut—more cattle—cut—cactus, sounds of chopping—cut—Fabiano chops cactus, etc. . . .

Of course, it is impossible for a film to physically transmit experiences such as dry heat and hunger to an audience, but *Vidas Secas* comes closer to this ideal than almost any other film. It is also very successful at leading us to empathise with its peasant characters, bringing us to an understanding of their attempts at living a dignified life despite their "culture of poverty." Moreover, *Vidas Secas* never sentimentalises their plight in the way that other films do—such as John Ford's adaptation of *The Grapes of Wrath* (1940)—even though, in leaving us with the family on the move, the film ends optimistically. Indeed, it is dos Santos' brilliant direction of the mostly non-professional cast and camera alike, especially his structuring use of motif, that leaves an indelible impression on the viewer of *Vidas Secas*. Most memorable of all is the squeaking sound of the family's oxcart wheel, which opens and closes the film. Initially, the piercing, grating, unpleasant sound is unaccompanied by an image. Thus, the audience struggles to understand the disturbing noise. When its source is revealed, we begin to realise that the ungreased axle is, like the silence, a sound-sign of dryness, of drought. We leave the theatre with the sound of "barren lives" ringing in our ears.

Peter Rist

1. Quoted by Ralph Edward Dimmick (trans.) in his Introduction to Graciliano Ramos, *Barren Lives* (Austin: University of Texas Press, 1987), xvii.

A Meia-Noite Levarei Sua Alma

At Midnight I'll Take Your Soul
Brazil, 1963, 81', b+w

Dir José Mojica Marins (b. 1929) *Scr* Mojica Marins *Cinematog* Giorgio Attili *Ed* Luiz Elias *Art dir* José Vedovato *Prod* Geraldo Martins Simões, Ilídio Martins Simões, and Arildo Iruam for Indústria Cinematográfica Apolo *Act* José Mojica Marins, Magda Mei, Nivaldo de Lima, Eucaris "Karé" de Morais, Valéria Vasquez, Ilídio Martins Simões

A Meia-Noite Levarei Sua Alma is, according to José Mojica Marins scholar Horácio Higuchi, the "first full-blooded horror film produced in Brazil."[1] Made one year before the military coup and the subsequent purging of dissident elements in Brazilian society, *A Meia-Noite* signalled the beginning of Mojica Marins' long-time battle with Brazilian censors, conservatives, and mainstream critics. (For example, *Ritual dos Sádicos*, made in 1969, was banned in Brazil until 1986.) It is not difficult to see why *A Meia-Noite* incurred such censorious wrath in a predominantly Roman Catholic country, soon to fall under military rule.

A Meia-Noite introduces the character Zé do Caixão (literally "Joseph the Coffin" but translated to "Coffin Joe" in North America), Mojica Marins' perverse alter ego/whipping boy. Zé do Caixão, played by Mojica Marins, is a sadistic, heathen undertaker dressed in black cape and top hat who terrorizes a God-fearing small community. Zé's wife, Lenita, is unable to bear him a son. This drives Zé to a series of vicious linked murders of his wife, his best friend Antônio, and the town doctor Rodolfo. In between the final two murders, he beats and rapes Antônio's fiancée Terezinha. After the rape, Terezinha hangs herself but not before she casts a curse on Zé and vows to return from the grave to "take his soul away." The film climaxes on "The Day of the Dead" with Zé stalked by his conscience through an atmospheric graveyard setpiece. Zé comes across the "Procession of the Dead" (a negative image) and sees his own corpse being carried in a coffin (shades of Carl Theodor Dreyer's *Vampyr*, 1932). Zé takes refuge in a crypt where he comes across the maggot-infested corpses of Antônio and Terezinha. The shock leaves him in a death-like state, upside down with eyes bulging. (He may have "died" in this film, but the popular Zé do Caixão was revived for subsequent films.)

The intensity of the murders and violence in the film were no doubt shocking for a 1963 Brazilian audience: Lenita is made unconscious with chloroform, tied up, then victimized by a (real) tarantula; Antônio is bludgeoned, then drowned in a bathtub; Dr. Rodolfo has his eyes gouged, then is set afire; and a minor character has a finger savagely severed with a broken wine bottle. The Sadean glee and Nietzschean moral superiority with which Zé commits this carnage makes it all the more horrific. Equally controversial is Zé's flagrant anti-Catholicism. Zé eats meat on Good Friday, taunts the dead, imbeds Christ's crown of thorns into a man's face, and refers to faith as a "symbol of ignorance." What is perhaps most subversive is that Zé's unbridled evil as it is played out in the film cannot be explained by his anti-Catholicism. No previous Brazilian film could have prepared the audience for the film's double-edged sword of intense violence and overt blasphemy. The subsequent controversy and distribution problems incurred by the film led the prominent Cinema Nôvo director Glauber Rocha, in a polemical gesture no doubt, to call Mojica Marins "the greatest moviemaker in the world."

As the first horror feature (and third film) from Brazil's preeminent horror filmmaker, *A Meia-Noite* is important for several reasons. It marked the beginning of Mojica Marins' enduring creative relationship with Italian-born cinematographer Giorgio Attili and editor Luiz Elias. (A third important collaboration, with screenwriter Rubens Francisco Lucchetti, began in 1966 with *O Estranho Mundo de Zé do Caixão.*) As such, it is Mojica Marins' first film to feature Attili's atmospheric and resourceful camerawork and to show glimpses of Elias' frenetic editing style. Other Mojica Marins touches include the creative use of postsynchronized sound and non-diegetic direct audience addresses by fictional characters (the two scenes by Zé do Caixão and the Gypsy woman which frame the credit sequence). The film also initiates many of Mojica Marins' recurring themes and imagery: anti-Catholicism, sadism, and misogyny. Most important, it introduces a character, the horror-philosopher Zé do Caixão, who has gone on to become Brazil's most popular cult-horror icon.

Zé do Caixão has become a virtual spin-off industry for Mojica Marins with public and stage appearances, spook-shows, comic books, songs, *fotonovelas*, television shows, and a horror phone-in service. The down side of such an effective shift from fiction to popular consciousness is that Mojica Marins has had difficulty separating himself from his fictional creation. So much so that in 1982, when Mojica Marins ran for Congress with the Brazilian Workers' Party (PT), he lost in his riding because his votes were split between José Mojica Marins and Zé do Caixão! As

Higuchi writes, "Now at the peak of his popularity, across different age and social groups, José Mojica Marins/Zé do Caixão is truly a national institution."

However one may feel toward Mojica Marins' use of explicit violence, gleeful sadism, or misogyny, one must come to terms with the incredible popularity he has achieved with the working class and underprivileged. Mojica Marins has claimed to be a champion for the underdogs of society. (He ran his brief political campaign with the motto "In defence of grave-diggers, garbage collectors and filmmakers!") Perhaps Brazil was a nation ripe for the mixed ideological underpinnings of Mojica Marins' films, part progressive—critiques of authority, anti-Catholicism—and part conservative—sexism, extreme individualism, instinct over reason. As a self-educated filmmaker in a patriarchal country with one of the lowest literacy rates in South America, one could understand his appeal to the "underdogs" of society.

Thanks to the collective efforts of Mike Vraney of Something Weird Video (the authorised dealer of Mojica Marins' video releases in the U.S., where he is known by the patronymic Marins) and Brazilian writers Horácio Higuchi (who supervised the subtitling of the video transfers) and André Barcinski, Mojica Marins' work can be properly situated within the peak of the horror film's international period. His large horror output gives further evidence that the cutting edge of horror in the 1950s and '60s was being produced outside of the U.S. (Italy, Mexico, Spain, Brazil, Great Britain, Japan).

Donato Totaro

1. Horácio Higuchi, "José Mojica Marins: The Madness in his Method," *Monster! International* 3 (October 1993): 7.

Os Fuzis

The Guns [The Rifles]
Brazil, 1964, 109', b+w

Dir Ruy Guerra (b. 1931) *Scr* Miguel Torres, Pierre Peligri, and Guerra *Cinematog* Ricardo Aronovich *Ed* Raimundo Higino and Guerra *Art dir* Calazans Netto *Mus* Moacir Santos *Prod* Jarbas Barbosa and Gilberto Perrone for Copacabana Filmes, Daga Filmes, and Embracine Filmes *Act* Átila Iório, Nelson Xavier, Maria Gladys, Ivan Candido, Hugo Carvana, Leonides Bayer, Paulo César Pereio, Maurício Loyola, Ruy Polanah, Joel Barcelos, Antônio Sampaio

By exploring relations between and within classes and groups during a campaign to protect a northeastern landowner's harvest against starving peasants and *beatos*, *Os Fuzis* deserves its acclaim as one of most important political and anti-militarist films ever made. It is also the quintessential film of Cinema Nôvo's "first phase." It mixes documentary and fictional modes and focuses on the interface of urban and rural proletariat, involving all four "problems" identified by Robert Stam and Randal Johnson as key issues: "starvation, violence, religious alienation and economic exploitation."[1]

Ruy Guerra is probably the most international and independent but least prolific of the major Cinema Nôvo directors, having directed only eleven features—in France, Mozambique, Mexico, and Brazil, as well as in coproduction with Spain—in the more than thirty years since his scandalous debut with *Os Cafajestes* (q.v.) in 1962. In 1976, he would film a follow-up to *Os Fuzis*, depicting the same characters fifteen years later in the city, in *A Queda* (q.v.). *Os Fuzis*, Guerra's second feature, was originally conceived in Europe as a story of a wolf pack's attack on a village. He had intended to make the film in Greece in 1958. The changes in subject and location to northeastern Brazil proved to be fortuitous. *Os Fuzis* begins with the cracked, anguished voice of a mystic (Antônio Sampaio) telling of the wrath of God. The dark screen is gradually brightened by the sun, and when the voice says that "there was an animal searching amongst the scraps of food," the camera tilts down to the barren ground. A tale is recounted of an animal facing great hardship and of the miracle of rain blessing the people to whom the animal belonged. But the film's images of a desolate landscape, empty of people, belie the account, except for the presence of an ox, which occasionally turns towards the camera and which is revealed again at the end of the sequence after a long pan past scrub and out-of-focus detail. The credits then appear on the screen.

The pre-credit tale is immediately alluded to in a shot where *beatos* follow a mystic who is leading an ox away from the camera along a dirt road. Throughout the film, peasants and other religious followers, who mostly remain silent and motionless, provide a commentary on hunger and blind faith and a backdrop to the main narrative line of a small army unit called to Milagres by the mayor, Vicente Ferreira, to protect food which is to be shipped elsewhere. At the end of the film a huge congregation is shown devouring the body of the sacred ox which has finally been slain. The people in these scenes are non-professional actors, inhabitants of Milagres, Tartaruga, and Nova Itarana where the film was made, but the participants in the interrelated story are professional actors. This difference is one of the key elements in *Os Fuzis*'s dialectical structure.

Roberto Schwarz and Randal Johnson have both written convincingly on how the use of non-professional and professional actors is part of a larger dialectical equation of documentary and fiction forms.[2] Yet both groups perform in a simultaneously stylized and realist manner. The soldiers are seemingly in continuous motion. When they are not actually moving, the camera shifts its perspective from one character to another and continues the dynamic feel and the sense of flux. In shots of Milagres' town square, where people have gathered to demand food, the soldiers wander amongst them, but the northeasterners are shown almost frozen in their standing or seated positions. The implacability and passivity of the northeast situation in the background is rendered timeless and thrown into sharp relief by the chaotic restlessness of the foregrounded soldiers, combined in long takes through the use of a wide angle lens. Indeed, the evidence of *Os Fuzis* confirms the assessment that Guerra is profoundly formalist.

Amongst the soldiers, boredom quickly takes over. They play games, in one of which Pedro accidentally kills a Milagres resident while aiming his rifle at a goat. A conflict develops between Mário (Nelson Xavier), who is becoming involved with a young woman from the town, Luiza (Maria Gladys), and the others. Mário befriends a truckdriver, Gaúcho (Atila Iório), who, while just passing through, meets up with the soldiers in a drinking establishment. Gaúcho gradually identifies himself with the plight of the northeasterners, and when a man carries his child, dead from hunger, into the town bar, he reacts. Dashing outside with a rifle, he tries to stop a truckload of food from driving away. In the ensuing sequence, rendered delirious by Ricardo Aronovich's rapidly moving hand-held camera and fast cutting, he is killed by a crazed Zé (Hugo Carvana). Mário, who tries to stop the killing, breaks down when he finds his dead friend, Gaúcho.

The raw power of the last scene in the narrative transmits the film's anti-militarist message and invokes the madness of the oppressive and repressive situation: denying the people their right to sustenance. Throughout *Os Fuzis*, cross-cutting invites the viewer to interrelate the story with the various pseudo-documentary scenes of neo-mythological gatherings and journeys and thus see blind religious faith in a political context: hunger caused by institutionalised repression. Mysticism is hence demystified. Also, one can understand that the characters of Mário and Gaúcho become politicised through the duration of the film. In effect, they experience a consciousness-raising (Paulo Freire's concept of *conscientização*). Ruy Guerra offers no concrete answers in his cinematic exploration of Brazil's northeast, but his brilliant, truly dialectical analysis engages both the emotions and the intellect in the process of struggling to feel and understand the alienating forces at work. We viscerally experience the burning sun and parched earth at the film's opening and the ugly, realistic violence of Gaúcho's slaughter near the end, while we are distanced enough to think through *Os Fuzis'* many dichotomies—such as country/city, poor/rich, past/present, and myth/reality—to comprehend Guerra's call for change.

Peter Rist

Awards: Special Jury Prize, Berlin, 1964.

1. Randal Johnson and Robert Stam, "The Shape of Brazilian Film History," *Brazilian Cinema*, Johnson and Stam, eds. (East Rutherford, N.J.: Associated University Presses, 1982), 33-4.
2. Roberto Schwarz, "Cinema and *The Guns*," trans. Randal Johnson and Robert Stam, *Brazilian Cinema*, op. cit., 128-33; Randal Johnson, *Cinema Novo X 5* (Austin: University of Texas Press, 1987), 99-105.

Deus e o Diabo na Terra do Sol

Black God, White Devil
Brazil, 1964, 125' (U.S. release 102'), b+w

Dir Glauber Rocha (1928–1981) *Scr* Rocha, Walter Lima Jr., and Paulo Gil Soares *Cinematog* Waldemar Lima *Ed* Rafael Valverde *Art dir* Soares *Mus* Heitor Villa-Lobos; songs by Sérgio Ricardo (music) and Rocha (lyrics) *Prod* Luiz Augusto Mendes for Copacabana Filmes *Act* Geraldo del Rey, Yoná Magalhães, Maurício do Valle, Othon Bastos, Lídio Silva, Sônia dos Humildes, Marrom, Antônio Pinto, João Gama, Milton Roda

Glauber Rocha's second feature, *Deus e o Diabo na Terra do Sol* ("God and the Devil in the Land of the Sun"), exemplifies both the director's unique style and the Cinema Nôvo movement's refreshing approach to Brazilian history and culture. It is a truly original work of fiction, combining syncretic *nordeste* myths, *cordel* literature, and indigenous Brazilian music—both classical (Heitor Villa-Lobos) and folk—together with an appropriately delirious mixture of tableaux staging and melodramatic acting, and filmed in realist long takes with strange, jerky camera movements interlaced with jump-cut montage.

The film begins with a high-angle camera tracking the *sertão*. After the credits, which accompany this image, the rotting skulls of cattle are viewed in close-up, followed by the puzzled face of a *sertanejo*, Manuel (Geraldo del Rey). He rides home on his donkey, passing a group of *beatos* led by the black mystic Sebastião (Lídio Silva). A documentary-like scene of daily life ensues, where Manuel and his wife Rosa (Yoná Magalhães) grind corn. Manuel travels to town to ask his boss, Colonel Moraes (Milton Roda), for payment of services, but he is told that the dead cattle count as his share. Beside a corral, the landowner uses his whip to fend off a confrontation, but Manuel kills him with his machete. The Colonel's men chase the *sertanejo* and kill his mother. Manuel is inspired at his mother's burial to become Sebastião's disciple. He makes the pilgrimage to Monte Santo with Rosa, but her scepticism provokes Sebastião's distrust. She kills the leader in the church after he has sacrificed a child, and the carnage escalates when a *jagunço*, Antônio das Mortes (Maurício do Valle), the "killer of *cangaceiros*," arrives on the scene. Miraculously, he spares Manuel and Rosa after slaughtering all the *beatos*, and the couple undertakes another journey to become disciples of Corisco (Othon Bastos), a *cangaceiro* who has assumed the identity of the legendary Lampião. At the end of the film, after the apparently invincible Antônio das Mortes shoots Corisco/Lampião, spinning to his death like a top, Manuel and Rosa escape once again. With Manuel running across the backlands, the camera tracks him in high angle like the opening sequence. Magically, the *sertão* is transformed into the sea, fulfilling Sebastião's (and Corisco's) prophesy.

It is clear from this description that *Deus e o Diabo na Terra do Sol* is full of violence, anguish, and painful suffering. A year after the film's release, Rocha wrote an important article, "An Aesthetic of Hunger," in which he claimed that the "most authentic [Brazilian Cinema Nôvo] manifestation of hunger is violence."[1] He argued that such a bleak view of Brazil's northeastern folklore has a political motivation when he said: "So we make these sad, ugly, desperate films that scream; films where reason does not always prevail. In this way, a culture of hunger, mirrored unto itself, becomes aware of its real structure and can actively begin the process of qualitative social change."[2]

Perhaps the most striking feature of *Deus e o Diabo na Terra do Sol* is its relentlessly contradictory nature. Stylistically, the film oscillates between the poles of realism and Expressionism. The near-documentary exposition of Manuel's family life is counterpointed by swirling camera movements and fast cutting on Moraes' death and its aftermath, scored to the dramatic *dansa* movement of Villa-Lobos' "Bachianas No. 2." Also, some individual stylistic elements contain contradictory dimensions: the use of the hand-held camera usually denotes *cinéma vérité* and the newsreel in its immediacy, but for Rocha, it is more akin to the painter's brush, and its deliberate trajectories have the feel of an ancient home movie. On the level of content, just as one begins to understand the nature of a character, s/he changes. The "Black God" of the English title, Sebastião, is also devilish in his violent quest, while the "White Devil," Corisco, in taking on the identity of the people's *cangaço*, Lampião, reveals a "good" side. Indeed, the original Portuguese title of the film better reflects an ambiguity of character and the sense that "God and the Devil" work side by side in the "Land of the Sun." In part, Rocha's polyvalent character construction can be seen as equivalent to the syncretism of Brazilian religion. For example, Sebastião seems to be a combination of the *beato* Sebastião of Pernambuco and Antônio Conselheiro of Canudos—the most famous Brazilian mystical leader. Both Sebastião and the "two-headed" Corisco/Lampião are related to St. George, and yet both are also closely related to "the dragon." Similarly, the hired killer Antônio das Mortes, who was based loosely on the real *jagunço* José Rufino, is part St. George (in comparison with Sebastião) but is decidedly dragon-like when he massacres the *beatos*. Even Manuel, when he is renamed Satanas by Corisco, displays a potential for evil by joining the activities of pillage and torture.

The critic Ismail Xavier has written that, "under the form of Destiny, the film paradoxically affirms the apparently opposite principle of human self-determination."[3] In this light, one can understand that the incredibly powerful forces of God and the Devil are balanced by the (successful) determination of the ordinary *sertanejos*, Manuel and Rosa, to survive. Here, the role of Antônio das Mortes as a catalyst and the ballad of the blind singer, Júlio (Marrom), who leads the couple to Corisco, are key elements. In sparing their lives, Antônio das Mortes enables Manuel and Rosa to determine their own futures, while Graham Bruce has noted astutely that the ballad, "composed by Sérgio Ricardo in the style of popular *cordel* literature . . . functions like a Greek chorus, foretelling and commenting upon the action contained in the images, and in addition, acts as a Brechtian distanciation device."[4] The last words of the ballad convey a similar openness to the final transformative images of the film:

> And I hope you've all drawn your lesson from it,
> That a world so badly divided
> Is headed the wrong way
> And that the earth is man's
> And not God's or the Devil's.

Peter Rist

Awards: Mexican Critics' Prize, Acapulco, 1964; Best Film, Mar del Plata, 1966.

1. Glauber Rocha, "An Aesthetic of Hunger," *Afterimage* (London), I (1970): no page numbers. First presented as a paper in Genoa, Italy, January 1965, and first published in Portuguese in *Revista Civilização Brasileira*, III (1965); also printed in a different translation by Burnes Hollyman and Randal Johnson in Johnson and Robert Stam, eds., *Brazilian Cinema* (East Rutherford, N.J.: Associated University Presses, 1982): 68–71, and in Michael Chanan, ed., *Twenty Five Years of the New Latin American Cinema* (London: British Film Institute, 1983), 13–14.
2. *Ibid.*
3. Ismail Xavier, "*Black God, White Devil*: The Representation of History," *Brazilian Cinema*, op. cit., 146.
4. Graham Bruce, "Alma Brasileira: Music in the Films of Glauber Rocha," *Brazilian Cinema*, op. cit., 298.

Menino de Engenho

Plantation Boy
Brazil, 1965, 110', b + w

Dir Walter Lima Jr. (b. 1938) *Scr* Lima Jr., based on the novel of the same title by José Lins do Rêgo (1932) *Cinematog* Reinaldo Barros *Ed* João Ramiro Mello and Júlio Bressane *Art dir* Alvaro Guimarães *Mus* Pedro dos Santos; Heitor Villa-Lobos; and João Nepomuceno *Prod* Lima Jr., Glauber Rocha, and Marcus Odilon Ribeiro Coutinho for Mapa Filmes *Act* Maria Lúcia Dahl, Anecy Rocha, Geraldo del Rey, Sávio Rolim, Antônio Sampaio, Rodolfo Arena

Walter Lima Jr. was born in Niteroi, a suburb of Rio de Janeiro. He studied law and history at university and entered the film world by becoming a critic. In 1963 he was assistant director on *Marafa* (directed by Adolfo Celi), and in the same year he assisted on Glauber Rocha's *Deus e o Diabo na Terra do Sol* (1964, q.v.), beginning a close association. (They became brothers-in-law when Lima married Rocha's sister Anecy.) It took less than two years for Lima to get an opportunity to direct his first feature-length film, an adaptation of the novel *Menino de Engenho*.

Like some films of the second phase of Cinema Nôvo, after the 1964 coup, *Menino de Engenho* was based on a literary classic, but unlike other key films of the period it is not set in the city and does not analyze the failure of the Left. Indeed, Lima's first film stands apart from other works of Cinema Nôvo in being perhaps the closest to the subjective lyricism of the French *nouvelle vague*. While reminiscent of the way Cinema Nôvo's first phase concentrated on the rural northeast, it takes the perspective of a boy born into the plantocracy who comes to criticise his class while remaining nostalgic about the past—an approach not unlike Jean Renoir's in *La Grande Illusion* (1937).

Menino de Engenho begins on a series of tracking shots through a derelict old building, gradually revealed to be a sugar mill. A voice-over recites a text on time winning out, as the narrative begins in "Paraibo 1920," following a low-angle shot of the mill's chimney, an image which later becomes a motif, emblematic of the paternalistic plantocracy. The boy Carlos (Sávio Rolim) witnesses his mother's death and is adopted by his uncle Joaquim de Melo—"Juca"—played by Geraldo del Rey, who runs the Santa Rosa plantation for Coronel Zé Paulinho (Rodolfo Arena), the boy's grandfather. Carlinho's mother's place is taken by his Aunt Maria (Anecy Rocha). She introduces him to the world of women and children while a young black man, Ricardo (Antônio Sampiao), becomes his friend and introduces him to Afro-Brazilian culture. Gradually, through subjective identification with Carlinho's character, we learn to view the patriarchy critically, especially Juca's philandering. Although this approach becomes ambiguous through our understanding of the grandfather's Old World honour system—where, for example, Carlinhos replicates Zé Paulinho's cane tapping, a gesture which potentially marks his masculine coming-of-age. When Aunt Maria leaves to marry into Colonel Lula's family, whose plantation is truly decrepit, Carlos is devastated. Sad scenes of loss and sickness are interspersed with exciting episodes, wherein Carlos is invariably linked with nature—often accompanied by camera movement and a range of music, from African drumming to sumptuous Heitor Villa-Lobos orchestral passages. The overall effect of the film is lyrical, especially at the end where the camera rapidly tracks past fields and rivers, as Carlos' point of view from a speeding train, intercut with flashbacks from his past.

Menino de Engenho is an extraordinarily dynamic film which in its rich combination of emotionally saturated cinematic style and historical-political awareness looks forward to Bernardo Bertolucci's *Il Conformista* (Italy, 1970). A number of elements, including the use of a train's sound and image to mark boyhood transitions, seem derived from Satyajit Ray's "Apu Trilogy" (India, 1955–59), and in its playful use of style, including the use of irises to depict Carlos' introduction to love, *Menino de Engenho* is strongly reminiscent of François Truffaut's early work. But the subject matter of Lima's film is decidedly Brazilian, and with its positive treatment of the bandit Antônio Silvino when he visits Santa Rosa, in its switching of musical genres, its use of the piercing sound of an ox-cart axle, and the exaggerated presence of natural phenomena—especially the flash flood—many echoes of other Cinema Nôvo films are produced.

Peter Rist

Awards: Honourable Mention, Brasilia, 1965; Best Screenplay, National Film Institute (INC), 1966.

Terra em Transe

Land in Anguish
Brazil, 1967, 115', b+w

Dir Glauber Rocha (1938–1981) *Scr* Rocha *Cinematog* Luiz Carlos Barreto and Dib Lutfi *Ed* Eduardo Escorel *Sound* Aluizio Viana *Art dir* Paulo Gil Soares *Mus* Sérgio Ricardo (original); Carlos Gomes; Heitor Villa-Lobos; Guiseppe Verdi; folklore *Prod* Barreto, Carlos Diegues, Raymundo Wanderly, and Rocha for Mape Filmes and Difilm *Act* Jardel Filho, Paulo Autran, José Lewgoy, Glauce Rocha, Paulo Gracindo, Hugo Carvana, Danuza Leão, Jofre Soares, Modesto de Souza, Mario Lago, Flávio Migliaccio, Telma Reston

Terra em Transe ("Land in a Trance"), Glauber Rocha's third feature, is the key film of what Randal Johnson and Robert Stam term the "second phase" of Brazilian Cinema Nôvo—between the coup d'état in 1964 and the "coup-within-the-coup" in 1968—characterized by analyses of failure and stylistically moving away from the realism of the "first phase" towards "self-referentiality and anti-illusionism."[1] *Terra em Transe* can also be characterised as one of the most sophisticated political films ever made.

Terra em Transe recounts the political involvements of a poet, Paulo Martins (Jardel Filho), in the fictional South American country of Eldorado. It can be understood as an allegory for Brazil's recent past in particular and Latin American politics in general. It can also be viewed as an exploration of the role of the artist in contemporary Brazilian society: Paulo works as a journalist and even makes a film, which functions as a film-within-the-film. The main body of *Terra em Transe* consists of Paulo's flashback reflections, after he is fatally wounded. Indeed, any attempt at recounting Paulo's "story" is fraught with difficulty because the film's narrative structure is mediated through a kind of poetic stream of consciousness, as Paulo's dying thoughts. Similarly to *Das Kabinet der Dr. Caligari* (Germany, 1919), where the sets were designed to reflect the madness of the storyteller, the style of Rocha's film is distorted in accordance with the narrator's perspective. But the distortions in *Terra em Transe* are much more subtle, being manifested in camera movements, sound mixture, and editing relations, as well as characters' gestures. And, as with Rocha's *Barravento* (1962, q.v.) and *Deus e o Diabo na Terra do Sol* (1964, q.v.) before it, *Terra em Transe* is deliberately contradictory.

The film begins in the state of Alecrim, where Paulo Martins frustratedly tries to persuade the populist governor, Felipe Vieira (José Lewgoy) to counter a projected coup attempt on the state of Eldorado by the rightist Porfírio Díaz (Paulo Autran). Paulo flees the governor's palace with Vieira's secretary, Sara (Glauce Rocha), in order to confront Díaz but is shot while driving through a police barricade. In the flashback we learn that Paulo had been Díaz's right-hand man four years earlier but deserted him to join forces with Vieira. Here, in Alecrim, he met Sara and her Communist associates, and together they wrote speeches in support of Vieira's gubernatorial campaign. Paulo falls in love with Sara but is disillusioned with Vieira after his election. After an apparent period in exile, he teams up with a media magnate, Júlio Fuentes (Paulo Gracinda), on his return to Eldorado and reunites with his former lover Sílvia (Danuza Leão). But, he regains his affiliation with the Communists and manages to betray both Fuentes and Díaz, now in cahoots. In the end, Paulo believes that only armed struggle can overcome the rightist alliance of media and politics and virtually commits suicide on his lone quest.

As with his previous films, Rocha created composite characters for *Terra em Transe*, in this case ones which combine archetypal traits of Latin American political figures. Porfírio Díaz was the name of the Mexican dictator before the revolution, and the character in the film personifies a despotic Latin American dictator. The key shot of Díaz, which is repeated often, shows him alone, braced against the wind, holding a flag in one hand and a cross in the other, proudly gazing skyward. This motif provides a succinct visual abstraction of the concepts of church and state united in a patriarchal leader. Paulo speaks of Díaz as the "god of his youth" and his presence in the film is often accompanied by operatic music. By contrast, the populist Vieira is invariably shown surrounded by people, wearing a white jacket and smoking a charoot. He combines characteristics of the lives of a number of Brazilian populist leaders, especially Getúlio Vargas (1930–45; 1950–54)—who moved far left from his oligarchic roots—and João Goulart (1961–64), who like Vieira was a *gaúcho* (and was deposed by a right-wing coup). And, like Goulart and other Brazilian leaders before the coup—Juscelino Kubitschek (1956–61) and Jânia Quadros (1961)—Vieira is supported by the Communists. As differently as Díaz and Vieira are depicted though, at the end of the film they are compared through the cross-cutting of their presidential campaigns—Vieira with *el povo* (the people) and Díaz alone against the sky and the cliffs, spouting about "infinite dawns."

"Politics" has a generally negative cast in *Terra em Transe*, but the character of Sara exemplifies the potential for pragmatic, radical change in Latin America, especially when she lectures Paulo on what it means to be genuinely political, telling him of her travails: she was jailed, tortured, and raped for her beliefs. Unfortunately, her strong voice diminishes as the film progresses, falling as she does for Paulo's "poetry." Nevertheless, *Terra em Transe* is far more effective as political analysis than almost any previous South American film. Even more strikingly innovative than the film's ambiguous political discourse is its narrative structure and strange style. For example, a scene is established by a dimly lit shot inside an unknown building. The camera tracks towards the street observing passers-by in slow motion, as Paulo's voice informs us that he has returned to Eldorado and that "nothing has changed." He continues "Once again I was lost in the depths of my feelings." There is an abrupt cut to a tightly framed shot of Paulo and Júlio Fuentes, who is introduced to us for the first time, at what appears to be an orgy. Characters drift in and out of the frame in movements reminiscent of Orson Welles' films and Sergei Eisenstein's *Ivan Grozny* (USSR, 1944–46). The combined effect of the hand-held camera, the close proximity of the subjects to the camera and each other, the diegetic jazz music, and Paulo's alternating gestures of rapturous embrace and rude rejection, is one of delirium. The effect is magnified when, after an apparent linear development of narrative—Paulo on the beach, then in his apartment—the orgy is returned to again, and then again following scenes involving Sara, Díaz, and others. Tellingly, many scenes are edited on gestures: Sara and Paulo embrace in a jungle setting—cut—the embrace continues, but they are now inside a house; when Alvaro (Hugo Carvana) leaks information to Paulo of Díaz joining forces with Fuentes, it is the gesture of him walking to Paulo's newspaper office, emphasized by a follow track, that is foregrounded through a flash-forward, before we learn of the betrayal. Rocha's narrative editing structure, which transcends the normal boundaries of time and space, is driven by the emotions of the protagonist Paulo and mediated through broad, sometimes operatic gestures. Indeed, with *Terra em Transe* Rocha brilliantly invented his own very distinctive, oneiric film form appropriate to the delirious political climate in which he lived.

Peter Rist

Awards: International Critics' Prize (FIPRESCI) and Luis Buñuel Prize, Cannes, 1967; Air France Prize for Best Film and Best Director, Rio de Janeiro, 1967; Critics' Prize and Young Filmmakers' Prize, Locarno, 1967; Cuban film critics' award for Best Film.

1. Randal Johnson and Robert Stam, "The Shape of Brazilian Film History," *Brazilian Cinema*, eds. Johnson and Stam (East Rutherford, N.J.: Associated University Presses, 1982), 36.

O Bandido da Luz Vermelha

Red-Light Bandit
Brazil, 1968, 92', b+w

Dir Rogério Sganzerla (b. 1946) *Scr* Sganzerla *Cinematog* Peter Overbeck *Ed* Sílvio Renoldi *Mus* Sganzerla *Art dir* Andréa Tonacci *Prod* José da Costa Cordeiro, José Alberto Reis, and Sganzerla for Urânio *Act* Paulo Villaça, Helena Ignez, Luís Linhares, Pagano Sobrinho, Roberto Luma, Maurice Capovilla, and cameos by Carlos Reinchenbach.

In the mid-1960s, a group of young directors, many of whom had been associated with Cinema Nôvo, began to break away from the movement. Arguing that Cinema Nôvo had become "Cinema Nôvo Rico" (Nouveau-riche Cinema), they proposed to return to and radicalise the movement's aesthetic and formal roots: they radicalised the "aesthetics of hunger" by turning out inexpensive black-and-white films in quick succession which rejected technical "perfection" for an aesthetics of *lixo* (garbage). Glauber Rocha ironically called them the *udigrudi* or underground; eventually the movement became known as Cinema Marginal and established two, fairly distinct, branches: the Rio de Janeiro group—Júlio Bressane, Neville d'Almeida, Luís Rosemberg, and others—always sustained a dialogue with the work of Cinema Nôvo, while the São Paulo-based group—Rogério Sganzerla, Carlos Reichenbach, and others—would effect a more radical break with what they called the "Europeanised and elitist language" of Cinema Nôvo. Some of the São Paulo group found financing through Boca de Lixo producers who provided small budgets for films designed to appeal to the public (via sex, violence, and action) and return profits.

Sganzerla's *O Bandido da Luz Vermelha* is usually considered the transitional film between Cinema Nôvo aesthetics and the Cinema Marginal break: while it still has traces of Cinema Nôvo-style allegorical representations of Brazilian history, its focus is on urban consumer society and the general social "garbage" it produces. According to Sganzerla, who was a twenty-three-year-old cinephilic film critic, the film is a "Western about the Third World." Jorge (Paulo Villaça) is an urban hustler who joins the marginal world of the São Paulo Boca de Lixo neighbourhood and who holds up—and often murders—the wealthy in their own homes. He is called the "red-light" bandit by the media because of his unusual criminal style: he carries a red lantern and has extended conversations with his victims as a sidebar of his unsentimental psychopathology. The police, despite their efforts, are unable to catch him, and Jorge enjoys his stolen money while the press sensationalises his exploits. When the police finally do entrap him, Jorge has already done himself in.

However, as Robert Stam has argued, a plot summary does not do justice to the narrative and cross-generic complexity of this film, in Sganzerla's words a "film-summa" that alludes to a panoply of Hollywood genres as well as to the B-movie homage of Jean-Luc Godard's *A bout de souffle* (1960). Alongside its moments of narrative action, violence, and explicit sexuality, the film includes a dizzying array of self-referential devices—including cameos by Sganzerla himself—within a fragmented episodic narrative that is even further off-centred by its off-screen narration. Sounding like radio announcers, the narrators acclaim the protagonist's "achievements," often anticipate on-screen events, contradict each other, and even lose the narrative thread altogether. As part of this thick intertextual universe, Sganzerla simultaneously cites Cinema Nôvo and criticises it—the famous Saint George triptych that begins *O Dragão da Maldade contra o Santo Guerreiro* (1969, q.v.) is set on fire, the *candomblé* music from *Terra em Transe* (1967, q.v.) is quoted early on (he must have seen the former film before it was released). Simultaneously, he refuses Cinema Nôvo's high-handed seriousness with satiric humour (such as the woman who, while being robbed, protests that she does not "talk to strangers") and challenges its focus on "folk" culture via the acerbic representation of the mass cultural universe that by 1968 could be said to constitute the "real" popular culture of Brazil.

The release of *O Bandido* unleashed the critical polemic that "defined" the movement. Sganzerla went on to make *A Mulher de Todos* (1969) and then moved to Rio and joined forces with Bressane at the Belair production company in 1970. Belair quickly produced six films before Sganzerla and Bressane were forced into exile in mid-1970. Their return to Brazil in 1972–73 also marks the end of the cycle: the Cinema Marginal directors moved either towards more personal and/or auteurist films or more commercial productions. In 1985 Sganzerla directed *Nem Tudo e Verdade*, a brilliant reconstruction and analysis of the unfinished Orson Welles' project *It's All True* (1941–42, q.v.).

Ana López

Awards: Best Film and Best Director, Brasilia, 1968; Best Supporting Actor (Pagano Sobrinho), Supporting Actress (Helena Ignez), Cinematography and Editing, National Film Institute (INC), 1968.

O Dragão da Maldade contra o Santo Guerreiro

Antonio das Mortes
Brazil, 1969, 95', colour

Dir Glauber Rocha (1938–1981) *Scr* Rocha *Cinematog* Affonso Beato *Ed* Eduardo Escorel
Sound Walter Goulart *Art dir* Rocha *Mus* Marlos Nobre, Walter Queirós, Sérgio Ricardo, and
Cego de Feira *Prod* Zelito Viana for Mapa Filmes *Act* Maurício do Valle, Odette Lara,
Othon Bastos, Hugo Carvana, Jofre Soares, Lorivel Pariz, Rosa Maria Penna, Emanuel
Cavalcanti, Mario Gusmão, Vinicius Salvatori, Sante Scaldaferri

After treating Latin American politics somewhat directly in *Terra em Transe* (1967, q.v.), Glauber Rocha returned to the mythical northeastern *sertão* of *Deus e o Diabo na Terra do Sol* (1964, q.v.) to produce his masterpiece of Brazilian tropicalist indirection, *O Dragão da Maldade contra o Santo Guerreiro* ("The Dragon of Evil Against the Holy Warrior"). It is a kind of second part of an "Antônio das Mortes" diptych, which perhaps justifies the mistranslation of the English title.

As had become customary in Rocha's work, the characters in *O Dragão* are composites, but here the mixture of Brazilian cultural referents is more complex than ever. For the non-Brazilian it is almost impossible to decode the network of allusions successfully. As René Gardies has shown in his analysis of the film, Rocha's characters tend to function politically rather than psychologically.[1] But the problem is compounded through some of the key characters switching "sides." Most significantly, the central personage, Antônio das Mortes, enters the narrative as a *jagunço*, a "killer of *cangaceiros*," but at the end he leads the remaining representatives of the people against the *latifundista*, his former employer.

Antônio das Mortes (played again by Mauricio do Valle) is brought to the town of Jardim das Piranhas by the police chief, Mattos (Hugo Carvana), on a mission to kill the *cangaceiro*, Coirana (Lorivel Pariz). He has been hired by the blind landowner, Coronel Horácio (Jofre Soares) and meets a local teacher (Othon Bathos) in a bar. In a ritual, *capoeira*-like sword fight, Antônio mortally wounds Coirana. The teacher is drunk most of the time, while Mattos plots with Horácio's wife Laura to kill her husband. Coirana, who speaks in verse and is tended by A Santa (Rosa Maria Penna) and Black Antão (Mário Gusmão), the mystic leaders of the *beatos*, takes almost the entire film to die. Meanwhile, Mattos kills

Horácio's devoted servant, Batista (Sante Scaldaferri) on the steps outside the bar, and Laura betrays her lover, stabbing Mattos repeatedly, also on the steps. A group of new *jagunços*, led by Mata Vaca (Vinicius Salvatori), arrives in Jardim das Piranhas on a truck and Horácio sends them to kill the remaining *cangaceiros* and *beatos*. As the dead bodies of Mattos and Corisco are simultaneously carried to the *sertão*, Antônio das Mortes forms a new allegiance with the teacher and the town's priest (Emanuel Cavalcanti). In the end, fighting together side by side like Randolph Scott and Joel McCrea in Sam Peckinpah's *Ride the High Country* (1962), Antônio and the teacher kill the *jagunços*, and Black Antão (riding a white horse) with A Santa slays the "dragon of evil" Horácio with his lance.

It is easy for a non-Brazilian, understanding the Western reference, to interpret *O Dragão* according to Hollywood mythology, but this would obscure the film's truly Brazilian nature. There are even resonances in casting and costuming decisions. Jofre Soares always played upper-class roles, so that Brazilian audiences would automatically understand the character of the Colonel that he plays. Odette Lara, who plays Laura, was a star of "classical" theatre and film in Brazil, thus her playing the part of an aging femme fatale—a Bahian ex-prostitute, no less—who is always dressed in violet, is somewhat scandalous, yet always riveting, and understandably melodramatic. Do Valle's large frame, covered by a cape, simultaneously conveys strength, an Amerindian dimension, and a flavour of "spaghetti" Westerns: part "good, bad and ugly." A Santa and Coirana wear their own, neo-mythological *beatos* and *cangaceiro* outfits, respectively, while Black Antão is posed mythically between the African god of war, Ogun, and St. George.

As with Rocha's previous films, the most disconcerting aspect of *O Dragão* is its narrative structure. For example, in the film's first six shots it is difficult to make clear connections between what appear to be four different scenes. Following an opening credit still of a painted triptych depicting St. George killing the dragon, we see an empty frame of the bleak *sertão*. As the credits roll, we hear gunshots and Antônio das Mortes enters the frame right. He exits left and then his *cangaceiro* victim crawls into the frame to replace him. The next shot depicts the teacher giving his young students a history lesson during which they recite dates including that of the death of the legendary *cangaceiro* Lampião. Later we learn that the location of this shot is the same as the next three—the town of Milagres, fronting as Jardim das Piranhas—which reveals Coirana, A Santa, and Black Antão initially dancing in the street and then posed together in front of a static camera. In both "scenes" they are surrounded by local people, presumably their followers, but the temporal and spatial connections are ambiguous, rendered more so by drastic changes in camera style and sound. The sixth shot re-introduces Antônio, in another town, amidst a street parade celebrating Brazilian independence. He is with Mattos, and they look out of place in their stylised timelessness amongst school children who look positively bourgeois, urban, and contemporary (and Americanised). We assume that the opening shot depicts Antônio's general mission in life at that time—killing *cangaceiros*—but retrospectively the shot of the teacher can be read as a flash-forward, since he is ostensibly politicised (though he still teaches archaically, by rote). The film's sixth shot, where Mattos hires Antônio, is chronological, but the three preceding shots could easily be understood also as flash-forwards to the scene of confrontation between Antônio and Coirana. Not only are the location (town square) and activities (dynamic, carnivalesque celebration followed by stylized tableaux) the same, but the characters' clothes never change either. Throughout the film, Antão and A Santa wear the same red/gold and white robes and conical headdresses. None of the principal characters change their emblematic costumes during the film, one of many examples of an odd temporality in the work. The most peculiar example is where the dying Coirana is apparently singing, surrounded by his followers, including A Santa and Antônio, adjacent to a rock face, while Antônio and A Santa appear simultaneously conversing in the *sertão*. While some observers might argue that the cross-cutting here is an instance of sloppy editing continuity, there are enough clues throughout the film to suggest that this is yet another example of Rocha's unique narrative style. We never learn how key locations—the town, the *sertão*, the cliff—are linked together. The editing straddles time and space to link the legends of Brazil's *nordeste* past with its U.S.-dependency present: near the end, for example, Antônio and the teacher suddenly appear at a rural truck stop. This jarring contact with contemporary reality is (perhaps) the encouragement they need to return to fight the "dragon of evil," although typically, and deliberately so, with Rocha we can never be sure.

Peter Rist

Awards: Four prizes including Best Director, International Critics' Prize (FIPRESCI), Luis Buñuel Prize, Cannes, 1969; Best Director, National Film Institute (INC), 1969; other awards in Belgium and Spain, 1969.

1. René Gardies, "Structural Analysis of a Textual System: Presentation of a Method," *Screen* 15 (1974): 12-19.

Macunaíma

[Jungle Freaks - U.S.]
Brazil, 1969, 108', colour

Dir Joaquim Pedro de Andrade (1932–1988) *Scr* Andrade, based on the novel of the same title by Mário de Andrade (1926) *Cinematog* Guido Cosulich and Affonso Beato *Ed* Eduardo Escorel *Art dir* Anísio Medeiros *Mus* Macalé; Mário de Andrade; Orestes Barbosa; Sílvio Caldas; Geraldo Nunes; Antonio Maria; Sady Cabral; and Heitor Villa-Lobos *Prod* Filmes do Serro, Grupo Filmes, and Condor Filmes *Act* Grande Otelo, Paulo José, Dina Sfat, Milton Gonçalves, Rodolfo Arena, Jardel Filho, Joana Fomm, Maria do Rosario, Maria Lucia Dahl, Miriam Muniz

Long out of distribution in North America, Joaquim Pedro de Andrade's *Macunaíma* is the great unrecognised political comedy of world cinema. Based on an important Brazilian "Modernist rhapsody"/novel of the same title written by Mário de Andrade (no relation) in 1926, the film is the key work of the "Tropicalist," third, and final phase of Cinema Nôvo. Continuing the political criticism of the first two phases, filmmakers in the third phase were forced by censorship and an oppressive regime to be indirect in their approach. While allegory and irony were used in *Macunaíma*, parody was its central strategy. The Brazilian B-movie tradition of musical comedy—*chanchada*—is recalled through caricature and the rediscovery of the great comedian Grande Otelo who, in his sixties, plays the title character, Macunaíma, as a baby. The film also comically satirises Brazil's illusory harmonious racial mix as well as its "Alliance for Progress" with the U.S. Indeed, the importance of Andrade's film version of *Macunaíma* lies in how the seriousness of its complex cultural and political encoding can be simultaneously enjoyed strictly as entertainment. *Macunaíma*'s gaudy, carnivalesque mise-en-scène, coupled with its absurd dialogue full of proverbs and accompanied by inappropriate folk songs, provide a rich commentary on contemporary Brazilian society. Most significantly, in the words of U.S. scholar Randal Johnson, "Its coded language of revolt represents an extremely aggressive attack on the continued exploitation of Brazil by the international capitalist system."[1] In *Macunaíma*, Andrade uses a metaphor of cannibalism as a parodic, excessive representation of his nation's response to an overwhelming foreign influence, and through juxtaposition and incongruence—e.g., a white male actor playing a mother giving birth to a middle-aged black Macunaíma—sets a highly charged ironic tone to the piece.

Joaquim Pedro de Andrade was born in Rio de Janeiro in 1932. While studying physics at Rio's Federal University, he became an active ciné club member, and in 1953 he made his first 16mm short film. He worked for a while as an assistant director, and in 1959 he directed two short documentaries for the National Book Institute about the sociologist Gilberto Freyre and the poet Manual Bandeira. He received grants to study film in Paris and then in London. While at IDHEC in 1961 Andrade finished *Couro de Gato*, which follows the lives of five Rio boys from the *favelas*, stealing cats to sell for carnival. This semi-documentary short provided the inspiration for and was included in the feature-length anthology film *Cinco Vezes Favela* (1962), which is considered to be one of the first works of Cinema Nôvo. After London, Andrade spent some time in New York City in 1961 learning direct cinema techniques with the Maysles brothers, and on his return to Brazil he put these lessons into practice by making a documentary feature film, *Garrincha, Alegria do Povo* (1963), criticising the alienating effects of Brazil's most popular pastime, soccer, on the poor. In directing his first full-length fiction film, *O Padre e a Moca* (1965), loosely based on a poem by Carlos Drummond de Andrade (no relation), Andrade revisited his first love, literary modernism. After making two short films in 1967 and 1968, he continued his work on 1920s Brazilian modernism with *Macunaíma*.

Mário de Andrade, who was an anthropologist as well as a literary figure, combined Amerindian, African, and Iberian legends with the literary genres of epic (out of the *Odyssey*), Rabelaisian comedy, grotesque realism, and satire to create his syncretic, truly Brazilian hero/anti-hero, Macunaíma. While retaining most of the novel's "tropicalist" elements, Joachim Pedro de Andrade dropped the positive attributes of the central character together with his transformational and rhapsodic powers.

A few magical connections and transformations occur in the film through cross-cutting and stop motion while a Kuleshovian "creative geography" is sometimes achieved through editing together various Brazilian regions as if they were contiguous. But the majority of carnivalesque, fantastical elements in the crazy quilt of the film's "tropicalism" are found in its colourful costumes, make-up, decor, and settings, and on the soundtrack. In the film's first scene, the Euro-Brazilian actor Paulo José (who later plays Macunaíma) is dressed in white and made up as an ugly, masculine old woman. S/he stands on the hard clay floor of a mud hut to give birth in Indian fashion (to the adult Afro-Brazilian Grande Otelo, whom we are told by the narrator was six years old when he was born!). Absurdly outfitted as a baby, complete with dummy, Otelo/Macunaíma has two adult brothers, one white, Manaape, and one black, Jiguê. Manaape, initially wearing black, performs strange rituals—such as carrying around a large stone—which mark him as a *nordeste*, perhaps *mestiço* mystic, while Jiguê, accompanied by a young woman, Sofará, wearing an Alliance for Progress flour sack and red underwear, is a hustler. We are told that Macunaíma eats ants and sleeps most of the time, "waking up only when he hears the word 'money' or when the family bathes in the river, naked." They all sleep in hammocks.

The accumulation of inversions parodies the Brazilian racial and cultural admixture and begins the film's criticism of the country's power imbalance (which encourages a dog-eat-dog mentality). On three occasions Otelo/Macunaíma is turned white, twice by a magical marijuana cigarette and once by a natural water fountain (which dries up as soon as Jiguê tries to use it). The three brothers travel to the city, where Macunaíma (now played by Paulo José) meets the revolutionary terrorist Ci (Dina Sfat). Domestic roles are inverted, as Macunaíma stays at home (mostly sleeping in his hammock) while Ci "goes to work" planting bombs. He even does the resting after she gives birth (to another Grande Otelo infant), and when mother and "child" are accidentally killed by one of her bombs, Macunaíma falls into the clutches of a grotesque corporate tycoon, Venceslau Pietro Pietra—i.e., "stone" in both masculine and feminine—played by Jardel Filho. Venceslau keeps people in cages and boils humans in his swimming pool turned *feijoada* pot—*Macunaíma*'s most overt representation of cannibalism as a metaphor for Brazil's greed and economic imbalance. Indeed, after Macunaíma returns home, to a now clearly Amazonian region, where the only colours are those of Brazil's national flag—green and yellow—he effectively commits suicide by jumping into a pool to chase after the elusive goddess Uiara (Maria Lúcia Dahl). Blood emerges from the (yellow) muddy water, seeping into Macunaíma's green jacket which floats alone on the water's surface, while a patriotic anthem mocks the action on the soundtrack. In this, the film's final shot, Andrade's own statement on his film is clearly represented: "*Macunaíma* is the story of a Brazilian devoured by Brazil."

Peter Rist

Awards: Best Actor (Grande Otelo), Best Art Direction, National Film Institute, 1969; seven prizes including Best Actor (Otelo), Best Screenplay, and Best Art Direction, Brasilia, 1969.

1. Randal Johnson, "Cinema Nôvo and Cannibalism: *Macunaíma*," *Brazilian Cinema*, eds. Johnson and Robert Stam, (East Rutherford, N.J.: Associated University Presses, 1982), 184.

Matou a Família e Foi ao Cinema

Killed the Family and Went to the Movies
Brazil, 1969, 64', b+w

Dir Júlio Bressane *Scr* Bressane *Cinematog* Thiago Veloso *Ed* Geraldo Veloso *Prod* Júlio Bressane for Belair Filmes *Act* Márcia Rodrigues, Renata Sorrah, Antero de Oliveira, Vanda Lacerda

Júlio Bressane had already directed several short films and a Cinema Nôvo-inspired feature (*Cara a Cara*, 1967) before erupting onto the 1969 Cinema Marginal scene with two films: *O Anjo Nasceu* and *Matou a Família e Foi ao Cinema*. Both of these films depart markedly from his previous work: they abandon the representation and analysis of history, narrative continuity, and coherent character development. *Matou a Família* is a brilliant example of meta-cinema which almost abandons narrative altogether. Although it does not make explicit references to other films, it is structured by a conceit already discernable in its title: Oedipal violence carelessly linked to mindless entertainment with a reflexive twist.

The event mentioned in the title occurs in the first five minutes: in grainy black and white and with an almost inaudible "live" soundtrack, a young man brutally kills his mother and father (who argue while watching TV) with a strap razor and goes to the movies to see a feature announced on the marquee as *Perdidas de Amor* ("Lost Women of Love"). From that moment on, the film indiscriminately combines footage and narrative events from the film-within-the-film and becomes, as film scholar Robert Stam argues, a "Chinese box of representations within representations."[1] The aggression implicit in the title and explicit in the first five minutes is worked, over and over again, on the desires of the spectator. Seeking narrative connection and/or clarity, the spectator must fumble for meaning and is able neither to separate the texts nor to connect them: there is simply no boundary. At the level of sound/image relations, the film often seems clearer, but is not. When scenes of urban squalor are juxtaposed to an uplifting *sambinha* sung by Carmen Miranda ("What a Great Country for Partying"), we impute a kind of social commentary. But that commentary is off-centred by the association of yet another popular *samba* with senseless death in another sequence. Similarly, we are driven to link the use of U.S. popular music on the soundtrack—from jazz to a pop male vocalist—to scenes of bourgeois decadence, but that same bourgeoisie is also represented to the accompaniment of classical music and Brazilian pop.

This disjunctive distanciation strategy is continued with the juxtaposition of scenes of violent death and murder to moments of utter banality or of fetishistic fascination: women washing dishes, ordering the maid, and combing their hair; a beautiful woman doing exercises wearing a form-fitting leotard; a woman who catches her husband committing adultery; two girls making love and being caught by one of their mothers. The juxtapositions climax in the last scene, when two of the female characters (from *Perdidas de Amor?*) slowly, with affection and strong erotic overtones, murder each other and fulfil a suicide pact established earlier.

Matou a Família will only allow us to take away from the film the perversity of our own drives for visual pleasure. An unmotivated scene halfway through the film illustrates this strategy clearly. With no transition, a playful scene in which two women (the two from *Perdidas de Amor?*) entertain themselves by play-acting and lip-syncing to a popular song is followed by a long and brutal sequence in which we see a man being tortured through increasingly more violent means (from cigarette burns and electric shocks to anal penetration while tied up with barbed wire) until he either passes out or dies. Without any further explanation or contextualisation, this scene is profoundly unsettling, responding to our visual pleasure and desperate search for narrative coherence with the torturers' satanic violence. This scene is perhaps incomprehensible to anyone but the Brazilian spectator of 1969, who was only too well aware of and unsettled by the increasing repression and violence of the military regime. As Fernão Ramos has argued, this was, perhaps, the only form of representation appropriate for a Brazil that was caught between the churnings of savage capitalism and the horrific practices of the military regime.[2]

After working with Sganzerla, Bressane went into exile in 1970. He lived in London and travelled throughout North Africa and Asia, often filming. Since his return to Brazil in 1973 he has directed seven films, slowly moving further away from Cinema Marginal and closer to a personal/auteurist mode.

Ana López

1. Robert Stam, "On the Margins: Brazilian Avant-Garde Cinema," *Brazilian Cinema*, eds. Randal Johnson and Stam (East Rutherford, N.J.: Associated University Presses, 1982), 321.
2. Fernão Ramos, *Cinema Marginal (1968-1973)* (São Paulo: Art Editora, 1987), passim.

Como era Gostoso o Meu Francês

How Tasty Was My Little Frenchman
Brazil, 1971, 84', colour

Dir Nelson Pereira dos Santos (b. 1928) *Scr* dos Santos, Tupi dialogue by Humberto Mauro *Narr* Célio Moreira *Cinematog* Dib Lutfi *Ed* Carlos Alberto Camuyrano *Art dir* Regis Monteiro and Mara Chaves *Mus* José Rodrix *Prod* Luiz Carlos Barreto, dos Santos, K. M. Eckstein, and César Thedim for Condor Filmes *Act* Arduino Colassanti, Ana Maria Magalhães, Eduardo Imbassahy Filho, Manfredo Colassanti, José Kleber, Gabriel Arcanjo, Luiz Carlos Lacerda de Freitas, Janira Santiago, Ana Maria Miranda, João Amaro Batista

Following the hugely successful *Vidas Secas* (1963, q.v.), Nelson Pereira dos Santos' next feature, *El Justicero* (1967), a comedy of manners, no less, was a relative commercial and critical failure. He then moved from what Randal Johnson terms a "sociological" phase to an "ideological" one with *Fome de Amor* (1968) and *Azyllo Muito Louco* (1970).[1] *Fome de Amor*, in its reflexive, anti-illusionist critique of the failure of the Brazilian intellectual Left, is also considered to be an important work of Cinema Nôvo's second phase. Shot partially in New York, on a trip ostensibly to make documentaries, *Fome de Amor* recalls the European art cinemas of Federico Fellini, Ingmar Bergman, Jean-Luc Godard, Michelangelo Antonioni et al, in alternating decadence, alienation, and analysis. *Azyllo Muito Louco*, based on Machado de Assis' classic Brazilian short story, "O Alienista," continued in this mode, and dos Santos' next feature film, *Como era Gostoso o Meu Francês*, brought him securely into Cinema Nôvo's third, Tropicalist phase.

    Como era Gostoso is possibly the most original Brazilian film made on the subject of the meeting of European colonisers and Amerindian natives. If seen as a straightforward narrative account, then dos Santos' intentions would be misinterpreted. Throughout the film, title cards, which represent extracts from diaries written by Europeans, ironically counterpoint the events unfolding. And as the critic Richard Peña points out, the viewer is uncharacteristically positioned, perhaps uncomfortably, as a Tupi native on the shoreline looking out to sea at the French and Portuguese when they arrive in Brazil.[2] But the director deliberately resisted encouraging the film's spectator to identify with any of the characters by staging most of the action in long and medium shots. Indeed, on one level, *Como era Gostoso* deconstructs ethnographic filmmaking while it contradicts written history and presents a satirical Tropicalist treaty on cannibalism as metaphor.

The plot of dos Santos' film is fairly simple. A Frenchman (played by Arduino Colassanti) is captured by Tupi Indians. He is to be killed by the Tupinambas, but they suspend his sentence when they discover that "Francês" is an expert on military technology. He helps them fight their rivals, the Tupiniquims (who support the French, while his captors support the Portuguese). Francês and a young Tupi woman, Seboipepe (Ana Maria Magalhães) become lovers, and together they discover some hidden treasure. But she chooses to not accompany him on a planned escape, and he unexpectedly stays behind with her. After the battle he is killed as part of the Tupinambas' victory celebration and then eaten in a ritual banquet. Seboipepe seems to delight in the cannibal feast more than anyone else.

Como era Gostoso was based somewhat on historical accounts. It is set circa 1557 somewhere in the Guanabara Bay region of Brazil, close to the Portuguese settlement of São Vicente (the site of which is near the modern city of São Paulo). Apparently the French, who settled around what is now Rio de Janeiro, divided the São Vicentians from other Portuguese colonials, and the two factions were often at war (siding with different native groups). Working with the legendary Humberto Mauro (*Ganga Bruta*, 1933, q.v.), dos Santos was careful to use authentic Tupi dialogue, and an attempt has clearly been made to represent Tupi culture accurately, including the rituals of cannibalism and body painting—most of the cast are naked for most of the film! In addition, many of the title cards that are used appear to reproduce text from actual historical journals and letters—by Mem de Sa, Brazil's Governor General; Portuguese Jesuit missionaries José de Anchieta and Manuel da Nobrego; the French admiral, Durand de Villegaignon; and other European chroniclers of the colonial, "first contact" experience. What is particularly interesting in the use of these anthropological and historical sources, though, is the degree to which they are ironically transformed. This is especially the case with the written accounts which, though they seem to be written mostly by men sympathetic to the Tupi, usually take a traditionally negative view—"In this country, no Governor, no Bishop or other authority could please God . . . for the evil is much impregnated in the customs" (Padre Nobrega). From the opening scene, where a man wearing a ball and chain is dragged into the ocean and a voice-over states that "he threw himself in the sea and drowned," the film spectator is led to question everything that s/he sees and hears—the dialogue shifts readily from French to Portuguese to Tupi dialect. Though initially we tend to relate closely to Francês as a "captive witness" (in Richard Peña's words), the narrative interruptions through intertitling, the distance created from the characters, and the sheer strangeness of the film's action cause us to question the validity of all colonial accounts of Brazil's history and culture. Eventually we find ourselves impossibly positioned vis-à-vis any sense of what it means to be "Brazilian."

Peter Rist

Awards: Four prizes including Best Screenplay, Brasilia, 1970.

1. Randal Johnson, *Cinema Novo X 5* (Austin: University of Texas Press, 1987), 184–5, 189.
2. Richard Peña, "How Tasty Was My Little Frenchman," *Brazilian Cinema*, eds. Randal Johnson and Robert Stam (Rutherford, N.J.: Associated University Presses, 1982), 193.

Os Inconfidêntes

The Conspirators
Brazil-Italy, 1972, 100', colour

Dir Joaquim Pedro de Andrade (1932–1988) *Scr* Andrade and Eduardo Escorel, based on the *Autos da Devassa* (late eighteenth-century official court record) and parts of the book of verse *O Romanceiro da Inconfidência Mineira*, by Cecília Meireles (1953) *Cinematog* Pedro de Moraes *Ed* Escorel *Art dir* Anisio Medeiros *Mus* Ari Barroso and Agustín Lara *Prod* Andrade for Filmes do Serro, Grupo Filmes, and Mapa Filmes (Brazil) and Radiotelevisione Italiana (RAI) (Italy) *Act* José Wilker, Luíz Linhares, Paulo César Pereio, Fernando Torres, Carlos Kroeber, Margarida Rey, Tereza Medina, Wilson Grey, Suzana Gonçalves.

This sometimes somber, often ironically humorous, and potentially bewildering film is as perfect an example of Brechtian allegorical filmmaking as Brazilian cinema has ever produced. On the heels of an Embrafilme call (backed by the military government) for historical films "with educational value" to commemorate Brazil's 150th anniversary but with the freedom of financing from Italian television (RAI, under the same program that also financed Jorge Sanjinés' *El coraje del pueblo* (Bolivia, 1971, q.v.) and other films), Joaquim Pedro de Andrade produced a "miracle": a film that was so faithful to the historical record of a central event in the struggle for independence from the Portuguese crown that it proved to be uncensorable despite its acerbic commentary on contemporary politics.

The "Inconfidência Mineira" was an unsuccessful eighteenth-century revolt in the state of Minas Gerais led by Tiradentes, who is now revered as a national hero: his birthday is a national holiday. (The incident had been the subject of an ill-fated earlier film, *Inconfidência Mineira*, the only film directed by the early screen actress and producer Carmen Santos, which was completed in 1948 after a decade's production, poorly received, and then lost.) The conspirators were all caught, tried, and punished according to their perceived culpability: all but Tiradentes were banished/exiled; he was sentenced to hang, after which his body was quartered and displayed as a warning, his house and possessions burned, and his descendants disgraced for five generations. Using only historically faithful material for its dialogues—direct quotations from the crown's records of the trials (the *Autos da Devassa*), the work of the various poets who participated in the conspiracy, and *O Romanceiro da Inconfidência* by Cecília Meireles (one of Brazil's most important modern poets)—*Os Inconfidêntes* nevertheless presents a reading of the events of the conspiracy that resonates clearly for the present.

The film's version of the conspiracy is doubly framed. First, because it is presented from prison, in a long series of involuted flashbacks that shift temporal planes with little warning (even within sequence shots) but also because that diegetic temporal continuum is itself framed by a series of non-diegetic (and not always visual) "inserts" presented without explicit commentary that begin and end the film. The very first shot of the film (pre-credits) is a close-up of a piece of red meat crawling with flies. It is followed by a series of unconnected shots in which one man hangs himself, another wastes away in jail, and another walks on a deserted island holding a yellowed manuscript. As the film will reveal, this was the fate of the conspirators: death and quartering for Tiradentes, banishment and/or madness for the others. But accompanying the last shot of this pre-credit sequence, we hear Ari Barroso's "Aquarela do Brasil" (the contemporary pop music surrogate national anthem) as we switch to a picture-postcard image of the photogenic Minas Gerais town of Ouro Preto (where the conspiracy took place). The irony, as Randal Johnson argues, could not be clearer—there is obviously a tremendous disjunction between the "official" historical record and the events themselves—but the film's barely veiled allegory is also already insistent: the "contemporary" moment of the twentieth-century song is the essential context to which the film is directed.[1]

As the narrative unfolds, we meet all the characters of the conspiracy—the intellectuals, pseudo-intellectuals, and poets who talked themselves into a rebellion, and Tiradentes (José Wilker), who galvanised them to action. From prison, the film alternates between flashbacks of the closed-door reunions that led to the conspiracy and scenes of the conspirators' interrogation by the crown. As the conspirators betray themselves and each other, the spectator cannot but make connections to the present and to the failure of the Left, especially the intellectual Left, in 1964. As the film details, the conspirators were all slave-owning members of an elite class whose heterogeneously motivated rebellion was unconnected to the people. And, perhaps because of their competing motivations, they all, perhaps even Tiradentes himself, fell apart under physical torture.

The film ends by echoing the pre-credit sequence. As Tiradentes is hanged, an abrupt cut presents contemporary Brazilian children applauding, as if at the end of a historical pageant, and black-and-white newsreel footage of a military parade in Ouro Preto, alternating with close-ups of red meat (Tiradentes' body) being chopped by a cleaver. "Aquarela do Brasil" surges up again on the soundtrack.

Although the implacable distanciation of its Brechtian devices (characters that speak directly to the camera, the appearance of meta-diegetic figures, abrupt temporal and spatial shifts, etc.) meant that *Os Inconfidêntes* would never attract a mainstream audience, the film was detained for three months by the censors. Apparently, however, Andrade and Eduardo Escorel had been right: the censors literally could not order cuts in the "texts" of Brazilian history. On the axis of high modernism and reflexive national expression, the film is an outstanding example of historical filmmaking that takes as its subject the critique of historical representation itself.

Ana López

Awards: Air France Best Film Award, 1972; Best Film, Rio de Janeiro, 1972; Award of the Arts and Letters Committee, Venice, 1972.

1. Randal Johnson, *Cinema Novo X 5* (Austin: University of Texas Press, 1987), 34–40.

São Bernardo

Brazil, 1973, 110', colour

Dir Leon Hirszman (1937–1988) *Scr* Hirszman, based on the novel of the same title by Graciliano Ramos (1934) *Cinematog* Lauro Escorel Filho *Ed* Eduardo Escorel *Art dir* Luis Carlos Ripper *Mus* Caetano Veloso *Prod* Marcos Farias for Saga Filmes *Act* Othon Bastos, Isabel Ribeiro, Nildo Parente, Vanda Lacerda, Mario Largo, Josef Guerreiro, Rodolfo Arena, Jofre Soares

São Bernardo is one of the most successful film adaptations of Latin American literature, retaining the ironic, distanced approach to character of Graciliano Ramos' source novel. It was also something of a surprisingly popular (as well as critical) success when it was finally released in Brazil two years after the start of the film's production and four years after its conception.

Leon Hirszman was born in Rio de Janeiro. While studying engineering in São Paulo, he got involved in theatre and organised some ciné clubs. He was one of the founders of the Students' Union's Centre for Popular Culture and was a prime mover at the beginning of Cinema Nôvo. His short film *Pedreira de São Diogo* was included as part of *Cinco Vezes Favela* (1962), and the second film that he directed was the important documentary about the Brazilian literacy campaign and its consequences, *Maioria Absoluta* (1964). He then directed two fiction feature films, *A Falecida* (1965), based on a play by Nelson Rodrigues, and a musical, intent on demystifying Rio's "Bossa Nova" image, *A Garota de Ipanema* (1967). After making three short documentaries in 1969, he began working on his most ambitious project, *São Bernardo*.

Paulo Honório (Othon Bastos) is an illiterate peasant in Brazil's northeastern *sertão* of the 1920s. He has dreams of being a *latifúndista* and ruthlessly focuses his entire life on becoming rich and powerful. In prison for stabbing a man, he learns how to read and write. After his release he becomes a travelling salesman and teaches himself mathematics, enabling him to add cheating to his repertoire of tricks. He is eventually able to take over the São Bernardo plantation which had been allowed to decline by its owner (Paulo's former employer). He meets a woman, Dona Gloria (Vanda Lacerda), on a train and learns about the good character of her niece, Madalena (Isabel Ribeiro), who is a schoolteacher. He decides to marry her not for her looks (which are remarked upon by other men) but for the supportive qualities that she would bring to the role of plantation wife.

Like the novel, the film is narrated in flashback by Paulo Honório. Whereas in Ramos' original Paulo is himself writing a novel and continually commenting on the process of writing, Hirszman has his narrator writing his memoirs. The viewer gradually learns that the impulse to do so has been triggered by Madalena's suicide and that he is writing in order to understand himself and become a better person. While the historical recounting is mostly rendered in long-take long shots, the scale of the recurrent images of Paulo Honório at his writing desk is much closer. Normally, with such an exposition, an audience would be encouraged to identify with the protagonist, but in *São Bernardo*, it is a real struggle for the spectator to see beyond the facial expressions and understand character. The deliberate injection of ambiguity by Hirszman here is reminiscent of many works by Jean-Luc Godard and Robert Bresson before him. Although such a strategy doesn't contain the cinematic reflexivity of the former director, it is ultimately more politically intentioned than the latter's work. Indeed, even though the concept of Brechtian distanciation leading to consciousness-raising is somewhat overused by the critics of Cinema Nôvo, it is clear from Hirszman's own comments on *São Bernardo* that he intended such an interpretation to be made and for his ambiguous narrative to work dialectically. Of Paulo Honório, Hirszman said that he "is a man who dedicates himself completely to a process of accumulating capital" and that this theme of "quantification," revealed through a "concrete analysis of a concrete situation," is as important as the "contradiction which exists between the fiction of the story and the confession of the character." Madalena is clearly the most sympathetic character in the film, even though she is observed mostly from Paulo's perspective. Much attention is paid to her attempts at democratising the plantation, which drive Paulo crazy with jealousy and suspicion of her "communist" leanings. He is ultimately shown to be a pathetic, lonely person at the end of the film, in contrast with his employees who work and sing together.

Randal Johnson and Robert Stam have written on how the dialectical structure of *São Bernardo* extends to the relationship between sound and image tracks, wherein one is dynamic while the other is static, allowing the film audience to shift its perspective from one element to another. They also state that, although the film is not essentially allegorical, the property of São Bernardo can be understood as the Brazilian nation in microcosm, with the central character representing the Brazilian people caught up unknowingly in their own destruction through their embrace of capitalism.[1] In fact, the release of Hirszman's film was delayed for seven months by the censor board, who sensed perhaps that Ramos' classic historical novel had been usurped as a vehicle to criticise contemporary society. The delay caused the production company to go bankrupt, but the filmmakers eventually persuaded the authorities that their adaptation of such an important work needed to be seen. It is also a tribute to Brazilian audiences that they would support such an original, austere (yet beautiful), challenging, and ambiguous film.

Peter Rist

Awards: Three prizes, including Best Director, National Film Institute (INC), 1973; three awards, including Special Jury Prize, Gramado, 1974.

1. Randal Johnson and Robert Stam, "*São Bernardo*: Property and the Personality," *Brazilian Cinema*, eds. Johnson and Stam (East Rutherford, N.J.: Associated University Presses, 1982), 207.

Toda Nudez Será Castigada

All Nudity Shall Be Punished
Brazil, 1973, 107', colour

Dir Arnaldo Jabor (b. 1940) *Scr* Jabor, based on a play of the same title by Nelson Rodrigues *Cinematog* Lauro Escorel *Art dir* Regis Monteiro *Mus* Astor Piazzolla and Roberto and Erasmo Carlos *Prod* Jabor for R. F. Farias Produções Cinematográficas and Ventania Produções *Act* Paulo Porto, Darlene Gloria, Paulo Sacks, Paulo César Pereio, Isabel Ribeiro, Hugo Carvana, Elsa Gomes, Henriqueta Brieba

In an era when state funding of films in Brazil was beginning to take hold but when such funding did not take a project's quality into account, Embrafilme's low-interest loans helped popularise *pornochanchadas* (erotic comedies). *A Viúva Virgem* ("The Virgin Widow," by Pedro Rovai), *A Infidelidade ao Alcance de Todos* ("Infidelity Within Everyone's Reach," by Aníbal Massaini Neto and Olivier Perroy), and *Os Mansos* ("The Lenient Husbands," co-directed by Rovai), all received loans in 1972, generally regarded as being the first year of *pornochanchadas*. But 1973 saw the release of *Toda Nudez Será Castigada*, perhaps the first important Brazilian film to treat adult sexuality in a serious albeit entertaining vein.

Arnaldo Jabor was born in Rio de Janeiro where he received his doctorate in law. He then worked in radio and television and also wrote theatre criticism. He began his career in cinema by working as a sound recordist for Cinema Nôvo directors such as Carlos Diegues and Leon Hirszman, and he directed his first short film, *O Circo*, in 1965. Jabor's first feature was a documentary, *A Opinão Publica*, which won a prize at the Pesaro film festival in 1967. His next film, *Pindorama* (1970), was his first fiction feature and represented Brazil at Cannes the following year. Jabor then made *Toda Nudez* in 1972. It was a very personal project for the director, because on the one hand he considered the author Nelson Rodrigues to be the greatest living Brazilian playwright, and on the other he wanted to address the contemporary problem of hypocrisy.

As the credits for *Toda Nudez* roll, we watch a rich, middle-aged man, Herculano (Paulo Porto) driving his convertible. The camera tracks with him as he carries flowers into his sumptuous residence looking for "Geni." When he finds a reel-to-reel tape deck, plays it, and learns that Geni has committed suicide, the film begins to recount Herculano's story in flashback. It begins with Herculano's brother, Patricio (Paulo César Pereio), plotting with his two aunts (Elsa Gomes and Henriqueta Brieba) and sister Irma (Isabel Ribeiro) to control Herculano's life (and hence his money) now that he is a widower. Herculano had sworn to his son, Sergio (Paulo Sacks), that he would never sleep with another woman, even after his cancer-stricken wife died. Nevertheless, Patricio is able to persuade his brother to visit a prostitute, Geni (Darlene Gloria), with whom he falls in love. Hypocritically, Herculano denies his attraction for Geni, claiming that he was drunk, but he is unable to resist her advances (prompted by Patricio). Before Herculano marries Geni, Sergio denounces him and is arrested for being drunk and disorderly. In jail, Sergio is raped by a "Bolivian thief," following which he gets revenge on his father by seducing Geni. Then, when she spies Sergio getting on a plane with the "Bolivian thief," she decides to commit suicide, in her (presumably) broken-hearted state.

The cinematic style of *Toda Nudez* is basically very conventional, but the mise-en-scène is quite expressive. In her free-spiritedness Geni is often shown outdoors (and baring her breasts), whereas stuffy interiors are associated with Herculano. Images of entrapment become more prevalent as the film progresses, while the film's colour scheme changes from dull brown to gaudy bright contrasts such as red/white and purple/emerald green as the melodrama intensifies. The most striking aspect of *Toda Nudez*, however, is its acting, which is uniformly strong. Darlene Gloria virtually explodes with passion in the role of Geni, while Paulo Porto perfectly captures both the sexual double standard associated with machismo and the hypocrisy of the Brazilian middle class. On the negative side, one could argue that there are narrative gaps—it's not exactly clear why Herculano's family wants him to marry a prostitute—and that the filmmakers are themselves using a "double standard"—criticizing society's sexual mores while displaying female nudity and not male. In any event, *Toda Nudez Será Castigada* is probably Jabor's most important film. He followed it with another Rodrigues adaptation, *O Casamento*, in 1975 and continued in the same vein with the popular *Tudo Bem* (1977). By the time that he directed his next film, *Eu Te Amo*, starring Sonia Braga, in 1980, it appeared that Jabor was aiming for more commercial success and caring less about social commentary. Indeed, through the presence of sexual icon Braga, *Eu Te Amo* was an international hit and brought Jabor closer to the mainstream albeit with a great deal of sophistication.

Peter Rist

Awards: Best Actor (Paulo Porto), Actress (Darlene Gloria), Supporting Actress (Elsa Gomes), and Art Direction, National Film Institute (INC), 1972; Second Prize, Berlin, 1973; Best Film, Actress (Gloria), and Music, Gramado, 1973.

Iracema, uma Transa Amazônica

Iracema
Brazil, 1974 (released 1980), 90', colour

Dir Jorge Bodanzky (b. 1942) and Orlando Senna (b. 1940) *Scr* Senna, Bodanzky, and Hermano Penna *Cinematog* Bodanzky *Prod* Wolf Gauer for Stopfilm *Act* Edna de Cássia, Paulo César Pereio, Conceição Senna, Rose Rodrigues

In 1972, during one of the most repressive periods of Brazil's lengthy military dictatorship (1964–85), the state film agency Embrafilme introduced incentives for filmmakers to shoot adaptations of the work of dead Brazilian authors. In 1974, in a brilliant and bitter comment on this initiative, Jorge Bodanzky and Orlando Senna named their journey into the squalor and despair of contemporary Amazonia *Iracema, uma Transa Amazônica*, borrowing the title and subverting the title character of nineteenth-century Romantic novelist José de Alencar's national literary classic, *Iracema, Lendo do Ceará* (1865). De Alencar's novel, whose first film adaptation was in 1917, depicts the indigenous princess Iracema—an anagram of America—as representative of her culture's noble virtues. Bodanzky and Senna's Iracema is an indigenous girl, circa 1974, who leaves her poor family and becomes a prostitute in the Amazon in the midst of the region's tumultuous "development." *Iracema*'s gritty depiction of the reality of the region's development, however, proved too much for the authorities, and like Ruy Guerra's *A Queda* (1976, q.v.), *Iracema* sat on the shelf for several years before it could be shown in Brazil, although it was seen abroad. In *Iracema*'s case the censors came up with the novel explanation that since it had been processed abroad (for budgetary and technical reasons it had been shot in 16mm, a format that many developing countries paradoxically lack laboratories to process adequately), it did not qualify as a Brazilian film nor, of course, was it foreign. *Iracema* languished in this legal limbo, denied a censor's certificate but not technically banned, until 1980, when the new government of General João Baptista Figueredo (1979–85) allowed it to be seen.

Wandering around the Amazonian port of Belém, where her family's river boat is moored, Iracema meets up with "Tião Grande Brasil," a loud-mouthed truck driver, and accompanies him into the interior on his lumber-hauling route. Tião is a caricature of Brazil's white southern working class, parroting the military's nationalist and developmentalist slogans and hoping to earn a fortune in the Amazon, oblivious to the environmental and human degradation around him. He soon tires of Iracema, however, and abandons her at a desolate truck stop with nothing but the clothes on her back: a bikini top and skimpy hot pants which exhort us to "Drink Coca-Cola." Thus begins Iracema's journey through the Amazonian landscape and her descent into prostitution and despair, followed relentlessly by Bodanzky's *cinéma vérité*-style hand-held camera.

Constructed as a documentary narrative, *Iracema* penetrates the Amazon like no other film in Brazilian film history, at a crucial time when rapacious "development" was well under way and the completion of the Trans-Amazonian highway the following year would bring even greater destruction. Paulo César Pereio, playing Tião, is the film's only professional actor, and the film combines documentary footage—forests being burned and clear cut, peasants, workers, and prostitutes speaking to the camera—with loosely-scripted or improvised narrative sequences using local non-professionals, such as the depiction of the sale of indentured labourers at auction. In the end a much worse-for-wear Iracema, old yet still a child, meets up with Tião again at another truck stop-cum-brothel, but he doesn't recognise her in her drunken and dishevelled state and roars off in his truck in search of ever-more-distant conquests. The film's metaphor of Brazil's development as a form of prostitution and the parallels it draws between sexual relations and a rapacious colonialism are now unmistakeable.

While the film has been praised for its *cinéma vérité* style and use of non-professional actors and as an exemplary treatment of its subject, this approach is not without its problematic aspects. The early part of the film, when Tião and Iracema are together, is completely dominated by Pereio's overblown, largely improvised performance, reducing the other characters to virtual silence. And while the decision to film in 16mm was made not only to allow filming in remote locations on a limited budget but also to convey (through the hand-held camera) a specific formal representation of the Amazon—chaotic, out of control—this formal representation, too, presents its own dilemmas. The camera is deliberately, exaggeratedly random and aggressive in its probing of its milieu, even in interiors, lending an uneasy sense of fatalism and irrationality to the characters' lives. While this may have been precisely the intention, it may be interpreted as a paternalistic, "southern" attitude, given form by a lack of structure in the film's editing and the chaotic camera movements.

Before they shot *Iracema* together, Bodanzky was a São Paulo photojournalist and cinematographer and Senna an accomplished screenwriter, later co-scripting *Coronel Delmiro Gouveia* (1978, q.v.), with one feature film to his credit. The two made one more film together in the Amazon, *Gitirana* (1976), while Bodanzky and *Iracema*'s producer Wolf Gauer continued to collaborate into the 1980s. In 1992, Senna was named director of the International Film and Television School in Cuba, an international centre administered by the New Latin American Cinema Foundation.

Timothy Barnard

Awards: Four awards, including Best Film and Best Actress (Edna de Cássia), Brasilia, 1980.

Guerra Conjugal

Conjugal Warfare
Brazil, 1975, 116', colour

Dir Joachim Pedro de Andrade (1932-1988) *Scr* Andrade, based on short stories by Dalton Trevisan *Cinematog* Pedro de Morais *Ed* Eduardo Escorel *Art dir* Anísio Medeiros *Mus* Ian Guest *Prod* Aloysio Salles, Walter Clark, and Luiz Carlos Barreto for Industria Cinematográfica Brasileira (ICB) and Filmes do Serro *Act* Lima Duarte, Carlos Gregório, Jofre Soares, Carmen Silva, Itala Nandi, Analu Prestes, Carlos Kroeber, Cristina Aché, Dirce Miglaccio, Maria Lúcia Dahl.

While Arnaldo Jabor's *Toda Nudez Será Castigada* (1973, q.v.) gave *pornochanchada* some respectability, *Guerra Conjugal* offered Brazilian audiences their first real critique of the popular genre. In fact, with *Guerra Conjugal*, Joachim Pedro de Andrade produced perhaps his most typical work, a striking forerunner to Pedro Almodóvar's dark sexual comedies of the 1980s, that united sex and death in ways that even the surrealists would have had difficulty imagining. In the director's own words, *Guerra Conjugal* combines "Domestic bondage, rotten kisses, varicose veins, open doors, arteriosclerosis, senile lust, slaps, delirium of flowering flesh, a bed with teeth, necrophiliac voyeurism, interior decoration, sexual doubts, asthmatic bronchitis, and even the final victory of prostitution over old age—[which] all indicate the possibility of redemption through excessive sin."

Three years after making his previous film, *Os Inconfidêntes* (1972, q.v.), Andrade returned to the bawdy, grotesque, "magical realist" fantasy world of *Macunaíma* (1969, q.v.) by adapting some sixteen short stories from Dalton Trevisan (known as the "Vampire of Curitiba"). Andrade combined these stories into three parts, focusing on Osiris, a lawyer who seduces his female clients; Nelsinho, a young man looking for ever more perverse sexual liaisons; and Joãozinho and Amália, an elderly couple engaged in "conjugal war." The stories are divided into various episodes and intercut, apparently in chronological order.

The first episode sets the tone with Joãozinho complaining of his wife's cooking and taking a bicarbonate in the kitchen. Then, Amália's complaint that he hasn't kissed her in years triggers thoughts of "bellies exploding" at death. On this grotesque mental image the scene shifts to the office of the lecherous Osiris who attempts to seduce the unfortunate Maria. She had been abandoned by her boyfriend when she was mistakenly diagnosed as being pregnant—actually her liver was swollen. Such a confusion of digestive and reproductive systems exemplifies *Guerra Conjugal*, as does the blurring of distinctions between food and human flesh (decaying and aging, respectively). Nelsinho is first seen kicking a dog, an action which equates with his disdain for others. He successively mates with older and older women, at one point leaving a young blonde woman for her mother, who offers him a "bonbon." His last sexual encounter is with a seventy-year-old prostitute. Meanwhile Osiris continues to turn clients into victims, successively meeting and tricking Olga and her husband, carrying on an affair with her virtually in front of him. But the tables are turned on the lawyer as first Olga encourages him to make love to her in front of her dead husband, and then Osiris meets up with a misogynist childhood pal who seduces him.

Amália is finally released from Joãozinho's habitual complaining when he dies—he thought she was poisoning him with her cooking—whereas Nelsinho believes himself to be redeemed after his final affair. Certainly the film ends ambiguously in this way, but the connections between the three main stories build to the extent that, young or old, most of the film's bourgeois characters are united in their grotesque, excessive appetites. The names João and Maria abound, so that they become synonyms for male and female. Most striking in *Guerra Conjugal*'s network of motifs, though, is Anísio Medeiros' colourful art direction. When Olga seduces Osiris after her husband dies, her bedroom, predominantly violet, is bathed in pink light. Her bed is in the shape of a mouth, with the bedcover as a huge tongue. Throughout *Guerra Conjugal* there is a proliferation of pink, mixed with purples, maroons, and blues. Indeed the colours of cheap romance are on excessive display, and our understanding of the scheme readily shifts to one of decaying flesh and carnality. This twist is marked by the film's credits: a heart surrounded by pink and blue flowers in the beginning is replaced by a purple wreath surrounded by insects at the end.

In an era when West Germany's Rainer Werner Fassbinder was criticising power imbalance within relationships by subverting traditional melodrama (including its use of colour), Andrade went one step further in brilliantly yet brutally exposing the sexual hypocrisy of the Brazilian middle class and set a standard of excessive mise-en-scène, for the likes of Almodóvar to follow. Like Glauber Rocha, Andrade died young. He was only able to finish two more films after *Guerra Conjugal:* the short *Vereda Tropical* (1977), made as part of the anthology film, *Contos Eróticos*—an even more excessive and reflexive attack on *pornochanchada*—and *O*

Homen do Pau-Brasil (1982). Perhaps his work will eventually receive the kind of major retrospective that it deserves, to enable it to be recognised as seminal cinematic "magic realism" disguising political commentary while reinventing genre.

Peter Rist

Awards: Best Film, Director, and Editing, Brasilia, 1974; Honourable Mention, Barcelona, 1975; Best Supporting Actress (Carmen Silva) and Best Screenplay, National Film Institute (INC), 1975.

Dona Flor e Seus Dois Maridos

Dona Flor and Her Two Husbands
Brazil, 1976, 118', colour

Dir Bruno Barreto (b. 1953) *Scr* Barreto, Leopoldo Serran, and Eduardo Coutinho, based on the novel of the same title by Jorge Amado (1966) *Cinematog* Murillo Salles *Ed* Raymundo Higino *Art dir* Anísio Medeiros *Mus* Chico Buarque and Francis Hime *Prod* Luiz Carlos Barreto, Newton Rique, and Companhia Serrador for Carnaval Films *Act* Sonia Braga, José Wilker, Mauro Mendonça, Dinorah Brillanti, Nelson Xavier, Nelson Dantas, Rui Rezende, Nilda Spencer, Arthur Costa Filho, Mario Gusmão

Dona Flor e Seus Dois Maridos is clearly the most commercially successful Brazilian film of all time. It grossed $5 million (U.S.) in its first five weeks of release in Brazil, eventually being seen there by over ten million spectators, and has grossed twice as much as any other Brazilian film in the U.S., $3 million. Indeed, *Dona Flor* was the most successful Latin American film ever at the U.S. box office until Luis Puenzo's *La historia oficial* (Argentina, 1985, q.v.) surpassed it (at $3.5 million).

In a year when more domestic films, eighty-seven, were released in Brazil than ever before, *Dona Flor*'s success is representative of a marked shift away from Cinema Nôvo's seriousness to soft-core pornographic entertainment. Well over half of the films produced in Brazil in 1976 had sex as the central component, and although not all the works are comic, it's clear that the *pornochanchada* had emerged as the dominant Brazilian genre; *Dona Flor* can be regarded as this genre's most sophisticated example.

Bruno Barreto was only twenty-three years old when he made *Dona Flor*. Encouraged by his producer father, Luiz Carlos, Bruno had directed his first feature film, *Tati a Garota* (1972), at the age of nineteen, having made his first film when he was only eleven. He then made another feature, *A Estrela Sobe*, in 1974 before adapting the popular novel, *Dona Flor e Seus Dois Maridos*, written by Brazil's most famous novelist, Jorge Amado. The more experienced Eduardo Coutinho (*Cabra Marcado para Morrer*, 1984, q.v.) helped Barreto write a screenplay which stayed close to the novel. The flashback structure was maintained, where Dona Flor thinks back over her life with her first husband, Vadinho, at his funeral. The film condenses Flor's memories into an extended flashback, in which we first learn of her cooking prowess and her devotion to Vadinho.

The first thing that happens in both film and novel is a young man, Vadinho (José Wilker), dies on the street at dawn during a bacchanalian carnival celebration, presumably of a heart attack. The setting of the film is Salvador, capital of Bahia, in the 1940s. Though partially in drag, Vadinho is the most macho of men, lusting after an Afro-Brazilian woman dancing at the head of a parade, and we quickly learn that he has died from a lifestyle of excess. In Flor's flashback she emerges as a kind and modest yet passionate and beautiful young woman, whereas Vadinho is represented as being a compulsive gambler and inveterate womaniser. After a period of mourning, Flor (Sonia Braga) is encouraged by her mother, Dona Rozilda (Dinorah Brillanti), and best friend, Dona Norma, to accept the advances of a prospective suitor and social opposite of Vadinho, the polite conservative pharmacist Dr. Teodoro (Mauro Mendonça). Every woman in Flor's acquaintance is thrilled by the prospect of a "good" marriage for her, especially her scheming mother (who is actually more sympathetic in the film than in the book). However, it is immediately evident on their wedding night that Flor's second husband lacks the sexual prowess of the first. She begins to consult a *macumba* priestess, not expecting her longing for Vadinho to be fulfilled. His naked ghost appears before her, quite tangible in her bedroom, and she then seeks to eliminate him through a *candomblé* ceremony. But when his image dissolves away and she cries out, the *babalão* (priest) shakes his head in a cross-cut *candomblé* scene, generating a return to Flor's house and a reincarnation of Vadinho. From here, Flor succumbs to Vadinho's pleas, and he lies in bed beside her, invisible to Teodoro on the other side. In the film's last shot we view the threesome emerging from the church, and as the camera pans left to follow them into the town square, we realise that Vadinho is totally naked yet invisible to the throng around them.

From this striking final shot we can appreciate that although Wilker is never viewed in full frontal nudity, he is as much a sex object as Braga, undercutting the sexism of the source material somewhat. Indeed, the reduction in length—the 520-page novel to less than two hours of film—removes a great deal of misogyny: Amado's prose retains and revels in stereotypes, male and female alike. The ugliness of Dona Rozilda's hatred is virtually eliminated in the film, while, inadvertently perhaps, Wilker's boyish demeanour and blonde Greek-god looks unconvincingly translate the novel's street-smart and rakish *malandro* Vadinho to the screen. Of course it is Braga's presence in *Dona Flor* which is most often discussed as the film's commercial driving force, and her performance certainly made her a star. She was born in 1951 in Maringa, Paraña state; her mulatto father died when she was six. She helped support her *mestiça* mother and six siblings by appearing on Brazilian television at fourteen, and at seventeen she performed on the São Paulo stage, leading to a role in a production of *Hair*. She became well known in *telenovelas* and played parts in numerous Brazilian films from 1970 on, before gaining an international reputation with *Dona Flor*.

Barreto's greatest strengths as a director can also be understood as weaknesses, especially in the contextual contrast of Cinema Nôvo and the search for a national cinema. He quickly became known as the most Hollywoodian of Brazilian directors for his technical accomplishments and the efficiency of his narrative style, which, given the fantastic subject matter of *Dona Flor*, is far more "realist" than "magical." His next film, a "true crime" drama, *Amor Bandido* (1979), confirmed his reputation and, like *Dona Flor*, was also released commercially in the U.S. He then produced an English version of *Dona Flor* for Hollywood, *Kiss Me Goodbye* (1982), and continued his quest to become a Hollywood personality by working as a Rio-based line producer on *Where the River Runs Black* (1986) and directing *A Show of Force* (1990), which was a relative failure with critics and audiences alike. During this time, though, Barreto continued to occasionally make films in Brazil, and his last real success came with another adaptation of a successful Amado novel, again starring an often-naked Sonia Braga, *Gabriela* (1983), which had the fourth highest gross of a Brazilian film in the U.S. at $1.2 million.

Peter Rist

Awards: Special Jury Prize, Taormina, 1977; three awards, including Best Director, Gramado, 1977.

Xica da Silva

Xica
Brazil, 1976, 117', colour

Dir Carlos Diegues (b. 1940) *Scr* Diegues and João Felicio dos Santos *Cinematog* José Medeiros *Ed* Mair Tavares *Art dir* Luis Carlos Ripper *Mus* Roberto Menescal and Jorge Ben *Choreog* Marlene Silva *Prod* Jarbas Barbosa for Terra, Embrafilme and Distrifilmes *Act* Zezé Motta, Walmor Chagas, Altair Lima, Elke Maravilha, Stepan Nercessian, Rodolfo Arena

Xica da Silva, based on the life of a legendary slave woman in eighteenth-century Minas Gerais, was by far the most successful of Carlos Diegues' films, drawing over three million spectators in its first 2½ months of release in Brazil. It is also the director's most colourful, carnivalesque film and one which was well received by the popular press. However, in presenting a comedy on slavery and in reinforcing the myth of the Afro-Brazilian as a predominantly sexual being, *Xica da Silva* has also been the object of much criticism—its U.S. release was delayed until 1982, presumably because the distributor was unsure of its reception.

Carlos Diegues followed *Ganga Zumba* (1963, q.v.) with two even more challenging feature films, *A Grande Cidade* (1966) and *Os Herdeiros* (1968). The former combines the interest of Cinema Nôvo's first phase in the northeast with the movement's shifting perspective to urban life by tracing the experiences of four different *nordeste* characters who have moved to Rio de Janeiro, while the latter allegorically presents forty years of Brazilian history. After the experimentation of *Os Herdeiros*, Diegues began to work in the mode suggested by his comments to Rogério Sganzerla in an interview in 1966, during which he discussed freeing Cinema Nôvo from its "youthful prejudices" and creating a new form of "spectacle that mixes politics and humour, Shakespeare and the *modinha de viola*. . . ." In *Quando o Carnaval Chegar* (1972), Diegues celebrated *chanchadas* and other popular forms of Brazilian culture as liberating forces, and produced his first work of the carnivalesque. In *Joana Francesa* (1974), a much-underrated, beautifully photographed film, he returned to the critical/historical mode. This film follows the progress of a French-woman (played by a *nouvelle vague* icon, Jeanne Moreau) from São Paulo bordello madame to decadent and despotic Dona of a sugar plantation. Set during the 1930s, *Joana Francesa* focuses on the self-destruction of the plantocracy, who are unable to adapt to Getúlio Vargas' industrialisation schemes. In its linear narrative and construction of a powerful and dynamic yet ambiguously regarded female central character, *Joana Francesa* prefigures Diegues' sixth feature and thirteenth film, *Xica da Silva*.

A young aristocrat, João Fernandes de Oliveira (Walmor Chagas) has been awarded the exclusive diamond mining contract in Arraial do Tijuco by the King of Portugal. Xica da Silva (Zezé Motta), a house slave, seduces him, and he buys her and frees her. She quickly comes to dominate society while incurring the wrath of the whites. By complaining that she has never seen the ocean, she gets João Fernandes to build her a boat to sail on a lake with her all-black entourage of attendants. An intendant, the Count of Valadares (Altair Lima) is sent from Portugal to investigate the strange goings-on and to end the extravagant abuses and scandalous behaviour. Xica dresses outrageously, complete with white make-up, to entertain the racist Count, but despite her entreaties, João Fernandes is sent back to Portugal. Xica's palace is destroyed by the revengeful whites, and she seeks refuge in a monastery where her young lover José (Stepan Nercessian) is in hiding. The film ends optimistically with José trying to convince her that they can continue to combat the king and his followers.

Amongst the real achievements of *Xica da Silva* is that a lavish costume spectacle was staged on a relatively small budget. On the artistic side, Diegues was able to realise his intention to construct a particularly Brazilian film reflecting a "people whose sensuality, exuberance, and creative imagination are capable of transforming reality in such an extravagant manner that it finally mixes with dreams. . . ." He was helped here considerably by the performance of Zezé Motta in the title role. With her unusual looks and abrasively frank manner, she was able to suggest the historical Xica's apparent ugliness and unpleasant demeanour while transcending these qualities with a brilliant energy. Although it is clear in the context of the film that a female slave's only route to power would be through her body, the treatment of Xica's sexuality—causing every man who makes love with her to scream, offscreen, while Jorge Ben sings the "Xica da Silva" theme song—unfortunately favours fantasy and myth over historical accuracy. On the one hand, such treatment brings a distinctive carnivalesque Brazilianness, but on the other, it reeks of Africana stereotype. Ultimately, though, Diegues' desire to put "the people on the screen and in the movie theatres" and the film's recognition that Brazilianness equates with Africanness and, especially, its gaudy colour palette and comic and musical energy redeem *Xica da Silva*.

Peter Rist

A Queda

The Fall
Brazil, 1976 (released 1978), 110', colour and b+w

Dir Ruy Guerra (b. 1931) and Nelson Xavier *Scr* Guerra and Xavier *Cinematog* Edgar Moura *Ed* Guerra *Art dir* Carlos Prieto *Mus* Milton Nascimiento and Guerra *Prod* Nei Sroulevich, Angela Lessa, Vera Mata Machado, Tereza Mascarenhas, and Flavio Bruno for Zoom Cinematográfica, Daga and Nelson Xavier Produções Ltda. *Act* Nelson Xavier, Lima Duarte, Isabel Ribeiro, Maria Silvia, Hugo Carvana, Paulo César Pereio

A Queda is a sequel, of sorts, to Ruy Guerra's *Os Fuzis* (1964, q.v.), a landmark film of the early Cinema Nôvo. *Os Fuzis*, an austere, slow-paced film in black and white, showed a group of young soldiers sent to the drought-stricken northeast to protect a landowner from starving peasants on the verge of revolt. *A Queda*, co-scripted, co-directed, and co-produced by *Os Fuzis'* star Nelson Xavier, takes up the soldiers' lives more than a decade later: Mário (Xavier) and José—"Zé"—(Hugo Carvana) are construction workers building Rio de Janeiro's subway system, while Pedro (Paulo César Pereio) is still a soldier. Using a hand-held 16mm camera and direct sound in a feverish style quite unlike that of *Os Fuzis*, *A Queda* immerses itself in its characters' new lives as urban proletariat, a terrain explored by surprisingly few Cinema Nôvo directors. Zé dies in a construction accident in the film's first scene because of a lack of safety equipment on the job, and for the rest of the film we follow Mário as he attempts to obtain compensation for his friend's widow. He is stymied not only by company officials, who bribe the widow's lawyer and exert pressure to keep the story out of the newspapers, but by his own father-in-law, a corrupt and aspiring foreman with the same company. When the widow settles for a pittance, Mário threatens the company bosses with a gun and then, apparently, commits armed robbery. Sought by the police, he takes shelter in the unfinished house he is building for his family, and in a final scene, intercut with silent images of shopping centres and consumer goods, his wife finds him there and they commit to an uncertain future together. Like *Os Fuzis*, *A Queda* has followed Mário on a journey of growing political awareness, one in which he and his class are far from sentimentalised or idealised.

U.S. scholar Robert Stam describes *A Queda* as "fus[ing] the visceral affectivity of a Cassavetes with the political cunning of a Brecht."[1] Guerra and Xavier employ a number of seemingly incongruous techniques to achieve this effect. The hand-held camera is extremely mobile, offering on the construction site the point-of-view of an invisible participant in the classic *cinéma vérité* style. In Mário and Laura's apartment, however, it intervenes in the action, crossing the actors' paths and then swinging around to reframe them, heightening the frustration and anger they are conveying. The acting itself is abrasive, at times violent, as when Mário returns home from drinking with Pedro and rapes Laura, or when Laura, in an improvised scene, explodes at her father's paternalistic behaviour. In contrast, the construction managers are shown discussing the accident's cover-up in their boardroom in freeze-frame, to avoid any psychological reading of their behaviour, Guerra notes. Perhaps the most novel technique is the frequent intercutting of images from *Os Fuzis* into the footage of *A Queda*, sequences that often have a narrative purpose, such as establishing the irony of Mário's efforts on behalf of Zé, who as a soldier in the earlier film had killed a man Mário had befriended who was leading the peasants' resistance to their oppressors. This alternation of footage from the two films is complemented by other experiments in montage, such as the final sequence cited above or the film's opening pre-credit sequence, a sort of Eisensteinian associational montage that shows an imploding building, garbage pickers, a slaughterhouse, and slaughter-house managers toasting each other with glasses of blood.

During the 1970s Guerra developed his theories concerning the need for a cinema that is both politically engaged and formalist. Since Cinema Nôvo's earliest days, he had warned against its eventual co-optation by the state and by the mainstream of the film industry, and in many ways *A Queda* is his working out of these concerns. To many, such a co-optation came in 1974 with the staffing of the state film agency Embrafilme (created in 1969) with Cinema Nôvo personalities under a military government. (*A Queda* was one of the few films of the period not to receive Embrafilme support, and Guerra maintained that the agency could not be expected to subsidise projects that fundamentally threatened the interests of the government.) It was at this time, too, that Guerra formulated his response to Nelson Pereira dos Santos' updating of Glauber Rocha's early maxim of the movement, "A camera in hand and an idea in mind," devised at the time of dos Santos' film *O Amuleto de Ogum* (1974) and of the movement's increasing interest in a "popular" cinema. "A camera in hand, an idea in mind, and the people in the forefront," dos Santos had said. Guerra, while conscious of criticisms that in the 1960s Cinema Nôvo had been an elitist experiment with little effect on the broad public, countered that "popular" should not be interpreted as "folkloric" or measured by box office success and riposted "The people in the forefront, certainly, but not only in their festivities." To Guerra, a truly popular cinema—and *A Queda* would prove to be his only opportunity to put such theories into practice—would establish a radical dialogue with the country's working class. In this way perhaps are the film's various formal strategies explained: *A Queda* was at the same time a corrosive drama, capable of holding the average filmgoer's interest, and structured to promote reflection and an understanding of the complexity of class relations and the intractability of the social behaviour they sustain.

A Queda was shot in 16mm in 1976, in three weeks on a small budget. Blown up to 35mm on faulty equipment, which caused permanent damage, it was Guerra's first film in five years since his return to Brazil from Europe with *Os Deuses e os Mortos* (1971); during this period he worked as a playwright, actor, and lyricist. The film was immediately banned, as *Iracema* (1974, q.v.) had been two years earlier. In 1978 *A Queda* was invited to the prestigious Berlin film festival, where it was allowed to be screened on a special 15-day permit. On the day of Brazilian president Ernesto Geisel's (1974–1979) official visit to Germany, *A Queda* won the festival's Special Jury Prize, as *Os Fuzis* had done 14 years earlier, making it impossible for the dictatorship to suppress the film any longer. Later that same year, prolonged labour strife began in the country for the first time since the beginning of the dictatorship. But by the time of the film's release in Brazil, Guerra had already left the country for his native Mozambique, which had achieved independence from Portugal in 1975, where he directed the country's first feature film, *Mueda Memória Massacre* (1978), and headed the country's new film institute. In 1983 he filmed the first of four somewhat insipid literary adaptations in the 1980s and 90s, *Eréndira*, an international co-production shot in Mexico and based on a Gabriel García Márquez short story. Only *Opera do Malandro* (1986) revealed a glimpse of his former stylistic brilliance and political concerns, but here, in this stylized song-and-dance adaptation of Brecht's *The Threepenny Opera*, set in Brazil during World War II, we are a long way from the proletarian cinema postulated by *A Queda*.

Timothy Barnard

Awards: Special Jury Prize, Berlin, 1978; Best Actor (Nelson Xavier), Brasilia, 1978.

1. Robert Stam, "Formal Innovation and Radical Critique in *The Fall*," *Brazilian Cinema*, eds. Randal Johnson and Stam (East Rutherford, N.J.: Associated University Presses, 1982), 240.

Mar de Rosas

Sea of Roses [A Bowl of Cherries]
Brazil, 1977, 90', colour

Dir Ana Carolina Teixeira Soares *Scr* Carolina *Cinematog* Lauro Escoral *Ed* Vera Freire *Art dir* Heloísa Buarque de Hollanda *Mus* Paulo Hurculano *Prod* Area Produções Cinematográficas, Mário Volcoff, Produçoes Cinematográficas, R.F. Farias, and Embrafilme *Act* Cristina Pereira, Norma Bengell, Otávio Augusto, Miriam Muniz, Ary Fontoura, Hugo Carvana

Unlike other Brazilian women directors of her generation, Ana Carolina received little formal instruction in filmmaking but learned her craft by working alongside male directors, such as Paulo Rufino and Geraldo Sarno. Her first feature-length work, *Mar de Rosas*, was the first feature by a woman director to successfully reach the screen following the 1964 military coup (Teresa Trautman's *Os Homens Que Eu Tive* (1973) was censored on "moral" grounds). And as it was co-produced by the state film agency Embrafilme, it received wide distribution throughout Brazil.

Mar de Rosas is the first in a trilogy of works narrating the coming of age of young, rebellious, middle-class women in the urban, industrialised central south of Brazil (it was followed by *Das Tripas Coração* in 1982 and *Sonho de Valsa* in 1986). Both "gynocentric" in generic influence (it borrows heavily from family melodrama) and increasingly "gynofocused" as its plot unfolds, this "instalment" follows the pre-pubescent protagonist Betinha (Cristina Pereira) through a series of confrontations with the adult world (and by allegorical extension, a repressive, patriarchal regime) while weathering a botched vacation with her parents.

Following an altercation between her father (Hugo Carvana) and mother (Norma Bengell) in a Rio motel bathroom, Betinha and her mother flee onto the Rio-São Paulo highway (a prime exemplar of the so-called Brazilian "economic miracle" touted by the military government). We are convinced that the mother (ironically named Felicidade) has stabbed the father to death. Yet instead of seizing the opportunity to seek anonymity and possible freedom in the hinterland of Greater Brazil, by force of habit (or, the film suggests, out of an atavistic masochism), the nervous pair head straight for "home." Soon, they are pursued by a moustached man (Otávio Augusto) wearing a suit and tie and driving a black Volkswagen. An "agent" dispatched by the surviving father, Mr. Barde takes the father's place behind the wheel, escorting them in the VW to ensure the proper restoration of familial—and social—order. After three attempts at escape, first by Betinha, then by mother and daughter during a stopover in a sleepy provincial town, the tireless escort corners them on a train, and, when he finally handcuffs Felicidade, Betinha chooses her own destination—and destiny.

Throughout, Betinha's irreverence serves as both the catalyst for, and vehicle of, transgression and critical commentary with regard to conventional social and screen norms of gender conduct. This is expressed by way of the dialogue (she cheerfully disrupts Mr. Barde's tedious, self-congratulatory monologue by prattling the word "clitoris" as though it were a childhood rhyme); in premeditated acts of physical revenge (in recurrent bouts of Electral frenzy, Betinha attempts to stab, burn, and bury her mother, then seriously wounds their smalltown host, Dr. Dirceu, by planting razor blades in a bar of soap); and in Ana Carolina's unconventional choreography and framing of the women characters in "unladylike" positions, exemplified in an unprecedented, low-angled close-up of Betinha squatting as she urinates by the roadside. Thus, in this film, the director introduces the *female* body as a privileged site not for the projection of male desire but for the somatization of sexual repression, torture, and resistance experienced under patriarchy and, more specifically, under the military regime supported by the upper middle class.

Ana Carolina's violation of social and sexual "taboos," her tendency to allow her characters to play out their death and sex drives (à la Freud) within otherwise banal settings, have prompted some critics to find aesthetic and thematic resemblances between her work and the cinematic surrealism of Luis Buñuel. On the other hand, her propensity for social satire by way of pointed euphemism as well as ridicule (trapped in the black VW, Felicidade exclaims in neo-colonial English, "My God, perhaps today is the best day of my life!"), coupled with the improvised concatenation of the characters' actions and repartee (as in the scene where the actors philosophise atop a sandpile in Dr. Dirceu's office) converts the film's dramatic space into a "theatre of the absurd." However, it is the director's innovative fusion of family melodrama with the road movie format which provides the strongest ground for articulating a doubly dystopian vision of married and middle-class life under the Brazilian military, in which the repeated acts of human domination and persecution (along with paranoia and frustrated resistance) figure as leitmotifs.

Catherine Benamou

A Lira do Delirio

The Lyre of Delight
Brazil, 1978, 105', colour

Dir Walter Lima Jr. (b. 1938) *Scr* Lima Jr. *Cinematog* Dib Lutfi *Ed* Mair Tavares *Art dir* Regis Monteiro *Mus* Paulo Moura *Prod* Lima Jr. and Roberto Farias for Embrafilme *Act* Anecy Rocha, Claudio Marzo, Paulo César Pereio, Antonio Pedro, Tonico Pereira, Othonial Serra, Pedro Bira, Isabela Campos

In the midst of Niteroi's *carnaval*, *A Lira do Delirio* functions like the swansong of Cinema Nôvo, echoing the flamboyant, fractured style of Glauber Rocha and the bad taste of Cinema Marginal and Joachim Pedro de Andrade. At the same time, in the delirium of its thematic and stylistic juxtapositions and its free-form proximity to the French *nouvelle vague*, it stands as a remarkably original example of Walter Lima Jr.'s work.

Ness Elliot, whose name is an inversion of Elliot Ness, the heroic lead detective in the hit U.S. TV series, "The Untouchables," is sought after by all the male members of A Lira do Delirio, a scruffy carnival troupe from Niteroi—a suburb of Rio de Janeiro, across Guanabara Bay. She works as a dancer at a dingy nightclub in Lapa, the bohemian quarter of Rio. One of her friends, Claudio, who is jealous of all the attention paid to her, hires a marginal to try and involve her in drug dealing. When this ploy fails he kidnaps her baby, Guri-Guri. Desperate, Ness seeks help from her police-reporter friend. Playing detective, he gets a lead after the hotel killing of a drag queen (who was a dancer at the Casanova club). But, Guri-Guri had already been sold through a doctor involved in the trafficking of stolen children! The film continually shifts in and out of dreams, memories, and other subjective visualisations, and here flashes forward to carnival, one year later. Ness has been re-united with her child, but she doesn't seem to be any happier.

A Lira do Delirio is unusual for a work by a Cinema Nôvo director in that the central character is a woman—played by Glauber Rocha's sister, Anecy, who is also Lima's wife. It also (unusually) provides a sympathetic portrait of homosexuality, and is perhaps the key Brazilian film set during carnival to use the spirit of carnivalesque inversion equated with freedom as a central theme and a structuring device. Lima was especially clever in subsuming transgressions of temporal and spatial continuity and apparent technical glitches and acting flubs to an "anything goes" narrative structure. At the beginning of the film we meet the police reporter (played by a shabbily bearded Paulo César Pereio) in bizarre whiteface. In short order, he appears without make-up, and then in whiteface again. Later, in a scene filmed in a hospital, he shows up in the background of a corridor shot focusing on the kidnapper/doctor (who is also incongruously bearded). The reporter's position is later revealed to be the beginning of another shot, in another sequence. We cannot be sure if such "jumps" are erroneous or intentional. Indeed, it is as if the transformations of carnival apply to the editing of the film.

A Lira do Delirio was produced on a very low budget, and this is obvious in a number of ways: the film stock is grainy and the camera mostly hand-held. But the actors seem never to change their attire during the course of the narrative, and the sound of the camera motor can often be heard—elements that would normally be regarded as mistakes. No retakes seem to have been done where one might expect them: A cop's gum won't stick on a post; the reporter bangs on a window causing it to open unexpectedly; a banner which is lit to start a fire is magically retrieved, intact. Again, such "mistakes" actually work in the context of the carnivalesque, and they also echo early films of the French *nouvelle vague*, especially *A bout de souffle* (Jean-Luc Godard, 1960) and *Tirez sur le pianiste* (François Truffaut, 1960) where the directors tried to emulate *films maudits* to some extent. The use of black-and-white footage as Ness directly addresses the camera, surrounded by light bulbs, provides a degree of cinematic reflexivity reminiscent of "new wave" film movements in general, while adding to *A Lira do Delirio*'s fragmented, carnivalesque form. The narrative flow of images is disrupted indiscriminately with visual representations of thoughts—Ness' flashback of her putting Guri-Guri in the crib prior to the kidnapping—illustrations of dialogue—a taxi driver talks of smuggling, and we see the smuggling—and dreams—a playboy imagines his own suicide by drowning. Indeed, the film itself seems "free" to transcend time and space in any direction, especially through the subjectivity of character. And here, Ness is clearly the central character; her desire to be liberated is equated with her ability to dance, and the deliriousness of *carnaval* with the equivalently delirious potential of cinema.

Peter Rist

Awards: Three prizes at the Brasilia Film Festival, including Best Director and Best Actress (Anecy Rocha), 1978.

Coronel Delmiro Gouveia

Colonel Delmiro Gouveia
Brazil, 1978, 90', colour

Dir Geraldo Sarno (b. 1938) *Scr* Orlando Senna and Sarno *Cinematog* Lauro Escorel Filho *Ed* Amauri Alves *Art dir* Anisio Medeiros *Mus* J. Lins *Prod* Thomaz Farkas and Sarno for Saruê Filmes and Embrafilme *Act* Rubens de Falco, Sura Berdichevski, Nildo Parente, Jofre Soares, José Dumont, Isabel Ribeiro, Magalhães Graca

Begun in 1976 and shown in foreign film festivals in 1978, yet not released in Brazil until 1979, *Coronel Delmiro Gouveia* can be thought of as being the last really significant work of the Cinema Nôvo movement. The film provides a historical reconstruction of the struggles of Delmiro Gouveia, a rich merchant and exporter from Recife, against foreign commercial interests. The film's nationalist perspective is amplified by the many allusions and references it makes to earlier works of Cinema Nôvo: an encircling camera reminiscent of Ruy Guerra and Glauber Rocha and the squeaking of oxcart axles (*Vidas Secas*, 1963, q.v.), while the narrative focus on the downfall of an entrepreneur is similar to that of *São Bernardo* (1972, q.v.). More originally, as Louis Marcorelles has noted,[1] *Coronel Delmiro Gouveia* combines elements of the Hollywood action film (specifically the Western genre) with a rigorous, somewhat Brechtian social analysis, opening as a documentary on an interview with an old worker (or an actor playing the role: it is never made clear).[1]

Geraldo Sarno was born in Pocoes (Bahia). He studied law in the state capital Salvador and moved to São Paulo where he began making documentary films produced by Thomaz Farkas in 1964 (inspired by the visit of Fernando Birri (*Los inundados*, 1961, q.v.) and his associates at the Argentine documentary film school). Sarno's first film as a director, the medium-length *Viramundo* (1965), has become recognised as one of the key works in the São Paulo documentary movement. Beginning with the arrival of migrants from the northeast at São Paulo's train station, *Viramundo* sequentially traces their decline: "Arrival in the city leads to work; bad working conditions lead to unemployment; unemployment leads to charity and marginality; marginality leads to religious catharsis and trance; the lack of resolution through the preceding means leads to the return to the Northeast."[2] The critics Jean-Claude Bernadet, Julianne Burton, and José Carlos Avellar all consider *Viramundo* a prototype of the

Brazilian "interventionist" documentary of the 1960s. After making two more short documentaries for Farkas, Sarno directed nine of the twenty-two short documentaries in a remarkable series that Farkas produced on Brazil's northeast between 1969 and 1971. The first of these, *Viva Cariri* (1969) documents the attempt to industrialise the *sertão* around Joazeiro (the city founded by Padre Cicero). Avellar considers this film to be representative of a move towards a more objective style of Brazilian documentary while recognising its creative use of sound. Elsewhere, Bernadet points to Sarno's *Iaô: A Iniciacão num Terreiro Gege-Nago* (1976) as being a kind of self-criticism of the earlier films wherein the director occupied an exalted position. In *Iaô*, Sarno's second feature-length film, an attempt was made to view *candomblé* uncritically, from within, unlike *Viramundo* which showed the *umbandistas'* naïve religious beliefs as contributing to their oppressed state.

In addition to working as a scriptwriter and production manager, Sarno had directed twenty films before undertaking *Coronel Delmiro Gouveia*. Only one of these, *O Picapau Amarelo* (1974), based on Monteiro Lobato's children's stories, was a fiction feature. Sarno's documentary background is clear from *Coronel Delmiro Gouveia*'s opening, apparently a documentary interview with the old worker who remembers the Colonel fondly. Delmiro Gouveia (Rubens de Falco) lives extravagantly but sides with the people and consequently suffers persecution by the Governor of Pernambuco state. He is rescued from jail by a band of *cangaceiros*, who are viewed individually in documentary-like close-ups and whose dramatic siege is also viewed in an observational, extreme long shot, nonfiction style. Gouveia hides in the *sertão* under the protection of Colonel Ulisses Luna (Jofre Soares), taking the Governor's stepdaughter with him. He builds a hydroelectric plant and a cotton thread mill and takes advantage of the blockade of English ships during World War I to conquer the Brazilian market. When Gouveia refuses to negotiate with the English owners of Machine Cottons in 1917, he is assassinated, at which point the film becomes highly stylised: the fast cutting on machines being destroyed appears to cause the Colonel's body to be riddled with bullets. This ironic echo of Soviet montage is reprised at the end of the film, when, in 1929, the new English overseers coldly gesture to workers who break up the mill, cart the pieces to the abandoned hydro project, and throw them into the churning waters of Paulo Afonso Falls—a metaphor for the exploitation and abandonment of Brazil.

As Avellar says, "Much of the most significant Brazilian cinematic production is situated exactly in [the] imprecise border between documentary and fiction."[3] *Coronel Delmiro Gouveia* is a clear example of this tendency and is also aligned with the best works of Cinema Nôvo in its dialectical and ambiguous treatment of characters and events. But Sarno goes somewhat further than Rocha and Guerra in being strongly critical of the central personage, Delmiro Gouveia, especially his treatment of women and his flamboyant lifestyle, while representing him as a national, anti-imperialist hero.

Peter Rist

Awards: Best Film (shared), Havana, 1979.

1. Louis Marcorelles, "Le nouveau cinéma brésilien veut rattraper le temps perdu," *Le Monde*, 30 March 1978.
2. Jean-Claude Bernadet, "The Sociological Model, or His Master's Voice: Ideological Form in *Viramundo*," *The Social Documentary in Latin America*, ed. Julianne Burton (Pittsburgh: University of Pittsburgh Press, 1990), 230.
3. Jose Carlos Avellar, "Seeing, Hearing, Filming: Notes on the Brazilian Documentary," *Brazilian Cinema*, eds. Randal Johnson and Robert Stam (East Rutherford, N.J.: Associated University Presses, 1982), 334.

Bye Bye Brasil

Bye bye Brazil
Brazil-France, 1980, 110', colour

Dir Carlos Diegues (b. 1940) *Scr* Diegues and Leopoldo Serran *Cinematog* Lauro Escorel Filho *Art dir* Anisio Medeiros *Ed* Mair Tavares *Mus* Chico Buarque, Roberto Menescal, and Dominguinhos *Prod* Lucy and Luiz Carlos Barreto for Aries Cinematográfica and Embrafilme (Brazil) and Gaumont (France) *Act* José Wilker, Bety Faria, Fábio Junior, Zaira Zambelli, Príncipe Nabor, Emanoel Cavalcanti, José Márcio Passos, Carlos Kroeber, Jofre Soares, Marieta Severo.

Bye Bye Brasil is the quintessence of the state film agency Embrafilme's success in the early 1980s. It was financed by Embrafilme, and more than recouped this investment, drawing close to 1½ million spectators (ranking tenth for all Brazilian films between 1980 and 1984). It was championed as being an ideal recipient of state money according to the 1975 National Cultural Policy, in its attempt to "create a national identity through the preservation of regional diversity";[1] and it was an international success—it was, for example, the third most successful Brazilian film of all time in the U.S., grossing $1.3 million.

After the enormous commercial success of *Xica da Silva* (1976, q.v.), Carlos Diegues made *Chuvas de Verão* (1978) which Randal Johnson calls "the first, maybe the only, Brazilian film to treat aging with the dignity and respect it deserves."[2] Having moved far from the radical experiments in both narrative style and ideological content that characterized his early works of Cinema Nôvo, with *Bye Bye Brasil* in 1979 Diegues produced the most satisfying example of his "new form of spectacle" which he had proclaimed in 1966. In following a group of travelling *carioca* performers, the Caravana Rolidei, through the northeast, northern Amazon, and central plateau regions of Brazil, Diegues manages to humorously entertain while creating metaphors of human prostitution and penetration, as well as criticising his own role of artist and producer of media.

The Caravana Rolidei includes the principals Lorde Cigane ("Lord Gypsy," played by José Wilker), "King of Magicians and Clairvoyants," Salomé (Bety Faria), "Queen of the Rumba," and Andorinha ("Swallow," Príncipe Nabor), the "Muscle King." They have driven their truck from Rio, and the film introduces them in the town of Piranhas (Bahia), on the banks of the São Francisco river. Here they pick up a budding accordionist, Ciço (Fábio Junior), and his pregnant wife Dasdô (Zaira Zambelli). At a roadside bar, Lord Gypsy learns about a new land of plenty in Altamira, which becomes his ultimate destination. In Maceió, the capital of Alagoas, they confront traffic and pollution, but farther up the coast in Paripueira they find an oceanfront paradise, suitable for setting up their tent. They head northwest through the *sertão*, and in Entremontes (Pernambuco) they encounter villagers praying for rain. Then, after passing through Piauí state, Dasdô's daughter is born on the side of the Trans-Amazonian highway in Maranhão state. From there they cross the Xingú River in Para state, and are disappointed by their intended El Dorado, Altamira, where the film shows the worst multinational exploitation of the rainforest region. While travelling on the Amazon River to the port city of Belém, Ciço asks his wife to become a prostitute. When they get there, completely out of luck and funds, the group splits up after Swallow is beaten at arm wrestling, and the re-united young couple fly to Brasilia. We learn that Ciço has become a successful *forró* musician, and he and Dasdô are surprised to meet up again with Lord Gypsy and Salomé who have Americanised and renamed their troupe Caravana Rolidey (an attempt at the English word "holiday"). The young couple bid goodbye to the troubadours who now head farther west towards Rondônia with Frank Sinatra's voice blaring on the truck's loudspeakers.

Diegues' humorous critique of popular Brazilian culture is achieved with a great deal of self-referentiality. Johnson claims that the narrative of *Bye Bye Brasil* functions as a metaphor for the history of Brazilian cinema—moving through the *sertão* of Cinema Nôvo to the compromises of commercialism and foreign exploitation in Amazonia—while others suggest that the film targets the "low culture" of Brazilian television. In Entremontes, Lord Gypsy meets a struggling yet relaxed travelling film exhibitor/projectionist, Zé da Luz (Joe of the Light), played by the Cinema Nôvo icon Jofre Soares. Zé is showing one of the most popular, "classic" black-and-white Brazilian films, *O Ebrio* (1946), written and directed by its female star, Gilda de Abreu. The lack of success of Zé's entrepreneurship is equated with Lord Gypsy's failure to lure audiences away from their communal television viewing. But, the Caravana is clearly moving with the times, in pretending to bring "other," specifically North American elements of entertainment to the Brazilian interior—at one point, a magical fake snowfall is created on stage. It is surely no accident that Globo TV stars Faria and Wilker were cast as the Caravana's key players, who become prostitute and pimp during hard times. Indeed, *Bye Bye Brasil*'s allusions to *pornochanchada* and the famed erotic allure of Globo TV increase with the truck's arrival in Brasilia—it is now full of "go-go girls."

Bye Bye Brasil is dedicated to Brazilians of the twenty-first century, and, according to the director, it presents a country in transition. Interestingly, though, the disappearing Brazil is not just represented by characters like Zé da Luz but also by the much younger Ciço and Dasdô, who stay in Brasilia performing traditional *nordeste forró* music. And although it is Cigane, the gypsy, who is posited as the most Brazilian of characters—wandering the country, prepared to sell anything and anyone in order to become successful—the more conservative, traditionalist alternative is championed to some extent through the character of Ciço, the nickname of the legendary backlands rebel priest, Padre Cicero.

"Caca" Diegues (as he is popularly known) is clearly the most successful of the Cinema Nôvo directors in adapting to the rapidly changing Brazilian cultural and economic climate, and *Bye Bye Brasil* remains his most sophisticated attempt at simultaneously indulging and criticising the contemporary situation. In 1984, he remade *Ganga Zumba* (1963, q.v.) on a big budget as *Quilombo*, gaining the financial success that the earlier work failed to achieve. He managed to continue making films during the virtual collapse of Brazil's film industry in the bleak late 1980s, with an attempt at teenage romance, *Um Trem para as Estrelas* (1987), and a very interesting carnivalesque parody of work in a dubbing studio, *Dias Melhores Virão* (1989), which brings his witty critique of Brazilian lowbrow culture right up to date.

Peter Rist

1. José Mário Ortiz Ramos, *Cinema, Estado, e Lutas Culturais* (Rio de Janeiro: Paz e Terra, 1983), 174-86. Quoted by Randal Johnson, *The Film Industry in Brazil: Culture and the State* (Pittsburgh: University of Pittsburgh Press, 1987), 154.
2. Randal Johnson, *Cinema Novo X 5* (Austin: University of Texas Press, 1982), 82.

Gaijin, Caminhos da Liberdade

Gaijin
Brazil, 1980, 105', colour

Dir Tizuka Yamasaki (b. 1949) *Scr* Yamasaki and Jorge Durán *Cinematog* Edgar Moura *Ed* Lael Alves Rodrigues and Vera Freire *Art dir* Yurika Yamasaki *Mus* John Neschling *Prod* Carlos Alberto Diniz for C.P.C., Sumiko Akiyoshi Yamasaki, José Gomez Frazão, and Embrafilme *Act* Kyoko Tsukamoto, Antonio Fagundes, Jiro Kawarasaki, Gianfrancesco Guarnieri, Alvaro Freire, José Dumont

Only twenty Brazilian feature films had been directed by women before Tizuka Yamasaki began shooting *Gaijin, Caminhos da Liberdade* in 1979, and none of these had been as ambitious—dealing with the oppression of immigrants and other marginals as well as women—or received as much critical acclaim: *Gaijin* won five awards, including Best Film at the 1980 Gramado film festival.

Yamasaki, who is of Japanese descent, was born in Porto Alegre. She studied film in Brasilia and Rio de Janeiro. She assisted Nelson Pereira dos Santos in 1974 on *O Amuleto de Ogum* and again in 1977 on *Tenda dos Milagres*. She was also an assistant to Glauber Rocha on his last film, *A Idade da Terra* (1980), before embarking on a solo directing career with *Gaijin*. Her first film was a personal project based on the experiences of her Japanese grandmother and Brazilian-born mother.

Gaijin—Japanese for "outsider"—documents the struggles of a shy young Japanese woman, Titoé (Kyoko Tsukamoto), who emigrates to Brazil in 1908. The film opens with a double framing device. First we see people on the streets of contemporary São Paulo, providing an urban multiracial perspective, and then we see Titoé and her fellow emigrées leaving Japan and arriving in São Paulo state to work on a coffee plantation, accompanied by Titoé's retrospective voice-over. She has an arranged marriage to Ryuyi Yamada (Jiro Kawarasaki), whom she gradually learns to love and respect, but he dies in a fever epidemic. The Japanese are virtual slaves. Their cultural heritage has nurtured them on obedience and hard work while their lack of Portuguese renders them even less able to protest. However, Titoé learns to be less passive and docile from the dissenting Ueno, the Brazilian migrant worker Ceara (José Dumont) and her Italian co-workers, especially the Calabrian Enrico (Gianfrancesco Guarnieri), who leads a strike. The forces of oppression are most clearly represented by British businessmen, discussing the need to hire Japanese labourers in order to fill the gap left by the abolition of slavery, and the brutal, roughly-bearded overseer, Chico Santos (Alvaro Freire). But, another Brazilian foreman, Tonho (Antonio Fagundes), becomes politically enlightened during the course of the film, and enables a group, including Titoé, to escape the Santa Rosa plantation by burning part of the neighbouring forest. At the end of the film, it is suggested that Titoé, who is working in a São Paulo factory, will begin a harmonious new relationship with Tonho, who is now a labour leader.

Among Yamasaki's real achievements with *Gaijin* was her ability to link Titoé's oppression as a subservient Japanese woman with that of other women, other racial minorities, other immigrants, and other workers.[1] She cleverly united all marginal groups in their class struggles. Also noteworthy was her representation of language. Every character speaks his/her own language: Japanese, Italian, English, Spanish, and Portuguese are all heard in *Gaijin*. During the course of the film, one can readily appreciate the difficulty with which people were communicating with one another, and it is only towards the end that Titoé et al. begin to speak and understand Portuguese. The range of languages is also a marker of the actual multi-ethnic formation of the Brazilian nation (and to the continuing dominance of English), which has rarely been recognised in other films. On the other hand, Yamasaki didn't shy away from criticising the myths of Brazilian racial and sexual harmony. In Titoé's first sexual liaison with Ryuyi, she is shown to resist, and faces the camera as if protesting her husband's forcefulness. One can extrapolate from this scene of women's sexual subjugation and others in the film, where Portuguese-speaking men are depicted as surly and sexually aggressive, that Brazilian miscegenation has emerged out of rape rather than love. Indeed, when the film returns to São Paulo, 1980, one understands that Brazil's economic growth has probably been achieved primarily through the exploitation of immigrant labour.

In other ways, *Gaijin* presents a very lyrical view of immigrant life. The cutting from one scene to another is often bridged with matched sounds. A montage showing the consummation of love in Titoé and Ryuyi's marriage is echoed with a similar montage at the end of the film where Tonho pursues Titoé. Her occasional flashbacks to Japan are rendered in soft focus and muted colours evoking nostalgia and loss, whereas Edgar Moura's colour cinematography of scenes in the coffee fields is sometimes too beautiful. But such lushness is perhaps justified in presenting the dignity of agricultural labour.

After making a medium-length film (*A Embaixada do Cinema*, 1982) and another feature (*Parahyba, Mulher Macho*, 1983), Yamasaki made a highly complex fiction feature using the backdrop of the 1984 mass movement towards direct elections, *Patriamada* (1985). Its central love triangle involving a young female reporter and two men is unusual, and its mixture of documentary political reality and fiction is audacious and innovative. But *Patriamada*'s treatment of gender relations is ultimately not especially progressive, and its experimental structure does not always engender coherence. Yamasaki continued to find Brazilian film work even in the worst of times: in 1991, she directed a Xuxa vehicle called *Lua de Cristal* when there were virtually no other feature film assignments in the country.

Peter Rist

Awards: Best First Feature, Honourable Mention, Cannes, 1980; five prizes including Best Film, Gramado (Brazil), 1980; Best Film, Havana, 1980.

1. See Zuzana Pick, *The New Latin American Cinema: A Continental Project* (Austin: University of Texas Press, 1993), 150–6, for this and other concepts to which I am indebted for my analysis.

Pixote, a Lei do Mais Fraco

Pixote
Brazil, 1980, 127', colour

Dir Héctor Babenco (b. 1946) *Scr* Babenco and Jorge Durán, inspired by the novel *Infancia dos Mortos* by José Louzeiro *Cinematog* Rodolfo Sánchez *Mus* John Neschling *Ed* Luiz Elias *Prod* Embrafilme *Act* Fernando Ramos da Silva, Marilia Pera, Jorge Jiliao, Gilberto Moura, José Nilson dos Santos, Edilson Linos, Zenildo Oliveira Santos

Following in the tradition of *Los olvidados* (Luis Buñuel, Mexico, 1950) and other films throughout the continent, *Pixote, a Lei do Mais Fraco* presents a tough, uncompromising view of the world of street children in São Paulo. Although director Héctor Babenco was born in Argentina, he first began making films in Brazil in the mid-1970s. His earlier works include *O Rei da Noite* (1975) and *Lúcio Flávio* (1978), a popular film about a well-known underground criminal. While both films were well received, it was *Pixote* that made him an internationally known director. After the success of *Pixote*, Babenco left Brazil for Hollywood where he made the English language features *Kiss of the Spider Woman* (1985, q.v.), based on the novel by Manuel Puig, *Ironweed* (1988), based on the novel by William Kennedy, *Foolish Hearts* (1990), and *At Play in the Fields of the Lord* (1991).

Babenco's first concept for *Pixote* was to make a documentary about a reform school, but the authorities denied him access to the school. Still intrigued by the idea of a film about children living on the margins of society, Babenco turned to José Louzeiro's novel, *Infância dos Mortos*, as the basis for a fictional film about street children. He spent over a year interviewing more than one thousand kids from the slums of São Paulo before deciding on 27 who would be featured in the film. They worked together for four months to improvise the parts they would play, with Babenco encouraging them to make up their own past histories of the characters.

The earlier idea of making a documentary carries over into the visual style of *Pixote*. The film opens with Babenco's direct address to the audience from a rooftop overlooking a *favela*. Citing statistics about the plight of homeless children in Brazil, this documentary-like introduction seems intended to impart a sense of realism to the rest of the film. He even goes so far as to point to Fernando Ramos da Silva, the boy who will play Pixote in the film, standing in front of a shack with his mother.

In the first part of the film we see Pixote's life in a juvenile detention centre. His routine incarceration is part of a generalised clean-up of the streets of São Paulo. Because he is only ten years old, he will soon be released along with his fellow detainees, who are all under eighteen years old. Life in the detention centre is a series of brutalising experiences. The older boys gang rape the younger ones, while the police routinely beat them in order to extract confessions. The only escape for Pixote, as for the other boys, is smoking dope and sniffing glue. In their free time the boys "play" by imitating police torture sessions which use fake electric shock devices and perform mock bank robberies with wooden sticks for guns. Da Silva was killed by police several years after the film was made.

After his friend Fumaca is beaten and killed by the police, Pixote escapes from the detention centre with a group of boys. Life on the outside has its moments of exhilaration, but he still faces a violent world where homeless boys are easy prey. He teams up with Dito and his transvestite girlfriend, Liliaca, and embarks on a life of petty crime. This pseudo-family, with Pixote as the child, survives by snatching wallets to get money to eat. Their chance at the big time comes when a drug dealer commissions them to deliver cocaine to Rio de Janeiro. Arriving in Rio, they are as giddy as any tourists, splashing on the beaches and fantasizing about what they will do with all the money from the drug deal. They are double-crossed, however, and lose a portion of the drugs and escalate the level of their crimes to include murder. With the money the trio salvages from the drug deal, they buy the rights to a prostitute, Sueli (Marilia Pera), who willingly complies with their scheme to rob her customers. Acting as decoys, they bring johns to Sueli and rob them, literally when their pants are down. When one of the robberies goes sour, Pixote panics and in the process kills both the john and his friend Dito. The scene where Sueli attempts to console Pixote is one of the most memorable of the film. While she begins to make sexual overtures toward him, he holds her and begins to suckle at her breast. Despite all of his bravado, Pixote reveals that he is still a child. After she rejects him, Pixote leaves and walks into the night alone.

Throughout the film, Babenco stresses the dichotomy between Pixote the boy and Pixote the man. At the age of ten, he has far more experience with sex and drugs than many adults; he is a criminal and has even committed murder. The life of the streets forces him to age quickly, yet at the same time we are always aware that he is still a child. At the time of its release Vincent Canby of *The New York Times* wrote that "Da Silva, who plays Pixote, has one of the most eloquent faces ever seen on the screen."

Pixote received considerable attention when it was first released, in large part because of its extremely graphic depictions of sodomy and physical brutality. As U.S. scholar Robert Stam has noted, one of the film's biggest failings is that it never puts Pixote's experiences into a larger political context.[1] Only the corrupt institutions of the police and the juvenile detention homes are criticised, not the society which produced them. Babenco himself has noted, "I never did *Pixote* because I wanted to convey a message. I knew I had all of the material for a political movie, but that didn't interest me at all."

Susan Ryan

Awards: Second Prize and Special Award, Locarno, 1981; Special Jury Prize, San Sebastián, 1981; two prizes, Biarritz, 1981; Best Foreign Language Film, New York Film Critics and Los Angeles Film Critics, 1981; Best Actress (Marilia Pera), National Society of Film Critics, U.S., 1981; Best Film, Sydney, 1982.

1. Robert Stam, review of *Pixote* in *Cineaste* 12, No. 3 (1983): 44–45.

Eles Não Usam Black-Tie

They Don't Wear Black Tie
Brazil, 1981, 120', colour

Dir Leon Hirszman (1938–1988) *Scr* Gianfrancesco Guarnieri and Hirszman, based on the play of the same title by Guarnieri (1959) *Cinematog* Lauro Escorel Filho *Art dir* Marcos Weinstock and Jefferson de Albuquerque *Mus* Radamés Gnatalli *Prod* Hirszman for Leon Hirszman Produções and Embrafilme (Brazil) *Act* Fernanda Montenegro, Gianfrancesco Guarnieri, Carlos Alberto Ricelli, Bete Mendes

Eles Não Usam Black-Tie, the fourth feature film by Leon Hirszman, is based on the play of the same title by playwright and actor Gianfrancesco Guarnieri. The idea to film this play about labour unrest and its impact on family relations first came to Hirszman after seeing the piece performed in the late 50s. Although the play was banned in Brazil from 1964 through 1977 by the military government, Hirszman began discussions with Guarnieri to write an adaptation. It wasn't until 1979 that they began to work together examining the original text and discussing it with sociologists, political activists, and those involved in popular theatre with the idea of not only updating it but also making it more relevant to the Brazilian social and political situation. Hirszman obtained even more information about the workers' movement in São Paulo through making a documentary on the 1979 metal workers' strike, *ABC da Greve* (1980). A political opening in the late 70s allowed the script for the film to be passed by the censors and shooting began in 1980.

The film focuses on a factory strike and the resulting repercussions on Tião, a young worker, and his father Otávio, a long-time labour activist, who also works at the plant. Tião will soon marry another worker, Maria, who is also pregnant with his child. His one desire is to avoid problems and have a decent life together with her. As tensions mount at the factory, Tião remains non-committal about the strike while his father organises with other union members to stop work when it is most advantageous. The film privileges Otávio's political activism but at the same time tries to give some understanding of the political circumstances which have created an apolitical person like Tião. His apathy is partially due to fifteen years of dictatorship and the pain he witnessed as a child in seeing his father imprisoned and the family torn apart. The constant oppression of a society which keeps working people living in poverty and has others brutalised by the police is shown to be why people like Tião decide to withdraw into their familial cocoon rather than confront the system.

Through the arguments between Tião and Otávio and the differing opinions of the others organising the strike, Hirszman succeeds in showing the complexities of organising within the labour movement. Otávio and his friend Bráulio are in favour of waiting until their organisation is stronger while a recently fired worker advocates an immediate strike. Once the strike is called, Tião surprises and angers both his father and Maria by crossing the picket line. The film ends with a violent confrontation between the striking workers and the police. Ironically, it is Bráulio, the advocate of non-violence, who is killed. According to Hirszman, this character was modeled after Santos Dias, a labour activist who was assassinated in 1980. The strike also brings an end to Tião's relationships with both Otávio and Maria, and Tião is forced to leave home to live with friends. The final shots of Braulio's funeral procession are a fitting end to this strong film which does not shy away from the contradictions of the working class.

Hirszman has said that he wanted to make a film which would attract not only the politically committed but also have popular appeal as well. *Eles Não Usam Black-Tie* uses emotion without being overly melodramatic and is effective largely because of the strength of the writing and the direction of performances by well-known stage actress Fernanda Montenegro (who also starred in Hirszman's *A Falecida*) as the mother, Carlos Alberto Ricelli as Tião, and the playwright Guarnieri as Otávio (he had previously played the role of Tião when the play was originally produced in the '50s). All of the main characters are shown with a complexity and depth which is rarely found in depictions of the working class in Brazilian feature films. By using drama and emotion without sentimentality, Hirszman demonstrated that it was possible to create a moving work while maintaining a commitment to political filmmaking.

Susan Ryan

Awards: Best Film, Havana, 1981; Best Film (shared), Special Jury Prize, Second International Critics' Prize (FIPRESCI), Third Agis Prize, Fourth OCIC Prize, Venice, 1981; Best Film, Nantes, 1981; Best Film, Valladolid, 1981; Critics' Award, Cartagena, 1983.

Cabra Marcado para Morrer

Twenty Years Later [Man Marked to Die]
Brazil, 1984, 119', colour and b+w

Dir Eduardo Coutinho (b. 1933) *Scr* Coutinho *Cinematog* Fernando Duarte (b+w, 1964) and Edgar Mouracol (colour, 1981) *Mus* Rogério Rossini *Prod* Produções Cinematográficas Mapa, Coutinho, and Vladimir Carvalho *Act* Elisabete Teixeira and family, João Virginia da Silva, and the workers of the Galiléia sugar refinery

In 1962, shortly after serving as production manager for the National Students Union on the Cinema Nôvo anthology film *Cinco Vezes Favela* (1962), Eduardo Coutinho accompanied a group of students from the Union's Centre for Popular Culture to the poor northeast of the country to film a short documentary on social conditions there. Among the footage they returned with, for a film that was never completed, were protests marking the assassination that year of peasant league leader João

Pedro Teixeira. From this footage grew the idea of making a feature film, *Cabra Marcado para Morrer*, about Teixeira and his league's struggles, with his widow Elisabete and league comrades playing themselves. Coutinho returned to the region in late 1963, but shooting was delayed when the area came under direct military control—a bad omen. After moving the production and thereby losing all the real-life actors except Elisabete, shooting began in late February; 40% of the script was shot and the footage sent to a laboratory in Rio de Janeiro when a military coup ousted President João Goulart on April 1. The film was an immediate target of the local military: the camp was raided on March 31, scattering crew and actors. A few crew members were jailed and all of Coutinho's equipment was seized; local newspapers heralded this blow against "communist subversion." Its actors in hiding and without equipment, *Cabra Marcado para Morrer* seemed marked never to be completed.

"Twenty years later," or almost, in 1981, Coutinho resolved to do something with the footage he had salvaged at the laboratory. He had made several television documentaries in the northeast in the late 1970s, and a political opening introduced by the new military president, General João Baptista Figueredo (1979–85) tempted him to try to locate Elisabete and the league activists who had gone underground in 1964. Transferring the surviving 35mm footage onto 16mm, he set out to find out what had become of them and to show them the fragments of the film they had acted in. The result is an unusually poignant human drama, both sobering and uplifting, that reveals the true human cost of military rule and repression. Easily mixing sentiment with a clear-headed look back at an era when, as Coutinho remarks in a prologue, there was "a sense that everything was headed towards a fatal convergence," *Cabra* creates its own intricate convergence between fact and fiction and past and present, constructing a dialogue between the urban intellectual and his country's most disenfranchised through these film fragments. The film was an unexpected critical and popular success, within Brazil and far beyond; Vincent Canby of *The New York Times*, the dean of mainstream U.S. movie critics, called it "incomparable."

Cabra Marcado para Morrer is a web of events and relationships, depicted by both "real" and "fictive" images, that articulate these poor northeasterners' resistance and loss. Coutinho carefully reconstructs, and himself spins, the threads that weave past and present together. As 1964 footage rolls he tells us in voice-over at the beginning of the film about his rediscovery of some of the people we are watching on screen, while another voice-off recounts the area's history, its labour strife, etc. Two actors from the film, poor peasants, have survived the interim and are interviewed, as are former associates of Teixeira's. One man, interrogated by the military after the raid, relates that they were looking for Cuban guerrillas and filmmakers. There is a dissenting voice, too, in an interview with a man who says that the league was too radical and that he regrets being a member because of the hardship it caused him. We hear about the film script being recovered in a prison in 1966, and about two league activists who "disappeared" shortly before the discovery of two bodies so badly mutilated that they could not be identified.

The central figure in this constellation is Elisabete, whom Coutinho found after considerable searching. After spending four months in prison, she changed her name and began a new life in a remote community, earning a bare living teaching children (she has a second-grade education) and taking in washing. The arrival of Coutinho with his film footage in this tiny place, which doesn't even have television, is a considerable event. Ringed by sober-looking friends and neighbours, who are finding out about the past life of this woman for the first time, Elisabete sits outdoors and tells Coutinho what happened to her and her family after the coup, a story Coutinho punctuates in the editing room with images from the 1964 film. Of her 11 children, one was murdered and another "disappeared," an eighteen-year-old daughter committed suicide, and the rest took shelter with relatives, some never to be heard from again. Coutinho then sets out to find these children, travelling as far afield as Cuba, discovering a son who thought his mother had been killed in 1964 and staging a surprise on-screen reunion between mother and daughter. By the end of the film this relentless insistence on the importance of each of his subjects' lives begins to drag a little for the audience—so many children to find and interview!—and some of the scenes seem a little maudlin and create a sense of unease in the spectator at being a privileged witness of such intimate moments made public. In the end, however, Coutinho's larger goal prevails, to help his subjects become not just the protagonists of their own drama, as he set out to do in 1964, but protagonists of Brazil's history, in which they are rarely mentioned.

Timothy Barnard

Awards: Best Film, Havana, 1984; Best Film, Rio de Janeiro, 1984; prizes at Berlin, 1985; other prizes.

Memórias do Cárcere

Memories of Prison
Brazil, 1984, 178', colour

Dir Nelson Pereira dos Santos (b. 1928) *Scr* dos Santos, based on the memoirs of the same
title by Graciliano Ramos (1953) *Cinematog* José Medeiros and Antonio Luiz Soares *Art dir*
Irênio Maia *Mus* excerpts from the national anthem by Louis Moreau Gottschalk *Prod* Luiz
Carlos Barreto Produções Cinematográficas *Act* Carlos Vereza, Glória Pires, Jofre Soares,
José Dumont

As censorship eased and Brazil emerged from two decades of uninterrupted military rule—José Sarney was named President by Congress in
1985 and state government elections were held in 1987—Nelson Pereira
dos Santos (*Rio Quarenta Graus*, 1955, q.v., *Vidas Secas*, 1963, q.v., *Como
era Gostoso o Meu Francês*, 1971, q.v.) turned to an incident from a half-
century earlier in order to examine, obliquely, the recent past. As he had
done with *Vidas Secas*, dos Santos adapted a work by the author
Graciliano Ramos, one of Brazil's leading literary figures, for *Memórias do
Cárcere*, a first-hand account of repression and resistance under another
lengthy period of dictatorship in the country's history, the first presidencies of Getúlio Vargas (1930–45 and 1951–54). Ramos, a member of the
"Generation of 1930" writers' movement in the early years of that
dictatorship, when he produced his finest work (*Vidas Secas* in 1938 and
São Bernardo (1972, q.v.) in 1934), was caught up in a wave of repression
and imprisoned in 1936–37. The "Generation of 1930" was concerned with
social conditions in Ramos' native northeast, where he was working as the
Director of Public Instruction in his home town of Alagoas at the time of
his arrest. Tarred with the brush of "communism" by the Right, he fell
victim to sweeping repression in the country following Vargas' crushing
of the left-wing National Liberation Alliance (ANL) in 1935. Arrested
without charge and sent to the Ilha Grande penal island, where political
prisoners would again be sent in the 1960s and '70s, Ramos kept a diary
of his experiences that formed the basis of his prison memoirs, written
from memory many years later and published posthumously in four
volumes the year of his death.

Vargas, like Juan Perón in Argentina (1946–55), was a contradictory
figure, an authoritarian populist who introduced limited social and
economic reforms—generally after the events depicted in *Memórias*—while
flirting with fascism and suspending constitutional rule. There is a sense,

in the first hour of the film, that Ramos' confinement will be brief and not unbearably uncomfortable, a rite of passage for a left-wing author. A prison guard asks for his autograph; bourgeois communists arrive in prison attended by servants; overnight visits with his wife and a host of necessities and small luxuries, including writing paper, are arranged through sympathetic or corrupt officials. There is even a celebration of the release of a book written before he was imprisoned (*Angústias*, 1936).

Everything changes, however, when Ramos is transferred from Ilha Grande to a rural labour camp. Not only do his own conditions worsen—he is sick with an ulcer, unable to obtain proper medical care, and cut off from sympathetic authorities—but his relationship with his fellow inmates begins to change. In the first prison he had shunned the Communist Party officials and developed friendships with the workers; here, exempt from the labour of rock-pounding because of his illness, he becomes a solitary figure, although he continues to take down his companions' life stories in his notebooks. He seems to scorn the collective decision-making process, the way a letter to Congress he has been enlisted to write is subject to interminable discussion and revision. Called upon to justify his purchase of a bed when sicker men are sleeping on the ground, he tells his fellow political prisoners "I bought it, it's mine. I'm a property owner." This part of the film is even more sombre, austere, and slowly-paced than the first, although like other films in its genre it achieves a sublime spirituality, affording a contemplation that is enhanced by its three-hour length and lack of musical effects. Finally, he is released (the film doesn't show us, but the following year he was appointed to the civil service in Rio de Janeiro under Vargas) but is forced to leave his notebooks behind with his fellow inmates, where they will be lost forever.

It is in this second part of *Memórias* that dos Santos addresses the vexing issues of privilege, complicity, and solidarity. While the film serves to reawaken popular memory and pay homage to those, like Ramos before them, who had suffered under the dictatorship, it also has the unsettling effect of questioning the relationship between a progressive cultural elite and those they speak for. This issue would have particular resonance in the Brazil of 1984: while it would be mistaken to speak of Brazil's dictatorship as benevolent, in contrast with its neighbours the country's successive military rulers did not seek a wholesale annihilation of national culture. The intellectual elite was generally able to continue working under constraint, and in this sense the image of Ramos, a solitary figure in the midst of so much human drama around him, scribbling in notebooks obtained through the connivance of fellow prisoners and prison guards, becomes a metaphor for the Brazilian intellectual. Dos Santos' ambivalence here is exemplary; it resonates throughout the work without intruding on the hermetic world of the film, Ramos' solitary prison existence. Critics have praised Ramos' work as achieving universality from "simple materials," and nearly thirty years after the release of his first feature film, dos Santos has achieved a similar effect, evidence of a mature vision. *Memórias* conveys a sense of timeless reflection through the minute examination of a single event, treating it with a wisdom that is neither complacent nor angry, sentimental or strident, but imbued with an awareness of life's complexities and compromises.

Timothy Barnard

Awards: International Critics' Prize (FIPRESCI), Cannes, 1984.

Kiss of the Spider Woman

O Beijo da Mulher Aranha
Brazil-U.S., 1985, 119', colour and b+w

Dir Héctor Babenco (b. 1946) *Scr* Leonard Schrader, based on the novel *El beso de la mujer araña* by Manuel Puig (1976) *Cinematog* Rodolfo Sanchez *Ed* Mauro Alice *Art dir* Clovis Bueno *Mus* John Neschling, in association with Nando Carneiro *Prod* David Weisman for H. B. Filmes (Brazil) and Sugar Loaf Films (U.S.) *Act* William Hurt, Raúl Juliá, Sonia Braga, José Lewgoy, Milton Gonçalves, Mirian Pyres, Fernando Torres, Herson Capri

Filmed in Brazilian studios and on location in São Paulo in 1984, *Kiss of the Spider Woman* is based on Argentine writer Manuel Puig's bestselling novel of the same title (also adapted as a play and a musical). Director Héctor Babenco (*Pixote, a Lei do Mais Fraco*, 1980, q.v.) shares Puig's birthplace but has spent his filmmaking career in Brazil and most recently in the United States (*Ironweed*, 1987; *At Play in the Fields of the Lord*, 1991). Babenco sets the film sometime around the novel's writing in a non-specified Latin American country ruled by a repressive military dictatorship. The film chronicles the growing relationship between two prison cellmates, a homosexual window dresser, Luis Molina (William Hurt), and a journalist turned revolutionary, Valentin Arregui (Raúl Juliá). Molina is serving an eight-year sentence for "impairing the morals of a minor," and Valentin is imprisoned for his involvement with a revolutionary group. Half-way through the film we discover that Molina is attempting to extract information from Valentin in exchange for a pardon. The gulf between these two completely opposed characters, a romantic, lower-class, Catholic homosexual and an atheist, upper-class, heterosexual revolutionary, slowly dissolves as their relationship grows from necessary tolerance, to respect and admiration, friendship, and love. The film employs several prison film conventions (homosexuality, brutality, informing, oppressive authority) but gives them a novel twist.

Kiss of the Spider Woman is suggestive stylistically and thematically of another prison film, Jean Renoir's *La Grande Illusion* (France, 1937). The opening shot of *Kiss* is a lengthy 360-degree pan/tilt of a prison room which introduces the central characters (Molina, Valentin) and location. The shot sets up a pattern of playing key scenes in long take, while also paralleling the camera strategy employed by Renoir (reframing, lateral depth of field, long takes). Both films are humanist dramas that reduce the political to the personal by concentrating on specific social barriers, national-class in *La Grande Illusion* and gender-sexual in *Kiss of the Spider Woman*.

To help ease the pain and boredom of prison existence, Molina narrates, for himself as much as Valentin, a (fictitious) World War II Nazi propaganda film, *Her Real Glory*. As in the novel Molina's narrated movie functions on several levels. The constructed fictional world parallels the socially-politically constructed "real" world which oppresses Molina and Valentin. Initially the movie signifies the ideological disparity between Molina (escapism) and Valentin (confrontation) but then develops into an emotional mirror of their inner conflicts and contradictions. In the narrated film Leni Laisson (Sonia Braga in one of her three roles), a composite camp parody of Hollywood B-movie queens, plays a Parisian chanteuse torn between the Resistance and her love for an enemy German officer. This echoes Valentin's love for Marta, a member of the "enemy" bourgeois, while Molina, like Leni, becomes a martyr for love.

In Puig's novel, the act of narrative reading is interrupted by the escapist B-movies that Molina narrates to Valentin, by the lengthy footnotes on social-psychological theories of homosexuality (all authentic except one), and by interjections of poetic reflection. Film is ill equipped to deal with all these discourses in one form (narrative); therefore Babenco compromises and appropriates the novel's postmodern form by incorporating different visual styles for the film's various locations: the prison cell (achromatic greys, blues, and the odd candle-lit gold to suggest a harsh reality), scenes outside the cell (conventional colour palette to portray a drab reality), and the flashback/subjective scenes (a stylized mixture of sepia and black and white to portray a fantasy world).

Disregarding minor plot changes, the film is a faithful adaptation of the novel's spirit and mood and Babenco finds cinematic equivalents for Puig's prose style. An example is the rendering of two key scenes which demonstrate the growing bond between Molina and Valentin and the symbolic merging of the political and the sexual. Puig's short, sparse dialogue and graphically rendered moments of intimate silence are translated by Babenco through mise-en-scène—warm, sensual lighting—sound and moving camera—long takes that move from medium shot to close-up. In the first scene a sick, incontinent Valentin soils his pants and Molina strips him, cleans his legs and buttocks, and dresses him. At this point Molina assumes the role he craves of the nurturing mother/wife (changing the diapers). But through the content—the concentration on the back of Valentin's legs and anal area—and the treatment—heavy breathing, hushed dialogue, and warm, intimate lighting—the scene sets up the (offscreen) sexual act—anal intercourse—which is consummated in the second "mirror" scene.

Although the film is in many ways progressive in its sexuality, some critics have taken its sexual politics to task (among them Vito Russo). They have interpreted the relationship as a retrograde homosexual seduction fantasy where Molina becomes a "man" after having had sex with Valentin. The film's critique of sexism may be less forthright than the novel, but Valentin's farewell plea to Molina that he no longer allow himself to be exploited can be read as both a critique of Molina's feminine, passive-destructive nature and an acceptance of his positive "feminine" traits. This is complemented by Babenco's unsympathetic portrayal of homophobia in the macho posturing of Valentin and the black policeman (Milton Gonçalves). The de-emphasis of sexual politics is due partly to the exclusion, for reasons of length, of Molina's narrated accounts of *The Cat People* (1942) and *I Walked with a Zombie* (1943), B-movies by Puig favourite Jacques Tourneur which function as meta-narratives on the novel's sexual politics.

Hurt's Oscar-winning portrayal of Molina is evidence of what a determined actor can achieve even when miscast. (Babenco wanted Burt Lancaster to play Molina originally; what a different film that would have been!) Hurt drew near-unanimous praise, but some were still critical of his portrayal. Hurt flirts with gay stereotype, but his detailed, nuanced performance suggests that much of it is role playing (the queen). Babenco's privileged direction of Molina (extreme close-ups and interior monologues) reveals a depth of character that makes Molina a very human and sympathetic character (funny, caring, hurting, smarter than he lets on). A more difficult critique to refute is that the film removes a layer of the novel's political complexity by eliminating the suggestion that Molina (the spinner of webs) and Valentin may have ulterior motives for their actions. Even with these criticisms, the film succeeds in bridging the gap between the political and the popular, a conscious strategy of many post-Cinema Nôvo Brazilian filmmakers.

Donato Totaro

Awards: Best Actor (William Hurt), Cannes, 1985; Best Actor (Hurt), Los Angeles Film Critics Award, 1985; Special Distinction (Foreign Film), The Independent Spirit Awards, 1985 (U.S.); Best Foreign Actor (Hurt), David Di Donatello Prizes, 1986 (Italy); Best Actor (Hurt), British Academy of Film and Television, 1986; Best Actor (Hurt), Academy of Motion Picture Arts and Sciences ("Oscar"), 1986.

A Hora da Estrela

The Hour of the Star
Brazil, 1985, 96', colour

Dir Suzana Amaral (b. 1933) *Scr* Amaral and Alfredo Oroz, based on the novel of the same title by Clarice Lispector (1977) *Cinematog* Edgar Moura *Art Dir* Clóvis Bueno *Mus* Marcus Vinicius *Prod* Raiz Produções Cinematográficas *Act* Marcélia Cartaxo, José Dumont, Tamara Taxman, Fernanda Montenegro

Suzana Amaral's first feature, *A Hora da Estrela*, successfully melds neo-realism with Cinema Nôvo to create an empathetic portrait of a rural northeasterner living in São Paulo. Amaral came to filmmaking late in life after raising a family of nine children. She returned to university in São Paulo (along with her eldest son) and, after graduating, began directing and writing documentaries for a local television station. In all, she made more than forty documentaries and short films before directing *A Hora da Estrela*.

Based on the novel of the same title by one of Brazil's foremost novelists, Clarice Lispector, the film is more a creative transposition than a literal adaptation. Ironically, the inspiration to transform the novel came to Amaral while she was studying filmmaking in New York City. After learning in 1977 that Lispector had died, she began rereading her novels and was immediately attracted to *A Hora da Estrela*, partially because it reflected some of her own experiences of living as an outsider in New York. After completing film school, she returned to Brazil to continue working in documentary (a 1979 documentary *My Life, Our Struggle* won an award at the Brasilia national film festival). It took nearly two years for Amaral and Alfredo Oroz to complete the screenplay for *A Hora da Estrela*, and shooting did not begin until 1985.

The novel and film both focus on the character of Macabéa, a homely, unkempt young woman who defines her existence in the film by declaring "I am a typist and a virgin, and I like Coca-Cola." Her personal hygiene leaves much to be desired, and her employers complain often about her dirt-smudged typing filled with errors. Amaral's identification with Macabéa is clear: we see and hear everything from her point of view. Although she is not much to look at, she is constantly observing others around her with a sense of innocent wonder. She listens in on the conversations of her roommates and her work colleague Gloria, whose vivacious and sexy personality is the opposite of her own. She learns about the world around her by listening to "Time" Radio, a program filled with trivial information. Her idea of fun on her day off is to ride the subways without any final destination. The life she leads is similar to this purposeless subway ride—day after day of work with no real aspirations or desires to change her way of being.

Despite her seeming lack of purpose and slovenly demeanour, the film reveals that Macabéa (Marcélia Cartaxo) does have an interior life, one in which she wishes she could be more like Gloria and the other girls. Although her sexuality is not evident in her appearance, Macabéa is sensual and longs for the relationships with men that Gloria has. A brief friendship with another displaced northeasterner, Olimpico, ends in rejection. He is as ignorant as Macabéa but has an arrogant manner which covers for his lack of knowledge. Her friend Gloria advises her to visit a fortune teller, where she learns that her life will change after meeting a foreigner. Sadly, the prophecy comes true quite suddenly when she is run over by a speeding Mercedes. It is here that Amaral takes the most liberties with the novel. Unlike the novel in which her death occurs without warning, the film cross-cuts between Macabéa's newfound sense of happiness upon learning her future and the impending doom of the car bearing down on her. For Amaral, the ending does not signify that

Macabéa has died; instead, there is a sense in which it might all be a dream, and that in this dream all of her hopes come true. In the final scenes, the realistic style of the rest of the film changes to brightly lit, slow-motion photography evoking a dream-state in which Macabéa is finally delivered from her miserable existence and achieves happiness.

In neo-realist fashion, Amaral focuses on the details of Macabéa's marginalised life to create her character: the dingy, run-down rooming house with its broken mirrors and chamber pots, her steady diet of hot dogs and Coca-Cola, and her pathetic attempts to look attractive with garish lipstick. The realistic mise-en-scène of the dimly lit and decrepit office and rooming house are as unappealing as Macabéa herself.

Amaral has called the original novel "a metaphor for the tensions between the two Brazils—the bustling lifestyle of the southerners which is contrasted to that of the underprivileged of the northeast, who may still claim their rights by force some day." This theme of contrasting rural and urban cultures can be traced back to the earliest days of Cinema Nôvo. In *A Hora da Estrela*, Amaral has created an inspired feminist adaptation of this familiar theme which received deserved acclaim at international festivals and in its commercial release in Brazil and abroad.

Susan Ryan

Awards: Eleven prizes, including Best Film, Director, Actress (Marcelia Cartaxo), Actor (José Dumont), Brasilia, 1985; Best Film (shared), Best Script, Glauber Rocha Prize (awarded by international press agencies), Havana, 1986.

Musica Barroca Mineira

Brazil, 1981, 26', colour

Dir Artur Omar (b. 1948)

O Inspetor

The Inspector
Brazil, 1988, 12', colour

Dir Artur Omar (b. 1948)

Video nas Aldeias

Video in the Villages
Brazil, 1989, 8', b+w and colour, video

Dir Vincent Carelli *Ed* Estevão Nunes Tutú *Narr* Virginia Valadão *Prod* Centro de Trabalho Indigenista (CTI)

A Arca dos Zo'é

Meeting Ancestors
Brazil, 1993, 21', colour, video

Dir Vincent Carelli and Dominique Gallois *Cinematog* Carelli and Kasiripinã *Ed* Estevão Nunes Tutú *Sound* Gallois *Prod* Centro de Trabalho Indigenista (CTI)

Opressão

Oppression
Brazil, 1993, 18', colour

Dir Mirella Martinelli (b. 1961) *Scr* Martinelli *Cinematog* Katia Coelho *Ed* Martinelli *Prod* Maria Ionescu and Zeca Ros for Orion Cinema e Video *Act* Gabriela Cardoso, Walderez de Barros, Norival Rizzo, Marcio Trinchinatto, Mario Cesar Camargo

National Film Council (CONCINE) Resolution 18 of 1977 mandated that a Brazilian-made short film would be part of each program of foreign films. "The short was to receive 5% of the gross box-office income, of which 40% would be returned to the exhibitor and 60% would go to the producer and distributor (of the short, not the foreign feature)." This measure provoked the anger of Hollywood's international overseer, Jack Valenti, and it backfired in the same way that the quota on Brazilian-made features stimulated the production of inferior films by exhibitors protecting their own interests. In 1984, after much public complaining about poor-quality short subjects, a jury was formed to select the films that would be shown, with a view to encouraging innovative, independent filmmaking.

With the precipitous decline in the quality and quantity of Brazilian features in the 1980s, short films increasingly stood out. Pornography accounted for over 80% of Brazilian feature production at the end of the decade, and state support ceased in April 1990 when Embrafilme finally closed its doors by decree of Fernando Collor de Mello's government. Over the next 2½ years a total of only 40 features were made in Brazil, and in 1991–92 only fifteen domestic features were released. But there was a virtual explosion of Brazilian short film production in the same period, and the São Paulo film festival increasingly became an important showcase for Brazilian short films. Another development over the same period of feature film decline (1984–94) is the advent of video, especially as it has functioned as a medium for groups and individuals excluded from the mainstream. Canadian video artist and curator Colin Campbell wrote in 1985 that there were more women working in video than men, and the low cost and portability of the medium has also enabled Brazil's indigenous peoples to document their own lives.[1]

Short filmmaking has long been an important tradition in Brazil, from Humberto Mauro (*Ganga Bruta*, 1933, q.v.), when head of the National

Institute of Educational Cinema (INCE) in the 1930s through the early days of Cinema Nôvo, where young directors found a training ground in the short film. São Paulo-based Thomaz Farkas especially produced a number of important short documentaries in the 1960s on the northeast. But in the 1980s a veritable "school" of short filmmaking emerged in Porto Alegre to parallel those in the major metropolises, São Paulo and Rio de Janeiro. According to Ana López, the "difference in the 1980s is that a number of filmmakers (especially someone like Jorge Furtado) actually think of themselves as 'professional short film makers' rather than as aspiring feature directors."[2] Obviously, it would be impossible to use a few works to provide a meaningful overview of one nation's short film and video output over a fifteen-year period or even to provide a representative sampling, so we have concentrated here on (i) the work of an important experimental filmmaker, Artur Omar, whose films were showcased at the 1989 Toronto Experimental Film Congress by Brazilian film scholar João Luiz Vieira, (ii) the (anti)ethnographic videotapes made by Tupi people and coordinated by Vincent Carelli, and (iii) a recent example of a São Paulo short narrative film directed by a woman, Mirella Martinelli's *Opressão* (1993).

Artur (or Arthur) Omar was born in Rio de Janeiro. From the very beginning of his filmmaking career, his work could be categorised as experimental. His third short film, *Congo* (1972), constructed like a semiotic text, begins to deconstruct the documentary form. Brazilian film scholar Jean-Claude Bernadet, who specialises in documentary, has written of *Congo*, which contains more writing than images (and which never actually shows its subject, the *congo* or *congada* dance), as being about "the relationship we have established with popular culture, since our only way of understanding it, because we will never be producers of it, is through the mediation of our print-based culture."[3] Omar's next film, his first feature, *Triste Trópico* (1974), mocks the audience's faith in documentary reality. It parodies Claude Lévi-Strauss' anthropological journey through Amazonia, documented in his seminal work of structural anthropology, *Tristes tropiques* (1955). In Omar's film, Professor Arthur becomes the messianic leader of an indigenous tribe who is diagnosed post-mortem by "scientists" to have been mad. Brazilian film scholar Ismail Xavier argues that "after equating the *sertão* and the sea and indelibly etching the omnipresent sadness of the tropics, Brazil is represented [by Omar] as the *locus* of a journey in a time when redemption is impossible."[4]

Whereas his earlier films had questioned the ability of filmmakers to document the unfamiliar and the veracity of documentary films in general,

Musica Barroca Mineira (1984) challenges the viewer's basic comprehension and interrelation of sounds and images. Ostensibly "about" eighteenth-century baroque music (composed by blacks) in the state of Minas Gerais, Omar's experimental film seems to question the status of Brazilian culture and history through a Borgesian mixture of things European, African, American, and, even Asian. In particular, it mocks the dominance of European religion—through the repetition of Christian icons—and its congruence with the music of colonial times—with Bach, Mozart, "Ave Maria," church organ, etc., on the soundtrack. Music is also represented visually through notations and terms, and the film initially forges connections between painting, music, and religion through montage. Editing, then, relates these elements to industrialisation: a shot of molten steel is complemented by the sound of a jack hammer which continues over the next shot where the camera tracks past a church organ in low angle. The perspective then shifts radically to show a man raking in shallow water accompanied by natural sounds of the tropics. Gradually, the action of gold prospecting and the figure of a black man are revealed, and, later, instruments of torture and slave shackles are juxtaposed between a statue of Jesus and a strange, possibly Japanese statue. One must infer connections across these various montages of incongruent sound and image "signs," a process which reminds us of Soviet film theory and structural semiotics (European, both), as well, of course, of Lévi-Strauss (a "Brazilianised" European). Minas Gerais was a centre of both colonialism and mineral exploitation, and one can understand from Omar's juxtapositions that their legacy still informs contemporary Brazilian culture—the sound mix also includes rhythmic African voices, "noise," whispers, and English punk-rock music. In any event, the "baroque" of the title is invoked throughout *Musica Barroca Mineira* in extravagant musical and cinematic gestures, grotesque images, and editing contrasts.

O Inspetor is a short, mock documentary about the methods used by crack police detective Jamil Warwar, who allegedly solved more than 3,000 cases of murder and other violent crimes in Rio de Janeiro. The film does contain a small amount of documentary footage, but it is most unusual in having Warwar, who was known as the Brazilian Baretta for his ability to disguise his identity, play himself. Beginning on close-up details—marijuana, a toothbrush—reminiscent of Fritz Lang's style of rendering clues in his seminal German crime films, *Die Spinnen* (1919-20) and *Dr. Mabuse der Spieler* (1922)—we hear a voice-over connect Warwar to Brecht and then see him cross-dress in order to solve crimes of rape. Allusions to master criminals of films past such as *Mabuse* and Louis

Feuillade's *Fantômas* (1913–14) are evident, except that here, Omar's "master" is fighting crime. Indeed, the concept of "performance" in life as well as film emerges as being a key subject of *O Inspetor*. Warwar also appears in *fotonovelas*, and one can understand his changing personalities through various forms of representation as a metaphoric artistic quest for identity. Warwar's downfall occurred during the infamous Claudea case when, following a series of arrests in the *favelas*, he discovered connections between international drug trafficking and prominent Brazilian business-men. Moving through the lower depths he discovered corruption at the highest levels of society and was exiled for being, in effect, too successful.

With *Raoni* being nominated for an "Oscar" as Best Documentary Feature in 1979, the world was introduced to the plight of the Amazonian Indian faced with the clearing of the rainforest. Although it was a Franco-American production, directed by Jean-Pierre Dutilleux, and narrated in its English version—subtitled *The Fight for the Amazon*—by Marlon Brando, *Raoni* also won the prize for Best Brazilian Film and three other awards, including Best Cinematography and Music, at the Gramado film festival in 1979. *Raoni* was a breakthrough film stylistically as well. Egberto Gismonti's music and Luiz Carlos Saldanha's widescreen cinematography combine to present a beautiful idyllic setting for Raoni's Megkronoti people on the banks of the Xingú River. Long observational passages depicting the "Indian way of life" are contrasted with statistics on the decimation of the native population and by sequences depicting growing resistance and solidarity amongst other Xingú basin tribes such as the Iavalapitis, Kréen-Akaóres, Suyás, and Jurúnas. Fighting back is clearly one of the film's messages, and at one point a discussion is documented on whether or not the filmmakers should be killed—it is decided that the filmmakers can help their plight. Presumably staged for the camera, the sequence suggests that the Amazonian people are aggressively determining their own future. In fact, *Raoni* is a rare example of a film which had some real political effect: In 1989, Raoni, Dutilleux, and others went on a world tour and started the Rainforest Foundation.

Raoni also began a legacy of native Brazilian peoples employing visual media to not only document their own, traditional ways of life but also to communicate with neighbouring peoples and engage jointly in struggle. Though a number of foreign filmmakers and anthropologists have concerned themselves with the plight of Amazonia—Adrian Cowell, Michael Beckham, and Geoffrey O'Connor in Great Britain, and Terence Turner and Laura Graham in the United States have done important work—it is Vincent Carelli working through São Paulo's Centre for Work with Indigenous Peoples (CTI) who has best continued in this spirit. *Video nas Aldeias* (1989) provides a brief overview of the project "Video in the Villages" which has worked since 1986 to furnish indigenous villagers with the equipment necessary for community members themselves to document and play back video images. The project seeks to bring indigenous Brazilians together with their own image, recording important ceremonies and hence reflecting their identity to themselves. The videotape begins with shots of people looking off-frame, in different directions, delightedly, then pointing off-frame. Eventually we see a television set, and the shot dissolves to a closer full screen image of the same scene that people were watching. *Video nas Aldeias* shows how the Nambiquára restaged a ceremony following their viewing of it, finding their first video rendition lacking in authenticity. In another segment we learn that the Kaiapó have made the most use of the video format, as a weapon to defend themselves: striking images depict the Kaiapó protesting at a Belém hydroelectric dam.

Some CTI videotapes, like *A Festa de Moca* (1988), provide ethnographic documentation, while others, like *Video nas Aldeias*, are more structured and reflect the Centre's mandate to promote the indigenous peoples struggle for self-determination and autonomy. *The Spirit of TV* (1990) shows the Waiãpi (who weren't "first contacted" until 1973) observing and interacting with other indigenous people, while *A Arca dos Zo'é* (1993) goes one step further in following some Waiãpi men, including the videographer, Kasiripinã, to visit their "ancestors," the Zo'é across the river in the state of Macapá. A Waiãpi man acts as a kind of guide for the visit to the Zo'é , claiming that "we knew these people from television images" and how this encouraged him to visit their village. Initially we see a video camera in each shot, marking the fact of indigenous people documenting their own reality, but when the plane bringing the Waiãpi visitors lands in Zo'é territory we receive both an inside and outside perspective. Thus, the videotaped apparent "first contact" between the two indigenous groups was somewhat staged—there must have been a crew on the ground when the plane arrived. In the background of a shot of people surrounding the new arrivals one can see a white woman (presumably Dominique Gallois, the co-director), who one assumes translates between the Tupi languages of the two groups. Interestingly, the viewer tends to identify with the Waiãpi "tour guide," who is more Western in appearance—the Zo'é are naked and sport wooden dowels through their lower lips—and who addresses the camera directly. It is easy to view the Zo'é's hunting and cooking practices as "primitive," though their guests remain uncritical and willing to share their own culture with their hosts. *A Arca dos Zo'é* does indeed present a very different perspective on documentary practice where the ethnographic subjects become ethnographers themselves. Yet, although the concept of "meeting ancestors" is well intentioned, it is clear until the end—with the plane taking off and one of the cameras staying on the ground to record it—that the structuring voice is still that of Vincent Carelli and his crew of (mostly) outsiders.

Opressão, produced by Orion Cinema e Video and apparently shot on video, looks like grainy 16mm or even Super-8 film. For its eighteen-minute running time, Katia Coelho's camera seems never to stop moving, relentlessly following its female protagonist through frustration and conflict to despair, persecution, and, eventually, to her senseless death. The camera records a young *mulata* (Gabriela Cardoso) trying to get her boyfriend to look after her baby for the evening in her drab apartment. She then visits her mother to beseech her to do the same, while the camera picks up pace, circling the subjects. With the front of her hair dyed pink, we are not surprised when she is revealed to be a dancer, fronting a punk band. Nazi skinheads disrupt the performance, beating up the band's black guitarist. The young woman seeks refuge with the club's seedy manager, who proceeds to give her a marijuana joint. They are both arrested and she is told by the police that she's going to be "fucked." Released from jail next morning, after being raped, she telephones her mother and pleads with her. But, in the bar where she makes the call, a drunken, apparently psychotic customer randomly shoots her. With no sentimentality at all, Mirella Martinelli matter-of-factly depicts the plight of a marginalised young Paulistana. Remarkably contemporary in its frenetic style and gritty nihilist realism, *Opressão* metaphorically suggests the bleak, marginalised state of Brazilian cinema today and the plight of young women, destroyed in and by a heartless, nightmarish urban environment.

Peter Rist

1. Colin Campbell, "Videotapes From Brazil and Chile: August 1–September 30 1985," catalogue of the National Gallery of Canada, p. 1.
2. Note to the author, February 1995.
3. Jean-Claude Bernadet, "The Voice of the Other: Brazilian Documentary in the 1970s," *The Social Documentary in Latin America*, ed. Julianne Burton (Pittsburgh: University of Pittsburgh Press, 1990), 89.
4. Ismail Xavier, "Cinema Nôvo and Post Cinema Nôvo—Appropriation of the Imaginary of the Discovery," *Mediating Two Worlds*, eds. John King, Ana López, and Manuel Alvarado (London: British Film Institute, 1993), 203.

Chile

El húsar de la muerte

Death's Hussar
Chile, 1925, 65', b + w, silent

Dir Pedro Sienna (pseudonym of Pedro Pérez) (1893–1972) *Scr* Sienna *Mus* (added in restoration) Sergio Ortega *Prod* Alfredo Wolnitziki for Andes Films *Act* Pedro Sienna, Clara Werther, Dolores Anzioni, Hugo Silva

"Eighty features were made in Chile between 1916 and 1931," a critic once lamented, "and nothing remains of them but press clippings and memories." Today, not even memories of Chile's lost silent films remain. Until 1962 only one film, Pedro Sienna's *Un grito en el mar* (1924), was believed to have survived. But that year an extraordinary opportunity presented itself: a copy of Sienna's *El húsar de la muerte* was discovered, in dreadful condition. Sienna was still alive and would be able to assist in its restoration. The print was purchased by the Experimental Film Centre of the University of Chile in Santiago, founded in 1959, and a technician spent an entire year laboriously restoring it. When he saw it, Sienna remarked that it was missing a few scenes and titles; the latter were redone, resulting in both intertitles and subtitles appearing in the final version. A "definitive" cut of the film was attempted with Sienna's help—silent films around the world were subject to cutting by exhibitors and distributors, making latter-day discoveries problematic—and a musical score commissioned by the Centre added in 1964. The film was subsequently seen throughout Chile's ciné club network and is stored in foreign film archives. It was Sienna's fifth and last film; after its filming he returned to work as a playwright, theatre actor, poet, and newspaper caricaturist.

217

El húsar de la muerte was one of 15 films produced in 1925, when Chilean silent cinema was at its zenith (this level of production has never been matched since), and enjoyed successful commercial release then. A silent film critic considered it to be the only film of the period to be "worthy of exhibition": production was dominated by rudimentary melodramas and historical films. Sienna's film, in contrast, reveals an intelligent use of the camera, with long-shot establishing shots giving way to medium shots from varying perspectives, and good narrative development and acting. A historical epic, it depicts a period of tumult and instability in Chilean politics, when the Spanish had for a time successfully suppressed attempts to declare independence and insurrections arose. The film focuses on the legendary guerrilla of the independence battles, Manuel Rodríguez, with Sienna in the lead role, between the Chilean defeat at Rancagua in 1814 and Rodríguez' betrayal and execution in 1816, two years before the Chileans finally triumphed under Bernardo O'Higgins. The film shows Rodríguez' meeting with the Argentine liberator José de San Martín in Mendoza just across the Andes before the former returns to Chile to organise guerrilla actions against the Spaniards. Along the way, a love interest develops and views of social life are presented. Finally, after meeting with San Martín again in Mendoza, Rodríguez is killed as he prepares to return with his "liberating army."

Chile's small film industry didn't recover from the devastating effect of the arrival of the sound film in the 1930s until the country's Popular Front government, elected in 1939 and the only such government outside of Europe during this period, embarked on an economic modernisation and import substitution program in 1941. As part of a program of state investment in the country's industrial infrastructure, the film agency Chile Films was founded in 1942 with 50% of its capital coming from the state. Chile Films then embarked on an ambitious attempt, not only to establish Chilean films in the domestic market but to create export markets as well. Throughout the 1940s, foreign directors, especially Argentine, with a couple of notable French directors (Pierre Chenal and Jacques Rémy), were attracted to work in the industry, which boasted modern new studios and technical assistance from Argentine producers. By 1947, Chile Films had collapsed, at about the same time as the Argentine industry's attempts to create a similar "international" cinema were proving unsuccessful and two years before Brazil began ill-fated efforts in the same direction with the Vera Cruz studio. Chilean film lay dormant until the late 1950s, when a group of young short film makers arrived on the scene with the support of the Experimental Film Centre, whose director, Sergio Bravo, the most prominent of these newcomers (*Banderas del pueblo*, 1964), had supervised the restoration of *El húsar de la muerte*. Chile Films would again play an important role in Chilean film under the Popular Unity government of Salvador Allende (1970–73), when filmmaker Miguel Littín (*La tierra prometida*, 1973, q.v.) again attempted an interventionist role for the agency.

Timothy Barnard

Valparaíso, mi amor

Chile, 1970, 90', b+w

Dir Aldo Francia (b. 1923) *Scr* José Román and Francia *Cinematog* Diego Bonacina *Mus* Gustavo Becerra *Prod* Cine Nuevo *Act* Sara Astica, Hugo Cárcamo, Rigoberto Rojo, Liliana Cabrera

Aldo Francia, the son of Italian immigrants to Chile, was educated in Italy before returning to his native Valparaíso, Chile's largest port. He became a doctor in 1949, beginning a 40-year career as a pediatrician in Valparaíso. Throughout the 1960s and until the overthrow of Salvador Allende in a military coup in 1973, he was a key figure in the growth of a film culture in Chile, especially in Valparaíso and the nearby resort of Viña del Mar. In 1962 he founded the Viña del Mar ciné club, tenaciously securing films and guest filmmakers for its series, and in 1967 he founded the Viña del Mar film festival, the site of many seminars and encounters between Latin American filmmakers. This festival played a critical role in the growth of the New Latin American Cinema, bringing together a new generation of filmmakers with their radical new themes and styles and tremendous longing for unity. He taught film unpaid in local schools, later becoming director of the film department of the University of Valparaíso, and founded the film magazine *Cine-Foro*.

Francia began filming, first for television and then in Super-8 and 16mm, in 1959, alone or in small groups brought together by the ciné club. With *Valparaíso, mi amor*, his first feature, he became an important figure in the nascent Chilean *nuevo cine*, the birth of which is dated to 1967, the year the Viña del Mar festival was founded. *Valparaíso, mi amor*, released before Allende's electoral victory in 1970, was shown at the Berlin film festival "Forum" and the "Quinzaine des réalisateurs" at Cannes. Francia would make one more film, *Ya no basta con rezar*, in 1972, before Allende's overthrow in 1973 and the end of the Chilean *nuevo cine* experiment, forcing his return full time to his medical career.

The idea for the film came from a story told him by a hitchhiking soldier concerning a cattle thief. From this anecdote Francia developed the story of González, jailed for cattle theft, leaving four children as symbols of a future without hope. For the children's characters Francia painted composite images based on other true stories people had told him, such as that of a street child who is taken home by a rich woman and treated like her own before being returned to the same spot she found him. His former gangmates, on seeing him arrive in a car with new clothes and a haircut, beat him up and steal his clothes, leaving him worse off than he was before. There is also an eleven-year-old girl who prostitutes herself to taxi drivers, a typically delinquent boy, and a younger boy inspired by Francia's own experiences at the Valparaíso's children's clinic, where poor children die for lack of money or a bed to treat them in.

Valparaíso, mi amor was inspired by Italian neo-realism, based on real events and reflecting social reality. The child actors were all non-professionals, found by Francia in a home for indigent children, and Francia studied police records to create his story. He reports that events were de-dramatised so that they would not appear excessive. An admirer of Vittorio de Sica (*Ladri di Bicicletti*, 1949), Francia wanted to provide the spectator an opportunity to engage actively in social analysis and reflection. He said at the time that "Film, in an underdeveloped country, should be closely tied to and committed to the process of social change. We can not make an escapist cinema. In the end, all film is political. If I were to attempt to make the spectator of my films a passive observer, I would be defending a political system, I would be promoting conformity. That too would be a political cinema. The other cinema, the kind that I make, the kind that interests me, consists of allowing the spectator to become aware of social problems."

Diego Bonacina's cinematography contains many well-executed long takes—Francia avoided close-ups because he had no experience in directing actors—but some technical "flaws" are apparent, such as the lighting, because sets were not used and Francia considered it "false" to light a room normally lit by a single dingy bulb. The film uses different voice-overs to tell the stories of the four González children. The most accomplished sequence begins in the children's clinic, crowded with people and short of staff, when a woman is refused care for her child because of a lack of beds. She returns to her home in the hills with her child in her arms, her gaze fixed on the funicular's rails.

Valparaíso, mi amor is a testament to injustice and to the inhuman treatment of children in large cities in underdeveloped countries. Valparaíso has a rich history of inspiring writers and artists; it is an exotic port to the east. The Dutch director Joris Ivens mythified it in *A Valparaíso* (1963), and it is evoked from a distance by Raúl Ruiz in *Les Trois couronnes du matelot* (1982, q.v.). Francia shows us Valparaíso's tortuous, narrow streets; the mansions of the rich and the jumbled, tumbledown shacks of the poor; the funiculars, going up and down the hillsides, marking time; the bars, markets, and even the port jail. This was Francia's homage to his birthplace, where as a doctor he had been exposed to its poverty and the poor children living in the hills. He called it a "Christian" film, "apart from all ideology," and as such it is a sensitive film, one representative of its day.

Marilú Mallet

El chacal de Nahueltoro

The Jackal of Nahueltoro
Chile, 1970, 95', b+w

Dir Miguel Littín (b. 1942) *Scr* Littín *Cinematog* Héctor Ríos *Ed* Pedro Chaskel *Mus* Sergio Ortega *Prod* Luis Cornejo and Luis Alarcón for Cine Experimental de la Universidad de Chile and Cinematográfica Tercer Mundo *Act* Nelson Villagra, Shenda Román, Marcelo Romo, Héctor Noguera, Luis Alarcón, Pedro Villagra, Luis Melo, Rubén Sotoconil, Rafael Benavente, Roberto Navarrete

El chacal de Nahueltoro, based on shocking real-life events from the early 1960s, is one of the most significant works of the New Latin American Cinema and has been seen by more Chileans than any other film made in Chile. Inspired by the Meeting of Latin American Filmmakers at the first Viña del Mar film festival in 1967, four Chilean directors began their first feature-length films in 1968: Helvio Soto, Raúl Ruiz (*La colonia penal*, 1971, q.v.), Miguel Littín, and festival organiser Aldo Francia (*Valparaíso, mi amor*, 1970, q.v.). Like Francia, Littín was associated with the

University of Chile. He was working in television and had been researching the "Jackal" project for over two years but had to stand in line to use
the same camera as Ruiz, Francia, and Carlos Elsesser (who began his first
feature in 1969). When finished, *El chacal de Nahueltoro* was exhibited
during Salvador Allende's successful election campaign by trade unions, at
schools, and in open air meetings and was later released to theatres in
35mm, eventually being seen by an estimated 500,000 people.

   El chacal is divided into five unequal parts. At the end of the credits,
which appear over optically printed images of anguished faces, appears the
title "On the childhood, regeneration and death of he who went by the
names of José del Carmen Valenzuela Torres, Jorge Sandoval Espinosa,
José Jorge Castillo Torres." We are thrown *media res* into an apparent
documentary of an angry mob surrounding the arrest of a man, shouting
"lynch him." The camera is jerkily hand-held, and the voice of a woman
(later revealed to be that of an official police recorder) begins to recount
the story of José/Jorge, the Jackal, a mass murderer. Then, the first
section of the narrative begins, entitled "José's Childhood." The visual
style changes abruptly with a nostalgic, slow pan across a silhouetted
skyline, accompanied by the sound of a flute and José's (Nelson Villagra)
voice-over. Another quick change occurs as a high-angle tracking camera,
representing the view of a horseback rider, appears to trap a small boy,
the young José. In successive short scenes, José is shown to be oppressed
by the military, the church, and the town mayor, following which he is
put to work carrying heavy sacks, and through a rapid Eisensteinian
montage repetition of the same image, the oppressive effect is magnified.

   Before the end of the flashback sequence, we are introduced to the
motif of José's wandering. We see him herding goats and learn of his
being sent from place to place as a child, from one adult guar-
dian/exploiter to another, as if no one wants him. The pseudo-documentary in the present tense resumes with the sound of a police siren and a
view through a fast-moving car's windshield. At Nahueltoro Bridge, José
is asked to re-enact the crimes. This triggers a return to his past, and the
title "José's Travels" introduces one of the two longest sections of the
film. José tells of his first prison term, a period spent with a woman
named María González, and his going back on the road again. We see him
drinking and a combination of hand-held camera and fast cutting project
a sense of deepening despair and delirium, leading to one of the most
interesting sequence-shots of the film, where he meets the widow Rosa
(Shenda Román). The shot begins on a fast pan to follow the chopping
motion of Rosa's axe and ends with the off-screen sound of José continu-

ing to cut firewood. In between, the camera reveals the drudgery of Rosa's quotidian peasant life but also caresses tenderly in its close framing of Rosa's face and hands, especially where it tracks to follow a glass of water she brings to José, her visitor. Continuing the flashback, we are invited to share Rosa's perspective, where her voice picks up the story, and through repetition of the image of uniformed officers throwing her out of her house, the viewer is able to identify Rosa's plight with that of José's. Nevertheless, at the end of this section of *El chacal*, where the film shifts from past to present more frequently, one cannot but be shocked at the realisation that José actually killed Rosa and her five children.

The film's remarkable achievement is to lead the audience to an understanding of the background to crimes that would seem heinous even to the most cynical observer. The killings are not depicted graphically, and it is clear that the "Jackal" is in a drunken stupor for all but the last of them. But, following the brief episode of the "Persecution and Arrest of José," Littín brilliantly analyses the forces surrounding the killer and indicts the Chilean system in the film's last two parts—"Education and Taming" and "The Death of José." Up until this point the film had regularly shifted modes from subjective to objective but had been predominantly located in the former with its engaged, *cinéma-vérité* camera style. Now, the camera is often static, and initially distanced, allowing space to observe the regimented routines of prison life. Echoing the earlier connection made between the church and the military, José is guided and taught by a man of the cloth (Héctor Noguera). Ironically, at the moment when he finally becomes "educated" in the full sense of the word—learning about his national history and culture as well as how to read and write—he is executed. A key moment in the film is that when a freeze-frame is used for the first time, where José is shown to smile, also for the first time. He kicks a ball and thus discovers the joys of the game of soccer, a key component of Chilean culture. He also seems to make friends in the prison, learning how to socialise. Indeed, *El chacal de Nahueltoro* constructs the argument that to be a marginalised person is to be ignorant of, and deprived of, all that it takes to be a complete person. At the same time that Cuban filmmakers were celebrating the achievements of their country's literacy program, Miguel Littín, a Marxist, was making an inspired critique of how the combined forces of Chilean authority—church, military, school, and state—continue to keep the peasantry marginalised in poverty of mind and spirit as well as substance.

Peter Rist

La colonia penal

The Penal Colony
Chile, 1971, 75', b+w

Dir Raúl Ruiz (b. 1941) *Scr* Ruiz, based on the short story "In der Strafkolonie" by Franz Kafka (1919) *Cinematog* Héctor Ríos *Ed* Carlos Piaggo *Prod* Dario Pulgar for Aleaman *Act* Mónica Echeverría, Luis Alarcón, Aníbal Reyna, Nelson Villagra

Raúl Ruiz is the most prolific Chilean filmmaker of all time who, after completing five features and seven shorts in five years (as well as co-directing another feature), continued to produce at this rate after ten years in exile. He was born in Puerto Montt, in southern Chile, and studied law and theology at university before becoming involved in theatre. He claims to have written over a hundred plays in the six years following the receipt of a Rockefeller grant in 1956. During this time he also shot his first (unfinished) film and in 1962 he attended Fernando Birri's documentary film school in Argentina. Then, after working for five years editing television news, he began his first fiction feature (which he was also unable to finish). But Ruiz's luck changed when he was able to get his hands on the shared camera first, before Aldo Francia and Miguel Littín, and finish shooting his next project, *Tres tristes tigres*, in 1968. He was thus the first of the Chilean *nuevo cine* filmmakers to get a fiction feature in release.

Tres tristes tigres (a tongue twister in Spanish), adapted from a play by Alejandro Sieveking, is an experimental narrative film dedicated to the sardonic Chilean "anti-poet" Nicarnor Parra. It provides a critique of the Chilean bourgeoisie (the "Three Trapped Tigers" of the title) who are unable to move with the changing political climate in their country, but Ruiz also attempted to criticise bourgeois form, placing the characters and the camera in awkward and unfamiliar places. Following an unsuccessful Chilean-U.S. co-production, *¿Qué hacer?* (1970), co-directed by Saul Landau, Ruiz embarked on his second fiction feature, *La colonia penal*.

Ruiz based *La colonia penal* on Franz Kafka's political fable "In der Strafkolonie" but changed the setting from Europe to a fictitious island in the Pacific Ocean off the coast of Peru. Once a leper colony, it had become a prison, and in 1950 a pilot community financed by the United Nations. According to Ruiz, the island became a free independent republic in 1972 (a year into the future). However, in what he calls "a kind of

Latin American Switzerland, divided into cantons," the prison rules were preserved. The inhabitants invented their own language, which contains old English and Spanish words, but they continue to behave like convicts.

The film opens on a black screen with a woman's voice-over, that of a reporter (Mónica Echeverría) visiting the island from the mainland. In the very first scene we view a dead body after she is driven away in a military vehicle, and her first experience of (in)hospitality is to be taunted by comic threats that her throat will be slit if she does anything wrong. Everyone, it seems, carries knives or swords and wears a uniform, and almost all of the occupants of the island are men. She interviews the president, who gives stock replies to her questions, and then, when she interviews someone else at the hotel, a pattern of distraction begins, reminiscent of Ruiz's *nouvelle vague*-inspired strategy in *Tres tristes tigres*. Attention is drawn to a secondary character, presumably sleeping in the reporter's bed, when he gets up and blocks off the camera's lens. The behaviour of the islanders becomes progressively more bizarre. Everyone drinks excessively, and the island culture would appear to consist only of singing and playing the guitar, practices made strange when the visitor is serenaded with the morbid lyrics of suicide (alluding to the anti-poetry of Parra). Even more strangely, performances are applauded by the clapping of swords. Music is effectively made using the instruments of the military.

The visitor's travels are made worse by her witnessing of torture and killings, which she reports in detail. But the surreal events that unfold lead us to question their reality, and by the time the president is shot, after he makes a statement to the press, we realise that the country's only export is *news*. Thus, *La colonia penal* works as an allegory of a neo-colonial military dictatorship, where the people have assimilated only the worst aspects of colonialism, leading to repression and chaos, and a *reductio ad absurdum* of the idea of media as an equivalent to a monoculture economy. Prior to making *La colonia penal*, Ruiz had begun another unfinished film, *Militarismo y tortura*, intended as a parody of a lecture/demonstration on how to torture. Looking back on this period, the director found it strange that while Chile was experiencing a period of democracy, he was dealing in his films with military rule and colonisation. While some observers find that he was representing a general Latin American malaise and the pre-Allende Chilean situation in particular, it is also clear that like Littín's *El chacal de Nahueltoro* (1970, q.v.), Ruiz was unfortunately prefiguring the horrors of the Pinochet regime.

Peter Rist

La tierra prometida

The Promised Land
Chile-Cuba, 1973, 105', colour

Dir Miguel Littín (b. 1942) *Scr* Littín *Cinematog* Affonso Beato *Ed* Nelson Rodríguez *Mus* Luis Advis and Grupo Inti-Illimani *Prod* Cinematográfica Tercer Mundo (Chile) and Instituto Cubano del Arte e Industria Cinematográficos (ICAIC) (Cuba) *Act* Nelson Villagra, Marcelo Gaete, Carmen Bueno, Rafael Benavente, Mireya Kulchewsky, Anibal Reyna, inhabitants of Santa Cruz, Colchagua

La tierra prometida is the most significant film produced during the period of Salvador Allende's government in Chile (1970–1973). Billed as Chile's "first widescreen colour spectacular," *La tierra prometida* is based on an actual incident in 1932, when for a short time the first socialist republic was established in the Americas: in Chile. Ironically, the film's tragic ending prefigures the military overthrow of Allende in September 1973, only two months after Miguel Littín completed it.

Having previously made the most successful Chilean film, *El chacal de Nahueltoro* (1970, q.v.), which had a decidedly leftist perspective, it is not surprising that following Allende's election in 1970 Littín was appointed head of Chile Films, the thirty-year-old nationalised film company. With Chile Films, Littín inherited dilapidated studios and a large, costly bureaucracy. He initiated filmmaking workshops and encouraged the production of documentary shorts (on no salaries). Littín directed a medium-length documentary record of a conversation between Allende and Régis Debray, *Compañero Presidente*, in 1971, but he stepped down from his position in 1972, frustrated by his inability to make Chile Films work effectively. However, he maintained good relations with the state-owned company as well as the Popular Unity government's State Office of Cinematography, while choosing to produce his next film, *La tierra prometida*, independently. *La tierra prometida* was filmed in central Chile, to the south of Santiago, in Littín's native province of Colchagua. It took eight months to shoot, often in terrible weather conditions, on steadily declining funds. Although Chile Films' sound studio was employed, no other Chilean facilities were adequate for the film's epic needs, and it was finished in Cuba.

An old man, Chirigua, narrates the events of *La tierra prometida*, and we are given a precise date of November 30, 1930, for the festivities of the feast of St. Emetrius. A group of peasants (played by the residents of Santa Cruz) are wandering the countryside looking for a place to settle. Gradually, José Durán (Nelson Villagra) emerges as the leader, and on their eventful journey they gather followers including Traje Cruzado—"Pin Stripe"—(Marcelo Gaete) who knows of some government land which he thinks they could claim as their own. They call their valley settlement Palmilla (the name of the Colchaguan village where Littín was born). The people engage in a number of pageant-like collective activities, and José Durán discusses politics with "Pin Stripe." The village prospers and grows and one day a red airplane distributes revolutionary flyers. The pilot announces that Marmaduke Grove (the name of an early-20th century Chilean military leader) is governing the country and has decreed that socialism must be installed everywhere. Inspired by the proclamation, José Durán and La Virgen del Carmen (Mireya Kulchewsky) lead the people to the regional capital of Los Huiques, while "Pin-Stripe" and the young Chirigua travel around the countryside re-distributing land and raising the people's political consciousness. Durán proclaims himself the new governor, but almost immediately the wealthy landowner Don Fernando and other dignitaries try to persuade him to step down, claiming that Grove's government was overthrown three months ago, having only lasted twelve days. Army troops arrive and Durán withdraws to the valley, where the peasants are massacred. Durán is dragged along the ground by horses and then shot while his female companion Meche (Carmen Bueno) dies by the sword. Nevertheless, the film ends hopefully with the young Chirigua, dressed in red, carrying José Durán's gun, and with Ernesto "Che" Guevara's words on those who fell and of "sacrifices with no retribution, [out of which] the revolution was also made."

Influenced mainly by the epic, long-take, choreographed style of Hungarian filmmaker Miklós Jancsó and also more directly by the moving tableaux of Brazilian filmmaker Glauber Rocha (whose cinematographer, Affonso Beato, was employed on the film), Littín tried to create his own Chilean historical epic form, simultaneously mythical and dialectical, in *La tierra prometida.* Like Rocha, Littín created characters based on historical and/or mythical figures, whose status is ambiguous, like the woman who plays the Virgin of the Carmen in the pageant—we must question if she actually is the Virgin. In casting Nelson Villagra as Durán, Littín was already tapping into Chilean film *typage:* as the Jackal, Villagra had become the archetypal Chilean peasant—oppressed yet defiant. Like Jancsó, Littín staged long-shot views of stylized collective activity, where music and movement combine to reflect the narrative thrust, but unlike his stylistic mentor, Littín used the panning camera, and the movement of people, horses, and an emblematic train to represent a positive sense of flux, more akin to Jean Renoir than Jancsó. As with Jancsó, and Sergei Eisenstein before him, Littín struggled to project fully rounded characters within their historical pageants, especially the women, and U.S. scholar Julianne Burton has complained that Meche and La Virgen remain distinctly stereotyped.[1] But, in using song lyrics and pointed dialogue, especially involving Durán, Littín was able to convey some key political ideas, such as the need for collective struggle and internal and transnational unity. It is impossible to tell whether or not Littín was completely successful in his ambitious attempt at creating a model of New Latin American Cinema, since *La tierra prometida* was never released in Chile, but partially in recognition of its experimental approach to socialism, his film premiered at the Moscow film festival in 1973 and was released in the U.S. following its North American premiere at the New Directors/New Films festival in New York City, March 1974.

During the 1973 coup of General Augusto Pinochet (1973–1989) Littín was able to escape almost certain imprisonment while visiting Chile Films by being mistakenly identified (deliberately) as a neighbouring resident by a friendly sergeant. He then successfully sought political asylum at the Mexican embassy and flew to Mexico City. But others who worked on *La tierra prometida* were not so fortunate. Many of the Santa Cruz residents who appear in the film were killed during the military regime's brutal campaign of reprisals. Carmen Bueno and Jorge Müller, a camera operator, were arrested in November 1973 by Chilean secret police and subsequently "disappeared" despite international efforts to save them. Littín has been able to continue successfully as a film director in exile, often by staging co-productions. His first Mexican-made film, *Actas de Marusia* (1976), received an Oscar nomination for Best Foreign Language Film, and his next two were based on works by great Latin American writers: *El recurso del método* (Mexico-Cuba-France, 1978), from the novel of the same title by the renowned Cuban author Alejo Carpentier, and *La viuda de Montiel* (Colombia-Venezuela-Cuba-Mexico, 1980), from the novel of the same title by the Colombian Gabriel García Márquez. For his next film, *Alsino y el cóndor* (1982), Littín assembled a group of Cuban, Mexican, and Costa Rican co-producers to make Nicaragua's first post-revolutionary feature. *Alsino* also received an Oscar nomination and was distributed in North America, making it the director's most successful project since *El chacal de Nahueltoro*. He then returned clandestinely to Chile to film a documentary with separate crews from Italy, France, and the Netherlands. The celebrated account of this dangerous, complex mission by Gabriel García Márquez, *La aventura de Miguel Littín clandestino en Chile* (1986) was published in English as well as Spanish, making the resultant film, *Acta General de Chile* (Spain, 1986), one of the most anticipated films in history. Littín continues to be an important figure on the world film scene, completing a television film on Agusto César Sandino (*Sandino*) in Spain in 1990, finally returning to his homeland to make a film which was screened in the "Un Certain regard" section of the 1994 Cannes film festival, *Los naufragos*.

Peter Rist

1. Julianne Burton, "*The Promised Land (La tierra prometida),*" in *Magill's Survey of Cinema: Foreign Language Films, Volume 5*, ed. Frank N. Magill (Englewood Cliffs, N.J.: Salem Press, 1985), 2471.

La Batalla de Chile: la lucha de un pueblo sin armas

The Battle of Chile
Chile-Cuba, 1974–79, 287', b+w

Part One: "La insurección de la burguesía"
(The Insurrection of the Bourgeoisie), 1974, 106'
Part Two: "El golpe de estado"
(The Coup d'Etat), 1976, 99'
Part Three: "El poder popular"
(Popular Power), 1979, 82'

Dir Patricio Guzmán (b. 1941) *Scr* Guzmán *Cinematog* Jorge Müller *Ed* Pedro Chaskel *Sound* Bernardo Menz *Prod* Equipo Tercer Año (Guzmán, Federico Elton, Müller, Menz, José Pino, Marta Harnecker) (Chile), in collaboration with Instituto Cubano del Arte e Industria Cinematográficos (ICAIC) (Cuba) and Chris Marker (France)

To say that *La Batalla de Chile: la lucha de un pueblo sin armas* is the most significant film made about Chile's history is an understatement.

Conceived by Patricio Guzmán in late 1972 as a dialectical record of the struggles of Salvador Allende's Popular Unity minority government, the "Equipo Tercer Año" continued shooting from February 1973 until the coup on September 11. Remarkably, all of the footage was smuggled out of the country, and the exiled Guzmán, with the valuable help of editor Pedro Chaskel, took five years to finish the monumental three-part documentary at ICAIC's facilities in Cuba. Like the model political film on the Left, *La hora de los hornos* (Argentina, 1968, q.v.), *La Batalla de Chile* was shot semi-clandestinely, but unlike its predecessor, Guzmán's film was well received by critics in North America (other than those necessarily committed to the same ideals as the filmmakers), even those as mainstream as Pauline Kael.

The five original members of Equipo Tercer Año met in December 1972 to discuss their filmmaking strategy. Understanding that, given the political instability inherent to a minority government, there would either be a civil war or right-wing coup (the latter, in fact, occurred), they felt the urgent need, in Guzmán's words, to "make a film about what was going on in the country from day to day." "Any fictional screenplay, any film structured around a plot, no matter how good, seemed to us to be completely upstaged by events themselves." They wanted to make the film primarily for the Chilean people, but also, especially in the event of defeat, for the benefit of workers' movements worldwide. Using Cuban filmmaker Julio García Espinosa's 1970 film *Tercer mundo, tercera guerra mundial* (filmed collectively and spontaneously in North Vietnam at the height of the U.S. assault) as a model, the group generated a theoretical outline for their analytical documentary. Eventually, the "screenplay" took the form of a wall "map" listing key points of the revolutionary struggle, accompanied by another list of elements which had already been filmed. The editorial collective of the journal *Chile Hoy*, including Marta Harnecker, joined the group at this stage. They filmed almost every day using their one Eclair camera and one Nagra portable sound recorder, with raw film stock (which was otherwise unavailable in Chile due to the U.S. economic embargo) sent to them from France by Chris Marker. They never granted interviews with other media and maintained their clandestine identity by carrying a range of credentials with them, sometimes posing as a French or Swiss TV crew, and by working on such a small scale.

The focus of Part One, "La insurrección de la burguesía," is on the right-wing forces opposing the government and mostly compiles footage shot before the end of June. A *cinéma vérité*-style, jerky hand-held camera, interviewing subjects in close-up, is used for interviews on the street with predominantly anti-Allende voters. When the camera then moves into bourgeois homes, one can detect Guzmán's influence, who by his own description stayed close by Jorge Müller's shoulder to direct "movements which are much more readily identified with fictional than with documentary filmmaking." Here the moving camera describes the ostentatious lifestyle of the Chilean rich, scanning cabinets full of useless artifacts. After showing Allende's failure to pass legislation in the House of Assembly, the use of style as rhetoric can again be detected in uncut flash-pans which increase the dynamism of a workers' rally and in the use of a very low-angled camera to represent Opposition speakers, as in Sergei Eisenstein's films, as grotesque. This first part ends by suggesting a jump ahead in time: an Argentine photographer is shot and the image blurs as he falls. The image is then masked and frozen on a Chilean soldier.

Part Two, "El golpe de estado," takes the viewer through the last three difficult months of the Popular Unity government and focuses much more on Allende and his followers than the first part. The differences within the Left are explored and at the centre of the piece is an extremely long take of an impassioned worker's speech at a small meeting. Allende ages visibly and becomes more desperate, but remains determined to abide by the democratic process. Part Two is graced by brilliant sound editing, reminiscent of Joris Ivens' *Spanish Earth* (1937). Here, the sound of a helicopter becomes a sinister motif, leading to aerial footage of the bombing of the government buildings marking the coup and Allende's death. Just before the denouement, a loud humming noise—presumably a technical flaw—perfectly complements the very grainy, poor-quality picture. The group shot footage of the bombardment directly off television, noting later that no one else thought to film the military's audacious broadcasting of its coup and assault on the National Palace.

Part Three, "El poder popular," was released much later than the other two parts, in 1979, and provides some nostalgic release from these with its almost exclusive focus on the forces of Popular Unity. This segment covers the time frame of both the previous films and shows the workers organising and discussing strategy around the Right's infiltration of the truckers' union, food distribution networks, factory and community organisations, and the redistribution of land. We see peasants, revolutionaries, and land owners arguing about the situation in long takes with the boom mike clearly in the frame. Such intrusions make the film audience more conscious of the processes of filmmaking, an attitude which is exaggerated towards the end of the film, when a professor is shown in class discussing the popular movements, and at the very end, when nitrate miners are framed against stylized white backgrounds and then replaced by an image of the empty landscape accompanied by mechanical sounds. In this final part the dialectical aims of Equipo Tercer Año are most clearly demonstrated: reflexive devices, the occasional distancing of the audience by having the camera move away into long shot, and analysis of the workers' strategies, are sharply contrasted with the activities of the Right.

After the coup, all of the filmmakers, with the exception of Jorge Müller, who with his companion Carmen Bueno "disappeared," were able to leave Chile clandestinely, in prearranged order. Guzmán had been arrested and held in the National Stadium for two weeks, while Federico Elton and Bernardo Menz were also detained for a while, but nobody panicked and everyone was re-united in Cuba after being invited there by ICAIC. Pedro Chaskel, though he had yet to work on the film, left Chile specifically to be the editor, and Marta Harnecker had already been in Cuba for two months when the others arrived. Chaskel stayed on in Cuba and became a successful director of documentaries (*Un foto recorre al mundo*, 1981). Guzmán followed the path of other Chilean exiles, directing the occasional co-production (*La rosa de los vientos*, Cuba/Venezuela/Spain, 1983), eventually settling in Spain. Most recently he has made a remarkable fictional representation of Latin American history for Spanish television, *La cruz del sur*, in 1992.

Peter Rist

Awards: Part One: Best Film, Grenoble, 1975. Part Two: Best Film, Grenoble, 1976; Best Film, Benalmadena, 1976; International Jury Prize, Leipzig, 1976. Part Three: Best Documentary, Havana, 1979.

Les Trois couronnes du matelot

Three Crowns of the Sailor
France, 1982, 117', colour

Dir Raúl Ruiz *Scr* Ruiz and Emilio del Solar *Cinematog* Sacha Vierny *Ed* Jeannine Vernea and Valeria Sarmiento *Mus* Jorge Arriagada *Sound* Jean-Claude Brisson *Prod* I.N.A.-Films and Antenne 2 *Act* Jean Bernard Guillard, Philippe Deplanche, Nadège Clair, Jean Badin, Lisa Lyon, Claude Dereppe, Frank Oger

After going into exile, Raúl Ruiz (*La colonia penal*, 1971, q.v.) continued to be an incredibly prolific filmmaker. Since 1974, when he made *Dialogues des exilés* in France, he has managed to direct about fifty works—films, videos, television programs, and series—including over twenty feature films. He has become the independent filmmaker *par excellence*, taking advantage of various kinds of opportunities to work, even minor television assignments, while forging a distinctive personality. Often, this "personality" involves the situation of "exile," and occasionally the films have recognisably Chilean and/or South American elements. Two of his most celebrated European-produced features from 1982 fit this description: *Het Dak van de Walvis* (The Netherlands) and *Les Trois couronnes du matelot*. The former was set in an imaginary Patagonia. Readily mixing English, Dutch, Spanish, French, and invented languages, this film constituted a mock scientific anthropological investigation in a decidedly Borgesian fashion.

Ruiz is often inspired by literature—both Latin American and European. In the case of *Les Trois couronnes*, the story of the ship "El Funchalense" appears to have been inspired by a legend from the south of Chile: "El Caleuche" is the story of a phantom ship which appears and disappears off the island of Chiloé, listening for the voices of its drowned sailors. The film begins with a narrator who tells of the murder of a professor by a student at a school of theology in Warsaw. In the dance hall, the student encounters a sailor who tells him a story in exchange for three Danish crowns. His story tells of a solitary sailor on the ship "El Funchalense." Although he has no family, in his travels he encounters his wife, his son, his best friend, his brother, his mother—all the people who should surround a normal individual, but who are, for him, dispersed throughout the world. The ship travels from port to port, visiting Valparaíso, Tampico, Dakar, Tangier, and Singapore. The sailor (Jean

Bernard Guillard) tries to unite the people in his life, but his attempt proves unsuccessful. A metaphor for exile, the film reveals well what happens to friends and family during one's exile: they are dispersed.

Les Trois couronnes proposes both a geographic exploration and an exploration of all the possibilities—in terms of narrative, visuals, effects, and sound—that film allows and incorporates the medium's accidents, its discoveries and surprises. There is a series of marginal secondary characters, who inhabit underground worlds and who, in one way or another, are connected with "El Funchalense" and its phantom sailors. Perverse and violent details abound: the sailors do not defecate excrement but issue worms instead; Mathilde (Lisa Lyon), the fascinating ballerina with whom the narrator falls in love, has only one bodily orifice—her mouth.

Visually, there are pictorial references to French Orientalist paintings of the nineteenth century, with their manner of illumination (Ingres and Delacroix can be cited from among the most well known of these painters as well as Marilhat and Decamps). For example, the young virgin prostitute who saves herself religiously for each man who passes through her door is someone we can recognise in the odalisques of Ingres. In terms of technique, the film constitutes an exploration of trick effects: in-camera superimpositions, changes in focus and direction of light in the same plane, as occurs, for example, in the depiction of a face behind a curtain. The film displays shadows, contrasting lights and filters to an excessive degree. Together with its use of wide-angle lenses and "trompe-l'oeil" depth of field, French cinematographer Sacha Vierny—known for his great work with Alain Resnais and Chris Marker—helps to create a baroque style reminiscent of Orson Welles. In the treatment of sound, Ruiz uses all kinds of voices; voices which sing like the captain who whistles Beethoven's Fifth Symphony or the forced diction of the sailor's narration and voices from afar.

Les Trois couronnes du matelot presents the evocative power of memory as a method of opposing death, desperation, and dispersion, with the ability to reconstruct in some nostalgic and obsessive way a world which has almost disappeared. Ultimately, the film suggests that one can indeed come forth from exile.

Marilú Mallet

Awards: First Prize, "Perspectives," Cannes, 1983.

Hijos de la guerra fría

Children of the Cold War
Chile-France, 1985, 80', colour

Dir Gonzalo Justiniano (b. 1955) *Scr* Justiniano *Cinematog* Jorge Roth *Mus* Jorge Arriagada *Prod* ARCA (Chile) and Out One (France) *Act* Eugenia Morales, Pachi Torrealba, Javier Maldonada, Sonia Mena, Hernán González

Following the bloody September 1973 coup that toppled Salvador Allende's government, filmmaking in Chile came to a near standstill under the military government of General Augusto Pinochet (1973–89). During Pinochet's 16-year rule, a new generation of filmmakers came of age, fresh from studies at foreign film schools, frustrated at merely making advertising commercials under the new consumer-based economic policies of the military regime. When Gonzalo Justiniano filmed *Hijos de la guerra fría* in 1985, years before Pinochet relinquished power but at a time when veiled criticism was becoming possible, it broke ground as the first feature to be shot in Chile since Silvio Caiozzi's *Julio comienza en julio* (1979) and ushered in a new wave of national films that criticised life under Pinochet from within, most notably *Imagen latente* (1987, q.v.) and *Historias de lagartos* (1988).

A quirky tongue-in-cheek comedy, *Hijos de la guerra fría* centres on the absurdly unromantic yet oddly passionate relationship between two middle-class office workers, Kafkaesque functionaries who are perfectly satisfied to live with their eyes closed during Chile's brief economic boom while ignoring all the warning signs of impending doom. They purchase a flashy new convertible and document their wedding on videotape. When the crash eventually occurs, the couple become unromanticised versions of Bonnie and Clyde, holding up small roadside diners in a spree of revenge against a system that has failed them. In the end, the man simply disappears into the landscape. (It is exactly this sweeping and oppressively empty landscape of Chile's particular topography that appears as a key element and isolating metaphor in many national films, including *Historias de lagartos* (1988) and *La frontera* (1991, q.v.).) With *Hijos de la guerra fría*, Justiniano presents a comic but critical look at middle-class complicity with the compromised morality of the Pinochet regime, while his later films mirror the frustrations of young people living within a grey environment.

Justiniano worked in advertising in Chile before moving to France to study cinema at the University of Paris and at the École Lumière. *Hijos de la guerra fría* was followed by the enormously successful *Sussi* (1988), a commercial tongue-in-cheek chronicle of the misadventures of a young woman who finds herself up for an advertising campaign as the ideal Chilean woman. Justiniano returned to the theme of boredom as a way of life in *Caluga o menta* (1990), which depicted the post-Pinochet generation wallowing in inactivity with petty crime and empty sex as the only alternative. Justiniano has been especially successful in raising co-production funds from European television, mainly France, Germany, and Spain.

In an interview, Justiniano noted that "what happened in Chile, which I tried to explain in *Hijos de la guerra fría*, was a complex political process. If there is a military government and a person like Pinochet in that government, in my opinion this process has not happened by coincidence. There is always a mentality behind it. There is a great sense of conformity among Chileans, who want to avoid problems at all costs. When I first decided to do a fiction film, I wanted to make it with a script that told the story of the people who fought against the dictatorship. Then I decided that this theme had been used too much already. What intrigued me the most about Chile were the hidden factors of daily life. I wanted to decipher what was happening, why there were people who ignored everything. I was not interested in making a didactic or moralistic film. Nor was I interested in making a film in which the good guys won and the bad guys were bad. The film also has a very grotesque and ironic side. I realised that this was the only way to talk and to communicate in a dictatorship. I am constantly referring to the issue of censorship. I tried to create a style of saying things without actually saying them. My idea in the film is to use these clichéd characters who live a kind of love story, are successful, and have a relatively good life. Everything they want in life comes to them, but in the same way, it goes, and everything finishes badly. This is why the film starts comically and finishes in a more symbolic and metaphoric way. The characters wind up in desolate landscapes. All their dreams are destroyed. It is a synthesis of the main features of my country's evolution."

Paul Lenti

Awards: Best Director, Cartagena (Colombia), 1986; prizes in Berlin, Turin, and Biarritz.

Imagen latente

Latent Image
Chile, 1987 (released 1990), 92', colour

Dir Pablo Perelman (b. 1948) *Scr* Perelman *Cinematog* Beltrán García *Ed* Fernando Valenzuela Quinteros *Art dir* Juan Carlos Castillo *Sound* Marcos de Aguirre *Mus* Jaime de Aguirre *Prod* Freddy Rammsy and Patricia Varela for Colectivo de Actores y Técnicos y Productores Chilenos and Ictus *Act* Bastián Bodenhöfer, María Izquierdo, Elena Muñoz, Gonzalo Roble, Gloria Munchemeyer, Shlomit Bayttelman

Imagen latente was the first feature film dealing critically with the Pinochet dictatorship to be made openly in Chile. But its public exhibition in Chile was prohibited by both the Film Classification Board and the court of appeals. However, its reputation abroad grew through screenings at film festivals, beginning with Havana in December 1987 where it won the International Critics' Prize. Then in 1990 after a civilian government was elected following 17 years of military rule, the censorship restrictions were relaxed somewhat, and *Imagen latente* was released along with six other Chilean-made features—a banner year to be sure.

Pablo Perelman studied film in Brussels and began working on documentaries and music videos. In 1974 he co-directed the feature *A la sombra del sol* with Silvio Caiozzi, after which he was forced to travel outside of Chile in order to continue to make politically controversial films. In 1976 he co-directed *Crónica de Tlacotalpan* with Miguel Littín in Mexico and in 1983 he photographed and co-directed (with Angelina Vázquez) the documentary *Fragmentos de un diario inacabado*, as a co-production with Finland. *Imagen latente* was his first solo feature.

Imagen latente is considerably autobiographical, with the central character, Pedro (Bastián Bodenhöfer) functioning as a surrogate Perelman. Pedro is a professional photographer who works in the world of advertising and whose brother vanished in 1975, approximately ten years before the main action of the film. Pedro and his wife, who is more engaged politically than he is and convinced that her brother-in-law has "disappeared," become estranged. He begins a search and although, as in Costa-Gavras' *Missing* (1982), the protagonist is initially conservative and sceptical, he becomes racked by guilt and obsessed with finding the truth. Pedro attends clandestine meetings of fellow searchers, and he interviews victims and relatives. Photographs of the "disappeared" add a documentary edge to the tale, and perhaps the strongest point of *Imagen latente* is where

Pedro clandestinely photographs (from a car) the carefully guarded, stately yet austere building where prisoners were held—presumably the actual site. After throwing his work and home lives into disarray, he eventually comes to terms with himself and becomes convinced of the reality of Pinochet's regime torturing and killing the "disappeared."

Like many Latin American films, *Imagen latente* is suffused with machismo, especially when Pedro starts an affair with his brother's former lover as a way of somehow "finding" him. But women are not stereotyped here as passive wives and lovers. They are equal to men in the political arena. In one of the film's strongest scenes, Pedro interviews a woman who recounts incidents of torture. The interview format suggests that the actress might indeed be a real victim of Pinochet's regime and is an example of the careful organic structure of the film, wherein the title itself resonates with meaning. Pedro is unable to capture the whole truth in his search and with his camera in the same way that the film—any film—can only provide a series of images, not reality itself. And here the revelation of the truth remains elusive and "latent." In fact, the film's title is meaningful in a number of ways. It resonates of "shooting in the dark" and of "drawing images out of the shadows," a photographic process of "latent image" where the image is "pushed" a number of f-stops in brightness.

The film was made on a very low budget, but a paucity of means was employed to advantage. Simple sets, lacking detail and depth, allow the camera to conceal rather than reveal, providing a claustral feel. This mood is also created through the continual use of close-ups, which additionally provoke an attitude of introspection—another appropriate stylistic choice. In achieving his remarkable synthesis of style and subject matter, Perelman was assisted greatly by the beauty and simplicity of Beltrán García's cinematography. And, in retrospect, it is hard to believe that Perelman was able to make *Imagen latente* in mid-1980s Chile at all.

Peter Rist

Awards: International Film Critics' Prize (FIPRESCI), Havana, 1987.

La luna en el espejo

The Moon in the Mirror
Chile, 1990, 75', colour

Dir Silvio Caiozzi (b. 1945) *Scr* José Donoso and Caiozzi, based on an idea by Donoso
Cinematog Nelson Fuentes *Prod* Caiozzi *Act* Gloria Munchemeyer, Rafael Benavente, Ernesto
Beadle, María Castiglione

Silvio Caiozzi's work straddles two eras of Chilean cinema, that of the
nuevo cine period of 1967–1973, whose major figures were exiled with the
repression of the coup d'état, and that of the industry's slow rebirth in the
late 1980s and early '90s, after the democratic elections of 1989. Caiozzi
studied film in the U.S. in the mid-60s, returning to Chile in time to
participate in the five-year renaissance of Chilean film that began in 1967.
He worked as cinematographer on *Nadie dijo nada* (1970), by Raúl Ruiz
(*La colonia penal*, 1971, q.v.), and *Ya no basta con rezar* (1972), by Aldo
Francia (*Valparaíso, mi amor*, 1969, q.v.), and as second camera on Costa
Gavras' *State of Siege* (1972). After the coup he was able to stay in Chile,
and his work in the lucrative field of filming advertising enabled him to
self-finance his first feature, *Julio comienza en julio* (1979), for which
shooting took place in 1976. *Julio*, safely set at the turn of the century,
came at a time when the Pinochet dictatorship was systematically razing
the country's film industry: schools and studios were closed, archives
destroyed, and filmmakers imprisoned. It was the only Chilean film to be
released commercially in Chile during the dictatorship, as a very few
independent experimental films or documentaries were produced but not
widely seen. These included *A la sombra del sol* (1974), co-directed by
Caiozzi and Pablo Perelman, whose first feature, *Imagen latente* (1987,
q.v.), was not seen in Chile until after the elections. In 1982 Caiozzi shot
a video adaptation of *Historia de un roble solo* by Chile's most prominent
author, José Donoso (who was living abroad at the time). Work on *La
luna en el espejo*, with an original script by Donoso and Caiozzi, began in
1985 but was not completed until 1990, when Gloria Munchemeyer won
a Best Actress award at the Venice film festival (the first time a Chilean
film had competed at this prestigious festival), and the film picked up
numerous awards at other festivals. Part of a planned trilogy based on the
work of Latin American authors, *La luna en el espejo* was the only one of
the three to be produced, and Caiozzi has not yet made another feature.

La luna en el espejo is set in Valparaíso, Chile's bustling port, with its distinctive funiculars leading from the port and commercial district up into the city's residential districts. A plain, dumpy-looking young couple like nothing better than to get together to create elaborate gourmet meals and to eat them with relish. Unfortunately, they have no privacy, as he lives in a small flat with his infirm father, a salty retired naval officer who demands constant attention, rails about modern society, and doesn't hide his dislike for his son's older girlfriend. The film opens on a television in the flat showing images of the Pope's controversial visit to Chile, our only indication throughout the film that it is set in the dictatorship's final years in the late '80s. Taking place almost entirely within the flat, *La luna en el espejo* creates a disorienting world focused on the rituals of cooking and eating at one end of the house and on the old man's attempts to maintain control at the other. The allegory for the change taking place in Chile, the old giving way to the new and the waning influence of the military, is fairly obvious, especially with the old man's presumed death from a fall outside the house at the end of the film. And yet there seems to be no attempt to create a "message" beyond this basic dichotomy, reminding us of Donoso's claim that he is "not interested in the novel of ideas." Instead, the film attempts to recreate his universe: constantly shifting and dark almost to the point of being macabre, illustrated by the title of his most famous work, *El obsceno pájaro de la noche*—"The Obscene Bird of Night." The viewer comes to feel, as does the reader of this novel, the uncomfortable sensation of having a viewpoint that is too close to the action.

Caiozzi deploys two stylistic devices to create this world on film: first, the network of mirrors the old man uses to survey everything going on in the flat from his bed, a disorienting set-up that is accentuated by our viewing events through yet another visual filter, the camera, with its own angles and perspectives. The result is a cinematic fun house, as another dimension is created in a small flat with a few mirrors and a camera. This dimension, perhaps, represents an elusive contentment, the moon seen only in the mirror of the film's title. Second, the couple's constant cooking is punctuated by close-up inserts of the food being prepared, in all its glorious sensuality. Theirs is a cuisine of rich abundance, of plump shellfish being shucked in close-up, of butter, cream, pastry. The viewer eventually becomes just a little bit repelled, and altogether fascinated, by the sensuousness of it all. The sustained effect of the juxtaposition of these two worlds of displaced viewpoints and close-ups is to lead the viewer into all manner of speculation, searching for narrative development where there is none: will the couple kill the old man? Their relentless chopping lets us imagine them, despite their simplicity, as seemingly perfect candidates for such a job. In the end, however, we are denied any such narrative outlet and are left with a world, as Donoso would have it, that signifies nothing. While the effect is more compelling in the self-contained world of Donoso's complex, feverish, and relentless prose, *La luna en el espejo* remains an interesting experiment in literary adaptation which creates a visual world that corresponds to the author's universe.

Timothy Barnard

Awards: Best Film, Trieste, 1990; Best Director, Cartagena (Colombia), 1990; Best Actress (Gloria Munchemeyer), Venice, 1990; Special Mention of the International Catholic Cinema Office (OCIC), Amiens, 1990; Special Jury Prize, Valladolid, 1990; Second Prize, Best Actor, ISA prize, Havana, 1990; Best Film, Best Iberoamerican Film, Montevideo, 1990.

La frontera

The Frontier
Chile-Spain, 1991, 122', colour

Dir Ricardo Larraín (b. 1959) *Scr* Larraín and Jorge Goldenberg *Cinematog* Héctor Ríos *Mus* Jaime de Aguirre *Prod* Cine XXI, Ion Producciones, Filmocentro Cine, Televisión Nacional de Chile (Chile) and Televisión Española (TVE) (Spain) *Act* Patricio Contreras, Gloria Laso, Alonso Venegas, Héctor Noguera

Young director Ricardo Larraín's first feature is post-Pinochet Chile's most accomplished and successful film to date, breaking attendance records for a Chilean film since the Popular Unity period of the early 1970s. *La frontera*'s script, by veteran Argentine scriptwriter Jorge Goldenberg (*La película del Rey*, 1986, q.v.), won a prize for new scripts at the Havana film festival, the festival's only cash award, to contribute to the production costs of promising projects. The film stars Chilean actor resident in Argentina Patricio Contreras in a powerful performance as a mathematics teacher sent into internal exile in southern Chile in the final years of the military regime. While the script follows the well-worn path of the mutual discovery of two very different elements of society, the urban intellectual and the isolated villagers, Larraín brings to it promising directing skills and a deft and intelligent sense of black humour. Despite the serious theme, the film is often quietly hilarious and it delights in the absurd.

Contreras' schoolteacher signed a petition late in the dictatorship for the release of a jailed colleague; he is obviously not a political activist, although some villagers refer to him affectionately as "the terrorist." His punishment turns out to be something of a blessing in disguise, as he not only discovers his own country but falls in love and recovers his zest for life whilst helping a deep-sea diver recover bric-a-brac from the ocean floor. His lover lives with her father, a Spanish Republican who transports himself daily back to his beloved Spain, while the deep-sea diver is never seen out of his diving suit, his enormous helmet under his arm, even when in church. More wry comedy is provided by the need for Contreras to sleep with the local priest, for lack of anywhere else in town to lodge him. His tragi-comic relationship with his compatriots is synthesized in a scene of lonely, drunken desperation in the town pub as he watches the local men dance together: "Don't you realise what's going on in the country? Don't you realise what's going on in the world? Queers!," he shouts, whereupon a man asks him to dance and, face set, he agrees.

The film's images of this southern town, its mist and shadows and rocky coastline, are beautiful, and veteran cinematographer Héctor Ríos (*El chacal de Nahueltoro*, 1970, q.v.; *La colonia penal*, 1971, q.v.) has done a masterful job of filming under low-light conditions, eschewing lighting even indoors: an enchanting blue gloom pervades the film. When news unexpectedly arrives of Contreras' freedom, he at first resolves to stay (throwing the local prefect into a quandary) and then attempts, unsuccessfully, to coax his lover and her father to return with him to Santiago. The old man perishes in a flash flood and his daughter, resisting Contreras' entreaties, stubbornly clings to his body as Contreras and the other villagers seek high ground. With the arrival of a helicopter, which the viewer is forgiven for assuming to be a rescue crew—in an insightful comment on contemporary society, it turns out that a TV news crew first reaches the scene—Contreras is recognised and asked to repeat his experience of internal exile. The film ends on this scene of Contreras speaking of his exile—as if it were not yet over—through the monitor of the video camera, his lover having chosen death with her daft Republican father to life in late 1980s Santiago.

Timothy Barnard

Awards: Second Prize, Berlin, 1990.

Colombia

Garras de oro

Dawn of Justice
Colombia, 1928, 45' (surviving fragments, at 16 fps),
b+w with some colour tinting, silent

Dir P.P. Jambrina *Cinematog* Arnoldo Ricotti (operator) and Arrigo Cinotti (assistant operator) *Prod* Cali Film

In the climate of the relative euphoria which reigned in Colombia in the 1920s, with the high prices obtained by its primary exports and the $25 million paid by the United States to indemnify the country for its loss of Panama, Colombian cinema saw its best days. While it never came to constitute a real industry, many film production companies appeared in several cities and towns of the vast, undeveloped country, with its poor communications. They generally set out to film feature-length productions of national literary classics such as *María, Aura o las violetas, Como los muertos,* and *Madre.*

With the founding of Cali Film in 1926, a group of investors, made up of professionals and merchants in the Cauca Valley, in the west of the country, embarked on the adventure of film production. Apparently this company's ephemeral existence gave birth to just one film, *Garras de oro,* which sought to reclaim Colombia's honour after it had been sullied by the events which culminated in Panama being separated from Colombia through U.S. military intervention in 1903.

The film's action takes place between 1903 and 1914 (the year the Panama Canal was completed) in New York City and Colombia, with a few images of the Canal interspersed throughout. Three themes develop

243

parallel to each other and eventually converge: the political evolution of U.S. President Theodore Roosevelt (1900–1908)—whose famous motto for his dealings with Latin America was "Walk softly and carry a big stick"; the campaigns and eventual court battles waged by some U.S. newspapers against the president's imperialist ambitions; and the romantic relationship between an American journalist and a Colombian woman, who are buffeted by the ups and downs of political events.

The film's argument is advanced through the use of long intertitles whose goal is to fashion a sometimes agitational denunciation of events. The style does not stray from the film language common to silent cinema the world over at this time, although there is evidence of greater technical resources being put to use than was usual in Colombia at the time. *Garras de oro* was also the only silent Colombian film to have had some scenes tinted by hand. These distinctive features may be explained by the possibility that the film's production was entrusted by Cali Film's shareholders to an Italian producer. It is not known with certainty whether or not this was the case, although various aspects of the mise-en-scène suggest that it was filmed in Italy. In any event, the film was evidently conceived and written entirely by Colombians.

More interesting even than the film itself was the way in which it came to be suppressed. In mid-1926 the Motion Pictures Producers and Distributors of America wrote to the U.S. State Department to warn it of the film's production ("is said to be highly injurious to this country," the letter states) and to solicit its intervention to prevent its distribution and exhibition in Colombia and elsewhere. The State Department's machinery was set in motion and sure enough the film disappeared. It was restored to Colombia's film heritage sixty years later, in 1986, when an incomplete print was discovered, consisting of the first and last and two intermediary reels, totalling 45 minutes in length.

In 1928 two public screenings of the film were reported by the Colombian press, one in Bogotá and the other in Medellín. Other news items of the day reported the film's censorship by Colombian authorities as a result of pressure from the U.S. embassy. The success of this pressure and the subsequent and overwhelming arrival of sound films in the country in 1929 were a devastating blow to the later development of Colombian cinema.

Jorge Nieto

La langosta azul

The Blue Lobster
Colombia, 1954, 29', b+w, silent

Dir Alvaro Cepeda Samudio (1927–1972), Gabriel García Márquez, Enrique Grau Araújo, and Luis Vicens *Scr* Cepeda Samudio, García Márquez, Grau, and Vicens *Cinematog* Nereo López and Guillermo Salvat *Art dir* Enrique Grau *Prod* Nueve-Seis-Tres *Act* Nereo López, Jeso Rum, Ramón Jessurum, Cecilia Porras, Enrique Grau, Luis Vicens, Alvaro Cepeda Jr., "El Mago"

For years Colombian intellectuals discussed a rare experimental film that involved several members of the Barranquilla group: the young journalist and critic Gabriel García Márquez, writer and filmmaker Alvaro Cepeda Samudio, and artist Enrique Grau. This trio was joined by the Catalan Luis Vicens, who ran a book distribution business in Bogotá. García Márquez has since dismissed *La langosta azul*, but Colombian film historians disagree with his assessment; Hernando Martínez Pardo went so far as to declare it the first serious effort to renew Colombian cinema.[1] Cepeda Samudio's widow Teresa de Cepeda suggests that García Márquez has washed his hands of the film because his original idea had been completely rewritten. Soon before the film was shot, García Márquez, then a young journalist and aspiring filmmaker, travelled to Europe to study film at the renowned Centro Sperimentale in Rome. The opening credits give all four participants equal recognition as authors of the work. Since Cepeda Samudio was the only member of this group to continue as a filmmaker, he is often credited as the director; yet Enrique Grau recounts that this was above all a group project and all decisions were made by consensus.

Although this short film had gone down in Colombian film legend, it remained largely unseen for almost four decades, the only print being that of the national film archive. A new print was struck for exhibition in New York in 1990, and it has since been screened at other archives and festivals. The film was shot by the three principal collaborators in over one week on 16mm reversal film stock, which gave a single print and no negative. Grau recounts that their film supply was so scarce that they discussed every shot laboriously before filming.

La langosta azul is part of a tradition of experimental cinema that includes such classics as Luis Buñuel's *Un Chien andalou* (1929) and Mario Peixoto's *Limite* (Brazil, 1930, q.v.). It is also reminiscent of works by contemporary pioneer filmmakers such as Maya Deren. A silent black-and-white film, *La langosta azul* documents a disturbing journey that questions a contemporary threat of the outside world, the radioactive poisoning of lobsters, discovered by the "Gringo," a stranger carrying a well-travelled bag, whose ominous presence possibly endangers the relative peace of a provincial coastal fishing village. The film is replete with many humorous scenes, offset by disquieting elements such as a man who spies on the stranger's movements through the town, the mysterious balloon-blowing manager of the Hotel Tal, or the egregious scoundrel who offers to find the lost lobster. These images are offset by documentary-like footage that depicts both daily life and startling poetic images that carry the film beyond its slim abstract narrative. Emphasis is often placed on unexpected details, highlighted by disturbing close-ups that give equal weight to all elements of the storyline.

Martínez Pardo called the film "a surrealist experiment whose best moments are not only symbolic but also function as film journalism. The work is important for two reasons: the first is strictly cinematographic and lies in the innovative concept of the film's structure. The storyline—the loss and search for the blue lobster—ceases to be important, the focus of interest, and instead it becomes a tenuous narrative thread that offers a reason to create the atmosphere of the town's daily life. The second shows the relationship between cinema and reality: Cepeda constructed a story that approaches science fiction and is simultaneously a story about life. In this sense, Cepeda Samudio advanced the development of Colombian cinema ten years."

Writer and filmmaker Alvaro Cepeda Samudio died in New York in 1972. Author of the novel *La casa grande* and two books of short stories, he made various films including *Noticiero del Caribe* (1968), *Carnival en el Caribe* (1969), and *Azilef* (1970).

Paul Lenti

1. Hernando Martínez Pardo, *Historia del cine colombiano*, Librería y Editorial América Latina, Bogotá, 1978.

El río de las tumbas

The River of the Graves
Colombia, 1964, 87', b+w

Dir Julio Luzardo (b. 1938) *Scr* Luzardo and Gustavo Andrade Rivera, with Pepe Sánchez
and Carlos José Reyes *Cinematog* Hélio Silva *Prod* Héctor Echeverry Correa, Alberto Mejía,
and Ismael Tello for Cine TV Films *Act* Carlos Duplat, Milena Fierro, Jorge Andrade,
Santiago García

"At a time when [Colombian] filmmakers gave no thought to the
peculiarities of film language, Luzardo addressed problems of structure and
style in his films. At a time when content was identified only with
subject, film with the representation of pre-existing action, and critique
with an explicit discourse, Luzardo created levels of signification and
placed the sense of reflexivity of the work in the atmosphere he created,"
film historian Hernando Martínez Pardo has written.[1]

The "time" was the beginning of the 1960s. Julio Luzardo returned to
Colombia after studying cinema at UCLA in the United States. His
parents had sent him there in the wake of the "Bogotazo" in 1948, when
the assassination of a politician caused a popular uprising and ushered in
a long period of political violence. By the time of Luzardo's return,
brimming with ideas suggested by his reading of new currents in Latin
American literature, the two warring political parties had entered into a
curious pact to alternate terms in office as a palliative to the upheaval.

Colombian cinema at the time was weaning itself off its great reliance
on local manners and was beginning to show the first signs of the vitality
which characterised Colombian, Latin American, and world cinema in the
1960s and '70s. Like other Latin American countries, Colombian cinema
felt the dominance of the Argentine and Mexican industries erode, viewed
the almost unknown Brazilian cinema with interest, enthusiastically
welcomed the first Cuban revolutionary films, and found a place for its
first generation of young filmmakers trained in Europe and the U.S.

Luzardo worked initially as an editor and assistant director on several
films. He directed two medium-length films, *Tiempo de sequía* and *La
sarda*, which, with another film, Alberto Mejía's *El zorrero*, were packaged
as a feature, *Tres cuentos colombianos* (1962). These films were produced
by Cine TV Films, where Luzardo worked filming advertising and
industrial shorts. *Tres cuentos colombianos* attracted more than 40,000

spectators which, while still not a lot compared to a major release of the day, gave rise to the notion that among Colombia's elusive public, a market might exist for such crude themes, almost pathetic in their realism.

Luzardo's work was uncompromisingly social, but he brought a sense of humour to his work. This approach lies at the root of *El río de las tumbas*. With this film he wanted to reveal the country through a typical village on the blazing banks of a large tropical river, where the inhabitants pass their lives in a state of perpetual torpor as a result of the climate. We see the priest deliver dreary harangues to his tiny congregation against the bad influence of the new mayor, who is protected by political figures not to the priest's liking. The indolent mayor is someone who tries to fulfil his obligations at the most leisurely pace possible.

Apathy is widespread, even when the town fool discovers a mysterious corpse floating in the river. An investigator arrives from the capital, full of enthusiasm for solving the crime. Nothing is solved, and the time for fiestas and the local candidate's visit arrives. The river then brings another, most inopportune corpse, but the mayor lets it keep floating so that the next town's mayor can deal with it. Violence exists, but it is elusive. This is the film's theme, and it becomes its principal defect. The subplot of the pretty waitress and the mysterious horseman, revealed through flashbacks to have been involved with the fool in attacks and banditry, does not entirely gel with the rest of the film. Its introduction breaks the film's stylistic and narrative threads, leaves gaps which are never resolved, and sows confusion like that caused by the abrupt ending.

Nevertheless, *El río de las tumbas* is still seen today as one of the most important Colombian films. The atmosphere Luzardo created is perhaps its greatest achievement, and contributing to this was the work of Brazilian cinematographer Hélio Silva, who had shot Nelson Pereira dos Santos' *Rio Quarenta Graus* (1955, q.v.). Despite the makeshift laboratory set up to process the film, the images reveal a purity and expressivity which contrast with the murky sound and the uneven acting. The film did not manage to attract large audiences, however: only 20,000 spectators went to its initial release. But it later became somewhat of a cult film and is a perennial component of Colombian film retrospectives abroad. Its portrait of the country and the people who inhabit it remains true today.

Diego Rojas Romero

1. Hernando Martínez Pardo, *Historia del cine colombiano*, Librería y Editorial América Latina, Bogotá, 1978.

Chircales

The Brickmakers
Colombia, 1967–72, 41', b+w

Dir Marta Rodríguez (b. 1933) and Jorge Silva (1941-1987) *Scr* Rodríguez and Silva *Cinematog* Silva *Sound* Rodríguez, Pierre Jacopin

Hidden away in the south of Bogotá is the zone of Chircales, whose residents make bricks using primitive techniques. For these inhabitants, life is little more than serfdom: they live in the owner's dismal dwellings and work from 5 a.m. to 6 p.m. under arduous and dangerous conditions. Marta Rodríguez and Jorge Silva found 50,000 people in the area involved in this primitive production of bricks. The voice-over narration explains that there are three classes of individuals: the landowners, those who rent this land and hire the work force, and the workers.

Chircales focuses on the Castañeda family, a couple with 11 children. In her prayers, one of the daughters begs God not to send her mother any more children. The film begins with the father explaining his political beliefs: "I am a Liberal," he proclaims, but without conviction. Rather, he is a Liberal because his father was. He finds his only comfort from work through drinking and abusing his family. The family's only joy appears to be a First Communion ceremony, celebrated for the children.

The filmmakers, in an almost timeless fashion, show the process of making bricks, from digging the clay and hand moulding bricks to loading the kilns where they are baked. The carbon monoxide from these kilns cripples workers and take the lives of many in the community. When a father of five dies, a neighbour complains that the boss doesn't even show up to pay his respects. The simple grave is ringed with bricks as its sole embellishment, and the family mourns its plight, knowing that without its breadwinner, the future will hold even more poverty. Silva noted that the film's rhythm tries to capture the community's internal rhythm, one that stands outside of time. "It is the rhythm of the countryside," he said, "the rhythm of repetition, of a repetitive life."

Through their six-month investigation of the Castañedas, Rodríguez and Silva assess religious, social, and political problems. An anthropologist, Rodríguez manages to get the family to forget the camera, even in its exposure of the father's drunkenness and his admission he mistreats his family. Like the contemporaneous Argentine film *La hora de los hornos*

(1968, q.v.), *Chircales* is a call to action, not an objective document. It begins with a quote from Marx and ends with a statement from Camilo Torres, Colombia's famous "guerrilla priest."

Rodríguez studied anthropology in Colombia and film for five years under Jean Rouch, who had filmed pioneering ethnographies in Africa in the 1950s, at the Museum of Civilisation in Paris, and film history at the Cinémathèque française. Rodríguez credits her meeting with Rouch as being decisive to her career: while others found her interest in anthropology and ethnology in opposition to her interests in filmmaking, Rouch offered a filmmaking course specifically aimed at anthropologists. She also notes the influence of the work of the French experimental filmmaker Jean Vigo, an influence seen in *Chircales'* poetic moments, such as when the young girl dresses for her First Communion, reminiscent of the scene of the woman dressing for the wedding in *L'Atalante* (1934).

Rodríguez returned to Colombia in 1966 and taught sociology at the National University of Bogotá. When she met Silva, her future husband and collaborator, she had already begun conducting research on the *chircaleros* in Bogotá's Tunjuelito neighbourhood and was putting together a film crew. Silva had studied literature and the plastic arts, particularly photography, and became involved with various ciné clubs in the 1960s, citing as influences Italian neo-realism and the French *nouvelle vague*.

The first version of *Chircales*, shot in 16mm and shown at the 1968 Latin American Film Forum in Mérida, Venezuela, was 75 minutes long. They followed this film with the medium-length *Planas testimonio de un etnocidio* (1970), about the persecution and torture of the Guahibo community in eastern Colombia. When that film won first prize at the 1972 Cartagena film festival, the filmmakers used the cash award to finance the editing of a definitive 41 minute version of *Chircales*, blown up to 35mm. In all, the couple made eight films together. After Silva's death in 1987, Rodríguez finished the editing of *Amor, mujeres y flores* (1989), concerning abuses of those working in Colombia's flower industry, whose pesticides cause early deaths and miscarriages. Rodríguez has since returned to her anthropological interests and in the early 1990s became involved with a video workshop with indigenous peoples.

Paul Lenti

Awards: Best Documentary, International Critics' Prize (FIPRESCI), Leipzig, 1972; Best Film, Tampere (Finland), 1973; Evangelischen Filmentrums Prize, Oberhausen, 1973; Best Film, Bilbao, 1976; Best Film, Festival de Cine Educativo, Mexico City, 1976.

Gamín

France-Colombia, 1978, 110', colour

Dir Ciro Durán (b. 1937) *Scr* Durán *Narr* Carlos Muñoz *Cinematog* Luis Cuesta and Durán *Mus* Francisco Zumaque *Prod* Claude Antoine for S.N.D.-l'Institut National de l'Audiovisuel (France) and Producciones Uno (Colombia)

In order to produce and promote national cinema in a coherent fashion, Colombia's Ministry of Communications introduced a government-administered production fund in 1971, requiring all feature films exhibited in Colombia to be accompanied by a nationally produced short film, which would be financed by a special box office tax on cinema tickets. As a result, over 600 shorts by more than 130 filmmakers were produced between 1970–80, giving national filmmakers a training ground to learn their craft and explore a variety of themes. The feature documentary *Gamín* began as part of this *sobreprecio*, or surcharge, system.

Appalled by the misery and indifference he found on the streets of Bogotá, especially by the number of abandoned street children, Ciro Durán decided to document this and, with money from the *sobreprecio*, made two short films, *Gamín I* and *Gamín II* (both 1976), which dealt with very young street kids, known as *chinches* (a type of small insect). The films were shot in 16mm and blown up to 35mm. The response was such that Durán decided to expand the film to investigate this environment further and include the destiny of older kids as continued conditions led to begging, thievery, prostitution, violence, and gasoline sniffing and alcoholism.

Gamín is divided into two sections. The first section is the most engaging because the children in it play to the camera. Dirty and dressed in tatters, the children mug for the camera and charm the audience with their vulnerability and unaffected openness. In one of the film's lighter moments, one little boy takes his first roller-coaster ride and soon realizes what he has gotten into. Through voice-over interviews and hand-held 16mm footage, we are also introduced to their families and given reasons for their children's abandonment on the streets. The second section is not so sympathetic, dealing with older children who have become hardened by their longer stay on the streets. The camera maintains a greater distance and we do not connect with the individuals as we do in the first section. The film attempts to work chronologically, showing the evolution from small children begging in the streets through to young thieves who pull off petty crimes, re-enacted for the camera.

With a grainy *cinéma-vérité* texture, *Gamín* utilizes a variety of methods, such as a hidden camera and a telephoto lens, to capture this world unobserved. Re-enactments and other documentary techniques are also used. Except for several short scenes, most of the film was shot without direct sound and features voice-over interviews of the kids and their families discussing their lives and conditions. Although sometimes effective, Francisco Zumaque's electronic score and jumble of voices tend occasionally to overpower and distract from the strength of the images. A dispassionate narrator occasionally breaks the continuity to supply information and statistics on the social and economic conditions of Bogotá. Yet the film offers no solutions, appealing to the audience's sympathy with an unstated criticism of the government's indifference. The film ends with a workers' demonstration through the streets of the capital, thereby casting the children's plight as an economic problem tied to underdevelopment and the exploitation of workers, who lack the funds to care for their families. It also delves into the mass migration of peasants into the capital, fleeing the violence and poverty of the countryside. At times, the viewer is manipulated through parallel montage, such as a sequence contrasting wanted and unwanted children.

Besides producing the occasional tourism documentary, Durán has continued to work with social and political themes. *Gamín* was followed by *Niño de dos mundos*, a documentary directed for East German television, included in the Colombian anthology film *Las cuatro edades de amor* (1980). He also made the feature-length documentary *La guerra del centavo* (1985), co-produced with German television, which dealt with public transportation. In 1988, Durán wrote and directed the fiction feature *Tropical Snow*, about cocaine smuggling and the desperation of young people who emigrate to the United States. Produced by Paramount Pictures and filmed in English, the film's international cast included David Carradine, Madeleine Stowe, and Nick Corri and was distributed internationally. He also directed a section of the international anthology film *How Are the Kids?* (1990), produced by UNICEF, about child abuse.

Paul Lenti

Awards: Outstanding Film of the Year, London, 1978; Best Film, Bilbao, 1978; Best Film, Huelva, 1978; Honourary Mention, Montréal, 1978; Second Prize, Leipzig, 1978; Best Director, Press Award, San Sebastián, 1978.

Tiempo de morir

A Time for Dying [A Time to Die]
Colombia-Cuba, 1985, 91', colour

Dir Jorge Alí Triana (b. 1942) *Scr* Gabriel García Márquez, with dialogue by García Márquez and Carlos Fuentes (1965) *Cinematog* Mario García Joya *Art dir* Carlos Parruca and Patricia Bonilla *Mus* Leo Brouwer and Nafer Durán *Prod* Compañía de Fomento Cinematográfico (FOCINE) (Colombia) and Instituto Cubano del Arte e Industria Cinematográficos (ICAIC) (Cuba) *Act* Gustavo Angarita, Sebastián Ospina, María Eugenia Dávila, Jorge Emilio Salazar, Reynaldo Miravelles

After implementing a box office tax in 1971 to fund short film production, the government responded to pressure by filmmakers and founded the state film agency FOCINE in 1978. At first FOCINE offered loans to filmmakers, but in 1985 it began to produce films itself. *Tiempo de morir* was among some ten feature-length projects slated for production in 1985–86. Jorge Alí Triana had studied theatre and film in Czechoslovakia before returning to Bogotá where he produced theatre, made short films, and directed series for national television. Triana had previously directed several acclaimed shorts and the 18 minute opening episode of the anthology feature *Las cuatro edades del amor* (1980).

Using an original 1965 screenplay by fellow countryman and Nobel Prize-winning author Gabriel García Márquez—according to García Márquez, it was his first film script not to be adapted from one of his stories—Triana first directed a 100-minute made-for-television version of *Tiempo de morir* in 1984 for the national television programmer RTI. The success of the TV version led Triana to direct a 35mm remake in co-production with the Cuban film institute, ICAIC. The script had previously been filmed in 1965 as a black-and-white Western by a young Arturo Ripstein, now one of Mexico's leading directors.

In theme and structure, the storyline is similar to García Márquez' 1981 novel *Crónica de una muerte anunciada* (adapted to film by the Italian director Francesco Rosi in 1987). Both stories are closed tales of revenge and destiny, in accordance with Jean Cocteau's definition of tragedy as an "Infernal Machine" that once wound up and put into place, must continue to its inevitable resolution. As in classic tragedy, fate is a key player and the audience is well aware of the outcome from the very beginning; destiny must be played out, despite all rational arguments and futile attempts to change it. The characters here are larger than life and make epic proclamations in an elevated and literary language that transcends everyday speech.

The film's storyline is simple: it begins with the return of a man to his home town after 18 years in prison for having killed another man in a duel. In the town he re-encounters his former love and his victim's two sons, who vow revenge. While the eldest son is a macho hothead who taunts the killer in much the same manner as his father had, the younger brother attempts to get to know the man and understand why his father was killed. Yet it is precisely this youngest son who eventually kills the man, despite the knowledge that he had killed his father in a fair fight and only after continued harassment.

There are those who argue which film—the Ripstein version or Triana remake, which gave the story a distinctly Colombian setting—is better. One is surprised by their similarity: at times both films can be compared on a frame-by-frame basis. Script differences are limited to minor details. Triana's film showcases Cuban cinematographer Mario García Joya's distinctive mobile camera work; yet Mexican camera operator Alex Phillips' imaginative tracking shots are equally impressive. Triana acknowledges his debt to Ripstein and gives a conscious nod to Mexican cinema by including a scene where the younger son and his fiancée go to a cinema to see the classic film *María Candelaria*.

As a critique of machismo and honour codes, the story is a closed circle without exit. Several characters comment that the past is merely repeating itself. Even the pharmacist's memories lead to a flashback that turns out to be present reality that only echoes the past without variation. The acting in the Colombian version is more natural and believable; the actors sweat and their clothes get dirty. The García Márquez script has a sense of timelessness, a feel of inevitability, of destiny, seen in the tarot cards that predict tragedy for the younger son and in the rumour that the man who killed his father is invulnerable. The past must repeat itself; destiny must be fulfilled. Noted Cuban composer Leo Brouwer has provided the film with an effective score, which ends with a Colombian *vallenato* based on the death of the sons' father, giving the tale a legendary feel and closing the circle, as if the story has already passed on into myth.

Paul Lenti

Awards: Best Film, Best Actor, International Critics' Prize (FIPRESCI), UNESCO Prize, Rio de Janeiro, 1985; Best Editing, Best Photography, Havana, 1985; Best Film, Biarritz, 1986; Manuel Murillo Toro Prize, Best Film, Best Actor and Actress, Acapulco, 1987.

La mansión de Araucaíma

The Araucaima Mansion
Colombia, 1986, 85', colour

Dir Carlos Mayolo (b. 1945) *Scr* Julio Olaciregui, based on the novel of the same title by Alvaro Mutis (1978) *Cinematog* Rodrigo Lalinde *Art dir* Miguel González *Prod* Bertha de Carvajal for Compañía de Fomento Cinematográfico (FOCINE) *Act* Vicky Hernández, Adriana Herrán, José Lewgoy, Antônio Sampaio, Luis Fernando Montoya, Alejandro Buenaventura, Carlos Mayolo

Produced entirely by FOCINE, the state agency which in 1985 became directly involved in film production using funds raised from cinema box office taxes, *La mansión de Araucaíma* was based on the novel of the same title by Colombian author Alvaro Mutis, which the author called a Gothic tale from the tropics. Mutis lived in Mexico, and both he and his friend Luis Buñuel shared a love of British Gothic novels. *La mansión* was originally conceived as a film project for the Spanish director, but Buñuel's advanced age prevented him from making the film. Mutis notes that "the idea of a Gothic tale set in the middle of the tropics emerged first as a film. The project eventually fell apart and the only thing that remained was this nub of a tale. The house and the atmosphere are from my family's estate in El Tolima. The characters are my most personal and profound and are completely invented."

The film depicts life in a mansion hidden within the jungle, a place where time has stood still, exposing the decadence of the rural aristocracy. The mansion is inhabited by a group of eccentric characters: the landowner, who inherited the house; a nameless priest; a pilot whose plane was downed by lightning; the servant, a cautious obedient Haitian; the mercenary Watchman (played by director Carlos Mayolo); a director (played by veteran filmmaker Luis Ospina); and Machiche, an erotic earth mother who apparently services the others while maintaining a certain control over them. With the declining power of the rural aristocracy, the servants now govern the mansion and the landowner. Within this closed world, the group repeats their daily routines almost mechanically, cultivating their eccentricities, until the fragile equilibrium is challenged by the arrival of a young woman, a beautiful model whose presence upsets this delicate equation and causes the film to erupt into eroticism and violence.

A veteran of many shorts and one feature film, Mayolo saw the project as a Latin American genre film—the tropical Gothic—that created a closed universe where everything revolves around a daily routine arising from the hermetic isolation of a remote estate. He points to literary examples such as *La casa verde* by the Peruvian author Mario Vargas Llosa and *La casa grande* by the Colombian author and filmmaker Alvaro Cepeda (*La langosta azul*, 1954, q.v.). Both these novels present the hacienda as a microcosm for society. By using two Brazilian actors (José Lewgoy and Antônio Sampaio), Mayolo emphasizes the universality of the film, suggesting that the story could take place in any Latin American country. Conflict emerges not through narrative development but through the interaction of clashing character types, and the film literally buckles under the weight of its oppressive atmosphere, where everything stifles within endless repetition without exit. *La mansión de Araucaíma* can ultimately be categorized as an "art film" that is a little too deliberately crafted. It would have been interesting to see what the director of *El ángel exterminador* (1962) and *Le Charme discrèt de la bourgeoisie* (1972) would have done with Mutis' original material.

Mayolo studied film in London in the 1960s and returned to Colombia in 1968, when he worked for an advertising agency in Bogotá making commercials and short films under the government's subsidy program for short films during the 1970s. Mayolo has often worked in tandem with other directors, making *Monserrate* (1971) with Jorge Silva (*Chircales*, 1967, q.v.) and co-directing with Luis Ospina a quartet of interesting shorts in the 1970s. His first feature, *Carne de tu carne* (1983), won eight international awards and established him as a director with an idiosyncratic approach to the medium, especially in his manipulation of generic codes. In 1989, Mayolo was hired by the television programmer RCN to direct the highly rated series *Azúcar*, an original story of a family told over three generations. He has since worked almost exclusively in television.

Paul Lenti

Awards: Special Jury Prize, Rio de Janeiro, 1986; Best Director, Best Actress (Vicky Hernández), Best Film, Bogotá, 1987.

Visa USA

Colombia-Cuba, 1986, 90', colour

Dir Lisandro Duque Naranjo (b. 1943) *Scr* Duque *Cinematog* Raúl Pérez Ureta *Art dir* Oscar Alzate *Mus* Leo Brouwer *Prod* Compañía de Fomento Cinematográfico (FOCINE) (Colombia) and Instituto Cubano del Arte e Industria Cinematográficos (ICAIC) (Cuba) *Act* Armando Gutiérrez, Marcela Agudelo, Gellver de Currea Lugo, Vicky Hernández, Diego Alvarez, Lucy Martínez, Gerardo Calero

Colombian cinema is distinctive in that, for the most part, it is a cinema of first works. Only a handful of contemporary filmmakers have followed up the promise of their first efforts with what might be considered a body of work. One of Colombia's most consistent and innovative filmmakers, Lisandro Duque Naranjo has made numerous short films, three features, and various television series that have received a degree of critical and commercial success at home and abroad. Duque studied anthropology at the National University after moving to Bogotá from the provinces in 1968, where he was exposed to ciné clubs. His interest in cinema led him to begin writing film criticism for newspapers while teaching film theory and aesthetics at several universities in the capital.

After writing the script for a short film in 1973, Duque directed the short *Favor correrse atrás* the following year, which won top prize in the short film competition at the Cartagena film festival, and co-directed *Lluvia colombiana* (1976), awarded third place in a national short film competition. Over the next five years Duque produced a consistent series of distinctive shorts before directing his first feature, *El escarabajo*, in 1982. Shot in his native Sevilla, the film dealt with a group of young cyclists and picked up a special prize from the organising committee of the Cartagena film festival and prizes for Best Script, Best Director, and Best Film at the Bogotá film festival.

In 1986, Duque followed *El escarabajo* with the genial feature *Visa USA*, co-produced by the Cuban film institute, ICAIC. Initially titled *Viajar a ningún Pereira* (a Colombian expression that means to travel nowhere), *Visa USA* is a refreshing love story marked by a gentle sense of humour and a sympathetic view of everyday provincial life. Also shot in Sevilla, the film centres on the charismatic son of a small poultry farmer who must choose between young love or his dream of travelling to the United States to become a famous deejay, despite his father's wishes that he go to university in Colombia.

Duque's character works announcing records at a local department store while teaching English in his spare time to earn extra money. His older brother had previously gone to New York on a tourist visa and now sends home ecstatic letters detailing his new life. He sends his younger brother money and advice on how to join him in the United States. While making his travel plans, he begins to court the vivacious daughter of a local banker, whom he tutors several days a week so she can pass her English exam. The girl's parents disapprove of him and, after discovering that his tourist visa has been denied, they plan to send the girl to stay with an aunt in New York in order to keep the two apart. He then plots to acquire an illegal visa in the capital.

Although presented as an entertaining love story, this commercial drama carries a deeper message about the extensive immigration of young people from Latin America to the United States in search of opportunities not available at home. Duque also underlines class frictions in Colombian society, seen in the parents' demand to arrange a suitable match for their daughter. The lead character is depicted as part of a new generation, one that has choices and, even if he decides to remain in Colombia, he is still able to control his destiny through diligent study. The well-developed script wisely places its emphasis on characterization and Colombian audiences responded enthusiastically to this upbeat film, making it a modest domestic success.

After *Visa USA* Duque directed the quirky *Milagro en Roma*, produced in 1988 by Spanish Television as part of a five-film package of works based on stories by Gabriel García Márquez, released under the collective title *Amores difíciles*. In recent years, Duque has worked extensively in national television: in 1990, he directed the 10-hour miniseries *La vorágine*, based on the novel by José Eustasio Rivera, followed by the nine-part series *María* (1991), adapted by García Márquez from the classic Colombian novel by Jorge Isaacs.

Paul Lenti

Awards: Best Film, Best New Actress, Alcatraz de Oro Film Club Award, Cartagena, 1986; Manuel Murillo Toro Prize, Best Film (shared), Bogotá, 1986.

Técnicas de duelo

Dueling Techniques [A Question of Honor]
Colombia-Cuba, 1988, 97', colour

Dir Sergio Cabrera (b. 1950) *Scr* Humberto Dorado *Cinematog* José Madeiros *Art dir* Enrique Linero *Mus* Juan Márquez *Prod* Abelardo Quintero for Compañía de Fomento Cinematográfico (FOCINE), Fotograma (Colombia) and Instituto Cubano del Arte e Industria Cinematográficos (ICAIC) (Cuba) *Act* Frank Ramírez, Humberto Dorado, Florina Lemaitre

Técnicas de duelo is based on an actual incident that was related to actor/scriptwriter Humberto Dorado by actor Jairo Hanibal Niño who, as a child, lived in the town where the episode took place. "Like the scene in the film, he was one of the students whose teacher announced to the class that he would probably die in a duel," Sergio Cabrera noted. "He told this story to Humberto, who was very impressed by it. Six years later, he and Humberto met again and Humberto asked him to repeat the story. This time it was completely different. So when Humberto wrote the script, we decided to keep the story open and not give the reason."

When Cabrera decided to film this story, the state film production agency, FOCINE, was practically paralysed. Exhibitors had questioned the constitutionality of raising production funds through an ever-increasing box office tax—16% in 1985—and the matter remained in the courts until 1990. FOCINE foundered with diminished funds, existing in near-bankruptcy while production ground to a slow halt and new institute directors entered and exited in revolving-door fashion. Cabrera knew the only way to find production funds was to win FOCINE's annual script competition, which would oblige the agency to produce the film. He noted that working with FOCINE at this time was crazy: "While production of *Técnicas* was under way, I went through six separate changes of directors. Each one had his own eccentricities . . . one liked the name of the film, another wanted me to change it. It was a mess."

A subtle comedy of manners, *Técnicas de duelo* is full of surprise and inventiveness. As a satirist of Latin life and mores, Cabrera strikes the target. He takes small-town society and Colombia's formal attitudes and eccentricities to task, along with particularly Latin American notions of honour, machismo, government bureaucracy, religious duty, and self-important petty officials, which all receive their share of jabs. The story is set in a small Andean town, where two former best friends—the school master and the town butcher—prepare for a duel. Although the duel's raison d'etre is never given, the film revolves around each man's actions as the fatal hour approaches and death seems imminent. Humberto Dorado's tight script retains a literary quality, and the formal elegance of the dialogue underlines the ritualistic nature of the impending duel, while counterpointing the inherent violence of the situation. José Madeiro's camerawork is rich and imaginative.

Sergio Cabrera began professional studies in philosophy at the University of Beijing, and his first film, the short *Hong Wei Bing*, was produced in China in 1973. After switching to film studies, he attended the London Polytechnic school where he made two short documentaries: *En verano* and *I Beg Your Pardon*. When he returned to Colombia, Cabrera devoted himself to filmmaking while working as a television actor and director of cinematography for more than 30 shorts and five feature films. In addition to directing popular mini-series for Colombian television, he directed and produced more than 500 documentaries, commercials, and promotional films for his advertising agency Fotograma. Cabrera also filmed FOCINE's final production, an award-winning ensemble comedy called *Estrategia del caracol*, which was finally finished in 1993 after four years in post-production. Since its founding, FOCINE had been plagued with economic and legal battles, forcing it finally to abandon production altogether in 1990 and dedicate its efforts to promoting Colombian films at home and abroad. Ironically, *Estrategia del caracol* was so popular that it outgrossed Steven Spielberg's *Jurassic Park* in Colombia.

Paul Lenti

Awards: Best First Film, San Juan (Puerto Rico), 1988; Best First Film (shared), Cartagena, 1989; Jury Prize, Festival Latino Film (New York), 1989; Best Film, Gramado (Brazil), 1992.

Rodrigo D. (No futuro)

Rodrigo D. (No Future)
Colombia, 1989, 90', colour

Dir Víctor Manuel Gaviria (b. 1955) *Scr* Gaviria, Luis Fernando Calderón, Angela María Pérez, and Juan Guillermo Arredondo *Cinematog* Rodrigo Lalinde *Mus* Germán Arrieta *Prod* Compañía de Fomento Cinematográfico (FOCINE), Tiempos Modernos and Foto Club 76 *Act* Ramiro Meneses, Carlos Mario Restrepo, Jackson Idrián Gallego, Vilma Díaz

The violent world depicted in Víctor Gaviria's first feature *Rodrigo D. (No futuro)* can be seen as a metaphor for the nation. In November 1990, FOCINE's director Maruja Pachón was kidnapped—after a little over a month in office—and was held for seven months before being freed in 1991. Pachón was taken because she was sister to Gloria Pachón Galán, widow of slain presidential candidate Luis Carlos Galán, who was killed by the drug cartels in August 1989. It was this murder that sparked the government's two-year war on the drug barons, and the subsequent violence took its toll on the country. National box-office attendance declined from 49 million in 1986 to approximately 37½ million in 1990.

With *Rodrigo D.*, Gaviria—a poet, writer, and short film maker—explored the bleak and precarious lives of working-class kids in Medellín. So dangerous is this world that six of the nine non-professional actors in the film were killed during or since the film's production. (Ramiro Meneses, who plays Rodrigo, has since taken up professional acting.) The naturalistic script, written in near-impenetrable Medellín street slang, won second prize in Colombia's annual screenplay competition in 1986. It is based on an article that appeared in a local newspaper in 1984 about a teenager, Rodrigo Alonso, who threatened to leap from the top floor of a downtown building. When asked why, the boy replied: "From the moment I was born, all I've done is suffer." Gaviria spent three years doing research for the film, greatly revising the original script to include real-life characterisations by the young non-professional actors. The film was shot in nine weeks and when released sold well internationally and was considered a critical and financial success at home, drawing 300,000 spectators nationally on first release.

Rather than following a linear plot, the film presents a slice of life as we follow Rodrigo and his teenage friends over a three-day period, exploring their world as they live it the best they can. Rodrigo can't sleep at night: he has headaches and thinks about his mother, who died sometime previous to the film's story. He is also looking for a drum kit so he can start a punk band with his chums, who sell cocaine to school kids, steal cars, listen to raucous punk music, or just hang around. Gaviria manages to capture the essence of this nether world through able camera work and a judicious selection of locations—the shantytowns that line the valley walls and overlook modern Medellín. The camera is often placed at high or low angles, reminding us that we are merely observers of this life. The raucous soundtrack by local punk groups also gives the film drive, while the nihilistic lyrics tend to underscore the emptiness of this daily routine. The story is unsettling, more often for things unsaid. Rodrigo's imminent suicide becomes an existential decision in the face of hopeless future.

Rodrigo D. is part of a Latin American film tradition about adolescents growing up and living amid poverty, which includes such classics as Luis Buñuel's *Los olvidados* (Mexico, 1950), *Pixote* (Brazil, 1980, q.v.), Ciro Durán's *Gamín* (1978, q.v.), *Crónica de un niño solo* (Argentina, 1965, q.v.), and *Gregorio* (Peru, 1986, q.v.). In addition to the film, Gaviria published a novel, *El pelaíto que no duró nada*, based on the story of another of the youths who appear in the film. Gaviria's production company, Tiempos Modernos, also shot two documentaries on the filming of *Rodrigo D.*: *Mirar al muerto, por favor*, a 20 minute video by Gavaria, Jorge Mario Alvarez, Pilar Cecilia Mejía and Javier Quintero, and *Cuando llega la muerte . . .*, a 30 minute video by Pilar Cecilia Mejía and Javier Quintero.

Filmmakers and FOCINE officials were pleased when *Rodrigo D. (No futuro)* was selected for official competition at the 1989 Cannes film festival, but this ebullience was short lived. In 1990, FOCINE was forced to abandon production completely, and the government announced FOCINE's official dissolution at the end of 1992. During its 15-year history, the Fondo produced approximately 200 features, medium-length films, shorts and documentaries. It also represented Colombian films abroad at film festivals or international showcases, provided funds to the national film archives, and aided Colombia's two annual film festivals in Santafé de Bogotá and Cartagena.

Paul Lenti

Awards: Best Film, Festival Latino Film (New York), 1990.

María Cano

Colombia, 1990, 104', colour

Dir Camila Loboguerrero (b. 1941) *Scr* Loboguerrero, Luis González, and Felipe Aljure *Cinematog* Carlos Sánchez *Art dir* Karen Lamassone *Mus* Santiago Lanz *Prod* Roy Martín for Comapañía de Fomento Cinematográfico (FOCINE) *Act* María Eugenia Dávila, Frank Ramírez, Germán Escallón, Diego Vélez, Jorge Herrera

Colombia boasts many talented women filmmakers, mostly in the field of documentary: Marta Rodríguez (*Chircales*, 1972, q.v.); the team of Patricia Castaño and Adelaida Trujillo; Clara M. Riascos and the prolific Gloria Triana. One of the country's foremost women working in fiction filmmaking is Camila Loboguerrero. Loboguerrero studied painting in Colombia in the early 1960s and later studied film in France, where she received degrees in cinematography from the University of Vincennes and art history from the Sorbonne in 1970. Between 1971 and 1985, she produced over a dozen distinctive short films in Colombia, and her first feature, *Con su música a otra parte* (1983), dealt with the confrontation between a mother and daughter. It achieved a degree of national success.

Loboguerrero's second feature, *María Cano*, is an ambitious biographical look at the independent and politically committed María Cano (1889–1963), who challenged conventions during a time when women didn't even have the vote. Cano's great uncle Fidel Cano founded the influential newspaper *El Espectador*, and as a poet she was respected by the local intellectual community. Born in Medellín, Cano gained notoriety during the turbulent years of the first half of the twentieth century defending workers, who voiced such unreasonable demands as an eight-hour day and better living conditions: at the time, workers laboured 16 hours a day, six days a week.

The film depicts the 1920s in Colombia, full of promise because the country had been indemnified by the United States for the loss of Panama, and also full of the ideals that socialism was encouraging worldwide. But the core of the film is the story of Cano and her relationship with union leader Ignacio Torres Giraldo, her long-time companion, helping organize people in their social struggle, often only one step ahead of law enforcement and local strong men. (In real life, some contemporaries believed this lifetime relationship to be merely a deep friendship based on mutual respect and shared ideals, while others speculated that the two were lovers. Loboguerrero opts for the latter, giving the relationship a complexity and personal commitment.) The film begins near the end of Cano's life, showing a woman broken by history and the forces she was dedicated to overthrowing, before flashing back to 1926, the year she first met Torres Giraldo, who fired her interest in the plight of the worker, beginning with helping tenants evicted from their dwelling. With Torres Giraldo, Cano undertook seven tours around the country, organizing workers and becoming a symbol of resistance.

Technically, the film is ambitious and Loboguerrero shows admirable control over the medium. Although costumes tend to appear too new, the varied locations give the film texture and the time periods depicted have been ably reconstructed. Also, some crowd scenes lack sufficient extras to give these moments the effective impact demanded by history. Furthermore, the episodic nature of the film requires a rhythmic narrative flow that occasionally falls flat with certain scenes seemingly devised merely to advance the exposition. And, although Loboguerrero tries to humanise the characters, Torres Giraldo, an unsentimental and dedicated revolutionary in real life, comes off politically strident and humourless, despite Frank Ramírez's efforts to give the character personality. Yet, *María Cano* succeeds in its efforts to reconstruct the life and times of one of Colombia's most vital personalities, one whose personal failures can be measured along with those of her public life.

Paul Lenti

Awards: Best Cinematography (shared), Cartagena, 1990; Best Film, San Antonio (U.S.), 1991; Best Actor (Frank Ramírez), Bogotá, 1990.

Ecuador

¡Fuera de aquí!

Get Out of Here!
Ecuador-Venezuela-Bolivia, 1977, 102', b+w

Dir Jorge Sanjinés *Cinematog* Jorge Vignati, Efraín Fuentes, Roberto Siso, Julio Lencina, and Ramón Arellano *Ed* Sanjinés and Beatriz Palacios *Sound* Marcel Milan and Freddy Siso *Mus* Los Rupay, Grupo Jatari, musicians in Tamboloma and Salasaka *Prod* Beatriz Palacios (Ecuador), Universidad de los Andes (Venezuela) and Ukamau (Bolivia) *Act* identity withheld

On a continent where exile is an endemic historical reality for whole sectors of the population as well as a potent cultural metaphor, *¡Fuera de aquí!* is *the* exile film par excellence. A film made in Ecuador by Bolivia's most famous filmmakers, Jorge Sanjinés and the Grupo Ukamau, *¡Fuera de aquí!* is *about* the roots and process of exile. The dispersion of a community, the ancestral unit of production and belonging, has been a classic theme of political filmmaking from Jean Renoir's *Le Crime de Monsieur Lange* (1936) to the U.S. documentarist Emile de Antonio's *In the Year of the Pig* (1969), but it here acquires a fierce concreteness as real people reconstruct for the camera the actual devastation of their own village (disguised in the film as "Kalakala" to prevent retribution). At the same time, *¡Fuera de aquí!* articulates in its narrative form the collectivist structure, values, and resilience of that community and of Andean indigenous culture as a whole.

Sanjinés and his collaborators had left Bolivia after the downfall of the progressive Juan José Torres regime (1970–71), pausing in both Chile and Peru, where they filmed *El enemigo principal* in 1973, before settling on Ecuador as the site of their next project. Although funded by the Venezuelan University of the Andes and the Central University of

Ecuador, the low-budget 16mm production was beset by problems. Ukamau cinematographer Antonio Eguino had been imprisoned in Bolivia during the 1975 pre-production period and another collective member had to jettison the project's stock acquisition. The filmmakers resorted to out-of-date stock and even then had to interrupt the shoot for eight months because of shortages. They undertook post-production abroad in two different countries, only to lose in air transit, after months of editing, the first cutting copy and the entire batch of synched-up sound tapes.

The title *¡Fuera de aquí!* is the Kalakala villagers' defiant challenge to their imperialist invaders, both the evangelical U.S. missionaries who demoralise and divide the community and the multinational mining corporation who, in cahoots with the national political oligarchy, ultimately destroy it. In its opening narrative of the Yankee missionaries' arrival with their guitar-led sermons and secret sterilisation campaign, *¡Fuera de aquí!* seems like a remake of *Yawar Mallku* (Bolivia, 1969, q.v.), complete with an update of that film's prefatory press clippings to authenticate the facts. The hymn-singers are followed by prospectors, mining executives, and finally soldier-escorted bulldozers, and the film moves beyond *Yawar Mallku* in the clarity and detail of its linking of religio-cultural colonialism with economic exploitation. The residents of Kalakala, uprooted from their homes and decimated by genocidal violence, regroup, bury their dead, and reflect on their defeat. The film concludes with the resilient exiles strategising their next battle and collectively building new homes. A ringing final slogan encapsulates Sanjinés' "film-as-weapon" aesthetics: "¡El pueblo luchará hasta la victoria!"—"The People Will Struggle Until Victory!"

¡Fuera de aquí! represents a new stage in Sanjinés' "search for a language in harmony with the culture of our people," as French critic Louis Marcorelles wrote,[1] namely a narrative film syntax that could both reconstitute his aboriginal subjects' historical struggles from their own cultural point of view and, at the same time, articulate their collectivist social ethos. Continuing to eschew the close-up, Sanjinés' mobile hand-held sequence shots are ever more fluid and graceful, hovering high-angle over group movements of social actors through landscape that would seem exquisitely choreographed did they not have the aleatory ring of documentary improvisation. The U.S. scholar Julianne Burton has compared Sanjinés to Ousmane Sembène in terms of their parallel development of narrative discourses that express an aesthetic equivalent of the "integrative interactional concept of being-in-the-world" proper to pre-industrial rural community life, whether in the Andes, in Senegal, or

elsewhere in the Third World.[2] In Teshome Gabriel's terms, Sanjinés' camera replicates the non-individualist subjectivity, the non-hierarchical political order, and the collective sense of social time and space of Third World societies.[3] The earlier scripts of both Sanjinés and Sembène rely extensively on visual coding and non-verbal communication rather than oral culture, inevitably raising questions of the political relationship of these urban Europeanised artists, both cosmopolitan Marxist intellectuals, to their indigenous subjects (Sanjinés is of Spanish-speaking mestizo origin).

Such questions are now at least relativised in *¡Fuera de aquí!* as sound acquires a new importance in the refinement of collectivist film language. Based for the first time on the extensive use of direct lip-sync dialogue by its non-professional performers, *¡Fuera de aquí!* offers a vivid inscription of the culture of collective speech that is rarely recorded in dramatised modes within postcolonial cinemas—and all too rarely even in documentary. Sanjinés' long takes both look and listen, and the communal process is unforgettable for its vivid mosaic of angry voices and babies' cries—an innovation on a continent where idealised peasant cultures are too often represented by impassive silent faces (*La hora de los hornos*, Argentina, 1968, q.v.) and aestheticised soundtracks of flute music and wind sounds. Above all, the ritualised debates between the community's two factions—and the two political strategies they espouse—presents a collective political process that is uniquely *audio*-visual.

According to Sanjinés, the incorporation of the debate scenes was, in fact, due in part to the production delays:

> This delay in filming allowed us to get to know the people better and a number of new elements were incorporated into the film. . . . Two opposing factions emerged: on the one hand there were the supporters of "Indianism," who are quite strong in Ecuador, and on the other the supporters of a materialist analysis based on the class struggle. . . . We had not laid down a precise scenario or imposed scripted dialogue but we agreed to write the scene on the basis of arguments that each group could use in favour of its connection to the problems. The camera played an important role and in long shots was careful to focus on those who were talking, but without imprisoning them in a closeup which could have prevented the other comrades from expressing themselves. . . .

¡Fuera de aquí! was selected for the "Quinzaine des réalisateurs" at the Cannes film festival in 1977. But the fashion for revolutionary Latin American cinema was on the wane, and, despite critical favour in Paris and Havana, only a modest non-commercial European and North American release followed; the film was never sub-titled in English. It was another case in the Andes, however, for over the next five years *¡Fuera de aquí!* is said to have reached a rural audience of millions in Ecuador alone. It would be several years before the Bolivian filmmakers could return home themselves, but their great film about exile found its own home within the culture whose voices it preserved and whose struggles it told.

Thomas Waugh

1. Louis Marcorelles, "Jorge Sanjinés et la réalité andine," *Le Monde*, Paris, 10 June 1977.
2. Julianne Burton, "Marginal Cinemas and Mainstream Critical Theory," *Screen*, 26, nos. 3-4 (1985): 17–18.
3. Teshome Gabriel, "Towards a Critical Theory of Third World Films," *Questions of Third Cinema*, Jim Pines and Paul Willemen, eds. (London: British Film Institute, 1989) 44–5.

La Tigra

[The Tigress]
Ecuador, 1989, 80', colour

Dir Camilo Luzuriaga (b.1953) *Scr* Luzuriaga, based on the short story of the same title by José de la Cuadra (1935) *Cinematog* Rodrigo Cueva and Diego Falconi *Mus* Sebastián Cardemil, Diego Luzuriaga, Santiago Luzuriaga, and Atahulfo Tobar *Prod* Grupo Cine *Act* Lissette Cabrera, Rossana Iturralde, Veronica García, Aristides Vargas, Virgilio Valero

La Tigra, Camilo Luzuriaga's first feature film, is also the first modern-day feature film by an Ecuadorean director. Ecuador is known largely for documentary shorts—by Luzuriaga (*Los Mangles se van*, 1984, *Así pensamos*, 1983, and *Don Eloy*, 1981), Mónica Vasquez (*Tiempo de mujeres*, 1988), Gustavo Guayasamín (*El Día de los muertos en Guangaje*, 1971, *Primero de Mayo*, 1974), and others. Luzuriaga began by studying engineering, then moved into theatre, photography, and finally film. His first documentaries were shot in Super-8. In 1981 he began working in 16mm. From 1982 to 1987 he taught photography at the Central University of Ecuador in

Quito. Since 1987 he has been the head of Grupo Cine in Quito. Besides the documentaries listed above, Luzuriaga has also directed the award-winning fictional short *Chacón maravilla* (1982).

La Tigra is the story of three beautiful sisters who maintain a farmhouse and small shop in Manabí. As a teenager, the eldest, known as "La Tigra," witnessed her parents' brutal murder by five renegade soldiers. Seizing her father's shotgun, she single-handedly killed their attackers. Now a woman, she continues to avenge herself on men, taking any man she wants, then forcing him out of her bed the next morning at gun point. Even her second sister's lover and fiancé is not exempt from her sexual appetite. The third sister, in contrast, is condemned by the two older to remain forever a virgin: a black sorcerer has told La Tigra that only her sister's chastity can save her from damnation for her sexual exploits.

Like the short story by José de la Cuadra that it is based on, the film begins when a travelling salesman files a legal complaint against La Tigra. The youngest sister's fiancé, he asks that soldiers be dispatched from town to guarantee she (and by extension himself as husband-to-be) will receive her share of the family assets. Beyond this opening allusion to property rights, however, Luzuriaga's film plays down the struggles between city (Guayaquil) and country (largely the *montuvio* region, but also, in passing, the *sierra*), civilisation and barbarism so important to Cuadra's work. Where Cuadra explores the barbaric sides of civilisation and ultimately paints all men, whether rapists or "protectors," sorcerers or salesmen, as exploiters of women, Luzuriaga instead accentuates the story's magic realism, emphasizing especially its romantic and erotic elements.

Dissolves, slow-motion hand-held camera movements, superimpositions, and flashbacks translate the "other," often traumatic, psychic realities called up by sorcery. Medium shots and close-ups of the half-naked older sisters, together with long-shots and extreme long-shots of the entirely naked Tigra, add a soft-core porn patina to a more traditional portrait of the cross-dressing *macha* à la *Doña Bárbara*. (Rómulo Gallegos' book (1927) was an inspiration for Cuadra's short story. The Mexican director Fernando de Fuentes' film (1943) has probably in turn influenced Luzuriaga.) La Tigra may smoke cigars, carry a rifle, wield a machete, and heft a whip, but her feminine "nature" is everywhere in evidence.

That the ending of Luzuriaga's film reverses that of Cuadra's story thus comes as no surprise: in the film La Tigra, the woman, is killed by soldiers but lives on as a woman/tigress; in the short story, she again vanquishes her attackers and lives on as *patrona*, not just *hembra* (i.e., as mistress and owner, not just as female creature). The film is thus less "about" any specific past or present Ecuadorean realities (a few references to a female guerrilla/Liberator have been added to the original story) than it is "about" mythic, and very much mass-mediated, images of Woman.

Chris Holmlund

Awards: Best Film and Best First Film, Cartagena (Colombia), 1990.

Paraguay

El pueblo

The Village
Paraguay, 1971, 40', b+w and colour

Dir Carlos Saguier *Cinematog* Saguier *Prod* Saguier

In a country with practically no film history, the documentary *El pueblo* appeared in 1971, directed by twenty-five year-old filmmaker Carlos Saguier. Its appearance was startling and, as far as is known, Saguier made no further films, nor was *El pueblo* followed by similar efforts.

Through images with great expressive qualities, *El pueblo* focuses on the daily rituals of a tiny Paraguayan community, one of many like it in the country. We see the morning fire lit and hear the prayers that accompany it; see the men leave for work; and watch clay being worked and corn flour prepared. Alongside these scenes of the work of the village, the film follows a group of villagers on their way to the village cemetery. Life and death confront each other in this community's poverty and neglect. Its difficult and monotonous existence is depicted in dramatic fashion in the heavy and striking sense of time the film imposes.

El pueblo attempts a different approach from other documentaries. It shows situations which affect the spectator's sensibility, and by alternating between black and white and colour a striking contrast is achieved which corresponds to the conflictive elements of the reality being depicted. At times its artistic virtuosity, a stylistic exuberance which tends to outdo itself, is somewhat excessive, but this doesn't lessen the film's achievement of joining expressive rigour with imaginative power.

Isaac León Frías

Miss Amerigua

Paraguay-Sweden, 1994, 93', colour

Dir Luis R. Vera (b. 1951) *Scr* Vera and Andrés Colman *Cinematog* Marten Nilsson *Art dir* Ricardo Migliorisi *Mus* Jan Tolf *Prod* Vera for PBN-Filmteknik AB (Sweden) and Latino Films HB (Paraguay) *Act* Raquel Baeza, Ayesa Frutos, Héctor Silva, Sonia Marchewka, Jesus Perez, Jorge Baez, Arturo Fleitas, Graciela Canepa, Carlos Cristaldo

Apart from an interesting period of independent, mostly 16mm, documentary filmmaking in the 1960s, culminating with the success of Carlos Saguier's medium-length *El pueblo* in 1969, local film production in Paraguay has been virtually non-existent. Part of the reason given for this absence by writers such as Rubén Bareiro-Saguier and John King is that General Alfredo Stroessner's authoritarian dictatorship (1954–1989) oppressed national initiatives in favour of foreign economic interests. Indeed, the only period when a number of feature films were made in Paraguay was in the late 1950s and early '60s, when Argentine filmmakers could find cheap film stock and exotic locations in Paraguay. Chief among these was Armando Bo, who began a series of erotic films with his wife Isabel Sarli, the "cinema's most hygienic actress"—so called because she was always on the point of bathing nude—in 1957 with *El trueno entre las hojas* (based on a novel by Paraguay's most celebrated author, Augusto Roa Bastos) and also directed her in an Argentine-Paraguayan "co-production," *La burrerita de Ypacarai*, in 1961. The only other period of Paraguayan film production was in the late 1970s when the government sponsored a series of propaganda films including a feature film on the national military hero Francisco Solano López, entitled *Cerro Cora* (1978, directed by Ladislao González), which was billed as the "first Paraguayan film."

Given this history, perhaps it is not surprising that *Miss Amerigua*, the first feature made in Paraguay under the new democracy, after the fall of Stroessner, was also a co-production. In fact, the director, Luis R. Vera, had lived in Paraguay for a while but was born in Santiago, Chile. He studied philosophy and worked for Chile Films until being forced into exile by the coup in 1973. He studied film and television production at the University of Bucharest in Romania, and in 1980 he moved to Sweden. In all he had produced and directed 18 shorts before making a feature, including *En el lugar . . . no muy lejano* (1980, Chile-Romania), which was in competition at the Havana film festival in 1983. His first feature, *Hechos consumados* (1984), partially shot in 16mm, edited and financed in Sweden, which spoke out against the horrors of General Augusto Pinochet's dictatorship, was showcased in the seventh Havana festival in 1985 as a Chilean film. His second feature, *Consuelo, una ilusión* (1988), a Chilean-Swedish co-production, focused on how the experience of exile changes a person inexorably.

In continuing a move away from straightforward political analysis and perhaps guided by the dictates of economics, Vera decided to make his next feature a satirical comedy. *Miss Amerigua* also recalls Brazilian *pornochanchada* and the 1950s exploitation period of Paraguayan film-making by having a beauty contest staged in the fictional town of Amerigua as its centrepiece. The main action of the film takes place over a twenty- four-hour period—the day of the pageant. At the beginning of the film we are given a flashback to a boy witnessing his father's death, at the hands of a military colonel. He returns home with his best friend, a poet, and we learn that they have both fought with the Sandinistas in Nicaragua. The prodigal son discovers that he has a beautiful sister who was born after his childhood flight. Conveniently his best friend falls in love with her, and, together with another contestant, the three of them escape on an oxcart at the end of the film after the colonel has been killed in revenge.

Miss Amerigua takes a traditional New Latin American Cinema political approach in using the character of the colonel as a corrupt, lecherous representative of the ruling oligarchy. But he, like most of the film's secondary characters, is comically drawn, which diffuses the critical edge. Also, the comedy veers dangerously close to stereotypical caricature at times: the Japanese jury president arrives in a Mercedes and speaks gibberish, provoking howls from the pageant's audience. There is certainly a great deal of local colour in costumes and decor, including the town's welcoming party for the arrival of dignitaries on a train running on apparently abandoned track. And, the idyllic background locale of a mountainous lakeside is rendered magnificently through Marten Nilsson's cinematography. Yet there are real problems with the racial component of the cast. Clearly one would expect the residents of the rural town to be predominantly native and Guaraní speaking, yet almost everyone is creole and only Spanish is spoken. To be sure, the director must be credited with bringing together technicians and actors from Sweden, Spain, Chile, Argentina, Uruguay, and Bolivia to join the over-50% Paraguayan contingent, yet in so doing he has badly misrepresented rural Paraguayan culture. Most strangely, the young brother and sister protagonists, who are clearly of European descent, have native American parents, the only obvious Guaraní. Thus, Vera presumably tried to valorise the indigenous population's contribution to Paraguay's history while completely selling out to commercial interests in casting his youthful protagonists. One must hope that future examples of Paraguayan filmmaking—co-produced or not—will better represent the true nature of its land, peoples, and culture, along the lines of Saguier's *El pueblo*, which is recognised as being the "first stone of an authentic Paraguayan cinema."

Peter Rist

Peru

Luis Pardo

Peru, 1927, b+w, silent

Dir Enrique Cornejo Villanueva *Scr* Cornejo Villanueva *Cinematog* Pedro Sambarino *Prod* Villanueva Films *Act* Teresa Arce, Enrique Cornejo Villanueva, Carmela Cáceres, Enrique Munillo, Rafael Villanueva

Actuality films—short views of current events—were plentiful during the silent era in Peru. Beginning at the turn of the century a great number of "views" were produced to be exhibited to the public—first in tents and later in movie houses. The first fiction films, the shorts *Negocio al agua* and *Del manicomio al matrimonio*, were produced in 1913. In 1922 a longer film, *Camino de la venganza*, was exhibited; it was a melodrama about the desires of a country woman who migrates to the capital. Later, the feature *Páginas heroicas*, about the Pacific War fought by Peru and Bolivia against Chile in 1879, was banned. This must have been the first Peruvian feature, but nothing more was ever heard about it, so that *Luis Pardo*, produced and released in 1927, became known as the first feature film in the history of Peruvian cinema. Only dispersed fragments of the film have survived, which remain unrestored.

Luis Pardo was inspired by the adventures of a turn-of-the-century bandit in the mountainous region of the country. He led an eventful life, becoming a sort of local Robin Hood and a legendary figure. The director and lead actor, Enrique Cornejo Villanueva, was a young amateur who never returned to film; the cinematographer Pedro Sambarino had directed Bolivia's first feature film, *Corazón Aymara*, in 1925. In the style of adventure films like *The Mark of Zorro* (Fred Niblo, 1920), *Luis Pardo* combined dynamic action scenes with romantic and comic situations and was filmed entirely on location. Despite the film's evident simplicity, we can appreciate the visual quality of its images, its sense of narrative continuity, and a tone which lies between playful and gentle. A similar style can be found in many other Latin American films of the period.

Although Cornejo Villanueva did not return to filmmaking, *Luis Pardo* was the first in a series of at least 13 other fiction features and a few feature-length documentaries in a period of stable film production which lasted until 1933. *Luis Pardo*, then, is representative not for its cinematographic merits, which are few, but for its status as a pioneering film, for having inaugurated a period of production at a time when the very notion of being able to produce films in Peru was widely doubted. After *Luis Pardo*, the production of feature films, one way or another, would be sustained uninterrupted until the 1940s, when various factors conspired to paralyse Peruvian feature film production until the 1960s.

Isaac León Frías

Gallo de mi galpón

Rooster in My Henhouse
Peru, 1938, approx. 75', b+w

Dir Sigifredo Salas *Scr* Francisco Diumenjo *Cinematog* Manuel Trullen *Prod* Enrique Varela La Rosa for Amauta Films *Act* Oscar Ortiz de Pinedo, Gloria Travesí, José Luis Romero, Esperanza Carrera

Gallo de mi galpón was one of the most successful productions of Amauta Films, which, between 1937 and 1940, produced 14 feature films, a record number for a single producer in Peruvian film history. That same period saw more films produced in Peru than in any other period before or since. A production boom was under way which might have been maintained but for the outbreak of war, which brought with it an interruption of raw film shipments from the United States. In subsequent years production dropped significantly.

The period of Amauta's zenith has become known by the phrase—born of exaggeration and an excess of enthusiasm—the "Golden Age" of Peruvian film. It was somewhat less of a golden age to those who lived through it, but, nevertheless, this artisinal cinema achieved a certain stability and succeeded in attracting attention from the public, both in Lima and in the interior. The films of the era tended to be melodramas, crime dramas, comedies, or musicals, genres which at times intermingled to paint a picture of everyday life in Lima in the second half of the 1930s.

Gallo de mi galpón was the Amauta film production to most ambitiously attempt a *costumbrista*, or mannered, view of life in Lima and the provincial towns on its outskirts. The story recounts the romantic quandary of the manager of a hacienda, incapable of choosing between two women. One of them, the daughter of the hacienda's owner, falls in love with one of the servants. The film was shot in Lima and in nearby towns, and abounds in comic moments and musical numbers, among them waltzes and *marineras* and *tonderos* (traditional coastal area folk dances). There is an evident eagerness throughout the film to exalt the food, song and dance, popular idiom, and cockfights of coastal Peruvian culture, all seasoned with the romantic twists of the plot.

Unlike earlier Amauta productions, such as *La bailarina loca, Sangre de selva, De doble filo, De carne somos,* and *El miedo a la vida,* all of which were flawed by defective story lines or poor technical quality, *Gallo* was proof of real progress in Peruvian film production technique. The photography was better than in earlier productions, as was the sound. The development of the plot, also, was better maintained, although it was still not free of those narrative gaps which, in general, marked the action of Peruvian films of this period. It must be remembered that these films were produced without foreign involvement entirely in Lima, which in those days had only makeshift laboratories and poor technical facilities.

Sigifredo Salas, the director, was a Chilean who directed eight other films for Amauta—three of them in 1938. The remainder of Amauta's production was directed by the Peruvian writer and director Ricardo Villarán, who had shot some silent films in Argentina in the 1920s. Salas identified completely with the creole aspirations of his films, and with *Gallo* he achieved one of the greatest tributes to creole life, an undertaking he would later resume with euphoric visions of creole manners in *Palomillas del Rimac, El guapo del pueblo,* and, to a lesser extent, *Tierra linda.* Of Salas, little is known other than his Chilean origins. He arrived in Lima in the mid-30s and left, reportedly for Ecuador or Bolivia, in the early 40s. However, researchers have found no trace of him in the region and it is not known if he is still living.

Isaac León Frías

Kukuli

Peru, 1961, 80', colour

Dir Luis Figueroa (b. 1929), Eulogio Nishiyama (b. 1920), and César Villanueva (1932–1974) *Scr* Hernán Velarde *Cinematog* Nishiyama and Villanueva *Mus* Armando Guevara *Prod* Enrique Vallve, Enrique Meier, Luis Arnillas, and Cine Club Cusco for Kero Films *Act* Judith Figueroa, Víctor Chambi, Emilio Galli, Lizardo Pérez

At the time of *Kukuli*'s release in 1961, thirteen years had passed since the last Peruvian feature had been released, apart from the complete commercial and critical disaster *La muerte llega al segundo show*, directed by José María Roselló in 1958. A relative hit with the critics and warmly received by the public, *Kukuli* suggested that a sort of renaissance in Peruvian cinema might be under way. Many earlier projects had failed and it seemed for a time that Peru would have to resign itself to the loss of a film industry whose output in the late 1930s has not been equalled since.

Interestingly enough, the film that was to launch this rebirth of Peruvian cinema wasn't made in Lima, the modern capital, but in Cuzco, the ancient capital of the Incas in the interior of the country. Prior to the release of *Kukuli*, Cuzco had been the site of the birth of a short film movement formed around the Cine Club Cusco, founded in 1955, which counted among its members *Kukuli*'s directors Luis Figueroa, Eulogio Nishiyama, and César Villanueva, and the brothers Manuel and Víctor Chambi (the latter with an acting role in the film), sons of the legendary photographer Martin Chambi, who was from the high altiplano region of Peru and had made Cuzco his home. All these young men were photographers and had found in the cinema a way to animate their portraits of life and nature in Cuzco and the surrounding region.

The Cine Club Cusco sponsored the making of various short films, the first showing the reality of the Peruvian Andes to be filmed by people of the region and not from Lima or abroad. *Kukuli* became their most ambitious project. It was filmed under innumerable difficulties and, after a long production period, was finally released in 1961. Despite the recognition it achieved in Peru and abroad, its directors were not able immediately to embark on new projects. The film which eventually took up the banner, *Jarawi*, co-directed by Nishiyama and Villanueva five years later, was a complete failure, thereby bringing an end to the Cine Club Cusco, for all intents and purposes already defunct.

Kukuli was inspired by a legend of the region which tells of a confrontation between a peasant and an *ukulu*—a mythological bear—because of their love for the same woman. The simple story was told the way it might have been had the film been made in the early years of sound film: the dialogue, spoken in the native language of the region, Quechua, was sparse; while the musical score, on the other hand, was conspicuous throughout the film. But the simplicity of the story was well served by the visual treatment, which focused on the natural beauty and local colour of the locations, the local dress and festivities. Here, the Andean universe was being empowered and with a strongly pantheistic and celebratory sentiment.

Kukuli presented, for the first time in a Peruvian feature fiction film, both a story set in the Cuzco region and a vision of the magical elements said to intermingle with daily life there. *Kukuli* was also an affirmation of the "indigenist" aesthetic, which had been expressed previously in Peruvian painting, photography, music, and literature. But this accomplishment proved to be fleeting, for *Kukuli* remains the only authentic Peruvian feature to perceive indigenous reality as something dazzling and magnificent. The sacred air of the compositions demonstrate this, with their strong desire to remark on the significance of what was being shown. In addition to examining a part of the country hitherto unseen in Peruvian cinema and to valorising the indigenist aesthetic, *Kukuli* retains expressive qualities that time has not eroded.

Isaac León Frías

Awards: Honourable Mention, Moscow, 1961; Diploma, Karlovy Vary, 1964.

La muralla verde

The Green Wall
Peru, 1970, 100', colour

Dir Armando Robles Godoy (b. 1923) *Scr* Robles Godoy *Cinematog* Mario Robles *Mus* Enrique Pinilla *Prod* Amaru Producciones Cinematográficas *Act* Julio Alemán, Sandra Riva, Raúl Martin, Jorge Montoro

La muralla verde was the third feature directed by Armando Robles Godoy, a writer and theatre director who also worked as a journalist and film critic. From the time he began to work as a critic and as a film programmer for the Film Culture Association, a group with a reputation for screening the best films made in the early 1960s, Robles Godoy revealed a preference for the *formal* aspect of the medium. Moreover, he was—and remains to this date—the only director to have created an auteur cinema in Peru. No other Peruvian director, before or since, has worked to create an *a fortiori* auteur cinema the way Robles Godoy has. Before him there was only the unaffected story, the *costumbrista* films, and indigenous recreations. After Robles, Peruvian film came to be dominated by a series of realistic themes drawn from the social problems of city and country alike.

But for Robles, references to Peruvian reality were always no more than the raw material, material which would dissolve in his fragmented stories, presented dischronologically in a heavily stylized manner. *La muralla verde* recounts the odyssey of a young man having to do battle with a crushing bureaucracy in order to obtain a plot of land in the Amazon jungle, where he must then struggle against nature, the "green wall" of the film's title. This story doesn't unfold in a linear fashion; rather, events alternate and, at times, bifurcate in different directions, like a puzzle that the spectator is obliged to put together. Robles Godoy's love of extreme expressive techniques is evident: close ups, lateral or point-of-view tracking shots, extreme angles, discontinuous editing, and out-of-sync voices and sounds abound, emphasizing the significance of the protagonist's extraordinary and almost superhuman efforts. For the average viewer, the film was confusing and disorienting, not to mention somewhat boring and pretentious, in its self-important techniques and in the sense it creates of having been made for a discriminating audience.

La muralla verde was the mature expression of an aesthetic Robles elaborated in his earlier films *Ganarás el pan* (1965) and *En la selva no hay estrellas* (1967), and which would continue to be worked out in the later films *Espejismo* (1973) and *Sonata Soledad* (1987), as well as in the many short films he directed between 1974 and the late 1980s. There was an undeniable evolution of his aesthetic through the four early films: while *Ganarás el pan* was a failure (despite being one of his few films, along with *Muralla*, to earn a small return), *En la selva*, despite giving the impression of being several films wrapped into one, was an improvement. *La muralla verde* was more coherent and in *Espejismo* he achieved a better fit between a somewhat fantastic story and his visual treatment, suggesting that he might obtain more satisfactory results with a more openly oneric or fantastic cinema.

La muralla verde is the film which won Robles Godoy the greatest recognition in foreign festivals and is the best known of his work, obtaining commercial release in the United States. The appreciation some U.S. critics feel for his work, evident in the awards the film won at the Chicago film festival, is due mostly to this film. It featured the cinematography of his brother Mario Robles and the work of several technicians who had studied at his private film workshop. His first four films were made before a general renaissance began in Peru in 1976, under the impetus of film production legislation, and constitute a radical affirmation of a personal style of filmmaking without antecedents or successors.

Isaac León Frías

Awards: Best Film, Best Director, Best Actor, Critics' Prize, Chicago, 1970; Best Film, Best Script, Best Actor, Panama, 1970; Dama del Paraguas Prize, Barcelona, 1970; Christopher and Candilejas Prizes, New York, 1972; Best Film, Cádiz, 1974.

Los perros hambrientos

The Starving Dogs
Peru, 1976, 100', colour

Dir Luis Figueroa (b. 1929) *Scr* Figueroa, based on the novel of the same title by Ciro Alegría (1939) *Cinematog* Kurt Rosenthal *Mus* Omar Aramayo *Prod* María Barea for Pukura Cine S.A. *Act* Juan Manuel del Campo, Rosalía Asencio, Olga del Campo, Gregorio Solano

Luis Figueroa has been the Peruvian director most faithful to peasant themes. After *Kukuli* (1961, q.v.), which he co-directed with Eulogio Nishiyama and César Villanueva, he had to wait 14 years before returning with *Chiaraje, batalla ritual* (1975), a feature documentary on traditional, violent rituals practised in the Andean highlands. *Chiaraje* was banned and has never been screened publicly in Peru. The following year, Figueroa directed *Los perros hambrientos* and, most recently, has made *Yawar Fiesta*, based on a story by one of Peru's best known authors, José María Arguedas, an important proponent of the "indigenist" aesthetic and an early supporter of the work of the Cine Club Cusco, around which *Kukuli* was made. Since *Yawar Fiesta*'s release in 1986, several years after it was made, Figueroa has been silent.

Los perros hambrientos wasn't the first Peruvian feature to take up the theme of the relations between landowners and peasants, but it was the first to do so emphatically, as the film's principal theme. A peasant drama based on the well known novel of the same title by Peruvian author Ciro Alegría, the film is dominated, however, not by the narrative but by a sense of the weight of the countryside and the spirit of the land. The narrative development is weak and erratic and, ultimately, without much force, unlike that of *Yawar Fiesta*, which goes to the other extreme of schematism and caricature. But in *Perros* the landscape acquires its own strength, as it did in *Kukuli* and *Chiaraje*, demonstrating perhaps the indigenous ancestry of its director and saving the film from its ineffectual dramatic element.

Like *Chiaraje* before it and *Yawar Fiesta* after it, *Los perros hambrientos* was an attempt to ditch the vision put forth in *Kukuli*. No longer was there an idealised image of the peasant world, no longer were scenery and folklore aesthetic effects which obscured the issues of social struggle in the Andes. The tendency towards a "postcard" aesthetic was left behind, as were the symphonic musical score and the slightest artistic pretence. Here

Figueroa opted for a realist representation with the appearances of a documentary. He aspired not to a "testimonial" cinema like that of Federico García (*Tupac Amaru*, 1984, q.v.) but to the sort of realism that the representation of social conflict seems to carry within it. Here the film came up against its own weaknesses, reminding us that the force of a film's material isn't automatically conveyed by its images.

The most valuable aspect of Alegría's novel, the dry and cruel vision of peasant life, mitigated by a certain sympathy and sadness, is virtually absent from Figueroa's film. Nevertheless, *Los perros hambrientos* bears the distinction of having begun a new current in Peruvian film, that of a return to a close examination of the problems of the countryside, preceding the films on similar themes by Federico García—*Kuntur wachana* (1977), *Laulico* (1980), and *El caso Huayanay: testimonio de parte* (1981)—as well as other films, such as *Un clarín en la noche* (1983) and *Los ronderos* (1987), which made the style seem his own.

Isaac León Frías

Awards: Special Jury Prize, Biarritz, 1979; Public Prize, Amiens, 1980.

Tupac Amaru

Peru-Cuba, 1984, 95', colour

Dir Federico García (b. 1937) *Scr* Yolando Rodríguez and García *Cinematog* Rodolfo López *Mus* Juan Márquez *Prod* Pilar Roca and Santiago Llapur for Cinematográfica Kuntur (Peru) and Instituto Cubano del Arte e Industria Cinematográficos (ICAIC) (Cuba) *Act* Reynaldo Arenas, Zully Azurin, César Urueta, Enrique Almirante

Tupac Amaru was the first big historical production in Peruvian film. "Big historical production," however, is an exaggeration, because the film shows signs that its production costs weren't as high as required by the scope of a project to film the story of the Inca Tupac Amaru, who, beginning in 1781, led the first battle for Peruvian independence. Nevertheless, in the context of Peruvian film, *Tupac Amaru*, one of the many films made possible only through co-production with Cuba's film institute, had a production finish much more polished than those films which had earlier covered historical themes.

Federico García was already a well-known director when he made *Tupac Amaru*. Along with Francisco Lombardi (*Muerte al amanecer*, 1977, *La ciudad y los perros*, 1985, q.v., *La boca del lobo*, 1988, q.v.) and Luis Figueroa (*Los perros hambrientos*, 1976, q.v.), he was one of the directors to inaugurate, with his *Kuntur Wachana* (1977), a major period in Peruvian film, under the impetus of film production legislation enacted in 1973. García was also the most lucid exponent of a "testimonial" cinema, one treating the problems of the countryside, through films such as *Kuntur Wachana, Laulico* (1980), and *El caso Huayanay: testimonio de parte* (1981). In *Kuntur Wachana* and *El caso Huayanay*, García adapted recent events to narrate, in a didactic fashion, stories in which peasants triumphed in their claims to land in the former film and, in the latter, to justify the cruel justice meted out in response to a foreman's abuses, who was sentenced to death by a community tribunal.

García first took up the theme of Peru's distant past in *Melgar, el poeta insurgente* (1982). Here the story told was that of Arequipian poet Mariano Melgar. But the film's dramatic deficiencies detracted from the character's tragic qualities and weakened the vision of the era the film tried to create. *Tupac Amaru* corrected this film's major defects. On the foundation of a more solid production, García centred the film on the trial scenes of José Gabriel Condorcanquí, the Cuzcan leader whose Incan name gives the film its title. With these scenes and through the use of flashbacks, an episodic reconstruction of the causes of the independence struggle develops. The film's argument is forceful and persuasive; the battle scenes are certainly the best of their kind ever filmed in Peru. The ending, like that of *El caso Huayanay*, is striking.

Not everything about the film was a success, however. There is an excess of information, a failing which became more serious in a later film, *El socio de Dios* (1986). Also, *Tupac Amaru* presents a grandiloquent aesthetic, imparting to the acting a rigidity common to many historical recreations. At the same time, it is arguably García's best film, and it is the one which had the greatest popular appeal. More recently, abandoning some of these pretences and working in a different vein altogether, García has made *La manzanita del diablo* (1990) and *La lengua de los zorros* (1992), both of poor quality.

Isaac León Frías

Awards: Saul Yelin Prize, Havana, 1979; Honourable Mention, Quito, 1986; Special Festival Award, Pyongyang, 1987.

La ciudad y los perros

The City and the Dogs
Peru, 1985, 144', colour

Dir Francisco Lombardi (b. 1949) *Scr* José Watanabe, based on the novel of the same title by Mario Vargas Llosa (1962) *Cinematog* Pili Flores Guerra *Mus* Enrique Iturriaga *Prod* Emilio Moscoso for Inca Films *Act* Pablo Serra, Gustavo Bueno, Juan Manuel Ochoa, Luis Alvarez

Francisco Lombardi wrote film criticism for the Peruvian film journal *Hablemos de cine* and the Lima daily *Correo* before beginning work as a director of short films after the introduction of film production legislation in 1973. His short films include sensitive portraits of blind children in *Al otro lado de la luz* and of the elderly in *Tiempo de espera*. In 1977 his first feature, *Muerte al amanecer*, was released, based on a true story which shook the nation in the 1950s, the trial of a man accused of raping and murdering a young boy. The film examined, a little rigidly, the conduct of the upper classes in Lima society.

His episode *Los amigos* in the anthology film *Cuentos inmorales* (1978) showed that he had become much stronger at directing actors and established two of the recurring themes of his work, imprisonment and the limits of reason. *Muerte de un magnate* (1980) is a lesser film, the chronicle of the murder of a fishing magnate. But the film established Lombardi as the leading exponent of an urban cinema, completely unlike his contemporaries Federico García (*Tupac Amaru*, 1984, q.v.) and Luis Figueroa (*Los perros hambrientos*, 1976, q.v.). In the 1970s discussion of Peruvian cinema turned on these two poles, a perspective which later lost currency. Next came Lombardi's *Maruja en el infierno* (1983), another claustrophobic tale, this time about a workshop where a woman exploits a group of mentally handicapped workers. Based on a novel by Enrique Congrains, the film took Lombardi further into the field of the social conflicts created by urban underdevelopment.

La ciudad y los perros, made in 1985, was Lombardi's most ambitious project to that date. It adapted a novel hitherto considered too difficult to film, one that had brought Peruvian novelist Mario Vargas Llosa to international attention, concerning the brutal conditions of life inside the country's military colleges. Lombardi stripped the story down and centred the action in the military college, where a young cadet is murdered and another tries to bring his killers to justice, and gave the story a linearity quite different from the temporal shifts of the novel. In this way, the film's drama increases in pitch throughout the film, culminating in a climax in the final moments. *La ciudad* also displays a good direction of actors and a fine recreation of the milieu, and these elements made it Lombardi's most accomplished film, to be surpassed only later with *La boca del lobo* (1988, q.v.).

In *La ciudad y los perros*—as in all of Lombardi's films—the story develops situations of extreme violence in order to emphasize social conflicts, injustice, and authoritarian hierarchies. At times there is a tendency toward a sensationalism that detracts from the overall dramatic coherence. Behind the director's gaze, which may at times seem somewhat distanced from the events he is presenting, one senses nonetheless a feeling of moral indignation, a sentiment present in all of Lombardi's films. The film works as a metaphor for Peru's social reality, even more so because this is not obvious from the flow of events.

La ciudad y los perros finished a period for Lombardi of using a hyperrealist approach, at the same time as he showed a propensity towards stylized decor, evident as early as 1983 with *Maruja*. Later, in *Caídos del cielo* (1990), which won the prize for Best Film at the Montréal film festival, he would return to an urban drama, recounting three stories simultaneously with an even greater stylization and with a black humour absent from his earlier films.

Isaac León Frías

Awards: Best Film, Biarritz, 1985; Third Prize, Havana, 1985.

Gregorio

Peru, 1985, 85', colour

Dir Fernando Espinoza (b. 1942), Stefan Kaspar (b. 1948), and Alejandro Legaspi (b. 1948) *Scr* María Barea, Espinoza, Kaspar, Legaspi, and Susana Pastor *Cinematog* Alejandro Legaspi *Mus* Arturo Ruiz del Pozo *Prod* Grupo Chaski *Act* Marino León de la Torre, Vetzy Pérez Palma, Augusto Varillas, Manuel Acosta Ojeda

Grupo Chaski was formed in the early 1980s and for a decade operated as a solid investigative team, producing and distributing its own films and, at one time, having as many as 50 people on contract, a considerable number for a Peruvian producer. This figure gives an idea of the diversity of activities it undertook. The group's production was rooted in the country's problems, working from a documentary base. This was the idea behind its medium-length films *Miss Universe en el Perú* (1982), *Caminos de liberación* (1983), *Imágenes para una democracia* (1986), and *Perú: ni leche ni Gloria* (1987). Similarly, a series of filmed newsreels under the rubric *Relatos de supervivencia* documented the various ways in which many people earn their daily bread and elude, if they so manage, the misery which abounds in the country.

But it was with its two features, *Gregorio* and *Juliana* (1989), that the group refined its concept of cinema. Both were collective productions, begun after careful research and scripting. In each film the fictional element is built on a tangible documentary foundation: the fiction appears as an extension of the lives of the ordinary people depicted in the film. Dramatisations of daily events, they could be considered docu-dramas or psycho-dramas. In each the norms of investigative journalism form the basis of the narrative.

Of the two, *Gregorio* is the film which most clearly adopts this approach. The film began as a documentary of a young boy who survives, barely, on the streets of Lima. In making the film, the group added a minimal dramatic element, using actors for scripted scenes. This is the framework for the boy's itinerary, from the time he leaves his home town in the Andes to the last corner of the city his wanderings lead him to. *Gregorio* was filmed almost completely in the city streets, capturing the feverish rhythm of a crowded and overpopulated city. This strategy was repeated in *Juliana*, marking it as something of a trademark of the group's style.

Gregorio's principal achievements lie in its documentary side, wherein the misery of the city and its inhabitants is shown, starkly but without sensationalism. But the fictional and documentary elements are not well combined, and at times the former seems like a fragile ornament dangling from a rough–hewn cloth. There are other times, above all in the direction of the children, when the camera achieves a sincere intimacy, a product of extensive rehearsals before filming because, as in other Peruvian films, the actors are not professionals. Not even the film's protagonist is professional, nor is the protagonist of *Juliana*.

Juliana isn't, strictly speaking, the feminine version of *Gregorio*. Rather, it is a continuation of a child's urban odyssey, only in this case by a girl. Here, as in the Argentine film *La Raulito* (1975, q.v.) by Lautaro Murúa, the hostile social environment forces her to assume the appearance of a boy. *Juliana* achieves a better equilibrium between the fictional and documentary elements, the lessons of *Gregorio* having been well learned. But while *Gregorio* offered a harsh view of the city and of the vicissitudes of the boy's life, *Juliana* is blander and tends to sentimentalise the story, stripping it of some of its more turbid and sordid aspects.

Grupo Chaski was dissolved in 1991. Its films constitute one of the most identifiable tendencies in Peruvian cinema in the 1980s, and its influence can be seen in films made since its demise, and not only by former members of the group.

Isaac León Frías

Awards: Best Film, Special Jury Prize and OCIC Award, Havana, 1984; Best Director and Best Actor, Bogotá, 1985; Mention, Huelva, 1985; Special Prize, Festival de Cinéma du Tiers Monde (Switzerland), 1986; Second Prize, Quito, 1986.

La boca del lobo

The Lion's Den
Peru, 1988, 123', colour

Dir Francisco Lombardi (b. 1949) *Scr* Augusto Cabada and Giovanna Pollarollo *Cinematog* José Luis López Linares *Mus* Bernardo Monessi *Prod* Lombardi and Gerardo Herrero for Inca Films and Tornasol Films *Act* Gustavo Bueno, Toño Vega, José Tejada, Gilberto Torres

When Francisco Lombardi (*La ciudad y los perros*, 1985, q.v.) made *La boca del lobo*, he already had a reputation as the most bankable Peruvian filmmaker. *La boca del lobo* confirmed this and is arguably the best Peruvian film of all time; it was certainly Lombardi's best received film.

Lombardi took up a delicate subject in telling the story of violence in an Andean village, torn by Shining Path guerrilla incursions and the subsequent military repression. The film is based on a massacre of civilians by military and police personnel, a common feature of the "anti-terrorist" campaign which had been in place eight years when the film was made. In *La boca del lobo*, a police unit, completely detached from the people it is there to protect, becomes increasingly tormented by guerrilla activities, whose perpetrators never appear on screen. Once more in Lombardi's work the story reflects the strategies of an invisible guerrilla movement that attacks without leaving a trace; for fifteen years now this movement has maintained a systematic harassment of village and city life alike.

Despite *La boca del lobo*'s specific social and political setting, that of Peru in the midst of a guerrilla insurgency in the 1980s, the film is also a "danger" film, which has a long history in the cinema, from *The Lost Patrol* (John Ford, 1934) to *The Thing* (Christian Nyby, 1951) and later *Assault on Precinct 13* (John Carpenter, 1976), to mention three U.S. films from different periods and genres which share this feature. Rather than being a critical account of Peru's internal war, then, like Marianne Eyde's *La vida es una sola* (1992), *La boca del lobo* is more accurately a genre film in which the most important thing, above all else, is the development of the tension affecting the members of the small police detachment. It's not that the film is uninterested in the political situation but that, unlike Lombardi's previous films, where he tried to recreate social reality, *La boca del lobo* seems more interested in the story line of men under siege, making it more like an adventure film in the mould of *Men in War* (Anthony Mann, 1957) than a truly political film.

It was precisely this dynamic that various critics objected to soon after the film's release. In this view, the film paid too little attention to the Shining Path phenomenon and offered instead a psychological view in which social conflict was presented and resolved in individual terms. These criticisms asked of the film something it didn't want to give: a testimonial of the political struggles in the Peruvian highlands. Instead, *La boca del lobo* used the war as a backdrop to create a climate of fear and anguish; as in all of Lombardi's films, this is the story of conflict between men, growing violence, and the loss of restraint. Seen in this light, the film reconciles the norms of a genre with the director's own concerns, a project never before undertaken in Peruvian film. *La boca del lobo* also reveals that, although Lombardi always returns to favoured themes, he is not an auteur in the sense of those directors who develop a conspicuously personal style. *La boca del lobo* remains to this date the most accomplished Peruvian film, despite its debatable perspective and a certain dramatic excess, not unlike a depiction of Russian roulette on screen.

Isaac León Frías

Awards: First Prize, San Sebastián, 1988; Second Prize, Glauber Rocha, OCIC, Radio Habana, El caimán barbudo and Giraldilla Prizes, Havana, 1988; Best Film, Cartagena, 1989.

Alias "La Gringa"

Peru-Spain-United Kingdom-Cuba, 1991, 93', colour

Dir Alberto Durant (b. 1951) *Scr* José Watanabe, Durant, and José María Salcedo *Cinematog* Mario García Joya *Mus* Pochi Marambio *Prod* Andrés Malatesta and Emilio Salomón for Perfo Estudio (Peru), Televisión Española (TVE) (Spain), Channel Four (U.K.), Instituto Cubano del Arte e Industria Cinematográficos (ICAIC) (Cuba), and Sociedad Quinto Centenario (Spain) *Act* Germán González, Gonzalo de Miguel, Elsa Olivero, Orlando Sacha

An influential figure in Peruvian cinema for the past 15 years, Alberto Durant has made several short films and three features: *Ojos de perro* (1981), *Malabrigo* (1986), and *Alias "La Gringa."* A filmmaker who gravitates to social themes, Durant has nevertheless tried to surmount a realist aesthetic in his films to incorporate magical or fantastic elements in the tradition of Latin American "magic realism." This tendency was already apparent in *Ojos de perro*, above all in the dream sequences, and in *Malabrigo*, where flashbacks reveal a magical element obscured in the narration of present-day events. It is also present, although in a more indirect manner, in *Alias "La Gringa,"* in the bizarre disappearances and escapes of the prisoner and in certain aspects of the mise-en-scène.

But the presence of these fantastic elements is relatively tangential in Durant's films, and they aren't developed the way they are in films by other Latin American directors. What predominates in Durant's films is the story, stories with a social resonance. *Ojos de perro* tells the story of the formation of the first trade union on a sugar cane plantation in the northern coastal region in the 1920s, making it the first Peruvian feature to take up a trade union theme. But here the story is weakly told because of Durant's taste for an aesthetic of long takes, vaguely inspired by the style of Hungarian director Miklós Jancsó, which doesn't give the images the force they need. *Malabrigo* is a sort of crime thriller, set in a port, also on the northern coast. A woman searches for her disappeared husband, a journalist who had gone to a small town to investigate strange goings-on reported there. His search leads him to discover political and economic dealings which dilute the principal story line, and the film ends in a particularly abrupt and confused manner. The first part of *Malabrigo*, however, is worthy of praise for its achievement of an atmosphere of constant threat in keeping with the thriller genre and also for certain sequences and mises-en-scène, such as the depiction of the hotel. Here, Durant's expressive powers are evident.

These expressive powers came to the fore in *Alias "La Gringa,"* the story of a criminal who escapes repeatedly from various prisons, particularly a penal island, where much of the film unfolds. This is Durant's best-told film; the narrative is smooth and fastpaced. Early in the film the centre of Lima is evocatively depicted as is, later, the penal island. There, in different areas, are found common criminals and Shining Path guerrillas. The image of an extraordinarily violent place beset by all sorts of social contradictions is well crafted. Along with its narrative strengths and impressive atmosphere, the film has fine acting, although some characters are not especially convincing, such as the imprisoned schoolteacher and the Shining Path leader in prison. Also, the final scene of the prison revolt, inspired by the crushing of uprisings in Shining Path–dominated prisons in 1986, occurs without sufficient dramatic justification and is one of the weak aspects of the film.

Alias "La Gringa" remains the most expensive Peruvian film produced to date, with a budget of approximately $400,000 U.S., provided mostly by the foreign co-producers. In addition to obtaining television sales throughout Europe and in the United States, and returning a profit to its investors, it won a few awards abroad and secured a better image there for Peruvian film, a well-made cinema capable of being distributed abroad at the same time as it bears witness to the country's turbulent social reality and gives a central place to the themes of marginality and terrorist violence. Although the Spanish public television network TVE, the foreign producer most heavily involved in Latin American co-productions throughout the 1980s, has largely withdrawn from such ventures since, co-productions now dominate Peruvian cinema. While co-productions used to entail a loss of control to the foreign investor, in the 1990s Peruvian directors have recovered almost complete artistic freedom under them.

Isaac León Frías

Awards: Best Film, Best Actor, and Best Cinematography, Bogotá, 1991; Radio Exterior prize, Huelva, 1991; Best Editing, Havana, 1991.

Uruguay

El pequeño héroe del Arroyo del Oro

The Little Hero of Arroyo del Oro
Uruguay, 1931 (released 1933), approx. 70', b+w, silent

Dir Carlos Alonso *Scr* Alonso, based on newspaper reports by José Flores Sánchez *Cinematog* Emilio and Humberto Peruzzi *Prod* Alonso *Act* Ariel A. Severino, Celina Sánchez, Juan José Severino, Vicente Rivero, Alberto Candeau

El pequeño héroe del Arroyo del Oro was the last of five silent features produced in Uruguay and remains the best Uruguayan film, a sort of primitive precursor to neo-realism. It was the only feature of Alonso's, an itinerant camera operator who, in the 1920s and '30s, travelled the country filming people, towns, and the countryside for silent newsreels of 10 to 20 minutes in length. *El pequeño héroe* was a considerable success, explicable in part because it reconstructed a murder which had captured popular attention and in part because it reflected a popular sensibility, gave oral history an image, and presented an immediate reality. The story was true: nine-year-old Dionisio Díaz, seriously wounded by a berserk stepfather and carrying his younger sister, walked several miles to a distant police post, where he died upon arrival. The film's early sequences depict daily life in the country; the drama then unfolds with a force which was no doubt impressive for the era. Uruguay at the time had only two million inhabitants, over half of them in Montevideo, and was undoubtedly less sophisticated then it would become. For the film's spectators it was a chance to see, like in a newsreel, the events they had read about in the newspapers, and the film was shot in the places where the events had unfolded, faithfully following the course of events.

293

With time Dionisio became a hero of such proportions that his story was taught in schools, and a sound version of Alonso's film, with a didactic voice-over replacing the intertitles, was released. The narrator hammered home what the images already showed more eloquently, and some tinny brass music was added to the soundtrack. The film's latter-day restoration was made from negatives of the day and two surviving prints, but the intertitles have been lost forever (the copy in the Cinemateca Uruguaya is the silent version without the intertitles). Nonetheless, the film still reveals that its language, elemental and unsubtle, was the one best suited to the task. Each sequence opens and closes like a descriptive unit. There are no cuts; the shots are elementally framed and the whole film maintains a rudimentary air which sustains the narrative development of this primitive drama. The film's actors were drawn from theatre; Alberto Candeau was one of the leading theatre actors of the day, and others went on to distinguished careers.

El pequeño héroe was begun in 1929, finished in 1931, and first seen publicly in 1933. Without studios and with makeshift laboratories, Uruguayan cinema came late to sound film, in 1936. Thirteen features were made between that date and 1952, representing half of the total national output. At that time a public for national films still existed, with international cinema not yet dominating the screens and the public still curious to see its reflection there. Between 1936 and '38 two labs and three studios were founded: a national film industry seemed viable. The possibility of co-productions (with neighbouring Argentina), the country's strong economy, and the high rate of film-going (11½ times annually per capita in 1951, the highest in Latin America) all suggested the industry would grow. With few exceptions, however, the films produced were imitations of Argentine films, and the public grew to prefer the original to a copy. In the 1980s other, more promising projects were frustrated: the public was already abandoning the cinemas.

Manuel Martínez Carril

Como el Uruguay no hay

There's No Place Like Uruguay
Uruguay, 1960, 9', b+w and colour

Dir Ugo Ulive (b. 1935) *Anim* Francisco Tastás Moreno

Carlos: Cine-retrato de un "caminante" en Montevideo

Carlos: Film Portrait of a Hobo in Montevideo
[Carlos]
Uruguay, 1965, 31', b+w

Dir Mario Handler (b. 1935) *Mus* Ariel Martínez *Sound* Enrique Almada *Prod* Instituto de Cine de la Universidad de la República (ICUR)

Elecciones

Elections
Uruguay, 1966, 36', b+w

Dir Ugo Ulive (b. 1935) and Mario Handler (b. 1935) *Cinematog* Jorge Solé *Sound* Conrado Silva and Carlos Camano *Prod* Instituto de Cine de la Universidad de la República (ICUR)

Me gustan los estudiantes

I Like Students
Uruguay, 1968, 6', b+w

Dir Mario Handler (b. 1935) *Mus* Coriún Ahoronián; songs "Me gustan los estudiantes" (Violeta Parra) and "Vamos, estudiantes" (Daniel Viglietti) sung by Viglietti *Prod* Altoverde and Cinemateca del Tercer Mundo

Uruguay has a long tradition of being an excellent place to view cinema, and in the 1950s and '60s an excellent network of ciné clubs existed, fuelling dreams by young Uruguayan intellectuals to make films. In 1954, on the eve of the birth of various film "new waves" throughout Latin America, the International Festival of Documentary and Experimental Film was founded in Montevideo by the State Broadcasting and Entertainment Service (SODRE). The SODRE festival would expose aspiring Uruguayan filmmakers to new work from throughout Latin America during this period: the 1958 festival, the year of the first Uruguayan short films of note, featured new films by the Brazilian Nelson Pereira dos Santos (*Rio, Quarenta Graus*, 1955, q.v.), the Bolivian Jorge Ruiz (*La vertiente*, 1959, q.v.), and the Argentine Fernando Birri (*Los inundados*, 1961, q.v.). Like these filmmakers, the Uruguayans professed to have been profoundly influenced by the Italian neo-realist movement of the period. However, lacking the industrial infrastructure, market, state support, and breadth of talent of neighbouring Argentina, which saw a short film movement produce some 250 films from 1958–1963 (*Prisioneros de una noche*, 1960, q.v.), Uruguay produced a handful of noteworthy films by three or four directors, of a total output of a few dozen, before film production ceased in the early 1970s in the face of increased political repression.

The two major figures of the period were Ugo Ulive and Mario Handler, both of whom eventually resettled in Venezuela. Ulive came to film from the theatre, shooting the 50' fiction film *Un vintén pa'l Judas* in 1958 and his best-known solo effort, *Como el Uruguay no hay*, in 1960. This nine-minute film, which included some rudimentary animation sequences, introduced collage as a strategy for Uruguayan filmmakers, who lacked proper production facilities, and established the movement's dominant film type, short agitational films satirising politics or, later, protesting repression in a long-democratic society. Ulive left Uruguay soon after this film to work at the newly formed film institute, ICAIC, in Cuba, where he co-scripted one of the most important early features of revolutionary Cuba, Tomás Gutiérrez Alea's *Las doce sillas* in 1962 and directed the feature *Crónica cubana* in 1963 before returning to Uruguay.

Handler studied film in Germany on a scholarship in 1963, making his first film, *En Praga*, in Europe before returning to Uruguay in 1964 to head the Film Institute of the National University (ICUR). Denied a budget and prevented from buying equipment, he surreptitiously shot his first Uruguayan film, *Carlos: Cine-retrato de un "caminante" en Montevideo* in 1965 with unused raw stock he discovered at the film institute. *Carlos* developed out of his encounter with a rural hobo who had travelled the country before becoming a *bichicome*, or vagabond, in Montevideo's old port district. Carlos was a lucid vagabond, professing to be "always reading" and preferring to call himself a *caminante*, or hobo, a more dignified profession than that of an urban tramp, and, Handler once commented, "understanding his profession to be a very ancient one." Handler spent considerable time with Carlos: "We became friends. We would drink beer and talk or we'd walk together for hours on end without saying a word. . . . I wanted to present a portrait of society through the study of a single individual, to arrive at the social through the personal." After filming was complete, Handler recorded a soundtrack based on questions he put to Carlos about his life, editing the material into a monologue that narrates the film. Production facilities were so primitive in Uruguay that Handler edited the film from the original negative without a moviola.

In 1965 Ulive and Handler collaborated on the film *Elecciones*, concerning the country's upcoming elections in 1966. This commentary on the inadequacy of the country's two political parties was prevented from being screened at the 1967 SODRE festival, prompting spirited protests and Ulive's definitive departure from the country. It was screened commercially in Montevideo, however, thanks to a new exhibition venture by Walter Achúgar, who later became a European sales agent for many of the continent's young filmmakers and a producer of some of their work.

There was to be one more major film during this period, Handler's *Me gustan los estudiantes*. This six-minute collage film, made partly with a faulty camera after police smashed his Bolex, juxtaposed student demonstrations and police repression in Montevideo with the meeting of the continent's government leaders, including U.S. president Lyndon Johnson, at the Uruguayan beach resort Punta del Este that year. The faulty Punta del Este footage was left silent, while the student demonstrations were accompanied by music by Uruguayan folk singer Daniel Viglietti, including the title song by the Chilean Violeta Parra, creating a bizarre effect. Again, technical facilities were so poor that Handler scratched the film's title onto the negative by hand, frame by frame. Despite its technical defects, the film's premiere at a film festival sponsored by the radical Uruguayan newspaper *Marcha* in 1968—at the height of student activism in Uruguay and around the world—was marked by a spontaneous outburst from the audience, which poured into the street and into the square opposite to protest the police repression depicted in the film.

As repression in the country increased, giving rise to armed insurrection in the form of the Tupamaros guerrillas, until the country's first military coup in 1973, Handler would film two more shorts. *El problema de la carne* (1969) is about a meat-packers strike and *Liber Arce, liberarse* (1970) is about a student shot dead by police who bore the unusual name Liber Arce, which when pronounced as one word, *liberarse*, means to free yourself. The production of these films was assisted by one of the projects of Uruguay's cultural Left, Third World Cinémathèque, dedicated to forging links with filmmakers throughout the developing world, which was closed down in 1971, two years after its founding. At that time, seven of its organisers were imprisoned briefly. In 1972, Third World Cinémathèque activist Achúgar was imprisoned for two months and tortured while another member of the organisation, Eduardo Terra, was held for four years. Handler has managed to shoot occasional shorts and fiction features in Venezuela, which have had limited international exposure and bear little resemblance to the agitational style and social themes of his Uruguayan short films.

Timothy Barnard

Awards: *Carlos: Cine-retrato de un "caminante" en Montevideo*: Best Experimental Film, Best Documentary (shared), Southern Cone Independent Film Festival (Montevideo), 1965; Uruguayan Film Critics Association Award, 1965; Honourable Mention for a Documentary Film, Viña del Mar, 1967.

Elecciones: Uruguayan Film Critics Association Award, 1966.

Mataron a Venancio Flores

They Shot Venancio Flores
Uruguay, 1982, 91', colour

Dir Juan Carlos Rodríguez Castro *Scr* Rodríguez Castro and Héctor Manuel Vidal, based on the script "A mediodía" by Rolando Esperanza *Cinematog* Humberto Castagnola *Art dir* Osvaldo Reyno *Mus* Carlos da Silva, with excerpts from Giuseppe Verdi's *Macbeth Prod* Henry Segura for Cinemateca Uruguaya *Act* Liber Rodríguez, Andrés Garrido, Antonio Cruz, Dante Alfonso

Uruguayan intellectuals and film-goers have long dreamt, if not of a national film industry, then at least of the occasional feature production in this country of three million people. While some 30 sound features were filmed there from the 1930s to the 1960s, these were either foreign (largely Argentine), filmed in Uruguay to lower costs, or were modelled on the Argentine industry's successful studio genres and heavily reliant on Argentine talent and money. In the 1950s and '60s several talented short film makers emerged (q.v.) but eventually withdrew from filmmaking or left the country to work in feature production abroad. The dream persisted, however, fed by Uruguay's exceptional accomplishments in theatre and literature and by a thriving culture of film criticism and exhibition, all of which earned the country a reputation as an intellectual hot house, where European art films had a devoted audience and per capita film-going was the highest in Latin America. In 1979, the feature *El lugar del humo* was filmed there by a local production company but using mostly Argentine technicians and directed by the Argentine Eva Landeck. This film's commercial failure ruined the small company that was set up to mount it. In 1980 the Uruguayan government joined with a U.S. producer to film a bucolic image of the country in *Gurí*, and in 1981 a lone filmmaker was able to produce a musical, *Sábado disco*, which despite its low cost and commercial appeal, did not recover its costs. Other projects during this period were never completed.

Finally, in 1982, a feature was produced which not only boasted entirely Uruguayan financing, actors, and crew but could be considered a serious project that offered the country's artists, in film and other disciplines, an opportunity to collaborate. *Mataron a Venancio Flores'* genesis was in a script competition held by the Cinemateca Uruguaya as part of its program of financing short films during this period. The winning script, Rolando Esperanza's "A mediodía," was developed to be shot as a feature film by *Mataron*'s director, Juan Carlos Rodríguez Castro, who had begun making short films in the late 1950s, and theatre director Héctor Manuel Vidal. The entire $100,000 budget was provided by the Cinemateca, which, since its founding in 1952 (making it one of the oldest cinémathèques in Latin America), has played an extraordinary role in the country's film culture. In addition to a cinémathèque's usual activities, archiving and documenting films—it has Latin America's largest film archive—and operating a public film library, it has published magazines and monographs, stages an annual international film festival founded in 1982, and operates a number of first-run and archival screening cinemas in Montevideo. In the early 1990s there were four such cinemas in the capital, accounting for one-fifth of all admissions there; at the time of the making of *Mataron* there were more, including one dedicated exclusively to screening new work from throughout Latin America, an undertaking not to be underestimated in a region where neighbouring countries' films are often unknown to each other. *Mataron*, for example, although screened in Moscow and Budapest, was never seen in Buenos Aires, across the River Plata from Montevideo.

After filming was completed in March 1981 in 16mm, *Mataron* was released by the Cinemateca in August 1982, on the anniversary of the country's independence. The film soon encountered controversy, however: it was not as warmly received by the country's demanding film critics as the Cinemateca would perhaps have wished, partly because of obvious technical defects, but also because the film could never, of course, hope to measure up to the major works of world cinema these critics were accustomed to reviewing. Worse, Rodríguez disassociated himself from the movie after he completed it—although his name remained on the credits—because of his dissatisfaction with the work of the Argentine film laboratory that processed the film, as the film had a faulty soundtrack and poor definition of its sepia sequences, which would later be partially corrected. In any event, the film attracted only 10,000 spectators—at this time in Montevideo, 50–100,000 admissions was a box office hit—and the Cinemateca did not recover its investment, forcing it to abandon plans for future features.

Mataron a Venancio Flores was filmed during the country's military dictatorship (1973–1985), which might suggest why the film was set in the mid-1800s. The tragic-farcical story could be interpreted as a sort of allegory for contemporary Uruguay, having lost its reputation as the peaceful and prosperous "Switzerland of Latin America" after years of confrontations between left-wing Tupamaros guerrillas and the military, and decades of economic decline. The film takes as its starting point the assassination of two former presidents of opposing political parties in 1868, one of them being Venancio Flores. The president writes to all his provincial military-political leaders, the *caudillos*, instructing them to "Gather your men and come," but one illiterate *caudillo* reads this as "Gather your men and take revenge," setting off a series of misadventures. Two criminals being transported by wagon across the pampas are intercepted by a band of soldiers. With their guardians they are abducted, and in the fashion of a Western, the band treks across the countryside, arguing for and against the execution of the criminals in their midst, mistaken for the assassins of Venancio Flores. The film ends ambiguously, after the criminals' execution and a final shoot-out between the two groups, as a woman surveys the lone survivor and rides off. The obscure historical incidents the film is constructed around, filmed in three sepia sequences interspersed with the film's colour "fiction" footage, are not clearly explained, reportedly causing confusion even for Uruguayan viewers.

Despite this lack of narrative cohesion and the film's other defects, such as its poor dubbing and lame editing, Rodríguez' stylistic aspirations, while not fully achieved, are clear. There is, first of all, the alternation of sepia and colour sequences, suggesting a manipulation of time and of fact and fiction that lends the film to an allegorical reading. Aware of the limitations imposed on him by his budget and the film's anomalous status as the country's first feature in a half a century, Rodríguez eschews spectacle. The acting, by the country's theatre professionals, is competent throughout, but the actors were so out of their element that their inability to ride horses caused numerous production problems. The camera at times films the same subject from a variety of perspectives, a stock low-budget innovation. Throughout we sense that Rodríguez is attempting to recreate the sort of "anti-spectacle" Western pioneered in the U.S. by directors like Sam Peckinpah and Monte Hellman, although in the case of *Mataron*, the line between anti-spectacle and rudimentary filmmaking is fine indeed. Little in the country's vaunted cultural traditions prepared aspiring filmmakers for the challenge of filming the country's monotonous landscape in an innovative way. *Mataron a Venancio Flores* took a small step in this direction, and it is unlikely that there will be another opportunity like it.

Timothy Barnard

Venezuela

Taboga y Hacia el calvario

"Taboga" and "Hacia el calvario" [Taboga]
Venezuela, 1938, 10'50", b + w

Dir Rafael Rivero (1904–1992) *Cinematog* Anibal Rivero and Carlos G. Ascanio *Sound* Antonio Plaza Ponte *Mus* Billo Frometa and his orchestra "Billo's Happy Boys" *Act* Eduardo Martínez Plaza, Enrique D'Lima, Pedro Martínez, Fini Veracoechea, Carlos Ascanio

National legend, with historical pretence, contentedly relates that Venezuela was among the first countries to produce "moving images." In 1897, two years after the first public screenings of the Lumière *cinématographe* in Paris, Manuel Trujillo Durán filmed two shorts in the oil town of Maracaibo with the picturesque titles *Muchachos bañandose en el Lago* ("Boys Bathing in the Lake") and *Un célebre especialista sacando muelas frente al Hotel Europa* ("A Famous Specialist Pulling Teeth in Front of the Europa Hotel"). With these films, of which nothing but newspaper notices remain, Venezuelan cinema was born. Later, others would follow Trujillo Durán's trail, but apart from the documentaries made by the government of Juan Vicente Gómez (1908–1935), the work of the pioneer Edgar J. Anzola, and the films produced by Amabilis Cordero in the 1930s in Barquisimeto, in the centre of the country, no films from Venezuela's silent period have survived. Nevertheless, it is difficult to date the end of Venezuela's film prehistory. And recently two rolls of original nitrate film of a feature entitled *Don Leandro el inefable*, directed by Enrique Zimmermann around 1915, were discovered. It appears to be a humorous and mannered recreation of Caracas of the day.

Venezuela was a poor country, and there were frequent clashes between rival *caudillos*, or rural fiefs. The Gómez dictatorship "pacified" the country between 1908 and 1935; most historians agree that Venezuela only entered the twentieth century with his death in 1935. Late nineteenth- and early twentieth-century Venezuela was poorly developed in every aspect: economic, political, cultural. Gómez, who triumphed over the regional *caudillos* in 1908 in a bid to "unify" and "stabilise" the country, was, like many dictators in world history, fascinated with the representation of his rule through moving images. All of his public acts, inaugurations and excursions were recorded by the camera. In 1911 Zimmermann began making numerous propaganda films for Gómez. In 1927 the National Laboratories were founded; there, overseen by the Ministry of Public Works, many documentaries and a newsreel service were produced, almost always showing the government's beneficence. Many young filmmakers, including Jacobo Capriles, Juan Avilan, Anibal Rivero, and Efraín Gómez, the president's nephew, began working in film there.

As far has been determined, the National Laboratories acquired an RCA truck with a Western Electric sound system and undertook the first attempts to make sound films in Venezuela. A short film with a music track, *La venus de nácar* (1932), by Efraín Gómez, has survived. The first sound test, spoken in English by a U.S. technician (with Spanish subtitles), has also survived, with the technician boasting of the future importance of this development for Venezuelan cinema.

The National Laboratories survived until 1937 when, two years after Gómez's death and in a period of transition to democracy, its equipment was apparently transferred to Estudios Avila. Estudios Avila was founded by the famous author and member of Congress Rómulo Gallegos, later to pass into the hands of Guillermo Villegas Blanco, founder of Bolívar Films, which has been in existence for more than 50 years and possesses the country's best laboratories.

Taboga y Hacia el calvario was directed by Rafael Rivero, a multi-faceted man, a humorist and writer, who began working in cinema with his brother Anibal. *Taboga y Hacia el calvario* is an extremely simple short film, a sort of "music video" *avant la lettre*. The film opens with Fini Veracoechea leading his friend (Carlos Ascanio) to a film editing room, to show him something he "couldn't imagine." There, on the small screen of the editing table, we see images of Billo's Happy Boys playing "Taboga" (which is the name of an island off Panama), alternating images of the orchestra's musicians and singer with those of the island "paradise." Research into National Laboratories by the contemporary critic José Miguel Acosta has revealed that the island scenes were filmed by Rivero's brother Anibal during the Panamerican Games in 1938.

When the orchestra concludes "Taboga," a worker with a *cuatro* (a four-stringed guitar) begins to play another song, "Hacia el calvario," in a carpentry shop. There, other workers are seen with their tools (hammers, saws, etc.), whose sounds we hear, and then comes the silence of the siesta. The film ends on a gag, when a can falls on the head of one of the sleeping workers.

Compared to other Latin American films of the period, *Taboga y Hacia el calvario* is not exceptional in any way. Its value lies in being a very rare surviving document from the beginnings of Venezuela's sound film history, restored in the early 1990s by the country's national film archive. Rafael Rivero went on to direct one of the country's most important early sound features, *Juan de la calle*, in 1941 (q.v.).

Oscar Lucien

Juan de la calle

Juan the Street Boy
Venezuela, 1941, 105', b+w

Dir Rafael Rivero (1904-1992) *Scr* Rómulo Gallegos *Cinematog* Antonio Bacé Flores *Art dir* Alberto Yunyent *Mus* Prudencio Esáa *Prod* Rómulo Gallegos for Estudios Avila *Act* Raúl Izquierdo, Domingo Hurtado, Luisa Silva, León Bravo

Juan de la calle was an anomalous film in the Venezuela of the 1940s, when national production, slow to become established after the introduction of sound the previous decade, was of the sort to satisfy the tastes associated with the popular foreign films of the day from Mexico, Argentina, and the United States. The delay in producing sound films in Venezuela was due mainly to the cost of equipping cinema theatres, but there were other factors. During the war, raw stock was in short supply, and in Venezuela electricity was rationed. Despite these obstacles, Estudios Avila, which had tentative beginnings in the production of short films, set out to make its first feature, *Juan de la calle*. Raw stock for the project came from another company, Rafael María Zambrano's Cóndor Films. When it was released in late 1941 it became a tremendous hit at home and was the first Venezuelan film to become well known abroad. Its success and the merits of its production, script, and acting gave birth to the dream of a national cinema with international exposure, a dream which went unrealised at the time and has never truly been achieved.

There were two main creative personalities behind the production of *Juan de la calle*, the scriptwriter Rómulo Gallegos and the director Rafael Rivero. Gallegos, a writer and educator who had lost a contest for the presidency of the country in 1941 to Isaías Medina Angarita, was well known for his novels *Doña Bárbara* (which earned him international stature), *Canaima*, and *Cantaclaro; Juan de la calle* was his first film script. Given the state of Venezuelan cinema at the time, the interest of such an author in the medium was remarkable. Rivero was a pioneer of Venezuelan cinema, directing the country's first sound film, *Taboga y Hacia el calvario* (1938, q.v.) after beginning as a camera operator and director of photography. Together, they created one of the enduring classics of Venezuelan cinema. Today, however, only fragments remain. Once believed to have been lost in a fire, some reels have been salvaged. Of eight original reels (of varying length), only the third is complete, with sound and image. Reels 1, 7, and 8 have survived without sound. The soundtracks of reels 5 and 6 have survived and reels 2 and 4 have disappeared completely.

Based on real events, *Juan de la calle* tells the story of a young orphan who enters a world of delinquency. On the advice of friends he gives himself up to police and is sent to a reformatory. Gallegos' script, while revealing a side of life little discussed in Venezuela in the 1940s, was nonetheless moralising and uplifting. The boys benefit from society's outstretched hand in order to regain the proper path in life, a solidarity it may still have been possible to believe in. The script's real merit lies in its engagement with social problems until then ignored by Venezuelan film, and here Gallegos' vocation as an educator is apparent, presenting an ethical vision of a social reality. The film is a sensitive story of the dispossessed, of lost childhood. The film's didacticism and hope prevailed over the tragedy of the lives it depicted. And although in the film good triumphs, Gallegos' script is not optimistic. It presented a social problem in a way that one became profoundly aware of a social reality that was plain to see, even if society preferred not to see it.

Liliana Sáez

La balandra Isabel llegó esta tarde

The "Isabel" Arrived This Afternoon
Venezuela, 1949, 100', b+w

Dir Carlos Hugo Christensen (b. 1916) *Scr* Guillermo Meneses and Aquiles Nazoa *Cinematog* José María Beltrán *Art dir* Ariel Severino *Mus* Eduardo Serrano *Prod* Luis Guillermo Villegas Blanco for Bolívar Films *Act* Arturo de Córdova, Virginia Luque, Juana Sujo, América Barrios, Tomás Henríquez, Juan Corono, Néstor Zavarce

The genesis of *La balandra Isabel llegó esta tarde*, one of the most celebrated Venezuelan films, is sometimes debated by film historians. A brief aside on its producer, Luis Guillermo Villegas Blanco, can shed some light on this genesis. From a young age Villegas Blanco, a restless and entrepreneurial soul, travelled widely, taking on a multitude of jobs and endeavours. At the age of 12 he was a proofreader for a Panamanian newspaper. He managed the artistic careers of his sisters in Venezuela and others in Colombia, Santiago de Chile, Buenos Aires, and Rio de Janeiro. In 1937 he was working in Mexico City as a journalist at the newspaper *El Excelsior*, which sent him to Venezuela to write a feature on the new government of General Eleazar López Contreras, which was giving the country its first taste of democracy after 27 years of dictatorship under General Juan Vicente Gómez. Two years later, in 1939, he had the idea of starting a film production company. He began by making industrial shorts and by travelling the country making documentaries. He founded Bolívar Films in 1940, when he was able to acquire the old equipment once used to film the public acts of the dictator Gómez. Soon afterwards he was able to add to his stock the equipment of Estudios Avila, owned by Rómulo Gallegos, after this producer went bankrupt after making *Juan de la calle* (1941, q.v.). A spirited project of filming the entire country ensued, giving rise to the newsreel series *Noticiario Nacional*, which became the foundation of an extensive exhibition circuit throughout the country. But Villegas Blanco's passion did not stop there: he aspired to produce feature films, and between 1944 and '45 Bolívar Films made its first two such features, *Aventuras de Frijolito y Robustiana*, a film version of a popular radio show, and *Barlovento*.

After a four-year silence, Villegas Blanco undertook the project of developing a real Venezuelan film industry with renewed vigour. He travelled abroad to buy equipment, to learn about new technologies, and to contact technical and artistic personnel. In visits to Mexico and Argentina he was able to hire some of the leading figures of these countries' film industries. Eight features resulted, among them *La balandra Isabel llegó esta tarde*, the second to be made.

La balandra Isabel llegó esta tarde drew together a varied and prestigious cast and crew. The script and dialogue were written by Guillermo Meneses and Aquiles Nazoa, respectively, both accomplished Venezuelan authors. The Argentine Carlos Hugo Christensen was hired to direct, and he arrived accompanied by the Argentines Leopoldo Orzali on sound and Ariel Severino as art director, as well as other members of the cast and crew. Mexico supplied the actors for the principal roles, Arturo de Córdova and Virginia Luque, who were supported by the no-less-well-known Argentine actress Juana Sujo. The cinematography was the work of the Spanish-born José María Beltrán, known in the 1940s as one of the leading figures of the Argentine industry (*La dama duende*, 1945, q.v.). *La balandra Isabel llegó esta tarde* has the distinction of being one of the first Latin American films to win a major European film festival prize, for cinematography at Cannes in 1950.

The film tells the story of a tormented love affair, with a dash of superstition and witchcraft, between Segundo Mendoza (Córdova) and Esperanza (Luque). Segundo, captain of a small freighter named after his wife Isabel, frequently hauls fish from Margarita Island, in the west of the country, to the port of La Guaira on the central coast. Through his travels he encounters the beautiful and bawdy prostitute Esperanza, a cabaret singer in the red-light district of Muchinga in the port, and is taken with her sensuality, her voice, her exoticism—and also by her trickery. The designs of the sorcerer Bocú (Tomás Henríquez) are realised when Segundo, after a half-hearted attempt to retire from his work, returns to La Guaira accompanied by his young son Juan (Néstor Zavarce), making his maiden voyage as his father's cabin boy. Once in port, Segundo disappears for several days on a spree with Esperanza. "La balandra Isabel llegó esta tarde" is what the whores sing when the boat is docked, anticipating a busy night with its crew.

Juan, in despair at the absence of his father, who had promised to return for him, leaves the boat and heads for Muchinga. He arrives at the bar and discovers his father in Esperanza's arms. This confrontation between father and son in the presence of Esperanza is perhaps the most moving scene in the film. "Don't get involved, lady," Juan tells her furiously, "because even though I'm not falling-down drunk I'm still a man." Segundo gives Juan a hard slap, and the boy returns to the ship disillusioned. That night Segundo discovers his lover's betrayal with the sorcerer Bocú. After coming to blows with Bocú and tearing from Esperanza's chest the necklace he once gave her, he returns at dawn to the ship, where it was believed he would never return. Taking the helm, he makes up with his son: peace and harmony reign after being undermined by the port sorcerer.

While the film is marked by a strong sense of the melodramatic, no doubt influenced by Mexican cinema of the day, its most important scenes are handled with great skill and sobriety. The realistic atmosphere of the port and the neighbourhood of Muchinga, the house of the sorcerer, and the bar are given great dramatic force by Beltrán's cinematography, which makes delicate use of chiaroscuro lighting. A stunning example of numerous attempts that were made to develop a film industry in Venezuela, *La balandra Isabel llegó esta tarde* was filmed in Bolívar Films' own studios and on location on Margarita Island and in the miserable port of La Guaira, just outside of Caracas. Despite the recognition it achieved at Cannes and its significant success at home, it failed to consolidate a national film industry. The reasons for this are unclear and present a challenge for future research.

Oscar Lucien

Awards: Best Cinematography, Cannes, 1950.

Araya

Venezuela-France, 1959, 90', b + w

Dir Margot Benacerraf (b.1927) *Scr* Benacerraf, with narration co-written by Pierre Seghers *Narr* José Ignacio Cabrujas (Spanish version, added in 1977); Laurent Terzieff (original French version) *Cinematog* Giuseppe Nisoli *Ed* Pierre Jallaud and Francine Grübert *Mus* Guy Bernard *Prod* Henry Nadler for Caroni Films (Venezuela) and Films de l'Archer (France)

Araya stands not only as a landmark film in Venezuela but is also one of the first major social documentaries in Latin America to anticipate what would eventually become known throughout the 1960s and '70s as the New Latin American Cinema. *Araya* is an epic lyric poem whose documentary-style narrative can be said to derive from Italian neo-realism and the Flaherty documentary tradition; it has been compared with Robert Flaherty's *Man of Aran* (1934), Luchino Visconti's *La terra trema* (1947), and Roberto Rossellini's *India* (1957). Benacerraf has called it "a cinematographic narrative shaped by scripted rather than spontaneous action, a fictionalised documentary if you will, the flip side of the Italian neo-realist style which had enjoyed such prominence." The impressive images, accompanied by a voice-over text written by Benacerraf and Pierre Seghers, depict the lives of three families from the remote and arid peninsula of Araya. The villages of each family form a triangle that covers the peninsula: the Pereda family, nocturnal salt workers, in Manicuare; the Ortiz family, fishermen, in El Rincón; and the Salazar family, who harvest salt by day in Araya. The three narratives woven together show a way of life unchanged since the Spanish conquest. Framed within a twenty-four-hour period, the film shifts between a denunciation of the hardships of salt mine labourers and fishermen, portrayed as living in a closed system without the possibility for change, and a romantic homage to the struggle of "Man against Nature." Evocative images of nature and the trajectory of the sun create a sense of the eternal, while at the same time "marking the hours" toward the encroachment of the modern world, when industry replaces manual labour at the end of the film.

Benacerraf began studying film at the Institut des Hautes Études Cinématographiques (IDHEC) in Paris in 1950. Back in Venezuela, on leave from her studies, she made the visually provocative short film *Reverón* (1952), a subjective portrait of the mysterious world of the well-known Venezuelan painter Armando Reverón, which garnered recognition at the first Berlin film festival in 1953. Benacerraf began production on *Araya* in 1957. Shooting lasted just four weeks and the crew consisted only of herself and her cinematographer, Giuseppe Nisoli, who worked for the Unidad Filmica Shell (part of the international British-based Shell Films). Benacerraf had decided to ship the completed film to a film lab in Paris and was unable to begin to view the footage until mid-1958 (after the fall of the dictator Marcos Pérez Jiménez), when she began the first edit. A partnership was formed with a French-Catalan producer, Belsollel, associated with the Parisian production house Films de L'Archer. An initial three-hour version was submitted to the Cannes film festival in 1959, but the festival pressured her to reduce the length for competition. While the long version was shown to Henri Langlois and Jean Renoir, who, Benacerraf relates, advised her "not to cut a single image," a team of three editors raced to meet the festival deadline. Today Benacerraf laments that the biggest mistake of her life was never to have made a dupe negative of the long cut.

The 1959 Cannes festival, premiering such important work as Marcel Camus' *Orfeu Negro* (Brazil, 1958, q.v), Roberto Rosellini's *India*, François Truffaut's *Les 400 coups*, and Alain Resnais's *Hiroshima, mon amour*, awarded *Araya* the Superior Technical Commission award for both sound and image, and it shared the International Critics' Prize with the Resnais film. Rights to the film sold well, and it was distributed widely, from Canada to China. Ironically, the film sold poorly in Spain and Latin America, the Venezuelan distributors claiming that the Venezuelan public would never understand such an "intellectual" film. Despite these sales and widespread festival exposure, it was not until 1977 that *Araya*, with a Spanish narration read by José Ignacio Cabrujas, was screened publicly in Venezuela. It was rewarded with a rare three-month run in several cinemas, often to packed houses.

For a complex combination of reasons, Benacerraf has not returned to filmmaking, but she has been active in the promotion of film culture in Venezuela. In 1965 she became director of cultural activities for the recently formed National Culture and Fine Arts Institute (INCIBA), and in 1966 she founded the Cinemateca Nacional. Three years later she established the Film School and Workshop Centre, dedicated to the promotion of film and film studies. A now-prominent art theatre was inaugurated in her name in 1987 as recognition of her contributions to Venezuelan film. Today, Benacerraf heads Fundavisual Latina, the Venezuelan arm of the New Latin American Cinema Foundation presided over by Gabriel García Márquez. In 1992 the agency inaugurated the biennial Latin American and Caribbean Short Film and Video Festival in Caracas, a further indication of Benacerraf's continued commitment to promoting Latin America cinema.

Karen Schwartzman

Awards: International Critics' Prize (FIPRESCI) (shared) and Superior Technical Commission Award for sound and image, Cannes, 1959; El Dorado Award, National Academy of Arts and Sciences for Film and Television, Caracas, 1978.

Cuentos para mayores

Tales for Adults
Venezuela, 1963, 100', b+w

Dir Román Chalbaud (b. 1931) *Scr* José Ignacio Cabrujas and Chalbaud *Cinematog* Abigail Rojas *Mus* Raimundo Pereira (in "La historia del hombre bravo"), Chelique Sarabia and Johann Sebastian Bach (in "Los ángeles del ritmo"), and Innocente Carreño (in "La falsa oficina del Supernumerario") *Prod* Continental Films and Avila Films *Act* Manuel Poblete, Messutti, José Antonio Gutiérrez, María García, Irene Inaudi, Josefina Briceño, Héctor Cabrera, Olga Henríquez

By the early 1960s, Venezuela still did not have a film industry. Government support would not come until the 1970s, when the first real infrastructure was established and commercial films first started to be made regularly. Until then, only occasional, often personal films would be made by directors unable to maintain a career. With Margot Benacerraf (*Araya*, 1959, q.v.), Román Chalbaud was the most promising young filmmaker to emerge in the late 1950s. Chalbaud had been a playwright and theatre director since the early 1950s. His first film, *Caín adolescente* (1959), based on his play of the same title, was a neo-realist look at Caracas' burgeoning shantytowns. He was able to make only one more film, *Cuentos para mayores*, in 1963, before returning to the theatre and to television until the mid-1970s, when he became a mainstay of Venezuela's small film industry into the 1990s, filming 15 more features. Most were scripted by José Ignacio Cabrujas and some were based on Chalbaud's own plays. None, however, seemed to fulfil the promise of these first films, which, although flawed in conception and execution, revealed greater aspirations than his later, more commercial work.

The anthology film, made up of several shorts by one or more directors and marketed as a feature, was a common fixture of world cinema in the early 1960s, from the famous examples of *Paris vu par . . .* (France, 1965) and *RoGoPaG* (Italy-France, 1963) in Europe, to films like *Tres veces Ana* (Argentina, 1961, q.v.), *Tres cuentos colombianos* (1962), and *Cinco Vezes Favela* (Brazil, 1962) in Latin America. Anthology films were an ideal way to expose new filmmakers, who perhaps lacked the experience, money, and technical resources to develop feature projects. Even in those films which were by a single director, like *Cuentos para mayores*, they made possible a heterogeneity of styles and themes impossible in a conventional feature.

Cuentos para mayores is made up of three parts. The first, "La historia del hombre bravo" ("The Story of the Angry Man"), recalls Chalbaud's debut with *Caín adolescente:* in a Caracas shantytown, a poor couple are unable to buy medication for their sick daughter (who never appears on screen). Simmering with impotent anger, the man decides to injure himself at the shoe factory where he works in order to get compensation. After thrusting his hand into the machinery, he bursts into the manager's office, bleeding, demanding compensation, and is then seen rushing home, only to discover that his daughter has just died. Exploding with rage, he loads a truck with his few belongings and drives off into the night, oblivious to the fact that his wife is able to join him only by running alongside the truck and jumping onto its running board.

The second part, "Los ángeles del ritmo" ("The Rhythm Angels"), is a tale of a group of young musicians who lead semi-delinquent lives—stealing from the church collection plate, sleeping in an auto junkyard—while attempting to get work as a popular band without the proper instruments. Needing instruments for a gig, two members of the group visit an elderly classical musician and ask to borrow instruments. He obliges them—with a harp, a tympanum, and a *cuatro*, a small four-stringed guitar. The episode ends when the boys are taken away by the police after stopping on the way to their performance to serenade their leader's girlfriend, whose mother has forbidden her to see him. Two members of the group are left in the deserted street with the old man, who exclaims "Only children, madmen and lovers will be saved!," whereupon the boys leave him alone in the street.

The third part, "La falsa oficina del Supernumerario" ("The False Office of the Supernumerary"), is set in the country's Congress, where a clerk is mistaken for a member of congress and is able to place an item on the agenda for debate to oblige his poor new "constituents." Seduced by the bribes, his own fantasies, and a misplaced sense of right, he sets up a thriving business helping the disadvantaged who come to Congress with their petitions and pleas for assistance and reform. When he is inevitably caught out, he flees on a city bus, only to be "recognised" and cheered by the common people on it.

Each "tale," then, presents an ambivalent view of contemporary Caracas and its inhabitants, competently experimenting with different narrative forms, moods, and styles. "La historia del hombre bravo" is the most successful, conveying a directness and sense of authenticity with its simple story that steers clear of sentimentality. Here, though, some of Chalbaud's formal devices, like a swinging light bulb in the couple's shack, are too self-conscious and serve to expose his limited resources. "Los ángeles del ritmo" contains his most extended experiment. When visiting the elderly musician, the boys enter his yard and walk the length of his ranch house in an extended tracking shot, accompanied by seemingly non-diegetic music by Bach. They find the musician out back, standing on a crate and "conducting" chickens on the ground in front of him. When, after talking to the boys for a moment, he descends from his crate and turns to an (until now offscreen) gramophone to stop the music, we realise that it indeed has been diegetic and that the boys have followed it to find him, but we are no less convinced of his eccentricity. Bach's music recurs at the end of the film as he stands in the street and asks the boys "Do you hear it?" before being left alone with his music and reveries. The third episode is the least successful. Meant to be a humorous and ironic look at Caracas' growing ranks of liberal professionals and a sly poke at politicians, it seems contrived and lacks conviction. As a whole, however, the stories work, not quite as "moral tales" (Chalbaud is too ambivalent for us to draw any conclusions) but as modest surveys of the social landscape, marked by generally intelligent and understated formal touches. This sort of personal, even intimate vision would not resurface in the commercial cinema that dominated Venezuelan production in the 1970s and '80s.

Timothy Barnard

Soy un delincuente

I Am a Criminal
Venezuela, 1976, 116', colour

Dir Clemente de la Cerda (1944-1984) *Scr* Luis Correa and de la Cerda, based on the book of the same title by Ramón Antonio Brizuela *Cinematog* José Jiménez *Mus* Miguel Angel Fuster *Prod* Proyecto 13 CA *Act* Félix Zarramera, Manuel Ferreira, María Escalona, Chelo Rodríguez, Emilia Rojas, María Gracía Bianchi, Carlos Alfaro

At the time of his death in 1984, Clemente de la Cerda was one of the most important figures to arise from the boom years of Venezuelan cinema. He began his career in 1964 with *Isla de sal*, which immediately established the focus on the politics of poverty and marginality which would characterise his later work. The political content of his films was considered subversive enough to warrant exclusion from state subsidies; it was only in the mid-70s that he began to receive government funding for his productions. *Soy un delincuente*, his first real commercial success, is a crucial film from the period of major growth in the Venezuelan industry. In fact, *Delincuente* proved to be the most successful domestic film in the history of Venezuelan cinema, outselling such big-budget Hollywood productions as *Jaws* in the year of its release.

As its title would suggest, the film is an exploration of criminality, that of Ramón Antonio, a youth born into the crushing poverty of a Caracas shantytown. His career is followed from his first efforts as a pickpocket (guided by his aunt, who also provides him with an early sexual education), through an adolescence spent as leader of a small gang of petty thieves, to the perhaps inevitable violence toward which his way of life leads. Based on the book of the same title, the film depicts a world determined by sex, drugs, and violence, following Ramón through a childhood that offers no more stability than his stays in prison or reform schools can provide.

The film reveals a complete failure of traditional institutions to offer alternatives to a life of crime. Although his mother objects to Ramón Antonio's way of life, she still accepts the money which that way of life provides: as his career progresses, the family home gradually acquires more and more possessions, culminating in a particularly ironic scene in which the mother tells her rosary in front of the family's new television. Most noticeably, fathers are entirely absent from the film. All of the families which we see revolve around a single mother struggling to raise her children. The male characters in the film are almost exclusively either criminals or police officers. And for all the film's violence, that violence is always carried out by the police.

What makes the film of particular interest, however, is the way in which de la Cerda escapes the temptation to allow *Soy un delincuente* to degenerate into a simple exploitation film. There is a strong but subtle political sense to the film: the ramshackle shantytown in which Ramón Antonio and his gang live is overshadowed by a huge, modern sports complex, thereby heightening the contrast between the richer urban centre and the slums which surround it; even within the Caracas underworld there are strong class divisions which ensure that the clearly mestizo Ramón Antonio will never escape the slums, just as his more middle-class friends will never fully venture into the richer neighbourhoods which they burglarise. De la Cerda never attempts to romanticise the criminal activities of his principal character but chooses instead to document the pressures and difficulties which force youths like Ramón Antonio to survive by any means necessary.

In a sense, *Soy un delincuente* manages to integrate the action film with a neo-realist style. For example, the majority of the cast is made up of non-professional actors taken from the streets in which the film's action takes place, which results in "realistic"—and, in the case of Félix Zarramera (Ramón Antonio)—riveting performances. Chase scenes tend to be shot from a great distance, often with the camera placed across the street from the action: when Ramón Antonio's closest friend is killed by the police, the camera is positioned in a tall building across the street; as a result, the dead youth quickly disappears into the crowds which surround his body. At the same time, voice-overs of radio news reports comment on his death and provide grim statistics for violent crime in the city. The result of this documentary-style distance is to contextualise the death of the character and to do so without romanticism or, surprisingly, cold detachment.

Ironically, the popularity of *Soy un Delincuente* may have inadvertently contributed to the decline in Venezuelan film which occurred later in the 1970s. As John King points out, after 1976 audiences began demanding "more and more 'delincuents' [sic]."[1] More dramatically, the films of 1976–77 were condemned by the reactionary press for their "irreverence, vulgarity and pornography"; this condemnation resulted in the gradual withdrawal of state subsidies to the film industry. Thus, *Soy un delincuente* can be seen as one of the watershed films from Venezuela, an exuberant and disturbing glimpse of Venezuelan street life which would point to the tremendous potential of the industry.

Mitch Parry

1. John King, *Magical Reels: A History of Cinema in Latin America* (London: Verso, 1990), 217.

El pez que fuma

The Smoking Fish
Venezuela, 1977, 115', colour

Dir Román Chalbaud (b. 1931) *Scr* Chalbaud and José Ignacio Cabrujas, from the play of the same title by Chalbaud (1968) *Cinematog* César Bolivar *Ed* Guillermo Carrera *Art dir* Guillermo Sabaleta and Enrique Zanini *Prod* Gente de Cine *Act* Miguel Angel Landa, Orlando Urdaneta, Hilda Vera, Haydée Balza, Arturo Calderón, Carla Luzbell, Rafael Briceño

Román Chalbaud is recognised as the most prominent Venezuelan auteur, who has established an impressive body of work in a number of different media. A self-taught filmmaker, Chalbaud's interest in film stems from his exposure to Mexican cinema of the 1940s—an exposure that has often shaped and defined his work in film, theatre, and television. He began his career in theatre, where he studied under Alberto de Paz y Mateos, a major figure in Venezuelan theatre. In 1953, at the age of twenty-two, Chalbaud staged his first play, *Muros horizontales*, followed two years later by the highly successful *Caín adolescente* (1955). His film career commenced shortly thereafter, with the film version of *Caín adolescente* in 1959 and *Cuentos para mayores* (q.v.) in 1963. Chalbaud turned away from film until 1974 and worked exclusively in theatre and television, devoting much of his energy also to cultural and labour activities.

El pez que fuma is based on Chalbaud's 1968 play of the same title; the title refers to the Caracas bordello in which the action takes place. The brothel is run by "La Garza" (Hilda Vera), who also sings old torch songs at the club, and her lover Dimas (Miguel Angel Landa). Jairo (Orlando Urdaneta), a quiet younger man, comes the brothel looking for work and quickly ingratiates himself to the couple. He begins by cleaning toilets in the club but rapidly moves his way up; at the same time, he cultivates both an apparently close friendship with Dimas and a sexual relationship with La Garza. He also initiates an intimate relationship with one of the women working at El pez que fuma (Haydée Balza).

As Dimas grows to trust Jairo, he begins to include him in various activities outside the club: Jairo is sent to humiliate Dimas' predecessor at the bordello (and as La Garza's lover) in prison; the younger man is also used to run cocaine provided (in a clever subversion of American cinematic clichés) by a U.S. drug dealer. Jairo gradually gains more power and authority at the bordello, eventually turning Dimas in to the police and assuming his position. Dimas is so outraged that he returns to the bar seeking revenge; during the fight which ensues he accidentally shoots La Garza. The film concludes with the funeral of La Garza and a single-shot coda in which Dimas is seen in prison with his predecessor.

Although the film is set in a bordello, Chalbaud's intention is clearly not to titillate. At the beginning of the film, the bartender at the bordello is seen peering at the surrounding neighbourhood through a rooftop telescope; later, a similar perspective is used during one of the club's striptease numbers, in which the dancer is barely visible in the spotlight's circle of light. As a result, the viewer is distanced from the action, which is denied any hint of eroticism in spite of its obviously voyeuristic quality. In fact, *El pez que fuma* is almost completely without erotic content, and on the whole the film emphasizes the sexual exhaustion of the club's inhabitants. Consequently, the film's emphasis falls on the power struggle which develops between the older owners of the club and their younger counterparts—an emphasis which clearly reflects Chalbaud's attitudes toward the political history of contemporary Venezuela.

Although much of Chalbaud's work has been drawn from his stage plays, *El pez que fuma* succeeds in escaping the restrictions of the stage. The film's conclusion is spectacular: when La Garza is shot, we see the incident several times, from various angles and at various speeds, as the tango "Sus ojos se cerraron"—"Her Eyes Closed"—is sung on the soundtrack. Suddenly the film abandons its slightly detached style and enters into a grotesque and stylized depiction of La Garza's funeral, at which sailors, dwarves, and blind men file past the coffin as the prostitutes pray for the deceased. A drunken mourner starts the jukebox and staggers off, stumbling and falling against doors which open to reveal that business at El pez que fuma is continuing as before. In an elaborate tracking shot, Chalbaud follows the drunk around the bar, passing from customer to customer, from dancer to dancer. John King has pointed out the influence of hyperbolic popular music on the films of Chalbaud;[1] during the funeral, it is as though the passionate and excessive tangos and *merengues* which La Garza performs at the club have suddenly taken over the style of the film.

Mitch Parry

Awards: Best Film, Cartagena (Colombia), 1978; Simón Bolívar Prize, Mérida, 1980.

1. John King, *Magical Reels: A History of Cinema in Latin America* (London: Verso, 1990), 220.

El cine soy yo

The Moving Picture Man
Venezuela-France, 1978, 94', colour

Dir Luis Armando Roche *Scr* Roche and Fabrice Helión *Cinematog* Jimmy Glasberg *Ed* Giuliano Ferrioli *Art dir* Manuel Mérido *Mus* Mauricio Reyna *Prod* Chabono Films (Venezuela) and Société Dimage (France) *Act* Azdrubal Melendez, Alvaro Roche, Juliet Berto, Manuel Poblete, Emilia Rojas

Poorly received when first released—"suspense is lacking" was the critic Jacobo Brender's response—and subsequently "lost," Luis Armando Roche's *El cine soy yo* was recently rediscovered in a cache of French pornographic films. That it should reappear in such dubious company is, perhaps, an ironically fitting way for *El cine soy yo* to resurface, given the film's focus on the incongruous and the absurd in the history of Venezuelan cinema.

Azdrubal Melendez plays an underemployed entrepreneur who jumps from job to job—welding, selling group portraits, hawking love potions in the street—in an effort to make a reasonably honest living. While watching a documentary on diamond mining in Venezuela (*La balla del diamante*, by Roche and J.J. Bichier), he decides to bring films to the distant mining villages, since, as he points out, "Movies can't reach those places." Claiming that, "Nowadays, movies have to go to the people," he purchases a truck; after some children tell him the truck looks like a whale, he attaches flukes to it and takes the "Audiovisual Whale" out into the country, stocked with a selection of old films.

Promising "The most beautiful girls, mermaids, sharks, cowboys, earthquakes, wild animals, magic, mystery and love," the Whale is initially welcomed to the small rural villages with great enthusiasm. Along the way Melendez is joined by Manuel (Alvaro Roche), a young orphan who lives on the street and earns his living by shining shoes, and Julietta (Juliet Berto), a French hitch-hiker they meet on a jungle road. Eventually, though, the audiences dwindle away and Manuel and Julietta, unable to cope with the increasing stress, leave Melendez to struggle on his own. Finally, the Whale is repossessed and towed away to the scrap yard.

El cine soy yo—a literal translation would be "I am the cinema"—is a capsule history of Venezuelan cinema, detailing in particular the difficulties encountered in the effort to bring a domestic cinema to rural audiences in the developing world. Initially caught up in the childlike imagination which allows the "Whale" to come into existence, Melendez is finally overcome by the financial difficulties of exhibition as audiences wane and monthly payments on the equipment become harder to make. As the Whale travels through the countryside, the camera concentrates on the omnipresent oil wells, reminders of the industry which made possible government subsidies in support of the Venezuelan film production; by the end of the film, when the Whale is repossessed, the successful towns of the past have been replaced by a ghost town dotted with rusting and abandoned oil wells.

More tellingly, Roche draws much of his satire from the film's reflexive moments. The film constantly reverses the positions of viewer and character: at one point, Melendez and Julietta appear in a two-shot while projecting a Josephine Baker film. "Let's pretend something," Julietta suggests, gesturing toward the camera; "Those are the live people and we are the people inside the screen." When Melendez asks if she likes the film, her response—"Yes, but I don't think the others do"—seems as much a criticism of the film in which she appears as it does a comment on the film she is watching. Later, when the trio encounters a film crew on a beach, "our" camera films the camera filming the romance which the crew is filming. The films which the Whale presents to the people often parallel the action of the film and even include earlier films by Roche.

Ultimately, Roche's vision of Venezuelan film is perhaps best captured by the image of the Whale itself, an image which is given further weight by the minor sub-plot which parallels the main narrative: a whale has become stranded in the Orinoco, having mistaken the river for the sea. Later, Julietta and Manuel stumble upon the rotting corpse of a whale on a beach and are told by a local fisherman that it should have gone "elsewhere to die, in the sea." This sequence is immediately followed by documentary footage, presumably from that night's screening, of a whale being hunted and killed. Roche suggests, then, that Venezuelan cinema is, like the Whale, incongruous and lost, in spite of the optimism of the mid-seventies. Even so, the satire is never bitter: when the whale is finally towed away, Melendez wishes it well, saying, "Goodbye, Friend. I hope you find your sea."

Mitch Parry

Bolívar, Sinfonía Tropical

Bolívar, A Tropical Symphony
Venezuela, 1980, 71', colour, no dialogue

Dir Diego Risquez *Scr* Gastón Barbou and Risquez *Cinematog* José Antonio Pantin *Ed* Ricard Jabardo *Mus* Alejandro Blanco Uribe *Prod* Luisa Mosquera and Producciones Guakamaya *Act* Antonio Eduardo Dagnino, Temístocles López, Lisandro Castro, Nelson Varela, Gilberto Rodríguez Berleche, Luis Alejandro González, Carlos Castillo, María Elena Roque, María Adelina Véra, Hugo Márquez, Diego Risquez

Orinoko, Nuevo Mundo

Orinoko, New World
Venezuela, 1984, 103', colour, no dialogue

Dir Diego Risquez *Scr* Luis Angel Duque and Risquez *Cinematog* Marietta Pérez, Andrés Agusti *Ed* Leonardo Henríquez *Mus* Alejandro Blanco Uribe *Prod* Blanco Baldó and Producciones Guakamaya *Act* Kosinegue, Rolando Peña, Hugo Márquez, Alejandro Alcega, Nelson Varela, Diego Risquez

Amerika, Terra Incógnita

Amerika, Unknown Land
Venezuela-France, 1988, 90', colour, no dialogue

Dir Diego Risquez *Scr* Luis Angel Duque and Risquez *Cinematog* Andrés Agusti *Art dir* Oscar Armitano and Nelson Varela *Ed* Leonardo Henríquez *Mus and Sound* Alejandro Blanco Uribe *Prod* Andrea Radonski and Producciones Guakamaya *Act* Alberto Martín, María Luisa Mosquera, Hugo Márquez, Luis Mariano Trujillo, John Phelps, Amapola Risquez, Blanco Baldó, Diego Risquez

Between 1930 and 1975, film production in Venezuela averaged two per year; from 1975 to 1977, that average leapt to eighteen per year, and dropped again to half that in 1978. This rapid and dramatic increase in the production of commercial films in Venezuela during the 1970s encouraged the establishment of a counter-cinema and allowed a remarkable movement of independent filmmakers working in Super-8 to offer their own, more radical contributions to Venezuelan cinema. Spearheaded by Julio Neri and Mercedes Márquez, these filmmakers adopted the format most commonly used for home movies, and developed a vibrant cinema made up of documentaries, experimental films, and shorts. Such was the quality of the resulting productions that Neri and Márquez organised an International Festival of Super-8 Avant-Garde Cinema in 1976; around the same time, Neri produced his first Super-8 feature, *Once Upon a Time in Venezuela*. Subsequent small-format films by Neri were blown up to 35mm in order to facilitate distribution.

In 1980 Diego Risquez, encouraged by the success of Neri's features, released *Bolívar, Sinfonía Tropical*, in Super-8, to considerable acclaim. For Risquez, the film "represents the poetic alternative to Venezuelan cinema," in which "the painter's brush has been replaced by the movie camera." *Bolívar* was followed in 1984 by *Orinoko, Nuevo Mundo*, also shot in Super-8 but blown up to 35mm, and by *Amerika, Terra Incógnita*, a Venezuelan/French co-production shot in the larger format; together the films form a trilogy of the New World. What makes this trilogy particularly striking is the ability of the films to recount and revise Venezuelan history without the use of dialogue and with only a musical score to provide sound effects. As a result, the films rely on stunningly rich and complex visual images reminiscent of the silent era—tableaux, highly expressive cinematography, densely allegorical mise-en-scène. If one were to compare these highly original films with the work of another director, it would have to be Hungarian filmmaker Miklós Jancsó. In a sense, the trilogy stands less as a retelling of the history of Venezuela and more as a "corrected" version of that history.

Bolívar begins with what serves as the unifying image of the trilogy: a conquistador emerges from the waves and claims the Venezuelan beach for Spain. Almost immediately the film leaps ahead to Simón Bolívar and the War of Independence in 1810, telling the story of this conflict in a series of highly stylized and symbolic images: following the decision to go to war, the conquistador wraps himself in black, concealing his face, and is transformed into a representation of Spanish rule. The war itself is presented in slow motion as the Venezuelan soldiers race through an abandoned building, waving their swords; eventually they launch a charge against the solitary figure in black, who is finally brought to his knees. Bolívar is portrayed by two actors: according to Risquez, "one represents a Bolívar known through text books, a superhero, an emperor in Napoleon's era; the other is the romantic warrior, the revolutionary, the lover, the man." The problems arising from the conflict between these two representations are dramatised as each pushes the other out of the frame. In an incredible shot near the end of the film, they coalesce into the painted image of Bolívar, which appears between the two actors, thus emerging as a synthesis produced by the dialectic between the other two.

Orinoko presents itself as a false anthropological documentary covering a 300-year period in the history of Venezuela. The film opens with the shaman Yanomami, who predicts the impending arrival of the Europeans; the appearance of Columbus at the Orinoco Delta in 1498 leads to a journey up the Orinoco and into the heart of the country. Along the way various characters from South American mythology emerge to warn the explorers that they are approaching the source of the river—the woman América, who gives birth to the Orinoco. Paralleling this mythical journey is the struggle between the competing forces which drive the process of European "exploration": Sir Walter Raleigh wishes to exploit the river in his search for Manoa y El Dorado; the German naturalist Alexander von Humboldt wishes to exploit the scientific possibilities which the Orinoco offers. In a sense, then, the river becomes the main character of the film and can perhaps be seen as the most dominant force of resistance to colonialism.

Amerika narrows the narrative focus to a single incident (the forced transportation of a Venezuelan native to the Spanish court), which serves as a metaphor for the entire process of colonisation practised by Europe in South America. In Spain, Amerika—here, a male character (Alberto Martín)—is presented as a curiosity, an exotic decoration to the court. Every effort he makes to define himself is thwarted by the members of the court, since his identity is determined by the desires of the Spanish. At the same time, the Princess (María Luisa Mosquera) falls in love with Amerika; as a result of their affair the Princess gives birth to a golden child. Throughout the film, which was filmed on a much larger budget than were its two predecessors, Risquez relies on stunningly sumptuous set design and elaborate camera movement. The film also presents highly stylized filmic parodies of various paintings by Velázquez (played by Risquez), including his most famous work, *Las Maninas*.

Risquez is most interested in providing the history of conquest and colonisation through the eyes of the people and mythical figures of Venezuela. Acknowledging the country's heterogeneity, a visual "chorus" of three characters representing "The Three Races" of Venezuela (native, black, and white European) rushes through the background of a number of shots in *Bolívar*, offering a more diverse view of the country's history than does that provided by the colonisers. It is, therefore, appropriate that the trilogy emphasizes the conflict between the Spanish and the people of Venezuela, since such an emphasis draws attention to South America's 500 years of resistance rather than to the continent's 500 years of victimisation.

Since the completion of the trilogy, Risquez has gone on to other, less politically charged, films. In 1994 he released *Karibe Kon Tempo*, a 35mm narrative film with sound; the result is considerably less intriguing than his earlier films, although it does manage to retain some of the stylistic achievements of the trilogy.

Mitch Parry

Macu, la mujer del policía

Macu, the Policeman's Wife
Venezuela, 1988, 90', colour

Dir Solveig Hoogesteijn *Scr* Hoogesteijn and Milagros Rodríguez *Cinematog* Andrés Agusti *Ed* José Alcalde *Art dir* Rubén Siso *Mus* Victor Cuica *Prod* Macu Films, C.A. and Cinearte, C. A. *Act* Daniel Alvarado, María Luisa Mosquera, Frank Hernández, Tito Aponte, Ana Castell

Solveig Hoogesteijn was born in Sweden and at the age of one emigrated with her family to Venezuela. She was educated in Caracas, graduating from the Central University in the late 1960s where she studied philosophy and literature. Continuing her studies in Germany, she enroled in the Munich School of Film and Television in 1970, during the height of the New German Cinema. In 1975, Hoogesteijn completed her thesis film, *Puerto Colombia*, a one hour documentary set in a small fishing village. A fascination with place and culture is demonstrated in the film. Throughout Hoogesteijn's oeuvre, rather than a particular theme or issue, the works are united through narrative and narrative structure as works of discovery—a discovery of identity, history, and memory, at both the individual and national levels, where the juxtaposition, or interpenetration, of "First" and "Third World" cultures is foregrounded. All the films embody a circular narrative structure, in contrast to a more conventional linear narrative, where the device of the "frame" or "flashback" is employed to create what Hoogesteijn calls "time as a round thing," intimating fluidity and movement but also a return. Her next film, *El mar del tiempo perdido* (1977), is based on the Gabriel García Márquez short story of the same title. The film was awarded Second Prize at the Havana film festival in 1981. Here, along with an exploration of culture, questions of national and pan-Latin American identities are raised, and fiction becomes "truer" than documentary. *Manoa* (1980) is Hoogesteijn's "road-movie" which follows the journey of two young men who travel through Venezuela. To the previously noted questions of culture and identity is added a third motif—history—in this journey through geography and time where the boys discover their collective and personal histories. The film represented Venezuela in the "Quinzaine des réalisateurs" at the Cannes film festival in 1980. In *Macu, la mujer del policía*, a preoccupation with women's issues is dealt with directly for the first time, and questions of gender and cultural constructs are at issue.

On initial viewing, the film appears to be typical of the police action genre. It narrates the story of Ismael, a police officer accused of murdering three teenage boys, one of whom was the lover of his wife, Macu. The story is based on a real event; there was even a documentary film made which the government censored at the time (Luis Correa's *Ledezma, el caso mamera*, 1982). The crime functions as a structural device for retargeting the "investigation" onto the cultural attitudes and structures of the country. As the events leading up to the crime and subsequent murder conviction one year later are revealed, so, too, are events in Macu's past via a complex formal strategy that juxtaposes a chronological narrative with a second non-linear narrative line. This construction serves to reveal more than just the assumed "primary" plot of the murder investigation and sets up an oppositional narrative within the film. We learn that Ismael was Macu's mother's lover, and that Macu was married to Ismael at the tender age of eleven. The stories of Macu and Ismael are interdependent, dialectical even, evidencing that both the male and the female share responsibility for the construction of gendered roles and identities. Furthermore, the film is concerned with images and moments of transition, suggesting a focus on the emergence and transformation of the subject. In this way, the film "gives birth," as it were, to a female subject and subjectivity by situating women as mutual participants, both subjects of and objects of a woman-to-woman discourse (via both semiotic and symbolic positionings), expanding the boundaries (if not breaking them, at least disrupting them) of History. It is Macu's story, the cinematic representation of the not-"real life" story (in contrast to the story of Ismael, based on the celebrated case) that remains, lingers in the memory, and that we identify with, locate, and experience as "real." The emphasis is on the telling of the untold, "forgotten" history of women's experience.

Production began in 1986 on a budget of approximately $70,000, the last low-cost film made before the continuing fall in the value of the currency brought film production in Venezuela to a near-halt. The euphoria of the so-called Saudi Venezuela of the 1970s ended with the sudden overnight devaluation of the Venezuelan currency on "Black Friday," February 18, 1983. During the second half of the 1970s, Venezuela, along with the rest of Latin America, amassed a huge foreign debt despite its oil revenues, and as a result, the economy went into a recession. Nevertheless, it was not immediately felt in the film industry, and in fact, feature film production peaked during 1984-85. The commercial success of some of these films fuelled a certain optimism within the film community during these years, but the economic realities finally prevailed and government subsidies to film had almost ceased by the late 1980s. *Macu* is on record as the most successful film at the Venezuelan box office in the year of its release, surpassing domestic records for *Rambo*, *Superman*, and *E.T., The Extra-Terrestrial*. Interestingly, the film became an issue at the time of its release and generated much discussion, and even a certain "audience participation" was achieved as Macu's "guilt" was argued. A commercial film that subverts the codes of its police-action genre and yet remains within the principal Venezuelan genre as a film of social denunciation, *Macu* successfully straddles the line between commercial and non-commercial cinema—today a divisive issue within the film community as national cinema is obligated to demonstrate its commercial viability in order to justify economic support from both government and private sectors. In late 1993 a National Film Law was finally enacted after a fight of 26 years; Hoogesteijn, then President of the National Film Directors Association (ANAC), was instrumental in lobbying this bill. At the writing of this entry, late 1994, Hoogesteijn had just finished shooting her new film, *Santera*.

Karen Schwartzman

Awards: Best Film and Best Actor (Daniel Alvarado), Consejo Municipal de Caracas, 1987; Best Actor (Alvarado) Premio ANAC, 1987; Best Film, San Antonio, Texas, 1988.

Jericó

Venezuela, 1991, 90', colour

Dir Luis Alberto Lamata (b. 1959) *Scr* Lamata *Cinematog* Andrés Agusti *Ed* Mario Nazoa *Sound* Nazoa *Art dir* Aureliano Alfonso *Mus* Federico Gaitorno *Prod* Thalia Producciones and Fondo de Fomento Cinematográfico de Venezuela (FONCINE) *Act* Cosme Cortázar, Francis Rueda, Doris Diaz, Alexander Milic, Luis Pardi, Yajaira Salazar, Amilcar Marcano, Wilfredo Cisneros, Luis Alberto de Mozos, Fanny Diaz

Made between 1988 and '90 with non-professional actors on a very low budget, *Jericó* is perhaps the most successful product of Venezuela's state film agency FONCINE (Venezuelan Film Production Fund). Released on the eve of the quincentenary of Columbus' "discovery" of the "New World," *Jericó* provides a powerful corrective to traditional Eurocentric notions of conquest, colonisation, and discovery by objectively observing a priest's transformation in captivity by native South Americans.

Born in Caracas, Luis Alberto Lamata studied history in university before becoming a director for Venezuelan television. He directed two prize-winning short films and then embarked on his ambitious first feature, *Jericó*. Lamata clearly did a great deal of research into indigenous histories, languages, and cultures before making his film, which interestingly switches perspectives in midstream and attempts to immerse the audience in culture shock of a different kind. In the early sixteenth century, Santiago, a Franciscan friar, arrives in South America with a group of conquistadors in order to bring God to the Indians. Almost immediately, he witnesses his companions' brutality and then tries to comfort an imprisoned native who has put his own eyes out. With blood on his robe, Santiago prays as he wanders towards a village, only to be overtaken by a bloodthirsty motley crew. He then joins an expeditionary force transporting gold, only to find that they are worse types than the others, resorting even to cannibalism (after their victim has been shown to catch a lizard as his prey). Following a battle, Santiago appears to be the only Spanish survivor. He is captured and involuntarily involved in a coca ceremony. Intoxicated, he strips and joins in a dance. Later, he shaves his beard and hair and marries a woman who bears his child. When a neighbouring tribe attacks the village, Santiago flees with his family. But he is captured by the Spanish and incarcerated in an isolated hut. When they realise his true identity—initially believing him to be indigenous, of course—they wait for him to tell them the whereabouts of the gold. But climbing up to the small window in the roof of his prison, he just laughs, like a madman.

During the period of his captivity, we, the film audience, have to struggle along with Santiago to understand the indigenous language, since no subtitles are provided. Lamata's decision enabled him to create one of the most remarkable extended passages of cinematic ethnography, where behaviour and customs have to be intuited without the aid of written or verbal interpretation. Indeed, *Jericó* is probably the most succesful fiction feature film made on the "New World" experience of first contact between Europeans and Native Americans—it is certainly the best of those made during the Columbus quincentenary "celebration." Disregarding the mainstream Hollywood epic, *Christopher Columbus: The Discovery* (1992) and Ridley Scott's slightly more revisionist *1492: The Conquest of Paradise* (1992), there are two other films of note. While it displays a similar degree of intensive research and strikingly original action and mise-en-scène, Nicholás Echeverría's *Cabeza de vaca* (Mexico, 1990) is stuck in exoticism and fails to really humanise the indigenous people. But, the Mexican film is far more palatable than the celebrated Canadian-Australian co-production, *Black Robe* (1991), which, unfortunately, won the Academy of Canadian Cinema's Best Film "Genie." Bruce Beresford's film on Jesuit missionaries in Québec demonises the Iroquois (Mohawks) in contrast to the peace-loving Huron who have been converted to Christianity. Lamata correctly avoided the neo-colonial pitfalls of *Black Robe*, which was based on Brian Moore's (perhaps racist) culturally appropriating novel by going to new and revisionist historical sources.

Peter Rist

Awards: Best Film and Best Director, Mérida, 1991; Best First Film, Biarritz, 1991.

Table of Films

Argentina

Bolivia

Brazil

Chile

Colombia

Ecuador

Paraguay

Peru

Uruguay

Venezuela

Original-language Film Title Index

English-language Film Title Index

337

Film Directors Index

Contributors Index

343

Name and Title Index

Names and titles in the technical credits and Awards sections of each entry are not indexed: these are indexed only when discussed in the main text of an entry. In this way many actors and technical personnel may be found to have been involved in more films than might be suggested by the following index. Although not distinguished in the index, other references may indicate only that a name or title has been mentioned.

Subject Index:
South American Cinema

Subject Index:
South American Society

Glossary of Brazilian (Portuguese or African) Terms

Terms in upper case are defined elsewhere in the glossary.

afoxé Highly rhythmic musical style and musical group from Bahia with strong African derivation and close ties to CANDOMBLÉ religion.

babalão CANDOMBLÉ priest; also called *pai de santo*.

Banto or **Bantu** Name for people of Southern African descent (e.g., Angola) and of their language group, who dominated the Palmares nation, but who were mistakenly believed to be the only African slaves in Brazil.

Barravento Tempest or turning wind. The title of a film by Glauber Rocha which, in his words, is "the moment of violence, when things of the earth and sky transform themselves, wherein sudden changes intervene in love, in life and in the social world."

beatos Portuguese word meaning "blessed," but mostly used to denote those who followed mystical, syncretic religious leaders in Brazil's northeast.

Bossa Nova Form of jazz that mixes North American and Brazilian musical influences.

bumba-meu-boi Carnivalesque dance/procession and musical form; traditionally the most important festival in Maranhão state.

caatinga Scrub vegetation, typical of the northeastern SERTÃO.

candomblé African word for a dance in honour of the gods, and the most orthodox of the religions brought to Brazil from Africa (by the Nago, Yoruba and Jeje peoples). A general term for Afro-Brazilian religions in Bahia.

cangaceiro Legendary bandits of the SERTÃO, who tended to rob from the rich and were often folk heros.

cangaço Social banditry of the NORDESTE; a gang of CANGACEIROS. Also a Brazilian film genre.

capoeira Martial art/dance developed by slaves in Bahia and performed to the rhythms of the *berimbau* stringed instrument.

carioca A person from Rio de Janeiro.

carnaval Carnival. A pre-Lenten celebration and the most important festival throughout Brazil.

conscientização Consciousness-raising. A concept developed by Brazilian anthropologist Paulo Friere in *Pedagogy of the Oppressed* in the 1960s.

cordel (literatura de) Popular literature in verse form from the northeast which is often sold in a pamphlet attached to a cord (hence, *cordel*).

Coronel   Colonel. Also any powerful man in Brazil, especially a rural landowner who typically controls the local political, judicial, and police systems.

favela   Slum or shantytown, especially on the hillsides of Rio de Janeiro.

favelado   Slum-dweller.

feijoada   National dish of Brazil: meat (usually pork) with rice, black beans, oranges, peppers, *farinha.* . . .

forró   Music of the northeast, combining Brazilian frontier and Mexican accordion-based influences.

frevo   Popular musical form from Pernambuco state.

futebol   Soccer. A sport so popular there was fear of revolt in the 1970s if the national team didn't win the World Cup.

Ganga Zumba or **Ganga-Zumba**   The "Great Lord" (in BANTU), the elected ruler of Palmares who lived in the capital, the royal enclave, Macoco.

gaúcho   Cowboy, originally from the state of Rio Grande do Sul (in the south of Brazil).

jagunço   Hired killer of the *NORDESTE.*

jangada   Small fishing boat with sail, usually with balsa wood hull, and built by the (northeastern) fishermen themselves.

jangadeiro   A *JANGADA* fisherman.

latifundista   Oligarchical landowning class.

lixo   Garbage.

macumba   Voodoo. A general word for an African-derived religious ceremony and percussion ensemble.

malandro   Urban vagabond, scoundrel or bandit. Originally *malandro do morro*, or scoundrel from the hills, a popular figure in Rio de Janeiro's mythology.

mestiço, mestiça   Person of mixed Amerindian and European ancestry.

mulato, mulata   Mulatto. A person of mixed African and European ancestry.

Nordeste   Brazil's northeast, a region of essentially Brazilian history and culture. Also a Brazilian film genre.

Ogun   A *CANDOMBLÉ orixá* (god, or patron saint) of war.

Oxumaré   A *CANDOMBLÉ* bisexual *orixá* (god) who is male for six months of the year and female for the other six. Associated with the river or the rainbow.

paulistano   Inhabitant of the city of São Paulo (a resident of the state is a *paulista*).

pivete   Child of the street; also a young delinquent.

povo   People. Also the common people, and a crowd of people.

quilombo   Community or village of runaway (escaped) slaves, the most famous of which was the Republic of Palmares in the seventeenth century.

samba   Quintessential Brazilian musical form, first performed at the 1917 Rio carnaval. A rhythm derived initially from Angola.

sambinha   A *SAMBA* musician or singer.

sertanejo   Inhabitant of the *SERTÃO.*

sertão   Backlands. The legendary, inhospitable, drought-stricken region of the northeast, also characterised by flash-floods and *CAATINGA* vegetation.

terreiro   A *CANDOMBLÉ* shrine, or place of worship.

umbandista   Practitioner of *umbanda*, a syncretic Rio-based religion combining African and spiritist elements.

vaqueiro   Cowboy of the *NORDESTE.*

Glossary of Film Terms

Terms in upper case are defined elsewhere in the glossary.

acetate "safety" stock RAW film STOCK with a cellulose acetate base which was the adopted replacement for highly inflammable NITRATE stock.

actuality The original term used for non-fiction film before "DOCUMENTARY film." Derived from the French term *actualité*, used by the Lumière brothers for their first films, which were comprised of un-edited OBSERVATIONAL shots of un-staged action.

aerial view Filmed from an aircraft, or giving the impression of being filmed from an airborne vehicle; a very high CAMERA POSITION and ANGLE.

agit-prop (film) Short for "agitational propaganda." Originally used in the Soviet Union for rhetorical political films wherein art and form are obedient to "social command" and immediate utility.

anthology film A FEATURE-LENGTH film which combines a number of short or medium-length episodes, usually directed by different people, and usually made around a common theme; also called "episode films." Especially popular in the 1950s and 60s in Italy and France and in Latin America.

archival footage Exposed and processed film, usually DOCUMENTARY, which is leased or bought from a film archive or stock footage company for use in another film, or television program. Also known as "stock footage," although it is assumed that "archival" material is readily identifiable, whereas "stock footage" may not be.

art cinema Film theatre (cinema), also called "art house cinema," which specialises in showing non-commercial, or foreign films, where the audience interest is in film as art rather than film as entertainment—hence, "art cinema" films. Came into prominence in the 1960s.

art director The person ultimately responsible for every aspect of film decor and set construction. On larger productions s/he could be called "production designer." In the studio era, the art director headed up a sizable production unit, including "set decorators," "scenic artists," "construction manager," and "property buyer."

auteur French word, now in common use, for "author," from the *politique des auteurs* ("authorship approach") developed by the critics of *Cahiers du Cinéma* in the 1950s which argued for the film director as principal "author" of a film, but can be applied to another individual whose personality most informs the finished film. Can also be used to distinguish "auteur" filmmakers from "less personal" *metteurs-en-scène* (see MISE-EN-SCÈNE). **Auteurist** refers both to followers of such an "auteur theory" and directors who strive to stamp their own personality on their work.

375

avant-garde cinema Unorthodox, EXPERIMENTAL films or ground-breaking film movements, e.g., French IMPRESSIONIST and SURREALIST avant-garde films of the 1920s. Work which constitutes a marked departure from convention, especially narrative form.

B-movie Originally, second-level Hollywood studio production in the 1940s, or films made by one of the smaller companies—e.g., Republic, PRC, Eagle-Lion—but which later came to be applied to all inexpensive films—e.g., "programmers" made by the Hollywood "majors" in the early 1930s—and sometimes used derisively.

blockbuster (production) Major studio film made on a very high budget, which is a huge success at the box office, and which is usually exhibited simultaneously in a number of large cinemas in key locales on its first run.

boom mike Microphone mounted on the end of a moveable pole (boom) above the subject being filmed, either carried by an operator (boom "man") or attached to the camera "dolly" (or CRANE).

Brechtian (distanciation) From Bertolt Brecht, German-born playwright, poet, screenwriter, and theorist of the theatre, whose ideas on "alienation effects" have profoundly influenced filmmaking and criticism, especially in the late 1960s and '70s. Distanciation is a politicised form of "defamiliarisation" or "making strange" where a work of art simultaneously reveals its own processes of production and those of society. More generally, in Brecht's "epic theatre," the spectator is intended to be active rather than passive and to remain outside of the drama rather than be emotionally tied to character, hence, made somewhat distanced from the work in order to be able to think through elements of form and content.

camera angle The angle of the camera's viewing axis in relation to the scene being viewed, usually in the vertical plane—see HIGH, LOW, and VERTICAL ANGLE—but also "oblique angle," where the camera is not level—one side being lower than the other, causing the effect of a "canted frame."

camera movement Where the camera moves about its own axes—PANNING or TILTING—or where it moves along the ground—TRACKING—or through the air—CRANING.

camera operator ("cameraman") Person on the film crew who actually operates the camera, and who normally works under the DIRECTOR OF PHOTOGRAPHY ("cinematographer").

camera position The height of the camera above the ground; thus a "low-position" camera is one which is close to the ground.

chanchada Most common popular Brazilian film genre, of musical comedy. Perhaps derived from *pachouada*, a word denoting incoherent speech, and thought to refer initially to comedy in very poor taste, but which has since come to be used as a general term for any Brazilian film comedy and musical.

choreography Direction of individual and group movement, especially dancing, for the camera. The **choreographer** plays an important role in many films, especially Brazilian, and not just musicals.

ciné club French. A group of cinéphiles who gather, often informally, to watch and discuss films, especially those unavailable through commercial DISTRIBUTION and EXHIBITION circuits.

cine publicitario Spanish. Filmed advertising, i.e., commercials, filmed in 35MM and intended principally or solely for EXHIBITION in cinemas before the FEATURE film. As such, an important training ground, and source of steady income, for many Latin American filmmakers.

Cinema Marginal Offshoot of Brazilian CINEMA NÔVO in the late 1960s; an even more independent and "marginal" movement than its predecessor, aggressively anarchistic, almost an "anti-cinema" movement.

Cinema Nôvo "New Cinema" in Portuguese. The most important Brazilian film movement, begun in the early 1960s, initially consisting of young filmmakers who wished to create a distinctive, truly Brazilian film production outside of a studio system, and independent of government restrictions and strategies.

cinéma vérité "Film truth" in French. Derived from Dziga Vertov's *Kino-Pravda*, DOCUMENTARY film series in the Soviet Union of the 1920s, wherein it was important that the film audience realised it was watching a film, not reality. The term was coined by Jean Rouch and Edgar Morin while making *Chronique d'un été* (1961) with newly developed, portable cameras and Nagra sound recorders. In this film interview subjects get to watch and comment on footage of themselves. The term also implies that the filmmakers try to avoid manipulating documentary truth, but it has often been confused with DIRECT CINEMA which is a movement which emphasized "objectivity" over the REFLEXIVITY of *cinéma vérité*. The term "verité" (sic) is used in Hollywood to denote a style of shooting to achieve the effects of veracity and immediacy—jerky, hand-held camera and GRAINY out-of-focus texture.

cinematic Of the cinema. Often used in the context of an element being typical of cinema rather than of one of the other arts, e.g., EDITING and the moving camera can be considered to be especially "cinematic" devices.

cinématographe The first operational film projector (which was also a camera), designed and built by the Lumière brothers in France in 1894, and first used as a projector in 1895.

cinematography A general term for the shooting of film in a "motion picture" film camera and/or its laboratory processing; time-based photography. Often incorrectly called "photography."

city symphony Type of DOCUMENTARY film using a day (and night) in the life of a city as a structuring device, where often shots depicting one aspect of city life—e.g., work on a factory production line—are grouped together in clusters—"categorical form," in David Bordwell and Kristin Thompson's terms. These films are often patterned on Walter Ruttmann's *Berlin—Die Symphonie einer Grosstadt* (Germany, 1927) but the genre is likely to have begun in France with Alberto Cavalcanti's *Rien que les heures* (1926).

classical (film) Term which is used far too loosely in reference to almost any type of film which has been established over a period of time, but which was most importantly used by André Bazin to refer to a refined American style of filmmaking employing "continuity editing" in the 1930s and '40s: **"Classical Hollywood Cinema."** This usage has most effectively been pursued by Bordwell and Thompson in a number of books and articles.

close shot, close framing A shot where the camera is close to the subject, but not necessarily a CLOSE-UP; usually somewhere between a MEDIUM SHOT and a close-up in scale.

close-up A shot in which the film FRAME shows only a detail of a person or object, usually the head and shoulders of a person.

collage Major technique in twentieth century art, first attributed to Pablo Picasso in the early 1910s and taken up by the European art movements Cubism, Futurism, Dada, and SURREALISM, it involves inserting into the art work extraneous and often "found" elements. Prefiguring its later use by filmmakers, the German artist John Heartfield used it in the late 1920s and early '30s to create social commentary through juxtapositions of photographic images. In cinema, the technique, surprisingly, only began to appear in U.S. EXPERIMENTAL circles, being first used by Joseph Cornell in the 1930s and '40s and later, most notably, by Stan Brakhage and Bruce Conner in the 1950s. In FEATURE filmmaking, Fernando Solanas in Argentina in the 1960s and Dušan Makavejev in Yugoslavia in the 1970s used FOUND FOOTAGE of various sorts which suggested associations with the films' other images. A certain "collage aesthetic," wherein radical formal juxtapositions and NON-DIEGETIC images INTERCUT with the narrative are employed, was more widespread, becoming quite common in the European AUTEUR cinema of the 1960s. In this sense "collage" in film can be understood in a broad sense as the juxtaposition of highly incongruous elements or the insertion of NON-DIEGETIC images.

comedia ranchera Spanish term for the most popular Mexican film genre of the 1930s and '40s: musicals with comedy which use a rural (often ranch) setting.

composition The visual arrangement of people or objects in the film shot or FRAME, as **compositional style**, e.g., "deep-focus composition." The term "composition" is less often used as a film term in the context of narrative—arrangement of story elements—or music.

continuity Mostly used in the context of narrative, where a smooth progression of time or action, or a continuance of detail—costumes, decor, colour—must be maintained from shot-to-shot or scene-to-scene. Hence "continuity editing" and "continuity person" (formerly "script girl"), who maintains continuity on the film set.

costumbrista Spanish. From *costumbre*, or habit; sometimes mistakenly rendered as "costumbrist" in English, which means nothing—"mannered" would be a better single-word definition. A cultural term referring to work which depicts the daily lives of people through comedy, romance, and music, while social and political problems and comment are avoided. In film, a genre common during the CLASSICAL sound period of the 1930s, '40s, and '50s, standing in contrast to the era's WHITE TELEPHONE films and MELODRAMAS and with which audiences of the day strongly identified because of the sympathetic depiction of common people and their popular culture.

crane up, down A CAMERA MOVEMENT where the camera moves through the air; usually achieved by having the camera mounted on a crane device, but could also be done, say, from an elevator or helicopter. A **crane shot** is one using a crane, or giving the effect of same.

credits Titles which appear at the beginning or end of a film (or both), listing the cast and crew.

cross-cut An "edit" from a shot in one location to a shot in another. Usually it is assumed that the action is occurring simultaneously (see PARALLEL MONTAGE) but not always. The device is known as **cross-cutting** and was developed in the early years of the century, especially in the context of a chase to the rescue.

cut, cutting A break in the film, usually intentional. An abrupt transition from one shot to another (also an "edit"), so-called because the process involves the use of scissors or a knife blade to "cut" the celluloid FILM STOCK.

cut-away An isolated shot, which is related in some way to the previous shot, but which is not usually in the same space or time frame.

cut on action A CUT from one shot to another which is made while something is moving in the FRAME, usually in the interests of smoothness or invisibility—to hide the cut—but sometimes done to increase the dynamism of the action, and on rare occasions to deliberately disorient the spectator.

cutting copy (also a "work print") A working copy of the film for the purposes of EDITING—when a final version is complete the original negative footage is edited to match and a new copy is made.

découpage French term, untranslatable into English, for an EDITING "plan" of a (sometimes finished) film which is like a visual version of a "screenplay," but not necessarily a "storyboard" or "shooting script" because these can't include a precise conception of movement within and between shots. Most notably used by film theorist Noël Burch and director Robert Bresson.

deep focus (cinematography) Where both immediate foreground and far background of a shot are sharply defined, achieved through a combination of choice of camera lens (WIDE ANGLE, short focal length), lighting (high intensity), aperture (wider, higher f-stop) and FILM STOCK (fast). Incorrectly thought to be introduced to Hollywood by Orson Welles and Gregg Toland with *Citizen Kane* in 1941, but occurred intermittently in American film much earlier, e.g., in the Sam Goldwyn production *Bulldog Drummond* (1929). Not to be confused with "staging in depth," or "deep space" MISE-EN-SCÈNE, where the intention to film in deep focus is not necessarily achieved, e.g., Jean Renoir's *La Grande Illusion* (France, 1937).

depth of field Range of distances from the camera lens which is in sharp focus, e.g., 10-20 ft. For an individual lens, the depth of field can be varied by changing the f-stop of the aperture and the distance at which it is focused.

detail (shot) Most often a CLOSE-UP of an inanimate object, but can also isolate a part of a person or animal for attention.

diegesis A term used in narrative film for the space and time (the world) of the story, both on and OFF SCREEN, and including events that are only inferred by the film spectator (never actually seen or heard), i.e., not just the "plot." Originally a Greek word for "recounted story."

direct address Where a person, either a fictional character or a DOCUMENTARY subject looks directly at, or speaks directly to the camera.

direct cinema An American DOCUMENTARY film movement in the late 1950s and early '60s where an attempt was made to record life objectively and directly, taking advantage of newly developed lightweight filmmaking equipment. The Québécois *cinéma direct* was similar but somewhat closer to the more REFLEXIVE French *CINÉMA VÉRITÉ* in sharing the services of the Québécois cinematographer Michel Brault.

direct sound Film sound and dialogue recorded on-site at the time of recording the image, as opposed to studio POST-SYNCHRONIZATION. Direct sound lends a DOCUMENTARY-like atmosphere to a film since it records ambient or "wild" sound, which is not always entirely predictable, whereas post-synchronization can lend an incongruous "canned" quality at odds with the goals of REALISM. New technology made its use practicable beginning in the late 1950s, and it also became a hallmark of a certain modernist AVANT-GARDE or NEW WAVE (e.g., Jean-Marie Straub and Jacques Rivette).

director of photography (d.o.p.) The head of the film crew's camera unit. A synonym for "cinematographer."

dissolve Slow EDITING transition from one shot to another where one "fades out" as the other "fades in," creating a full SUPERIMPOSITION at the middle of the transition; achieved either "in-camera"—where the operator gradually closes down the aperture (fading to black), rewinds the film and opens up the aperture to overlap the next shot, fading in—or through OPTICAL PRINTING.

distribution Intermediate stage between film production and EXHIBITION, supplying the finished film to the places where it will be shown. The **distributor** works for a percentage of profits, or for a flat fee, or as a rental agency—a distribution company (distributor) may buy the rights to a film for a country or area and rent out prints of it to EXHIBITORS.

documentary The term most often used for non-fiction films, those depicting real events and real people; factual films. Derived from the French term *documentaire* which was used for travel films, and first used in English by John Grierson in a review of Robert Flaherty's *Moana* (U.S., 1926), a poetic record of traditional Polynesian life. Debate continues on questions of "objectivity"; on what should constitute a "true" documentary film; on the degree to which filmmakers should be able to manipulate the source ACTUALITY material, especially pertinent in the light of Grierson's belief in the "creative treatment" of reality. See also DOCUMENTARY NARRATIVE.

documentary narrative Used to describe a hybrid between DOCUMENTARY and narrative film, wherein certain documentary material or techniques (e.g., interviews and DIRECT ADDRESS, ACTUALITY, or ARCHIVAL FOOTAGE, etc.) are deployed in a fictional narrative which aspires to a certain documentary fidelity or REALISM. Not to be confused with "docu-drama," which is a dramatic reenactment of real events, often in a sensational style using *CINÉMA VÉRITÉ* techniques. Somewhat analogous to the "historical narrative" literary genre, although usually set in the present. See also DOCUMENTARY and FLAHERTY DOCUMENTARY TRADITION.

editing The process of selecting, assembling ("splicing"), and arranging shots and their corresponding sound elements, sometimes used as a synonym for CUTTING. Tasks performed by a film "editor," working in an "editing room," on an "editing table," which is often of a "flatbed," horizontal type, allowing for a number of magnetic soundtracks to be edited together with the film strip.

Eisensteinian montage or editing Referring to Sergei Eisenstein, whose filmmaking theory and practice in the Soviet Union of the 1920s foregrounded dynamic EDITING, wherein a juxtaposition of contrasting elements within and between shots (initially termed a "montage of attractions") dynamised the film and the film watching experience alike. Interested in emotional and physiological "affects" in MONTAGE, Eisenstein was also the most significant theorist and practitioner of "intellectual montage."

episodic A term used in narrative film, often used to distinguish linear, "tight" narratives where almost every plot element ties together neatly from much "looser," "episodic" narratives where separate episodes in one or more characters' lives are linked sometimes sequentially, sometimes thematically.

establishing shot A shot which begins a scene or film, providing an introduction to setting, location, or mood of the upcoming action (and possibly main characters as well). It is most often a LONG SHOT or EXTREME LONG SHOT.

ethnographic filmmaking A genre of DOCUMENTARY film which shows cultural practices from an OBSERVATIONAL perspective, often of a "disappearing world," and most often made by filmmakers from outside the culture (predominantly European or Euro-American filmmakers). Also called "anthropological filmmaking." Sometimes the footage remains un-edited.

exhibition The process of showing finished films to audiences. The **exhibitor** owns or operates a film theatre or chain of theatres.

experimental film A film in which any kind of formal or stylistic experimentation takes place and could even be one which shows ground-breaking subject matter. Often used as a synonym for "AVANT-GARDE film."

Expressionism Early twentieth century art style in Europe, especially Germany, where inner states are expressed outwardly. Used (incorrectly) as a general term for German cinema of the 1920s, following the release of *Das Kabinett des Dr. Caligari* (1919) which contained highly stylized abstract set design and decor. As an adjective the term is usually used to denote aggressively stylized design, often angular, high in contrast and pessimistic in connotation.

extreme close-up A DETAIL shot in very large scale showing just a portion of an object or person, especially the face, e.g., eyes or mouth only.

extreme long shot A shot where the scale of what is shown—usually a landscape—is very small; sometimes an AERIAL or "bird's-eye" VIEW.

feature, feature-length (film) A long film, usually fictional, which runs for an hour or more. (Some commentators give a shorter 50 minutes running time as the minimum length, while others go even further—Ephraim Katz gives 34 minutes, or 3,000 ft.) Films between thirty minutes and one hour in length are sometimes referred to as "medium-length" films.

film maudit French term for "bad" or "disreputable" film, used by critics of *Cahiers du Cinéma*, ironically in support of low-grade Hollywood films and against highbrow French films in the "tradition of quality."

film noir French term, now in common English use, for American films of the 1940s which were much "darker" than the Hollywood norm, both stylistically—LOW-KEY LIGHTING, extreme angles, "night-for-night" shooting (rather than "day-for-night")—and thematically—"anti-heroes," underworld milieu, narratives of entrapment.

film stock Cellulose-based "film strip," on which a series of still photographs is registered. The clear base is coated on one side with light-sensitive emulsion.

film-within-a-film A SHORT film which is shown, sometimes partially, during the film, usually to comment on, or gain insight into the main body of the film which contains it. Also a narrative device which depicts the making of a film within the narrative of the film being viewed.

filter A clear or coloured piece of glass or "gelatin" placed in front of the camera or printer lens to modify the tone or colour balance of the film image.

Flaherty documentary tradition Referring to the American filmmaker Robert Flaherty, whose *Nanook of the North* (1922) pioneered the structuring of non-fiction material in narrative form and of re-staging action for the camera as if it were ACTUALITY—most notably, Flaherty and his subjects, unable to light effectively inside an igloo, built a dummy igloo wall (like a "set") on location. See also DOCUMENTARY NARRATIVE.

flashback A scene or shot which depicts a time earlier than the one currently being represented.

flash-forward A scene or shot which depicts an event imagined, projected, or expected to occur later.

follow track A CAMERA MOVEMENT where the camera follows a moving subject, keeping them on-screen (and often centred in the FRAME), usually following from behind the person.

found footage "Stock footage," usually DOCUMENTARY material, which is purchased or "found" another way, e.g., during World War II, the British would "steal" or "capture" German footage to use in their own propaganda films.

fps Frames per second. The rate of "film transport" through the camera and projector; 24 fps is the normal, "sound speed."

frame The smallest unit of film. One of the successive individual images that are shown at a rapid rate to provide the illusion of a "motion picture". Also means the space that the photographic image occupies, like the frame of a painting. **Framing** is the process of composing a shot by using the edges of the frame to select what will be visible on screen and a synonym for COMPOSITION.

freeze frame The effect of repeatedly printing a single FRAME of film: it appears that motion is suspended and that the action is frozen on the screen.

gaucho Spanish. A term for a figure in South American and particularly Argentine history who is roughly analogous to the American cowboy. The nomadic cattle-herding gauchos were finally driven from the land at the end of the nineteenth century when the vast pampas were parcelled out. In film, an action genre similar to the U.S. Western, often depicting the gauchos' battles against the colonising Spaniards (thus inverting the Western's glorification of colonisation and representing strongly nationalistic sentiments). The genre's heyday was in Argentina in the 1940s; a minor Brazilian *gaúcho* genre also existed.

grainy (film stock) When the small particles of metallic silver, which are formed during film processing, become visible to the eye. This occurs when the FILM STOCK is very "fast"—usable in low light conditions—or where the image is blown-up on the screen, especially from a small gauge, e.g., SUPER-8 to 35MM.

graphic(ally) match(ed) Where two successive shots are edited together to create a strong similarity of compositional elements, e.g., line, colour, shadow.

Griersonian aesthetic Referring to Scottish film producer John Grierson (see DOCUMENTARY), who believed that all films should be socially affective, and who is best known for setting up the G.P.O. Film Unit in the U.K., where he encouraged the making of "poetic documentaries" in the mid-1930s, and the National Film Board (NFB) in Canada, where he oversaw the production of World War II propaganda films employing Lorne Greene's "voice-of-God" VOICE-OVER NARRATION and bombastic music.

guerrilla cinema Term coined by Argentine filmmakers Fernando Solanas and Octavio Getino in their 1969 manifesto "Hacia un tercer cine" ("Towards a Third Cinema"), written to accompany their 1968 film *La hora de los hornos*. Guerrilla cinema was conceived as participating directly in the leftist national liberation movements then under way in Latin America, both as a critique of neo-colonialist rule and as an incitement to political action.

high angle A CAMERA ANGLE where the camera is looking down on the subject. Also, "very high angle," or "extreme high angle," where the camera is almost directly above the subject.

high contrast When the difference between light and dark areas of a shot or scene is relatively large. In lighting, it usually means predominantly (LOW) KEY LIGHTING is used. In black-and-white there tends to be a lack of distinction in the grey tones, whereas in colour the bright tones veer towards the gaudy. "High contrast" is also associated with "fast," GRAINY FILM STOCK.

Impressionism Late-nineteenth century art movement in France which inspired French AVANT-GARDE filmmakers of the 1920s—e.g., Abel Gance, Louis Delluc, Marcel L'Herbier—who used film style—EDITING, CAMERA MOVEMENT, SUPERIMPOSITION, and "special effects" to poetically abstract the real world in which their CINEMATOGRAPHY was based, and to search for the CINEMATIC essence (and to separate film from its traditional base in drama and narrative literature).

industrial (short, or film) A commissioned film, usually a SHORT, for public relations or publicity purposes, usually intended not for public EXHIBITION but for viewing by a special, limited audience (e.g., clients, etc.). In the silent period, often shown publicly as part of a program of films.

insert A shot, usually NON-DIEGETIC, and often in CLOSE-UP or EXTREME CLOSE-UP, which is placed within a scene somewhat incongruously, in order to make a point, or help explain the action. Such "inserts" became commonplace in Soviet cinema of the 1920s, where directors such as Sergei EISENSTEIN developed MONTAGE tropes of metaphor and simile leading towards a truly "intellectual cinema" where audiences had to think through chains of insert-type shots in "intellectual montage." According to Barry Salt it can also refer to any "shot of an object or part of a person other than the face," and that "before World War II this term was also used to describe anything CUT into the main scene such as INTERTITLES and CLOSE SHOTS of faces."

intercut The EDITING between shots of two or more different people, usually in different spaces, and usually to infer simultaneous action, but with a wider usage than PARALLEL EDITING and CROSS-CUTTING, since the spaces being joined are not necessarily disparate. Also used for the "cutting in" to a scene of any extraneous material, e.g., INSERTS, INTERTITLES, and LEADER.

intertitle Words, phrases, or sentences appearing within and between film sequences to describe the setting, mood, or action, or to represent dialogue or thoughts. A silent film technique, which was gradually abandoned after the coming of sound.

iris See MASK

jump-cut A seemingly "bad CUT" where there seems to be a piece missing from the film. Either the character's position changes abruptly, or, in special cases, the background changes completely while the character's foreground position remains relatively stable. The technique has been used deliberately for effect—most notably by Sergei EISENSTEIN in *Octyabr'* (USSR, 1927)—but, generally speaking, until Jean-Luc Godard used the technique extensively in *A bout de souffle* (France, 1960), it occurred accidentally.

Kuleshovian creative geography In the late 1910s, Lev Kuleshov, while teaching at the Soviet State School on Cinema Art, conducted a series of MONTAGE experiments. In one of these, by EDITING together NEWSREEL footage filmed in a variety of

Soviet cities he was able to "create" a totally new, composite city with its own "geography."

lateral depth of field Term coined by André Bazin to characterise Jean Renoir's particular brand of REALISM, where the camera TRACKS or PANS laterally (from right to left, or vice versa), while the action is staged in depth and beyond the film FRAME.

lateral tracking shot Where the camera TRACKS or "dollies" in a direction across the FRAME, from right to left, or left to right, usually to follow the subject's movement.

leader Blank FILM STOCK, usually black or clear, which normally begins (or "leads") each reel of film for the purpose of threading the film onto the projector. In EXPERIMENTAL cinema, sometimes used within the film itself, e.g., creating a prolonged image of pitch black or pure white on the screen during the film.

lip-sync dialogue Accurate synchronization of the sound of speech with the lips of the speaker. Also the term for the simultaneous recording of voice and image, rather than shooting with no sound at all or sound recorded independently, "wild sound."

long shot A shot in which the scale of the person(s) being depicted is relatively small. (Some observers consider a shot where the figure just fills the FRAME—also called a "full shot"—to be a "long shot," while others believe that the figure(s) can be very small, e.g., where, according to Katz, "the camera is positioned at a distance that allows general recognition of the subject matter at the expense of detail.")

long take A shot that continues for an extremely long time. (In the 1920s and '30s, a shot longer than 20 seconds could have been considered "long," but now, post-Miklós Jancsó, a shot needs to be upwards of two or three minutes to be so designated.) In the shooting phase, a "take" is an in-camera version of a shot. There can be any number of "takes" of a particular shot to produce the desired material for the finished film.

low angle A CAMERA ANGLE where the camera is looking up at the subject from below. An "extreme low angle" or "very low angle" is where the camera tends to provide a very strange distorted image of a person or object.

low-key lighting A lighting set-up which uses high intensity key lights (or SPOT LIGHTING) rather than "fill light" (which floods the set with low intensity light from above) and which creates a strong contrast between light and dark areas of the shot, where the shadows tend to be deep. Characteristic of FILM NOIR.

mask(ing) Process of blocking out part of the photographic image. Any shape of mask can be used, the most common being a circular "iris."

medium shot A shot intermediate in scale between a LONG SHOT and a CLOSE-UP. Understanding of what the "medium" scale is varies from a full body shot (sometimes called a "medium long shot") to a shot where the character is FRAMED from the waist to the top of the head (sometimes called a "medium close-up"). A framing from the knees to the top of the head is sometimes called an "American shot."

melodrama Popular genre in film as well as theatre throughout the world, but especially so in Latin America, traditionally in the Mexican and Argentine industries, where the pessimistic (evil) forces of melodrama have been far stronger than in contemporaneous Hollywood films, and most recently on television, especially the Brazilian *novelas* of O Globo TV.

meta-cinema From "metalanguage," coined by the logicians of the School of Vienna, which is, according to Robert Stam, Robert Burgoyne, and Sandy Flitterman-Lewis, "the higher-level language used to describe language itself as an object of study." Thus "meta-cinema" can be understood as an intensely REFLEXIVE cinema.

mise-en-scène French term, now in common English use, meaning literally "put in the scene." Unfortunately almost everyone has their own understanding of what this term means: derived from theatre terminology, it includes the action of the characters, and the staging and directing of this action in relation to the setting. For Bordwell and Thompson it is "all the elements placed in front of the camera to be photographed: the settings and props, lighting, costumes and make-up, and figure behaviour," in short, all the "pro-filmic" elements, and yet lighting affects the photographic quality and texture of the finished film, should arguably be discounted. Bazin used the term to separate mise-en-scène filmmakers from MONTAGE filmmakers while the *NOUVELLE VAGUE* critics of *Cahiers du Cinéma* contrasted AUTEUR film directors with *metteurs-en-scène* who had great control over the medium but who lacked individual personality.

monitor Video term for television screen/unit which allows the recorded image to be viewed (and sound to be heard) while the video is being shot.

montage Originally a French term, meaning "mounting up," and adapted by Soviet filmmaker/theorists of the 1920s for film EDITING, providing an elevated sense to the process commensurate with their understanding that montage/editing was the essential property of cinema (hence, "Soviet montage"). Any dynamic or intellectually stimulating application of editing. Sometimes even used as a direct synonym for "editing."

Movietone optical sound One of the two successful sound processes adopted in the late 1920s and developed by the Movietone company, where sound is produced optically on photographic film strip and electrically converted into sound via a beam of light.

music video A SHORT film—ironically, rarely made on video—which runs the length of a musical piece on record (or audio cassette or CD) and which allowed for a great deal of CINEMATIC innovation when the form first became popularised by MTV in the U.S. during the early 1980s. Music videos have since become more and more like "commercials" for popular recording stars.

neo-realism New realism. Used initially in describing Luchino Visconti's *Ossessione* (Italy, 1942) and then in conjunction with Italian films made immediately following World War II which worked deliberately against the pre-war, fascist-run studio system. Italian neo-realist films were characterized by their EPISODIC dedramatised action, focus on quotidian working class life, being shot predominantly on location (rather than in the studio) and employing non-professional actors.

New Latin American Cinema General term, *Nuevo Cine Latinoamericano* in Spanish (see also *NUEVO CINE*), most often used in relation to films—often documentaries or fictionalised reconstructions—made independently, on the Left, especially in Argentina, Bolivia, Brazil, Chile, Cuba, and Uruguay, during the late 1960s and '70s. The pan-continental movement is generally thought to have been instigated through the film festival organised by the Cine Club del Uruguay in 1965 and the first Viña del Mar Film Festival in Chile in 1967. The Cuban revolution and Allende's election in Chile were political catalysts for the "movement" (as was, conversely, activism against military dictatorships elsewhere). Retrospectively,

Fernando Birri's pioneering work in Argentina along with Uruguayan and Chilean SHORTS of the 1950s and early '60s and Brazilian CINEMA NÔVO have been included under the rubric of "New Latin American Cinema," while the incorporation of an annual international film festival in Havana in 1979, using this name, resurrected the "movement," which had gone into decline following the military coups of the 1970s (in Bolivia, 1971; Chile and Uruguay, 1973; and Argentina, 1976).

new wave General term, first used for the French *NOUVELLE VAGUE* in 1958, but later used to describe flourishing film movements throughout Europe and Latin America in the 1960s, and in the rest of the world in more recent years, e.g., the Taiwanese "new wave" of the late 1980s.

newsreel A journal of news events on film; effectively introduced at the beginnings of cinema with the single shot ACTUALITIES made by the Lumière brothers, but formularised newsreel series, conceived as such, started late in the first decade of the century. They became regular inclusions in film programming, but began to disappear in the late 1950s with the advent of television news programs.

nitrate (film stock) Short for "cellulose nitrate base," the material most commonly used in the manufacture of FILM STOCK until 1950. Highly inflammable and quick to decompose (and hence become combustible, and even more dangerous). The world's film archives are still working to transfer surviving nitrate prints onto ACETATE "SAFETY" stock.

non-diegetic Outside the DIEGESIS, i.e., space of the (usually narrative) film's action. Typically, "non-diegetic sound" is often music, played by musicians who do not appear in the film; an INSERT is often "non-diegetic." Also called "extra-diegetic."

nouvelle vague The French NEW WAVE of the late 1950s and early '60s, a youthful movement inspired to use CINEMATIC techniques (such as EDITING and CAMERA MOVEMENT) very freely and influenced by Italian NEO-REALISM, American FILM NOIR (and B-MOVIES) and a few favoured directors, including Jean Renoir and Robert Bresson, but actively against other French directors "of quality."

nuevo cine (also *nueva ola*) Spanish. General terms for NEW WAVE, especially common in Argentina and Chile.

observational (style) Where the camera strictly observes the action, from a distance, with no apparent intervention. An ideally "objective" DOCUMENTARY style typical of ETHNOGRAPHIC films.

off screen Implied space beyond the screen or film FRAME, including that beyond the set and behind the camera. Often used in the context of "off-screen sound" where the audience is cued to infer something that is happening simultaneous with "on-screen" action, e.g., an off-screen gunshot might cause a body to fall on screen.

oneiric (film) Dream-like film structure, where a strict, linear narrative interpretation of the unfolding events in the film is not always possible. Dream sequences in narrative films which are marked as such are "oneiric" but so are "poetic" film passages where time is suspended, as well as SURREALIST, "magical realist," and various EXPERIMENTAL films.

optical printing The **optical printer** is a combination camera and projector which can duplicate images on previously processed film, reduce or enlarge images, and create a variety of visual effects.

optical sound See MOVIETONE OPTICAL SOUND

ostraneniye   Russian (phonetic transliteration; also *ostrenanie*) for the concept of "defamiliarisation" or "making strange" introduced by the Russian Formalist Victor Shlovsky in the mid-1910s, who cited the example of Tolstoy describing the human system of ownership through the eyes of a horse. Cubism and Futurism were key visual art movements in which paintings were revelatory through seeing ordinary things in strangely new ways. In film, Fernand Léger and Dudley Murphy's *Ballet mécanique* (France, 1924) exemplifies the processes of defamiliarisation.

pan   A CAMERA MOVEMENT where the camera swivels horizontally about its own axis to the right or the left (it doesn't move along the ground). Short form of "panorama" or "PANORAMIC," because among the first camera movements in ACTUALITIES were panoramas scanning between 180 and 360 degrees of viewing angle. Sometimes similar movements along the camera's vertical axis are called "vertical pans" (rather than TILTS).

panoramic   A static camera view which overlooks a large angle of observation, generally a cityscape. An early word for a PANNING CAMERA MOVEMENT.

parallel montage   CUTTING between two separate scenes in disparate spaces, whereby the EDITING creates the illusion of the two actions occurring simultaneously.

photo-montage (documentary)   A style of filmmaking which, for practical, aesthetic, or budgetary reasons, constructs a film out of still photographs. These photographs are often made to appear more dynamic by PANNING or TILTING the camera across them or by employing a ZOOM lens. Usually found in DOCUMENTARY and often accompanied by a VOICE-OVER NARRATION, it is a common technique for making films on historical topics where no filmed ARCHIVAL footage exists or is available. In the ART CINEMA tradition, the best-known example is Chris Marker's *La Jetée* (France, 1963), a sort of intellectual and Romantic science-fiction story. In 1958, Fernando Birri in Argentina made a photo-montage documentary, *Tire dié*, on poor children as a class project at a new film school in Santa Fe (which was later reshot on 16MM film in 1960).

pixillation   A section of film which is made "FRAME by frame," but by using live action rather than drawn, painted or otherwise constructed figures, is **pixillated**. A person or object moves in between frames being recorded, so that it appears as if impossible movement occurs, e.g., a person slides along the ground without moving his/her feet. Pixillation is an "animation" technique.

play back   Video term for a procedure, not available to filmmakers, of "playing back" a video recording immediately after its production, especially to show the results to cast and crew.

poetic realism   First used to describe French films made in the late 1930s where mood and setting had equal importance to story (hence "poetic") and where REALISM was of the literary kind (e.g., Zola), resulting in a quite pessimistic attitude to human nature and society couched in "romantic fatalism," especially in the combined work of director Marcel Carné and writer Jacques Prévert, where nighttime, rain, and fog (and industrial smog) are often prominent aspects of the MISE-EN-SCÈNE.

point of view   General term for subjectivity which has a special application in film, being used for perceptual subjectivity where **point-of-view shots** show exactly what a character sees from his/her perspective. **Point-of-view editing** is the oscillation between point-of-view shots and REACTION SHOTS.

pornochanchada Slang term for Brazilian "erotic comedies" (which are rarely erotic), often made cheaply, and which dominated national production in the late 1970s and '80s. The name is a perversion of the term used for Brazilian musical comedies, CHANCHADA, though the crudeness of much of the work reflects the original meaning of the source term.

post-production All the work that is done on the film after it is shot; mostly EDITING.

postsynchronized sound The recording of sound in attempted synchronization with the picture after filming has been completed. Dialogue is also "dubbed" into another language using this procedure.

pre-code Before the Hollywood Production Code (censorship) came into full effect in 1934, clamping down on explicit sexual and racial references. American pre-code films tend to be especially fast-paced and hard-edged in accord with the "raciness" of the material, especially in comparison with the blandness of Hollywood films from the mid- to late 1930s.

pre-credit sequence Device which became popularised in the 1970s, where a film begins with a narrative sequence before the CREDITS appear, done either to shock the audience into the action, *media res*, or to provide background information prior to the main body of the film's story.

pre-production Everything that is done before a film is shot, including all the phases of scriptwriting, art direction, casting, funding, etc.

quota quickie Slang term for films made to fulfil a quota placed on theatres to show a percentage of nationally-made films. Typically, they are made very cheaply and quickly, e.g., Brazilian *PORNOCHANCHADAS*.

raw stock FILM STOCK which is yet to be exposed to light (run through a camera) and processed.

reaction shot A shot of a person reacting to what s/he sees, typically following a POINT-OF-VIEW SHOT. Often it is this shot rather than the subjective view which causes audiences to identify with character.

realism Literary and art term, adapted for film, and which can apply to style, subject matter, or both. André Bazin theorised that CINEMATIC realism involved the use of LATERAL DEPTH OF FIELD wherein, no matter where the camera spins there is life continuing beyond the screen (involving a complex staging of action OFF SCREEN.) Critics often refer to a **realist** acting style, and sometimes the term is used to connote a negative side of human behaviour or as a corollary for "humanism" or "naturalism."

reflexive The process by which films reflect themselves, foregrounding their own production, their authorship, their stylistic elements, their reception, or their "intertextuality". A key process in "modernist" art which tends to be more "about" itself than the external world, reflexivity is also "post-modernist" when extended to the intertextual realm. Also called "self-referentiality," but mis-termed "self-reflexive."

reframing Where the camera moves to consciously change the COMPOSITION of the FRAME/shot; in mainstream narrative films the camera often moves to **reframe** a character when s/he moves in order to maintain their centrality.

reversal film A type of FILM STOCK which, when processed, yields a single positive print and not a negative. While this reduces laboratory costs, it makes it impossible to strike multiple copies of the film and creates the perilous situation of having a single, original print.

RUSHES Unedited footage fresh from the laboratory, viewed immediately, often daily, to ensure that there are no technical glitches, unsatisfactory performances, etc. and that no scenes need to be reshot while cast, crew, decors, etc. are still in place.

sequence shot A shot, invariably a LONG TAKE, which is the same length as the film scene or "sequence." Common in the early days of narrative film, before sequences were broken down through EDITING into a series of shots, it re-emerged in NEW WAVE films of the 1960s.

shooting ratio The relationship between the amount of footage shot for a film and the actual length of the finished film. A 4:1 or 5:1 ratio is typical for narrative films, but DOCUMENTARY shooting ratios can be much higher, even greater than 20:1.

short subject (or film) A film, whose duration is relatively short, generally less than 30 minutes.

shot-counter shot Term used for an EDITING situation where a shot of one person (or group of persons) is INTERCUT with another. Where the camera takes the position of the successive characters, the operation is also called shot/reverse shot; "over-the-shoulder" FRAMINGS are common in shot/reverse-shot editing.

silent speed The "film transport" rate—passing through the camera and projector—before sound was introduced: normally 16 FPS (frames per second) or 18 fps, but when films were made on hand-cranked cameras (and projected by hand) the rate was always variable, from 12 to 24 fps.

single-frame (exposure, shooting) The procedure of exposing the film "frame by frame" rather than at a continuous rate of speed; used in "stop motion" and "time lapse cinematography."

16mm A film "gauge" (of 16mm in width) which was introduced for the amateur market in the 1920s and which came into widespread use for DOCUMENTARY and television production as well as other kinds of independent and EXPERIMENTAL filmmaking in the late 1950s.

slow motion When the camera is run at a faster-than-normal rate, and then when the film is projected at this normal rate, the motion of the action on screen will be slowed down. The opposite of slow motion is "fast motion" or "accelerated motion."

soft focus An effect achieved either by shooting slightly out of focus, or by placing a special FILTER or gauze (or other diffusing material, like grease) in front of the camera lens. The resultant image is "diffused" or lacking sharp definition.

sound effects Natural, or artificially created sounds (other than speech or music) that are added to the film's soundtrack.

sound on disk See VITAPHONE SOUND

"spaghetti" Western Films in the Western genre made in Europe (mainly in the 1960s and '70s), so-called because Italian production predominated (but German and Spanish Westerns were also plentiful).

spot lighting Using lights which project intense, narrow beams of light directed to specific areas of the set; also called spots.

stop motion See SINGLE FRAME.

Super-8 Film "gauge," slightly wider than 8mm, which became the most popular amateur (and "home movie") gauge in the 1960s and '70s. Just before the advent of video in the '80s, much interesting EXPERIMENTAL work was done in Super-8, especially, in Latin America, in Venezuela.

superimposition The printing or photographing of one film image on top of another so that they appear simultaneously on the screen. Can be achieved "in-camera," or by a "glass-shot," or by multiple printing (especially with an OPTICAL PRINTER).

super-production Very high budget film, usually produced by a major studio.

Surrealism Important movement in 1920s French literature and painting whose practitioners loved the **surrealist** possibilities of the cinema, especially the ability of EDITING to freely transcend normal boundaries of time and space, and the absurd MISE-EN-SCÈNE (action and sets) of American silent comedians such as Buster Keaton. Aggressive and radical, Surrealist artists believed in the play of free thought and the primacy of the world of dreams over the "real world." Many Surrealists were obsessed with the connections between love and death. The most prominent filmmaker associated with the movement was the Spanish-born Luis Buñuel, who, through the work he did in Mexico in the 1950s, bridges the connection with "magic realism" in Latin American film.

swish-pan Very rapid PANNING of the camera which causes the image to be blurred on the screen, often used to make an EDITING transition (sometimes to hide the CUT, but sometimes to make it more dramatic); also called "flash pan" or "zip pan."

tableaux (grouping or framing) Used to describe an early narrative style used by filmmakers like Georges Méliès who created scenes in single shots (which may include "special effects") where figures would be grouped in LONG SHOT scale, and where the fixed camera would view the action straight on at a 90 degree angle. Some contemporary filmmakers have adopted the style (sometimes to work deliberately against Hollywood CLASSICAL style).

Technicolor Trademark for the best known and most widely used film colour process, invented by Herbert T. Kalmus and Daniel F. Comstock in the U.S. during World War I, but which is often (incorrectly) used as a synonym for colour film. Originally, Technicolor was a "two-color" system which couldn't reproduce the full colour range of the spectrum (and where blues tended to be green and reds had an orange/pink hue). The more natural "three-color," or **three-strip** process was introduced in 1932.

telenovela Spanish and Portuguese term for television "serial narrative" (the "soap opera" in English), extremely popular throughout Latin America, which some observers find to be to be often more sophisticated than their American daytime television counterparts. According to Ana M. López, the most significant difference between the two forms is that *telenovelas* "have always had clear-cut stories with definite endings that permit narrative closure." She adds that *telenovelas* are "prime-time entertainment for all audiences, . . . widely exported, and definitive of the Latin American star system."

telephoto lens A camera lens with a long focal length that magnifies the image like a telescope, making it possible to take CLOSE SHOTS of distant objects and people; it reduces perspective and flattens images.

35mm The standard "gauge" for professional filmmaking since the early days of cinema.

tilt up, down A CAMERA MOVEMENT where the camera swivels vertically about its own axis, up or down; also called "vertical pan."

tinting A process where the developed film is dipped into a bath of dye. The dark areas remain black and grey, while the lighter ones pick up the colour. **Toning,** which is often misnamed "tinting," is where the dye is added during the development of the positive print: the darker areas of the FRAME are coloured, while the brightest areas of the image remain white. Sometimes the effects of hand colouring and the use of FILTERS with colour stock are also called "tinting."

track A CAMERA MOVEMENT where the camera moves along the ground in any direction. Initially the term **tracking** referred only to camera movements where the camera was mounted on a wheeled device (sometimes called a "truck") running on tracks. Such movements had a very pronounced, single directionality. Later, when the rubber-wheeled "dolly" was introduced, which allowed the camera to move smoothly in any direction, the meaning of the term "tracking" was expanded to include such movements.

tracking shot A shot which includes tracking or "dollying" CAMERA MOVEMENTS.

travelling shot A shot where a camera is mounted on a moving vehicle (usually a car or a train) on which the film's action is also taking place. Also used for shots where the camera is mounted on a vehicle which is travelling in the same direction as the vehicle on which the action occurs (although strictly speaking such shots are "tracking shots").

two-shot A shot containing two characters in the FRAME, who predominate visually. Similarly, a "three-shot" contains three main characters, a "four shot" four, etc.

typage A film acting term devised by Soviet theorists of the 1920s for a system of performance whereby an actor possesses features believed to characterise a social class or any other group or type.

udigrudi Brazilian slang term for "underground," used by a breakaway group of filmmakers in the late 1960s who were even more radical than the directors of CINEMA NÔVO, being almost Dadaist in their self-destructive and anti-art tendencies. See also CINEMA MARGINAL.

vertical angle A CAMERA ANGLE where the subject is directly underneath the camera lens; also called "overhead angle" (or "shot").

videographer Video equivalent of "cinematographer": the person responsible for operating the video camera. Can also be used for "video director."

Vitaphone sound One of two successful sound systems introduced in the late 1920s, where sound emanated from a separate wax disk in synchronization with the film. Promoted by Warner Brothers, the SOUND-ON-DISK system was abandoned in 1931 after problems in maintaining synchronization after film print breakage or damage.

voice-over narration, monologue An OFF-SCREEN (often NON-DIEGETIC, and authoritative) voice which fills in details of what is being shown, or places the images in a wider context, especially in DOCUMENTARY films, but also used for a character's thoughts, visions, or FLASHBACKS in fiction films.

Wellesian Reminiscent of films directed by Orson Welles, often implying a stylistic connection, usually of flamboyant or "baroque" camera articulation or DEEP FOCUS CINEMATOGRAPHY.

white telephone (genre) First used (pejoratively) to characterise family MELODRAMAS and light comedies in luxurious settings made in Fascist Italy during the 1930s (*telofoni bianchi*). So called because the upper-middle class decor often featured white telephones.

wide angle lens A camera lens with a short focal length, which exaggerates the sense of depth perspective, and distorts lines at the foreground FRAME edges. In 35MM filmmaking, a lens with a focal length of 30mm or less is a "wide-angle lens."

widescreen Any film "aspect ratio"—expressed as a relationship between screen height and width—that is greater than the standard "Academy ratio" (established by the American Academy of Motion Picture Arts and Sciences) which was, until recently, 1.33:1. (Now that it has been set at 1.85:1, the understanding of what is a "widescreen" ratio has changed.) The best-known widescreen process is CinemaScope (2.35:1), an "anamorphic" process developed by 20th Century Fox in 1953.

zoom An apparent camera movement which is achieved by using a **zoom lens** which has the capability of changing focal length during a shot. A **zoom-in** to the TELEPHOTO position magnifies the object of view and flattens the perspective, while a **zoom-out** towards the WIDE-ANGLE position reduces the scale of the subject and increases the sense of depth.

Works Consulted

This list is limited to film books and articles consulted in the course of preparing this book.

General

Alea, Tomás Gutiérrez. *The Viewer's Dialectic*. Translated by Julia Lesage. Havana: José Martí, 1988.

Armes, Roy. *Third World Film Making and the West*. Berkeley: University of California Press, 1987.

Bentley Hammer, Ted. *International Film Prizes: An Encyclopedia*. New York: Garland, 1991.

Bergan, Ronald, and Robin Karney. *Bloomsbury Foreign Film Guide*. London: Bloomsbury, 1988.

Bordwell, David, and Kristin Thompson. *Film Art: An Introduction*, 4th ed. New York: McGraw-Hill, 1993.

Burton, Julianne. *Cinema and Social Change in Latin America: Conversations with Filmmakers*. Austin: University of Texas Press, 1986.

———, ed. *The Social Documentary in Latin America*. Pittsburgh: University of Pittsburgh Press, 1990.

Chanan, Michael, ed. *Twenty-five Years of the New Latin American Cinema*. London: British Film Institute/Channel Four Television, 1983.

Cowie, Peter, ed. *International Film Guide*, annual, 1969–89. London: Tantivy, 1969–89.

———, ed. *Variety International Film Guide*, annual, 1990–93. London: Andre Deutsch, 1990–93.

———, ed. *Variety International Film Guide 1994*. London: Hamlyn, 1994.

de Usabel, Gaizka S. *The High Noon of American Films in Latin America*. Ann Arbor, Michigan: UMI Research Press, 1982.

Fusco, Coco, ed. *Reviewing Histories: Selections from New Latin American Cinema*. Buffalo: Hallwalls Contemporary Art Center, 1987.

Gumucio-Dagron, Alfonso. *Cine, censura y exilio en América Latina*, 2nd ed. Mexico City: Sindicato de Trabajadores de la Universidad Nacional Autónoma de México (STUNAM)/ Centro de Integración de Medios de Comunicación Alternativa (CIMCA)/ Federación Editorial Mexicana (FEM), 1984.

———, and Guy Hennebelle, eds. *Les Cinémas d'Amérique Latine*. Paris: Lherminier, 1981.

Hojas de cine, Testimonios y documentos del nuevo cine latinoamericano, 3 vols. Mexico City: Fundación Mexicana de Cineastas, 1988.

Katz, Ephraim. *The Film Encyclopedia.* New York: Perigee, 1979; 2nd ed. New York: Harper Perennial, 1994.

King, John. *Magical Reels: A History of Cinema in Latin America.* London: Verso, 1990.

——, Ana M. López, and Manuel Alvarado, eds. *Mediating Two Worlds: Cinematic Encounters in the Americas.* London: British Film Institute, 1993.

"Latin American Cinema/Le cinéma latino-américain." *Iris* no. 13 (Summer 1991).

López, Ana M. "An 'Other' History: The New Cinema of Latin America." In *Resisting Images: Essays on Cinema and History,* ed. Robert Sklar and Charles Musser, 308–30. Philadelphia: University of Temple Press, 1990.

——. "Our welcomed guests: Telenovelas in Latin America." In *To Be Continued . . . Soap operas around the world,* ed. Robert C. Allen, 256–75. London: Routledge, 1995.

Luhr, William, ed. *World Cinema Since 1945.* New York: Ungar, 1987.

Lyon, Christopher, ed. *The International Dictionary of Films and Filmmakers: Volume I Films.* Chicago: St. James Press, 1984.

Magill, Frank N., ed. *Magill's Survey of Cinema: Foreign Language Films,* 8 vols. Englewood Cliffs, N.J.: Salem Press, 1985.

Marcorelles, Louis. *Living Cinema: New Directions in Contemporary Film-making.* New York: Praeger, 1973 [1970].

Pick, Zuzana M. *The New Latin American Cinema: A Continental Project.* Austin: University of Texas Press, 1993.

Roud, Richard. *Cinema: A Critical Dictionary,* 2 vols. New York: Viking, 1980.

Sadoul, Georges. *Dictionary of Film Makers.* Translated, edited, and updated by Peter Morris. Berkeley: University of California Press, 1972 [1965].

——. *Dictionary of Films.* Translated, edited, and updated by Peter Morris. Berkeley: University of California Press, 1972 [1965].

——. *Histoire du cinéma mondiale.* Paris: Flammarion, 1981 [1949].

Salt, Barry. *Film Style and Technology: History and Analysis.* London: Starword, 1983.

Schnitman, Jorge A. *Film Industries in Latin America: Dependency and Development.* Norwood N.J.: Ablex, 1984.

Stam, Robert. "Rewriting 1492: Cinema and the Columbus Debate." *Cineaste* 19 no. 4 (1993): 66–71.

——, Robert Burgoyne and Sandy Flitterman-Lewis. *New Vocabularies in Film Semiotics: Structuralism, post-structuralism and beyond.* London: Routledge, 1992.

Toledo, Teresa. *10 años del nuevo cine latinamericano.* Spain: Verdoux, 1990.

Trelles Plazaola, Luis. *South American Cinema: Dictionary of Film Makers.* Río Piedras: Editorial de la Universidad de Puerto Rico, 1989.

Argentina

Barnard, Tim. *Argentine Cinema.* Toronto: Nightwood Editions, 1986.

Barney Finn, Oscar. "Luis Saslavsky, Del esplendor a la soledad." *Cine Libre* (Buenos Aires), no. 2 (1982): 34–6.

Bendazzi, Giannalberto. *Cartoons: Il cinema d'animazione 1888–1988.* Venice: Marsilio, 1988.

Beycero, Raúl. *Ensayos sobre cine argentino.* Santa Fe: Universidad Nacional del Litoral, 1986.

Birri, Fernando. *La escuela documental de Santa Fe.* Santa Fe: Universidad Nacional del Litoral, 1964.

——— . *Fernando Birri, Pionero y peregrino.* Buenos Aires: Contrapunto, 1987.

Bonitzer, Pascal. "Cinéma politique." *Cahiers du Cinéma,* no. 222 (1970): 33–37.

Calistro, Mariano, Oscar Cetrángolo, Claudio España, Andrés Insaurralde, and Carlos Landini. *Reportaje al cine argentino, Los pioneros del sonoro.* Buenos Aires: America Norildis, 1978.

Ciria, Alberto. *Más allá de la pantalla: cine argentino, historia y política.* Buenos Aires: Ediciones de la Flor, 1995.

——— , and Jorge M. López. "Literatura, cine e historia en Leopoldo Torre Nilsson." *Cine cubano,* no. 129 (1990): 15–28.

Colombres, Adolfo, ed. *Cine, antropología y colonialismo.* Buenos Aires: Ediciones del Sol, 1985.

Couselo, Jorge Miguel. *El negro Ferreyra, un cine por instinto.* Buenos Aires: Freeland, 1969.

——— . "El aporte de Alcides Greca al cine argentino." *Todo es historia* (Buenos Aires), no. 49 (1971): 74–79.

——— . *Leopoldo Torres Ríos, El cine del sentimiento.* Buenos Aires: Corregidor, 1974.

——— , ed. *Historia del cine argentino.* Buenos Aires: Centro Editor de América Latina, 1984.

——— , ed. *Torre Nilsson por Torre Nilsson.* Buenos Aires: Fraterna, 1985.

Cozarinsky, Edgardo. *Borges in/and/on Film.* New York: Lumen, 1988 [1980].

di Núbila, Domingo. *Historia del cine argentino,* 2 vols. Buenos Aires: Cruz de Malta, 1959/60.

Feldman, Simón. *La generación del 60.* Buenos Aires: Legasa, 1990.

Ford, Aníbal, and Nora Mazziotti. "José González Castillo: cine mudo, fábricas, y garçonières." In *Los invertidos* by José González Castillo (annotated edition), 77–96. Buenos Aires: Puntosur, 1991.

Getino, Octavio, ed. *Notas sobre cine argentino y latinoamericano.* Mexico City: Edimedios, 1984.

——— . *Cine latinoamericano, Economía y Nuevas Tecnologías.* Buenos Aires: Legasa, 1988.

——— . *Cine y dependencia, El cine en la Argentina.* Buenos Aires: Puntosur, 1990 [1979].

López, Ana. "Argentina, 1955–1976: The Film Industry and its Margins." In *The Garden of Forking Paths: Argentine Cinema,* ed. John King and Nissa Torrents, 49–80. London: British Film Institute, 1988.

López, Daniel. *Catálogo del Nuevo Cine Argentino 1984/1986.* Buenos Aires: Instituto Nacional de Cinematografía, 1987.

——— . *Catálogo del Nuevo Cine Argentino 1987/1988.* Buenos Aires: Instituto Nacional de Cinematografía, 1989.

Lozano, Jaime L. *El síndrome del cine nacional.* Buenos Aires: Sindicato de la Industria Cinematográfica Argentina (SICA), 1984.

Mahieu, José Agustín. *Historia del cortometraje argentino.* Buenos Aires: Editorial Documento/Instituto Nacional de Cinematografía/Universidad Nacional del Litoral (Santa Fe), 1960.

——— . *Breve historia del cine argentino.* Buenos Aires: Editorial Universitaria de Buenos Aires, 1966.

——— . *Breve historia del cine nacional.* Buenos Aires: Alzamor, 1974.

Martín, Jorge Abel. *Cine argentino, Historia, Documentación, Filmografía. Cine Libre* (Buenos Aires), no date.

——— . *Diccionario de realizadores contemporáneos.* Buenos Aires: Instituto Nacional de Cinematografía, 1987.

Morris, C.B. *This Loving Darkness: The Cinema and Spanish Writers 1920–1936.* Oxford: Oxford University Press, 1980.

Romano, Eduardo. *Literatura/Cine: Argentinos sobre la(s) frontera(s).* Buenos Aires: Catálogos, 1991.

Rossi, Juan José, ed. *El cine etnobiográfico de Jorge Prelorán.* Buenos Aires: Ayllu, 1987.

Solanas, Fernando. *La mirada, reflexiones sobre cine y cultura* (interview with Horacio González). Buenos Aires: Puntosur, 1989.

———, and Octavio Getino, "Towards a Third Cinema," *Cineaste* 4, no. 3 (Winter 1970–71): 1–10.

Bolivia

Gumucio-Dagron, Alfonso. *Historia del cine boliviano.* Mexico City: Filmoteca UNAM, 1983.

Sanjinés, Jorge. *Teoría y práctica de un cine junto al pueblo.* Mexico City: Siglo Veintiuno, 1979.

Susz, Pedro. *La campaña del Chaco, El ocaso del cine silente boliviano.* La Paz: Universidad Mayor de San Andrés/Instituto Latinoamericano de Investigación, 1990.

Brazil

Avellar, José Carlos. "Conversación indisciplinada." *Cine cubano,* no. 116 (1987): 1–5.

Bernadet, Jean-Claude. *Trajetória Crítica.* São Paulo: Polis, 1978.

Cavalcanti de Paiva, Salvyano. *História Ilustrado dos Filmes Brasileiros, 1929–1988.* Rio de Janeiro: Francisco Alves, 1989.

Ciment, Michel. "Ruy Guerra" and "Glauber Rocha." In *Second Wave,* ed. Ian Cameron, 99–119. New York: Praeger, 1970.

Elsaesser, Thomas. "Tales of Sound and Fury: Observations on the Family Melodrama." *Monogram,* no. 4 (1973).

Esteve, Michel, ed. *Le «cinema nôvo» brésilien (1). Études cinématographiques,* nos. 93–96. Paris: Lettres Modernes, 1972.

Fowler, Alexander. *Orson Welles.* London: Pendulum Publications, 1946.

Gardies, René. *Glauber Rocha. Cinéma d'aujourd'hui,* no. 79. Paris: Seghers, 1974.

———. "Structural Analysis of a Textual System: Presentation of a Method." *Screen,* 15, no. 1 (1974 [1973]): 11–31.

Higuchi, Horácio. "José Mojica Marins: The Madness in his Method." *Monster! International,* no. 3 (October 1993): 5–19.

Johnson, Randal. *Cinema Novo x 5: Masters of Contemporary Brazilian Film.* Austin: University of Texas Press, 1984.

———. *The Film Industry in Brazil: Culture and the State.* Pittsburgh: University of Pittsburgh Press, 1987.

———, and Robert Stam, eds. *Brazilian Cinema.* East Rutherford, N.J.: Associated University Presses, 1982.

Marcorelles, Louis. "Le nouveau cinéma brésilien veut rattraper le temps perdu." *Le Monde,* 30 March 1978.

Monteiro, José Carlos. *80 ans de cinéma brésilien*. Paris: Embrafilme/Cinémathèque française, 1978.

Mulvey, Laura. "Notes on Sirk and Melodrama." In *Visual and Other Pleasures*, 39–44. Bloomington: Indiana University Press, 1989.

Paranagua, Paulo Antonio. "Brésil, 20 ans après." *Positif*, no. 300 (1986).

——, ed. *Le Cinéma brésilien*. Paris: Centre Georges Pompidou, 1987.

Ramos, Fernão, ed. *História do Cinema Brasileiro*. São Paulo: Art Editora, 1987.

——, *Cinema Marginal (1968–1973): A Representação em seu Limite*. São Paulo: Editora Brasiliense, 1987.

Rocha, Glauber. "Humberto Mauro and the Historical Position of Brazilian Cinema." Translated by Jon Davis. *Framework*, no. 11 (Autumn 1979 [1963]): 5–8.

——. "An Aesthetic of Hunger." *Afterimage* (London), no. 1 (April 1970 [January 1965]): no page numbers.

Salles Gomes, Paulo Emílio. *Cinema: Trajetoria no Subdesenvolvimento*. Rio de Janeiro: Paz e Terra/Embrafilme, 1980.

——, and Adhemar Gonzaga. *70 Anos de Cinema Brasileiro*. Rio de Janeiro: Expressão e Cultura, 1966.

Stam, Robert, and Ismael Xavier. "Recent Brazilian Cinema: Allegory/Metacinema/Carnival." *Film Quarterly*, 41, no. 3 (Spring 1988): 15–30.

——, and Ismail Xavier. "Transformation of National Allegory: Brazilian Cinema from Dictatorship to Redemocratization." In *Resisting Images: Essays on Cinema and History*, eds. Robert Sklar and Charles Musser, 279–307. Philadelphia: Temple University Press, 1990.

Turner, Terence. "Visual Media, Cultural Politics and Anthropological Practice." *The Independent Film and Video Monthly*, 14, no. 1 (Jan./Feb. 1991): 34–40.

van Wert, William F. "Ideology in the Third World Cinema: A Study of Sembène Ousmane and Glauber Rocha." *Quarterly Review of Film Studies*, 4, no. 2 (1979): 207–226.

Vieira, João Luiz, ed. *Glauber por Glauber*. Rio de Janeiro: Embrafilme, 1985.

Willemen, Paul, ed. "Brazil - Post Cinema Novo." *Framework*, no. 28 (1985).

Chile

Caiozzi, Silvio (interview). *Hablemos de cine* (Lima), no. 73–74 (1981).

Chanan, Michael. *Chilean Cinema*. London: British Film Institute, 1976.

Christie, Ian, Malcolm Coad and Raúl Ruiz. "Exile and Cunning: Raúl Ruiz." *Afterimage* (London), no. 10 (Autumn 1981): 70–127.

Francia, Aldo. *Nuevo Cine Latinoamericano en Viña del Mar*. Santiago: ARTECIEN/CESOC, 1990.

García Márquez, Gabriel. *Clandestine in Chile: The Adventures of Miguel Littin*. Translated by Asa Zatz. New York: Henry Holt, 1987 [1986].

Mouesca, Jacqueline. *Plano sequencia de la memoria de Chile, 25 años de cine chileno (1960–85)*. Madrid: Ediciones del Litoral, 1988.

Pick, Zuzana. "Chilean Cinema in Exile." *Framework*, no. 34 (1987): 39–57.

——, ed. "A Special Section on Chilean Cinema." *Ciné-Tracts*, no. 9 (Winter 1980): 18–55.

Rosenbaum, Jonathan. "Mapping the Territory of Râúl Ruiz." Unpublished article, which appeared in shortened form as "Râúl Ruiz." *10 To Watch: Ten Filmmakers for the Future*, ed. Piers Handling, 32–34. Toronto: World Film Festival of Toronto, 1985.

"Spécial Raoul Ruiz." *Cahiers du Cinéma*, no. 345 (March 1983).

Vega, Alicia, ed. *Re-visión del cine chileno*. Santiago: Centro de Indagación y Expresión Cultural y Artística (CENECA), 1979.

Colombia

Alvarez, Carlos. *El cortometraje del sobreprecio, datos 1970–1980*. Bogotá: Archivo Fílmico de la Cinemateca Distrital, 1982.

García Aguilar, Eduardo. *García Márquez, La tentación cinematográfica*. Mexico City: Filmoteca de la UNAM, 1985.

Gaviria, Víctor Manuel. *El pelaíto que no duró nada*. Bogotá: Planeta Colombiana, 1991.

Martínez Pardo, Hernando. *Historia del cine colombiano*. Bogotá: Librería y Editorial América Latina, 1978.

Nieto, Jorge, and Diego Rojas. *Tiempos del Olympia*. Bogotá: Banco de Colombia/Fundación Patrimonio Fílmico Colombiano, 1992.

Ecuador

Burton, Julianne. "Marginal Cinemas and Mainstream Critical Theory." *Screen*, 26, nos. 2–4 (1985): 2–21.

Estrella, Ulises, ed. *Historia del cine en el Ecuador, Cronología de la cultura cinematográfica (1849–1986)*. Quito: Nueva Editorial, 1986.

Gabriel, Teshome. "Towards a Critical Theory of Third World Films." In *Questions of Third Cinema*, eds. Jim Pines and Paul Willemen, 30–52. London: British Film Institute, 1989.

Marcorelles, Louis. "Jorge Sanjinés et la réalité andine." *Le Monde*, Paris, 10 June 1977.

Villacres Moscoso, Jorge W. *Historia del cine ecuatoriano*. Guayaquil: Instituto de la Cinemateca Ecuatoriana, 1973.

Waugh, Thomas. "'Words of Command': Notes on Cultural and Political Inflections of Direct Cinema in Indian Independent Documentary." *Cineaction* (Toronto), no. 23 (Winter 1990–91): 28–39.

Peru

Bedoye Wilson, Ricardo. *100 años de cine en el Perú, historia crítica*. Lima: Universidad de Lima, 1992.

Carbone de Mora, Gianvarlo. *El cine en el Perú, 1897–1950, Testimonios*. Lima: Universidad de Lima, 1992.

———. *El cine en el Perú, 1950–1972, Testimonios*. Lima: Universidad de Lima, 1994.

Nuñez Gorritti, Violeta. *Pitas y alambre, La época de oro del cine peruano 1936-1950.* Lima: Colmillo Blanco, 1990.

Perla Araya, José. *Censura y promoción en el cine.* Lima: Universidad de Lima/Unión Latina, 1991.

Uruguay

Alvarez Olloniego, José Carlos. *Historia del cine uruguayo.* Montevideo: Cinemateca Uruguaya, 1957.

———. *Breve Historia del Cine Uruguayo.* Montevideo, 1973.

Gandolfo, Elvio. *"Mataron a Venancio Flores,* El intento de un cine nacional." *Cine Libre* (Buenos Aires) nos. 3-4 (1983): 30-3.

Hintz, Eugenio, and Graciela Dacosta, eds. *Historia y filmografía del cine uruguayo.* Montevideo: Ediciones de la Plaza, 1988.

Pastor Legnani, Margarita, and Rosario Vico de Peña. *Filmografía Uruguaya 1898-1973.* Montevideo: Cinemateca Uruguaya/Cine Universitario del Uruguay, 1975.

Venezuela

Aguirre, José M., and Marcelino Bisbal. *El nuevo cine venezolano.* Caracas: Editorial Ateneo de Caracas, 1980.

Caropreso Ponce, Luis. *Breve historia del cine nacional (1909-1964).* Caracas: Consejo Municipal del Distrito, 1966.

Díaz S., Raiza. *Reconocimiento de los generos y los temas en el cine venezolano 1975-1988.* Caracas: Fondo de Fomento Cinematográfico, 1988.

Schwartzman, Karen. "A Descriptive Chronology of Films by Women in Venezuela, 1952-92." *Journal of Film and Video,* 44, nos. 3-4 (Fall 1992 and Winter 1993).

———, Harel Calderón and Julianne Burton-Carvajal. "An Interview with Margot Benacerraf: *Reverón, Araya,* and the Institutionalization of Cinema in Venezuela." *Journal of Film and Video,* 44, nos. 3-4 (Fall 1992 and Winter 1993): 51-75.

Tirado, Ricardo. *Memoria y notas del Cine Venezuelano: 1897-1959.* Caracas: Fundación Neumann, 1988.

———. *Memoria y notas de Cine Venezuelano: 1960-1976.* Caracas: Fundación Neumann, 1989.

Notes on Contributors

(As current in the 1996 publication)

Timothy Barnard has edited a monograph on Argentine cinema (*Argentine Cinema*, Toronto, 1986) and translated a memoir of the tango (*The Bandonion: A Tango History*, London, Canada, 1988). He has prepared a three-hour radio documentary on political film censorship West, East, and South (CBC Radio IDEAS, 1985) and published articles, primarily on Latin American cinema, in a number of international journals and anthologies. He has managed international film and human rights projects and worked as a translator, interpreter, and English as a Second Language instructor. He holds a B.F.A. in Cinema Studies from Concordia University in Montréal.

Catherine Benamou was born in Suresnes, France. A long-time devotee of travel and research in Latin America, she has curated screenings and produced cable television programs concerning Latin American film and video in New York City, and was co-founder of "Punto de Vista: Latina," a special Latin American women's distribution project. She is currently a Ph.D. candidate in Cinema Studies at New York University, and teaches film history and criticism at the College of Staten Island—CUNY. Her dissertation research on Orson Welles' unfinished film *It's All True* led to her work as associate producer and senior research executive on the completed version released through Paramount Pictures in 1993. She has published articles and reviews in *Afterimage, Cahiers du Cinéma, Cineaste, Discourse, Frontiers*, and *Persistence of Vision*.

David Douglas is currently writing his Ph.D. thesis on Canadian experimental film and teaches "Third World," Canadian, and Contemporary Film courses at Concordia and McGill Universities in Montréal.

Alfonso Gumucio-Dagron is a poet, essayist, filmmaker, and film historian. His film writings include the encyclopaedia *Les cinémas d'Amérique Latine* (Paris, 1981), co-edited with Guy Hennebelle, *Cine, censura y exilio en América Latina* (La Paz, 1979), *El cine de los trabajadores* (Managua, 1981), *Historia del cine boliviano* (Mexico, 1983), and *Luis Espinal y el cine* (La Paz, 1985). He studied film at IDHEC in Paris and his films include the feature-length *Señores Generales, Señores Coroneles* (France-Bolivia, 1976), and numerous short films. He founded the Centro de Integración de Medios de Comunicación Alternativa (CIMCA) in Bolivia. He was a member of the Ukamau film collective in Bolivia in the 1970s and was assistant director on *¡Fuera de aquí!* (Ecuador, 1975). He currently works for UNICEF.

Federico Hidalgo was born in Argentina and has lived in Montréal for over eleven years. He has a B.A. in Political Science and a B.F.A. in Cinema (Film Production). He is currently a graduate student in Cinema at Concordia University.

Chris Holmlund is an Associate Professor in the Department of Romance and Asian Languages at the University of Tennessee-Knoxville. She writes on French, North American, and Latin American film and video. She is currently co-editing a book entitled *Between the Sheets, In the Streets: Lesbian/Queer/Gay Documentary*.

Paul Lenti (1949–1994) worked as a freelance journalist specialising in Latin American cinema. He spent eight years as a film critic for *The Mexico City News* and worked for the trade publication *Variety* between 1983 and his death in 1994, where he was responsible for compiling the annual Latin American film and television supplement. He also coordinated the film section of the New York Festival Latino from 1990–1993. He translated the book *Objects of Desire: Conversations with Luis Buñuel* for Marsilio Press (New York, 1993). He contributed commentary on Jacques Vaché and translations of letters by Vaché and an article about Vaché by André Breton for the book *4 DADA Suicides* (London, 1995).

Isaac León Frías studied Literature and Sociology. He was editor of the Peruvian film magazine *Hablemos de Cine* between 1965 and 1985, when it ceased publication. He is presently director of the Filmoteca in Lima and professor of film studies and Dean of the Faculty of Communication

Studies at the University of Lima. He also writes film criticism for two weekly publications in Lima. He is a member of the editorial board of the new film magazine *La gran ilusión*, published by the Faculty of Communication Studies at the University of Lima.

Ana López is Associate Professor of Communications at Tulane University, New Orleans where she teaches film and cultural studies with a Latin American focus. In addition to numerous articles and book chapters on Latin American film, media, and Latino/a representation she has recently co-edited a special issue of *Quarterly Review of Film Studies* and the book, *Mediating Two Worlds: Cinematic Encounters in the Americas* (London, 1993).

Oscar Lucien is a Venezuelan filmmaker and scriptwriter. He studied Sociology in Venezuela and France and cinema in France and since 1980 has worked as a researcher at the Instituto de Investigaciones de la Comunicación in Caracas and taught cinema at the Universidad Central between 1983 and 1992. He was Director of the Cinemateca Nacional in 1991–92 and President of the same institution from 1992–94. He has written the books *Fiebre, una historia sin tiempo: proposición metodológica para el estudio del film* and *El documental en la encrucijada* and co-authored *Pensar el cine*. His films include documentary and fiction shorts and the fiction feature *Un sueño en el abismo* (1991).

Marilú Mallet was born in Chile where she became a filmmaker and an architect. She studied anthropology in California. After spending some time in Cuba, she settled in Montréal, where she received an M.A. from the Université de Montréal. She has been granted a number of filmmaking awards including a John Simon Guggenheim Filmmaking Award in 1988 and the "Meilleur Documentaire d'Essai à Création" and FIPA prizes at Cannes in 1991 for her film *Cher Amérique*. Two collections of her short stories have been published and she is currently on the Full-Time Cinema Faculty at Concordia University.

Manuel Martínez Carril has worked as a journalist and film producer and served as director of the Montevideo Film School. He has published three books on film and served on numerous film festival juries. He has written film criticism since 1958 for numerous publications. Currently director of Cinemateca Uruguaya and the Festival Cinematográfico Internacional del Uruguay, he has served on the executive of the

International Federation of Film Archives (FIAF). In 1990 he was named a Knight in the Order of Arts and Letters by the French government and in 1992 was admitted to the Gabriela Mistral Order in Chile.

Jorge Nieto is a journalist and film critic who has been involved for the past twenty years in Colombia and internationally in the work of moving images preservation, as an archivist, researcher, and film archive official. He is presently Curator of the Colombian national film archives at the Fundación Patrimonio Fílmico Colombiano and is a member of the Executive Committee of the International Federation of Film Archives (FIAF). His recent book, *Tiempos del Olympia* (1992), is a historical chronicle of the beginnings of cinema in Colombia. On the occasion of the centenary of cinema in 1995 he produced and directed a series of television programs on the history of Colombian cinema.

Mitch Parry studied English literature at the University of Western Ontario, where he also taught film studies. In 1991 he left Canada to teach English as a Second Language; he returned to Canada in 1993. His first novel, *Vacant Rooms* (Anvil Press, 1994) co-won the International Three Day Novel Contest. At present he is living in Montréal, where he is working on a second novel.

Peter Rist was born in Croydon, England. He worked as a Mechanical Design Engineer in England and Canada, and then, while teaching Mathematics at the St. Vincent Technical College in the Leeward Islands, developed a strong interest in African-based cultures. He received his Ph.D. in Cinema Studies from New York University and is currently the Chair of the Department of Cinema at Concordia University in Montréal.

Diego Rojas Romero has been involved in the formation of ciné clubs in Colombia and has written film criticism for specialised journals and taught film studies at the university level. He worked on the production of the film *En busca de María* (1985) and was producer of *La carta* (1987). He has made numerous educational and industrial videos. He was a member of the editorial team for the book *Manual de apreciación cinematográfica* (1986) and co-authored the books *Colombia, the Set* (1987) and *Tiempos de Olympia* (1992). He developed a cataloguing system for Colombian cinema, *Modelo de catalogación de la filmografía nacional* (1994) and recently participated in the production of a television series on the history of Colombian cinema.

Susan Ryan teaches Caribbean cinema at Rutgers University and is currently completing a doctoral dissertation on Nicaraguan video production at New York University.

Liliana Sáez studied Cinema at the Universidad Central in Venezuela. She is a researcher at the Cinemateca Nacional, in charge of the Venezuelan Audiovisual Memory program, and a member of the Venezuelan Film Critics Association (AVCC). She has been a contributor to the film and photography magazine *Encuadre* since 1985 and contributed to the publication *Objeto visual, Cuadernos de investigación y documentación de la Cinemateca Nacional*.

Karen Schwartzman is a Doctoral Candidate in the Department of Cinema Studies at New York University. She is co-curator of the film series "Venezuela: Forty Years of Cinema, 1950–1990," presented at the Museum of Modern Art, New York (1994). She lives in New York and Caracas.

Donato Totaro lives in Montréal and teaches Film Studies at Concordia University. He has an M.F.A. in Film Studies from York University, Toronto (1990). Research interests and publications include Andrei Tarkovsky, temporality in cinema, and the horror and comedy genres.

Thomas Waugh has been teaching film studies since 1976, and more recently interdisciplinary gay and lesbian studies, at Concordia University in Montréal. He has published frequently on political documentary, Canadian film and video, Indian film, and gay media in such periodicals as *Jump Cut*, *Cineaction*, and *The Body Politic*. He edited the anthology *"Show Us Life": Toward a History and Aesthetics of the Committed Documentary* (Metuchen, NJ: Scarecrow Press, 1984), and is author of *Hard to Imagine: Gay Male Eroticism in Photography and Film from their Beginnings to Stonewall* (New York: Columbia University Press, 1996). His doctoral dissertation was on Joris Ivens.

Films burning in a fire at the Cinemateca Brasileira in São Paulo in 1957. Films made on nitrate stock—the standard material until the 1940's—can spontaneously combust when in a state of decomposition; applying water actually feeds the chemical reaction that produces the flame.